Empire and Power in the Reign of Süleyman

Kaya Şahin's book offers a revisionist reading of Ottoman history during the reign of Süleyman the Magnificent (1520–66). By examining the life and works of a bureaucrat, Celalzade Mustafa, Şahin moves beyond traditional, teleological approaches and argues that the empire was built as part of the Eurasian momentum of empire building and demonstrates the imperial vision of sixteenth-century Ottomans. This unique study shows that, in contrast with many Eurocentric views, the Ottomans were active players in European politics, with an imperial culture in direct competition with that of the Habsburgs and the Safavids. Indeed, this book explains Ottoman empire building with reference to the larger Eurasian context, from Tudor England to Mughal India, contextualizing such issues as state formation, imperial policy, and empire building in the period more generally. Şahin's work also devotes significant attention to the often-ignored religious dimension of the Ottoman–Safavid struggle, showing how the rivalry redefined Sunni and Shiite Islam, laying the foundations for today's religious tensions.

Kaya Şahin is Assistant Professor of History at Indiana University, Bloomington. His research and writing have been supported by the Andrew W. Mellon Foundation, the Newberry Library, and the Social Science Research Council.

Cambridge Studies in Islamic Civilization

Editorial Board

Published titles are listed at the back of the book.

Empire and Power in the Reign of Süleyman

Narrating the Sixteenth-Century Ottoman World

KAYA ŞAHİN
Indiana University

 CAMBRIDGE
UNIVERSITY PRESS

CAMBRIDGE
UNIVERSITY PRESS

32 Avenue of the Americas, New York NY 10013-2473, USA

Cambridge University Press is part of the University of Cambridge.

It furthers the University's mission by disseminating knowledge in the pursuit of education, learning and research at the highest international levels of excellence.

www.cambridge.org
Information on this title: www.cambridge.org/9781107529885

© İ. Kaya Şahin 2013

First published 2013
First paperback edition 2015

A catalogue record for this publication is available from the British Library

Library of Congress Cataloguing in Publication data

Şahin, Kaya, 1974– author.
Empire and power in the reign of Süleyman : narrating the sixteenth-century Ottoman world / Kaya Şahin, Indiana University.
    pages cm. – (Cambridge studies in Islamic civilization)
Includes bibliographical references and index.
ISBN 978-1-107-03442-6 (hardback)
1. Mustafa Çelebi Celâlzade, d. 1567.   2. Mustafa Çelebi Celâlzade, d. 1567 – Political and social views.   3. Mustafa Çelebi Celâlzade, d. 1567 – Criticism and interpretation.   4. Turkey – Officials and employees – Biography.   5. Historians – Turkey – Biography.   6. Turkey – History – Süleyman I, 1520–1566 – Historiography.   7. Historiography – Turkey – History – 16th century.   8. Turkey – History – Süleyman I, 1520–1566.   9. Imperialism – History – 16th century.   10. Power (Social sciences) – Turkey – History – 16th century.   I. Title.
DR509.M87S34   2013
956'.015–dc23   2012031961

ISBN 978-1-107-03442-6 Hardback
ISBN 978-1-107-52988-5 Paperback

Contents

Figures and Maps

Figures

Maps

Acknowledgments

As a political science major at Boğaziçi University, my curiosity about Ottoman history was initially spurred by debates around the transition from the empire to the republic. I was fortunate enough to take Ottoman language lessons with Metin Berke and Yücel Demirel, who instilled in me a more holistic view of Ottoman history and culture. At Sabancı University, Metin Kunt, Hülya Canbakal, and Tülay Artan, with their focus on early modern Ottoman history, were the best teachers I could hope to find at a critical juncture in my academic formation. I should also mention, among my first and formative influences, Halil Berktay's lectures and conversations on historiography and comparative history. At the University of Chicago, thanks to Cornell Fleischer, I was able to further concentrate on the fifteenth and sixteenth centuries, within a perspective that placed the Ottomans into a larger geographical, cultural, and political environment. Everything I write is, in a way, a dialogue with Professor Fleischer's own writings, lectures, and personal conversations. I am eternally grateful for his sage advice, unflagging encouragement, incomparable intellectual stimulation, and, above all, infinite patience. Robert Dankoff's help and guidance were instrumental in unlocking Celalzade Mustafa's dense prose and eventually enjoying his style. Next to being members of my dissertation committee, Constantin Fasolt and Fred Donner have encouraged and supported me over the years, and I continue to aspire to the scholarly example they have set in their own works. Courses taken with John Woods, Rachel Fulton, Adrian Johns, Constantin Fasolt, and Tamar Herzog helped me rethink various issues related to Ottoman history. The Early Modern Workshop was a fertile meeting and debating ground for early modernists of all stripes. Although the process of writing is often a lonely pursuit, I developed many ideas through ongoing conversations with my fellow Chicago graduate students and now colleagues Mehmetcan Akpınar, Nikolay Antov, Abdurrahman Atçıl, Evrim Binbaş, Snjezana Buzov, Ertuğrul Ökten, James Tallon, James Vaughn, and Nükhet Varlık.

The research and writing for my dissertation and book were supported by grants from the University of Chicago's Department of History and its Center for Middle Eastern Studies, the American Research Institute in Turkey, the Andrew W. Mellon Foundation, Tulane University's Department of History, and the Newberry Library. I would like to thank Nevzat Kaya and Emir Eş at the Süleymaniye Library, Ayten Ardel at the Prime Ministry Archives, Ülkü Altındağ at the Topkapı Palace Archives, İlknur Keleş and Melek Gençboyacı at the Millet Library, Esra Müyesseroğlu at the Topkapı Palace Library, and Ayda Perçin at the Türkiye Yazma Eserler Kurumu Başkanlığı for their help during my research and with publication permits. I used the collections and interlibrary loan services of the Joseph Regenstein Library at the University of Chicago, the İSAM Library in Istanbul, the Northwestern University Library, and the Newberry Library. I turned my dissertation into a book thanks to a Mellon postdoctoral fellowship at the Newberry in 2010–11, and as an affiliate of the Buffett Center for International and Comparative Studies at Northwestern University. Daniel Greene, Diane Dillon, Carmen Jaramillo, Paul Gehl, and the Newberry fellows created a stimulating intellectual environment that made me rethink many an argument. At the Buffett Center, Andrew Wachtel, Hendrik Spruyt, Brian Hanson, and Rita Koryan provided a vibrant academic hub. The book took its final shape in the spring of 2012, thanks to the suggestions of two anonymous reviewers for Cambridge University Press, and under the guidance of my editor, Marigold Acland. Sarika Narula and Anuj Antony greatly facilitated the production process and kindly answered every question. Christopher Markiewicz prepared the book's index, and offered several helpful suggestions at the proofreading stage. Especially in the writing and proofreading stages, I often remembered, and relied upon, the guidance I received from Müge Gürsoy and Semih Sökmen as a junior editor at Metis Publishers in the late 1990s.

During my research in Istanbul, I benefited from the hospitality of Kerem Ünüvar, Setrak Eryazı, the Koryan family, and my sister and brother-in-law, Ayşegül and Ulaş Güvenç. Istanbul, a city of many attractions, is particularly enjoyable in the company of Burak Onaran and Mehmet Beşikçi. In New Orleans, the Brancaforte family (Benito,

Charlotte, and Elio) gave me a home away from home. At Tulane and in New Orleans, I enjoyed the friendship and support of Thomas Adams, George Bernstein, James Boyden, Donna Denneen, Eli Feinstein, Kenneth Harl, Jana Lipman, Colin Maclachlan, Elizabeth McMahon, Lawrence Powell, Samuel Ramer, Randy Sparks, Eric Wedig, and Ferruh Yılmaz. Several friends and colleagues read parts of the manuscript and offered suggestions, helped with my research, and answered my queries about various issues. I would like to mention here Meltem Ahıska, Sebouh Aslanian, Günhan Börekçi, Erdem Çıpa, Emine Fetvacı, Hakan Karateke, Sooyong Kim, Kıvanç Koçak, Baki Tezcan, and Kahraman Şakul. At Indiana University, I am grateful for the warm welcome I have been given by my colleagues and the staff at the history department.

Despite the emotional cost of physical distance, since the day I left my hometown of Burhaniye for boarding school, my parents Fatma and Hasan Şahin never failed to express their faith in me and the work I do. I wouldn't find much comfort and pleasure in my research and writing without the constant presence and support of Rita Koryan, who kindly allowed Celalzade Mustafa to become a mainstay of our everyday life since 2005. I am eternally grateful to her for showing me that there is a whole life to be enjoyed beyond the issues and personalities of the sixteenth century and outside manuscript libraries and archives.

Abbreviations, Transliteration, Dates, and Pronunciation

The following abbreviations are used throughout the book:

BOA: Başbakanlık Osmanlı Arşivleri
BSOAS: *Bulletin of the School of Oriental and African Studies*
JTS: *Journal of Turkish Studies. Türklük Bilgisi Araştırmaları*
KK: Kamil Kepeci
EI 2, EI 3: Encyclopedia of Islam 2 and 3, electronic edition.
IJMES: *International Journal of Middle East Studies*
IJTS: *International Journal of Turkish Studies*
IrSt: *Iranian Studies*
İA: *İslâm Ansiklopedisi*
JEMH: *Journal of Early Modern History*
SK: Süleymaniye Kütüphanesi
StIsl: *Studia Islamica*
TDVİA: *Türkiye Diyanet Vakfı İslam Ansiklopedisi*
TSAB: *Turkish Studies Association Bulletin*
TSMA: Topkapı Sarayı Müzesi Arşivi
TSMK: Topkapı Sarayı Müzesi Kütüphanesi
TTYY: *Tarih ve Toplum Yeni Yaklaşımlar*
WZKM: *Wiener Zeitschrift für die Kunde des Morgenlandes*

Quotes from Celalzade Mustafa's works and titles of Ottoman Turkish, Arabic, and Persian works are fully transliterated through a slightly modified version of the *IJMES* transliteration system. (After their first mention, titles of Mustafa's works are repeated in a shortened form and without any special characters.) Excerpts from Mustafa's writings are shortened as much as possible; the longer versions can be found in my dissertation.

With the exception of the index, Ottoman Turkish words are provided in the modern Turkish orthography in the text, in italics; the *'ayn* and *hamza* are marked with an apostrophe. For Arabic and Persian personal names, a simplified version of the *IJMES* transliteration system, without the diacritical signs, is utilized. For Ottoman personal and geographical names, the modern Turkish orthography is adopted, except when there is an English equivalent for the latter: hence, for instance, Istanbul instead of İstanbul, Aleppo instead of Halep, Rhodes instead of Rodos, and Belgrade instead of Belgrad. Long vowel markers (â, î) are minimally used. Whenever possible, Anglicized versions of Ottoman, Arabic, and Persian words are used as they appear in the Merriam-Webster dictionary: Sharia, waqf, vizier, Sunni, Shiite, and so forth, the exceptions being madrasa instead of madrassa, and Quran instead of Koran.

Although the original sources discussed here use the *Hicri* calendar, which is based on the lunar year and begins at 622 CE (the date of Muhammad's exodus from Mecca to Medina), the dates are given in Common Era throughout the book. The original *Hicri* dates are provided in my dissertation.

For a Turkish pronunciation guide, the readers are kindly referred to a webpage by Erika H. Gilson:

http://www.princeton.edu/~ehgilson/alpha.html.

MAP 1. Central Europe ca. 1570 (Paul R. Magocsi, *Historical Atlas of East Central Europe* [Seattle: University of Washington Press, 1993], 14).

Ottoman and Safavid Wo

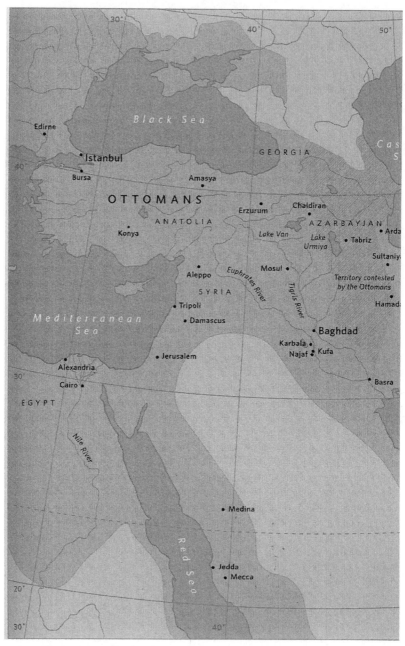

MAP 2. The Ottoman and Safavid worlds in the sixteenth century (Massumeh Farhad and Serpil Bağcı, eds., *Falnama: The Book of Omens* [London: Thames & Hudson, 2009]).

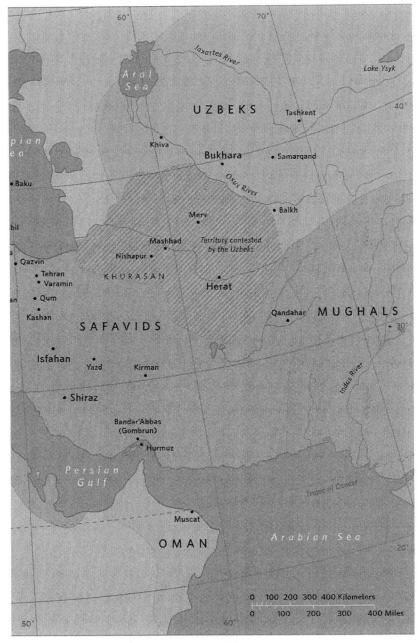

MAP 2 (*continued*)

FIGURE 1. Celalzade Mustafa's tomb, from M. Şinasi Acar, *Ünlü Hattatların Mezarları: Gelimli Gidimli Dünya* (İstanbul: Gözen, 2004), 26. The epitaph is by his acquaintance Deli Kadı.

Introduction

Revisiting Celalzade Mustafa

On a torrid August day in 2009, I visited Celalzade Mustafa's final resting place in Istanbul's Eyüp district, in a neighborhood called Nişanca. The chancellor (*nişancı*) is buried in the cemetery adjoining the small mosque built for him by Sinan, the chief imperial architect. His brother Salih, a teacher, judge, and religious scholar, is buried nearby, but the sepulchers of poets who received plots from this patron of poetry have disappeared. The mosque, adorned with glazed tiles, has changed significantly since the mid-sixteenth century. It was damaged in a fire in 1729 and was rebuilt following a more devastating fire in 1780.[1] The mansion where Mustafa composed his works, welcomed fellow literati, and provided advice to young and aspiring secretaries is long gone, probably destroyed in the fire of 1780, if not before. The bathhouse and dervish lodge he had commissioned do not survive either. After reaching one of the highest administrative positions of the empire and enjoying the unanimous respect of his fellow administrators and literati, Mustafa now sleeps in a modest working-class neighborhood, away from the bustling avenues, familiar landmarks, and popular locales of imperial and republican Istanbul.

Mustafa (ca. 1490–1567) entered the Ottoman scribal service in 1516, at a time when an embryonic corps of secretaries was about to expand

---

[1] Tarkan Okçuoğlu, "Nişancı Mustafa Paşa Camii," *Dünden Bugüne İstanbul Ansiklopedisi*, vol. 6, 86–87; Suphi Saatçi, "Observations on Sinan's Mosques and Masjids in Eyüp," in *Eyüp Sultan Symposia I-VIII: Selected Articles* (Istanbul: The Municipality of Eyüp, 2005), 135–36.

1

considerably. He was initially taken on as a secretary of the imperial council (*divan katibi*). He became chief secretary (*re'isülküttab*) in 1525 and chancellor in 1534, a position he held until his retirement in 1557 and then briefly in 1566–67. He devoted the last decade of his life to his writing and produced, most notably, two major works on the reigns of Selim (r. 1512–20) and Süleyman (r. 1520–66)[2] and a treatise on politics and morals.[3] Thanks to a stellar bureaucratic career and widely respected, influential works, Mustafa was recognized by his contemporaries as well as by future generations as the ideal Ottoman litterateur who combined service to the dynasty, defense of the empire, and literary prowess under a single mantle.[4] Beyond these lauds, the function of Mustafa's bureaucratic career and literary production is better understood within the global dynamics of the sixteenth century. Mustafa came of age in a time characterized, for the Ottomans as well as the inhabitants of the entire Eurasian continent, by sudden and radical changes in political organization as well as cultural and religious identity. The end result was the creation of new empires that have been characterized by Sanjay Subrahmanyam:

> (1) as states with an extensive geographical spread, embracing more than one cultural domain and ecozone; (2) as states powered by an ideological motor that claimed extensive, at times even universal, forms of dominance, rather than the mere control of a compact domain; (3) as states where

[2] The versions used throughout the book are the following: *Geschichte Sultan Süleymān Ḳānūnīs von 1520 bis 1557, oder, Ṭabaḳāt ül-Memālik ve Derecāt ül-Mesālik / von Celālzāde Muṣṭafā genannt Ḳoca Nişāncı*, ed. Petra Kappert (Wiesbaden: Steiner, 1981) (hereafter *Tabakat*); *Tārīḫ-i Sulṭān Selīm*, ms. British Museum Add. 7848 (hereafter *Selimname*). For *Tabakat*, page numbers followed by the letters a or b refer to the original manuscript, whereas numbers without letters refer to Petra Kappert's critical introduction.

[3] *Mevāhibu'l-ḫallāḳ fī merātibi'l-aḫlāḳ*, ms. SK, Fatih 3521 (hereafter *Mevahib*).

[4] Abdülkadir Karahan, *Fuzûlî'nin Mektupları* (Istanbul: İbrahim Horoz, 1948), 4–7, 31–38; Cornell H. Fleischer, *Bureaucrat and Intellectual in the Ottoman Empire: The Historian Mustafa Âli (1541–1600)* (Princeton, N.J.: Princeton University Press, 1986), 30–31; Âşık Çelebi, *Meşā'irü'ş-şu'arā*, ed. G.M. Meredith-Owens (London: Luzac, 1971), 135a, 228b; İsmail Hakkı Uzunçarşılı, "Onaltıncı Asır Ortalarında Yaşamış Olan İki Büyük Şahsiyet: Tosyalı Celâl zâde Mustafa ve Salih Çelebiler," *Belleten* 22, no. 87 (1958): 400–04; G.M. Meredith-Owens, "Traces of a Lost Autobiographical Work by a Courtier of Selim II," *BSOAS* 23, no. 3 (1960): 459; Christine Woodhead, "After Celalzade: the Ottoman Nişancı c.1560–1700," in *Studies in Islamic Law: A Festschrift for Colin Imber*, ed. Andreas Christmann and Robert Gleave (Oxford: Oxford University Press and Manchester University Press, 2007), *Journal of Semitic Studies*, supplement 23: 295–96; Ahmed Resmi Efendi, *Ḫalīfetü'r-rü'esā* (Istanbul: n.p., 1853), 4–6.

the idea of suzerainty was a crucial component of political articulation, and where the monarch was defined not merely as king, but as "king over kings," with an explicit notion of hierarchy in which various levels of sovereignty, both "from above" and "from below," were involved.[5]

The Ottoman polity was inaugurated by a small group of militarized nomads in northeast Anatolia around 1300, and it subsequently evolved into a frontier principality and a dynastic kingdom. The conquest of Constantinople in 1453 was a turning point in terms of dynastic prestige and political ideology, but it is only in the sixteenth century that we can fully perceive an imperial set of mind and a leap forward in institutionalization. Looking at this period through Mustafa's career shows that, next to a few elements of continuity, new Ottoman administrative practices reflect an impressive level of invention and creativity. This is not the achievement of a particular political and organizational genius but, rather, the outcome of pragmatic measures, adopted under the pressures of a world-historical process of empire building and interimperial rivalry. In the Ottoman case, these pressures are represented by the near-simultaneous expansion of the Safavid (1501–1722) and Habsburg (1526–1918) Empires. Selim's contribution to these developments was the invasion of large territories in the Middle East. Süleyman continued his father's anti-Safavid legacy and adopted an aggressive foreign policy on the European front. Military campaigns required the deployment of increasingly larger financial resources, which in turn necessitated a better management of various revenue sources. Revolts in the Middle East in the first decade of Süleyman's reign exposed the weaknesses of Ottoman control in newly acquired territories and motivated the sultan and his men to develop better methods of management. While searching for the means to prevail over two fronts, field large armies and navies, collect taxes, put down rebellions, ensure the compliance of local elites and communities, and supervise their own ruling elite, the Ottomans contributed to a dialogical process of empire building by constraining their rivals to engage in similar activities. Secretaries were necessary for the creation and deployment of technologies and instruments of control such as land surveys, law codes, and various registers recording expenses, the distribution of land grants (*timar*), the decisions of the imperial council, and so forth. Mustafa played a

---

[5] Sanjay Subrahmanyam, "Written on Water: Designs and Dynamics in the Portuguese Estado da Índia," in *Empires: Perspectives from Archaeology and History*, ed. Susan E. Alcock et al. (Cambridge: Cambridge University Press, 2001), 43.

prominent role in the introduction of new administrative practices and attempted to control and manage both the realm and the members of the Ottoman ruling elite in the name of the sultan.

Imperial rivalries in this period involved a crucial ideological dimension and led to an intense political and cultural competition. The Ottomans competed with the Habsburgs over claims to universal monarchy and with the Shiite Safavids over the definition of true Islam and the leadership of the Muslim community. The Ottoman sultan legitimized his rule by claiming to provide justice, security, and prosperity to his subjects. Documents produced by secretaries in a relatively standardized and sophisticated idiom served the task of creating and propagating particular images of the sultan and particular notions about the Ottoman Empire. Despite the fact that they remained the smallest group within the Ottoman ruling elite, secretaries constituted a very vocal minority whose function was to act as the surrogate of the sultan in bringing order to the realm and in explaining and defending the new empire. In addition to the documents he produced or supervised as chancellor, Mustafa expounded his own ideas about empire and bureaucratic identity in his historical and political writings. He believed that his career as a servant of the dynasty qualified him over other historians who did not know the inner workings of the Ottoman administration. He was also concerned about presenting what he believed to be the correct historical, religious, and cultural position vis-à-vis the Habsburgs, the Safavids, and other enemies and rivals. Although he proudly witnessed the sudden rise to prominence of secretaries in the midst of a newly centralizing early modern dynastic polity, he also worried about their vulnerability vis-à-vis the military class. In his political treatise, he claimed that a well-educated, freeborn service class could manage the empire better than the military men. Mustafa was one of the builders of a new imperial identity according to which the Ottoman realm, ruled by a law-abiding and justice-dispensing dynasty that protected Sunni Islam against enemies from within and without, constituted the epitome of Islamic civilization.

This powerful fiction was subsequently hailed as an Ottoman "classical age," an idealized period that continues to occupy a privileged place in the rhetoric of Turkish political Islam. The Ottoman sixteenth century is widely accepted as a formative stage in the empire's organization and cultural production. Apologetic approaches portray the reigns of Selim and Süleyman as the culmination of a march from tribe to empire. The proponents of the "decline theory" interpret Süleyman's empire as an ideal construction and see the aftermath of his reign as the beginning of an inescapable descent into imperial dissolution.[6] These approaches have the merit of realizing that the first half of the sixteenth century is a critical period; however, they fail to explain its specificity. They refrain from developing more comprehensive models within which the sudden imperial expansion would become more meaningful. There is a "classical age obsession" among Ottoman historians. At the same time, there is a conspicuous absence of works studying the "classical age" with a critical eye.[7]

Studying Mustafa's career and writings allows us to discuss the singularity of early modern empire building and emphasize the parallels and differences between the Ottomans and the other early modern empires. While Mustafa the bureaucrat worked to establish administrative institutions, Mustafa the litterateur, the historian, the political writer created, circulated, and debated universalist political ideas that ranged from claims to universal monarchy over East and West to messianism, from the promotion of Sunni Islam to Mongol/Timurid concepts of ecumenical sovereignty. These activities placed him on the same level with his peers from Henrician England to Mughal India. Despite the considerable differences in political outlook, educational background, and religious belief among individual cases, Mustafa was part of a Eurasian expansion in bureaucratic action, a trend that included his fellow Ottomans Ramazanzade Mehmed (d. 1571) and Feridun Ahmed (d. 1583), the Safavids Qadi Ahmad Qummi (d. after 1606) and Iskandar Munshi (1560/61–1633), and the Mughal Abu'l-fazl ibn Mubarak (1551–1602). On the Western part of Eurasia, this new era was represented by figures such as Thomas Cromwell (1485–1540) and William Cecil (1521–98) in England, Michel de l'Hospital (1507–73) in France, and Mercurino Gattinara (1465–1530), Nicolas Granvelle (1486–1550), and Francisco de los Cobos (1477–1547) in the Habsburg domains.[8] In the sixteenth

---

[6] For a concise critique of these approaches, see Jane Hathaway, "Problems of Periodization in Ottoman History: The Fifteenth through the Eighteenth Centuries," *TSAB* 20, no. 2 (Fall 1996): 25–31.

[7] Oktay Özel, "Modern Osmanlı Tarihyazımında 'Klâsik Dönem:' Bir Eleştirel Değerlendirme," *TTYY* 4 (Fall 2006): 273–94.

[8] For a few relevant studies, see Stephen Alford, *Burghley: William Cecil at the Court of Elizabeth I* (New Haven: Yale University Press, 2008); Hayward Keniston's somehow old but still very useful *Francisco de los Cobos: Secretary of the Emperor Charles V*

century, the number of secretaries and their purview increased throughout Eurasia; the volume and content of administrative records expanded;
an imperial grand policy was formulated in the palace and put into practice on the battlefield; the political center began to infiltrate the lives of its
subjects through law, architectural projects, politicized ceremonies, and
the supervision of religion; quasi-sacral notions of sovereignty were created and circulated as part and parcel of imperial expansion. Mustafa's
life and career illustrate the objectives, yearnings, illusions, achievements,
and failures of a group of Ottoman administrators and literati who are
very similar in outlook to their English, French, Habsburg, Safavid, and
Mughal peers. Süleyman's empire is not the outcome of a Near East-
ern/Islamic/Turkish historical *Geist* that realized its political and civilizational potential. Rather, it is a creative answer to a global crisis that
radically changed the political, cultural, and religious landscape of early
modern Eurasia.

Ottoman Empire Building and Early Modern Eurasia

The term *early modern Eurasia* provides a meaningful geographical and
cultural space within which the histories of the new empires may be
placed. *Eurasia* denotes a zone, from Western Europe to East Asia, which
has been connected through various commercial and ecological cycles
since the Bronze Age Revolution; this zone was even more thoroughly
connected through economic and political/cultural exchanges from the
last decades of the fifteenth century onwards.[9] The appellation *early modern* was created by Europeanists seeking a label for the period between
the Renaissance on the one hand and the rise of the nation state, industrial
capitalism, and European modernity on the other. Jack A. Goldstone's
criticisms about the Eurocentric and modernity-centric limitations of the
concept are still relevant,[10] and certainly, the histories of non-European

---

(Pittsburgh: University of Pittsburgh Press, 1958); Denis Crouzet, *La sagesse et le malheur: Michel de l'Hospital, Chancelier de* France (Seyssel: Champ Vallon, 1998); John
M. Headley, *The Emperor and His Chancellor: A Study of the Imperial Chancellery
under Gattinara* (Cambridge: Cambridge University Press, 1983).

[9] See Jack Goody, *The Eurasian Miracle* (Cambridge and Malden, MA: Polity, 2011).

[10] Jack A. Goldstone, "The Problem of the 'Early Modern' World," *Journal of the Economic
and Social History of the Orient* 41, no. 3 (1998): 249–84. For inspiring discussions on
the positive and negative aspects of the term *early modern* in the case of Qing China, see
Lynn A. Struve, ed., *The Qing Formation in World-Historical Time* (Cambridge, MA:
Harvard University Asia Center, Harvard University Press, 2004).

societies cannot be reduced to their progress toward European modernity or their failure to do so. However, it is also true that the early modern era can still be defined as a global moment that included the active participation of various polities that may or may not be geographically situated in Western Europe. By adopting the term *early modern*, my aim is not to subsume the Ottoman experience under the European one, but rather reinsert the Ottomans and, in comparison, other Eurasian polities, cultures, and societies, into a shared time and space that have been taken over and dominated by industrial-capitalist European imperialism and Eurocentrism. Discussing the onset of a global early modernity in the first half of the sixteenth century is a remedy against both Eurocentrism and various defensive, apologetic, proto-nationalist approaches that focus on the particularities (or merits) of non-European and non-Christian societies. In this book, it also serves the purpose of engaging the "global turn" in recent historiography through an analysis of the Ottoman case.[11]

Indeed, there was a period of relatively integrated political and economic developments and relatively dialogical cultural exchanges in Eurasia from the late fifteenth century onward, until the supremacy of Western/European societies was dictated to the rest of the globe through the twin forces of industrial capitalism and new forms of imperialism after the last decades of the eighteenth century.[12] Parallel and near-simultaneous trends, such as "territorial consolidation; firearms-aided intensification of warfare; more expansive, routinized administrative systems; growing commercialization . . . wider popular literacy, along with a novel proliferation of vernacular texts," were observed.[13] These were supported, between 1450 and 1600, by a favorable climate, an improvement

---

[11] See Jerry H. Bentley, "The Task of World History," in *The Oxford Handbook of World History*, ed. Bentley (Oxford: Oxford University Press, 2011), 12–13: "The global turn facilitates historians' efforts to deal analytically with a range of large-scale processes such as mass migrations, campaigns of imperial expansion, cross-cultural trade, environmental changes, biological exchanges, transfers of technology, and cultural exchanges, including the spread of ideas, ideals, ideologies, religious faiths, and cultural traditions."

[12] John Darwin, *After Tamerlane: The Global History of Empire since 1405* (London: Allen Lane, 2007), 50–99; Charles H. Parker, *Global Interactions in the Early Modern Age, 1400–1800* (Cambridge: Cambridge University Press, 2010), passim. The break that occurred from the late eighteenth century onward is discussed in C. A. Bayly, *The Birth of the Modern World, 1780–1914: Global Connections and Comparisons* (Malden, MA: Blackwell, 2004).

[13] Victor Lieberman, "Introduction," in *Beyond Binary Histories: Re-Imagining Eurasia to c. 1830*, ed. Lieberman (Ann Arbor: University of Michigan Press, 1999), 14.

in agricultural production, and an expanding international trade, which allowed the expanding empires to have access to resources needed for administrative consolidation and militarism. In an article that traces the pedigree of the term *early modern*, Jerry H. Bentley identified three global processes that created an early modern ecology: "the creation of global networks of sea-lanes that provided access to all the world's shorelines, global exchanges of biological species that held massive implications for human populations as well as natural environments, and the forging of an early capitalist global economy that shaped patterns of production, distribution, consumption, and social organization around the world." These processes led to "demographic fluctuations, large-scale migrations, intensified exploitation of natural environments, technological diffusions, consolidation of centralized states, imperial expansion, and global cultural exchanges."[14] These cultural exchanges included the reformulation and circulation of ideas on universal/ecumenical sovereignty.[15] Joseph Fletcher, one of the pioneers of global perspectives in history writing, adds to these trends the growth of regional cities, the rise of urban commercial classes, religious revival and reformations, and rural unrest.[16]

The Ottoman polity deserves to be studied within the larger context of early modern Eurasia because it exhibits most of these transformations in the first half of the sixteenth century. Joseph Fletcher's view that the early modern period has a "quickening tempo" is relevant for Ottoman history as well: if for nothing else, the first half of the sixteenth century is worth studying due to the palpably quickening pace of political, military, economic, and religious activity in the Ottoman realm. Next to the attempts at administrative consolidation and cultural competition, the Ottoman realm felt the impact of global ecological and epidemiological dynamics; the Ottoman ruling elite took an active interest in overland and

[14] Jerry H. Bentley, "Early Modern Europe and the Early Modern World," in *Between the Middle Ages and Modernity: Individual and Community in the Early Modern World*, eds. Charles H. Parker and Bentley (Lanham: Rowman & Littlefield, 2007), 22–23.

[15] Sanjay Subrahmanyam, "Connected Histories: Notes towards a Reconfiguration of Early Modern Eurasia," in Lieberman, *Beyond Binary Histories*, 289–316. For a further illustration of this argument see Subrahmanyam, "Turning the Stones Over: Sixteenth-Century Millenarianism from the Tagus to the Ganges," *The Indian Economic and Social History Review* 45, no. 2 (2003): 129–61.

[16] Joseph Fletcher, "Integrative History: Parallels and Interconnections in the Early Modern Period," in *Studies on Chinese and Islamic Inner Asia*, ed. Beatrice Forbes Manz (Aldershot: Ashgate Variorum, 1995).

overseas travel and communication and engaged in a veritable activity of expansion and exploration.[17]

In recognition of the wider world within which the Ottomans dwelled, Ottoman historians have utilized the term *early modern* to demarcate a historical period (ca. 1450 to ca. 1850) and raise questions about space, legitimacy, knowledge, and religious and cultural identity.[18] Cemal Kafadar was one of the first scholars who discussed affinities and differences between early modern European and Ottoman histories and noted the emergence of new forms of literature, identity, and sociality as the features of a distinct era.[19] More recently, it has been argued that the Ottomans took part in a European or Mediterranean early modernity, especially with regard to the building of military and political institutions and the circulation of universalist politico-religious ideas.[20] Under the impact of Marshall Hodgson's global Islamic history vision or Marxian debates on the particularities of "Asian" societies, the Ottomans have also been studied together with the contemporary Islamic empires of the Safavids and the Mughals (1526–1857).[21] In this book, on the other hand, sixteenth-century Ottoman empire building is presented both as a

[17] Sam White, *The Climate of Rebellion in the Early Modern Ottoman Empire* (Cambridge: Cambridge University Press, 2011); Nükhet Varlık, "Disease and Empire: A History of Plague Epidemics in the Early Modern Ottoman Empire (1453–1600)" (PhD diss., University of Chicago, 2008); Giancarlo Casale, *The Ottoman Age of Exploration* (Oxford: Oxford University Press, 2010).

[18] Metin Kunt and Christine Woodhead, eds., *Süleyman the Magnificent and His Age: The Ottoman Empire in the Early Modern World* (London: Longman, 1995); Virginia Aksan and Daniel Goffman, eds., *The Early Modern Ottomans: Remapping the Ottoman Empire* (Cambridge: Cambridge University Press, 2007); although it focuses on the 1600–1800 period, Virginia Aksan, "Locating the Ottomans among Early Modern Empires," *JEMH* 3, no. 2 (1999): 103–34.

[19] Cemal Kafadar, "The Ottomans and Europe," in *Handbook of European History, 1400–1600. Late Middle Ages, Renaissance, and Reformation*, eds. Thomas A. Brady Jr., Heiko A. Oberman, James D. Tracy, vol. 1, *Structures and Assertions* (Brill: Leiden, 1994), especially 615–25.

[20] Daniel Goffman, *The Ottomans and Early Modern Europe* (Cambridge: Cambridge University Press, 2002); Linda T. Darling, "Political Change and Political Discourse in the Early Modern Mediterranean World," *Journal of Interdisciplinary History* 38, no. 4 (Spring 2008): 505–31; Tijana Krstić, *Contested Conversions to Islam: Narratives of Religious Change in the Early Modern Ottoman Empire* (Stanford: Stanford University Press, 2011).

[21] Metin Kunt, "The Later Muslim Empires: Ottomans, Safavids, Mughals," in *Islam: The Religious and Political Life of a World Community*, ed. Marjorie Kell (New York: Praeger, 1984), 113–36; Halil Berktay, "Three Empires and the Societies They Governed: Iran, India and the Ottoman Empire," in *New Approaches to State and Peasant in Ottoman History*, eds. Berktay and Suraiya Faroqhi (London: Frank Cass, 1992), 242–63; M. Athar Ali, "Political Structures of the Islamic Orient in the Sixteenth and

subset of the new Eurasian empires and as a hinge that connected (*pace* Sanjay Subrahmanyam and his concept of "connected histories") the eastern and western parts of Eurasia. This process had two facets: the first consisted of practical attempts at establishing territorial and economic control from western Iran to the Hungarian plains, whereas the second involved the production of universal and transcendental political concepts that ranged from Timurid notions of divinely sanctioned sovereignty and European ideas of universal monarchy to a newly imagined Sunni identity.

Discussing empire building and administrative consolidation inescapably creates the risk of overemphasizing intentionality at the expense of contingency, or "efflorescence" at the expense of "crisis."[22] My aim is not to argue that Ottoman empire building was completed in this period or that it reached an "ideal" form. As shown by Rifa'at Abou-El-Haj, Karen Barkey and Baki Tezcan, the post-Süleymanic Ottoman polity continued to manifest a tremendous political and economic dynamism, a pervasive pragmatism, and an important level of social mobility and mobilization.[23] Moreover, a large land-based empire such as the Ottoman subset is a collection of various mechanisms of adaptation that develop several vulnerabilities over time, especially when they fail to transform themselves according to new circumstances.[24] As Sam White has demonstrated, in

---

Seventeenth Centuries," in *Medieval India 1: Researches in the History of India, 1250–1750*, ed. Irfan Habib (Delhi: Oxford University Press, 1992), 129–40; Stephen J. Dale, *The Muslim Empires of the Ottomans, Safavids, and Mughals* (Cambridge: Cambridge University Press, 2010). For a discussion of Dale's work from an Ottoman perspective see Kaya Şahin, Review, *IJTS* 17, nos. 1–2 (2011): 196–99.

[22] I borrow this dichotomy from Jack Goldstone: "While a crisis is a relatively sharp, unexpected downturn in significant demographic and economic indices, often accompanied by political turmoil and cultural conflicts, an efflorescence is a relatively sharp, often unexpected upturn in significant demographic and economic indices, usually accompanied by political expansion, institution-building, cultural synthesis, and consolidation" ("Neither Late Imperial nor Early Modern: Efflorescences and the Qing Formation in World History," in *The Qing Formation*, 252).

[23] Rifa'at Ali Abou-El-Haj, *Formation of the Modern State: The Ottoman Empire, Sixteenth to Eighteenth Centuries*, second edition (Syracuse: Syracuse University Press, 2005); Karen Barkey, *Bandits and Bureaucrats: The Ottoman Route to State Centralization* (Ithaca: Cornell University Press, 1994); Baki Tezcan, *The Second Ottoman Empire: Political and Social Transformation in the Early Modern World* (Cambridge: Cambridge University Press, 2010).

[24] See W. G. Runciman, "Empire as a Topic in Comparative Sociology," in *Tributary Empires in Global History*, eds. Peter Fibiger Bang and C.A. Bayly (Basingstoke, Hampshire: Palgrave Macmillan, 2011), 99–107. For the variety of administrative units organized by the Ottoman center as a reflection of local context, see Gábor Ágoston, "A

the first half of the sixteenth century, Ottoman expansion was supported
by a suitable ecological environment; the success of the Ottoman elite
depended on its ability to develop creative ways to benefit from this
environment. However, "as they grew in scale and scope, Ottoman systems of provisioning and settlement faced mounting problems. Just as
the Ottomans proved especially precocious at building these systems,
so they became particularly dependent on their stability and suscepti-
ble to their failures," particularly when they began to feel the impact
of "population pressure, inflation, and diminishing returns from agriculture" in the 1570s.[25] The imperial subset that was imagined and created by Mustafa and his contemporaries thus entered, relatively soon, a
period of severe challenges and major transformations. Nevertheless, the
first half of the sixteenth century needs to be revisited to understand the
dynamics behind the first relatively organized Ottoman thrust at establishing more expansive administrative structures and more sophisticated
cultural and ideological discourses. This process is too rich to be confined to the straightjacket of nationalist and teleological approaches that
interpret it as a prelude to the Turkish nation state or as the culmination
of a Turko-Muslim spirit. At the same time, with its emphasis on rationality, rule of law, efficient government, government-controlled religion,
and political economy, the first Ottoman experience of early modernity
also proves that European early modernity, often defined alongside the
aforementioned concepts, is not superior or unique, but part of global
trends.

My book is not a work of comparative history but, whenever appropriate, it refers to other early modern Eurasian polities, because one of
its objectives is to discuss the Ottoman case as a subset of early modern
empire formation. This allows me to emphasize convergences and diver-
gences and, more importantly, to render the "Ottoman experience" more
meaningful and relevant within a larger context. This period could (and
should) be discussed through the perspective of various individuals and
communities and by using different methodologies. I bring together the
perspective of the empire's chief bureaucrat through a mixture of revisionist political history and a close reading of the chancellor's works. The
book is divided into two parts. Part 1 (Chapters 1 through 4) offers a
revisionist reading of sixteenth-century Ottoman history that takes into

Flexible Empire: Authority and Its Limits on the Ottoman Frontiers," *IJTS* 9, nos. 1–2
(2003): 15–31.
[25] White, *Climate of Rebellion*, 19.

account both internal tensions within the Ottoman ruling elite and the international context. Mustafa's experiences and observations, gleaned from his works of history, form the main thread of the narrative in the first part. Part 2 (Chapters 5 through 7) discusses the evolution and functioning of the new empire's institutions and the cultural and political discourse that accompanied them.

PART ONE

CELALZADE MUSTAFA AND THE NEW OTTOMAN EMPIRE IN EARLY MODERN EURASIA

1

The Formative Years (1490–1523)

Mustafa belonged to a new generation of Ottomans that included the future sultan Süleyman, the future grand vizier İbrahim, and the future chief jurisconsult (*şeyhülislam*) Ebussu'ud. This generation came of age during a period of exceptional political and religious upheaval in early modern Eurasia. The tremendous challenges of the time, such as the thorough revision of religious and cultural identities, the emergence of a more destructive form of warfare based on gunpowder weapons, and the near-simultaneous rise of rival empires, also provided opportunities. Between the last decades of the fifteenth and the first decades of the sixteenth centuries, a global stage was set for the creation of imperial entities and discourses. Under different circumstances, Mustafa, like his father, would probably become a judge or a madrasa teacher. In a period when secretaries became the closest collaborators of empire builders, however, he was asked to play a different role.

Entering the Ottoman Ruling Elite

Reconstructing the first decades of Mustafa's life must rely on conjecture. Almost all autobiographical references found in his works are concerned with his professional career. Contemporary biographical dictionaries (*tezkire*), which were mostly compiled for poets and scholars, present him as a patron of poetry and a litterateur and do not dwell on his early years. It is generally agreed that his family hails from Tosya, a mid-sized township in northern Anatolia, and that his father, Celaleddin, worked as a madrasa teacher and then as a judge.[1] The first modern study of Mustafa's life assumes, on the basis of these sources, that he was born in Tosya, ca. 1490–91.[2] His father was indeed born and raised there, but he left his hometown to continue his education in Istanbul, probably in the late 1470s or early 1480s. Mustafa was either born in Istanbul or, like his brother Salih, somewhere in the Balkans where his father worked as a judge (kadı).

In the mid-fifteenth century, around the time when Celaleddin was coming of age, the majority of Tosya's population was Muslim, and the inhabitants were mostly agriculturalists, growing rice and producing timber. The town's artisans, especially the textile craftspersons, enjoyed a degree of financial prosperity. The area had entered Ottoman control for the first time in 1392, under Bayezid I (r. 1389–1402). After Bayezid's defeat by Timur (r. 1370–1405) in 1402, the Candaroğlu family, the hereditary ruler of the area, was briefly restored to power. Tosya was reoccupied by Mehmed I (r. 1413–21) in 1417; the remainder of the Candaroğlu domain was decisively annexed by Mehmed II (r. 1444–46, 1451–81) in 1462 and reorganized as the province (sancak) of Kastamonu. The capture of the area was a crucial part of the Ottoman policy to expand into Western and Central Anatolia and the Black Sea littoral in the fourteenth and fifteenth centuries to control the considerable agricultural, mineral, and commercial potential of the region.[3] By this time, most of the Ottoman rivals in Western and Central Anatolia had been subdued, and anti-Ottoman coalitions among Muslim Anatolian princes had lost their power. Moreover, the Ottomans had become more adept at implementing methods of conquest and annexation such as the cooptation of the local ruling elites, the granting of various financial incentives to

---

[1] Âşık Çelebi, Meşāʿirüʾş-şuʿarā, 134a; Latifi, Tezkiretüʾş-şuʿarā (Istanbul: İkdam Matbaası, 1896–97), 335; Riyazi, Tezkire-yi Riyāżī, ms. Millet Genel Kütüphanesi 765, 133a; Beyani, Tezkire-yi şuʿarā-yı Beyānī, İstanbul Üniversitesi m.s. T.Y. 2568 (Halis Efendi), 92b; Kınalızade Hasan, Tezkiretüʾş- şuʿarā, ed. İbrahim Kutluk (Ankara: Türk Tarih Kurumu, 1978), 988. Later works repeat the information found in these near-contemporary sources: Ahmed Resmi, Ḥalīfetüʾr-rüʾesā, 5; Müstakimzade Süleyman Saʿdeddin Efendi, Tuḥfetüʾl-ḫaṭṭāṭīn (Istanbul: Devlet Matbaası, 1928), 525; Hüseyin Hüsameddin, Nişancılar Durağı, ISAM manuscript, 82. Also see Celia Kerslake, "Celalzade Mustafa Çelebi," TDVİA, vol. 7, 260–62; Şerafettin Turan, "Celal-Zade," İA, vol. 3, 61–63, for condensed accounts of Mustafa's biography.

[2] Uzunçarşılı, "Celâl zâde Mustafa ve Salih Çelebiler," 392.

[3] J.H. Mordtmann, "İsfendiyar Oğlu," EI 2; C.J. Heywood, "Kastamonu," ibid.; Yaşar Yücel, Anadolu Beylikleri Hakkında Araştırmalar 1, 2nd ed. (Ankara: Türk Tarih Kurumu, 1991), 53–142 passim.

producers and merchants, and the establishment of Ottoman control through the appointment of judges and the allotment of land grants (*tımar*).[4] The Ottomanization of Kastamonu was the first step in Mustafa's family's rise in Ottoman service. Rather than entering the service of another Anatolian Muslim ruler, Celaleddin traveled to the recently conquered Ottoman capital, Istanbul.

After graduation, Celaleddin became a lecturer at his alma mater, the madrasa of Hacı Hasanzade.[5] The school was situated at the lowest echelon of the school hierarchy, and its lecturers received modest stipends. Probably because judges were paid higher than lecturers, Celaleddin transferred into the legal branch and became a judge in the Balkan provinces.[6] His son Salih, Mustafa's younger brother, was born there, in Vulçitrin (Vučitrn/Vushtrri in modern-day Kosovo), in 1493.[7] The family then moved to Sarajevo. In his only anecdote about his youth, Mustafa tells his readers the story of Ottoman raiders who abrogated an Ottoman-Hungarian peace treaty by attacking the neighboring Hungarian territory. Celaleddin, the judge of Sarajevo at the time, intervened on their behalf with Firuz Bey, the governor of Bosnia, and saved them from being executed. Because Firuz Bey became governor after 1506, the anecdote places Celaleddin and his family in Sarajevo around the first decade of the sixteenth century.[8] The family relocated to Istanbul a few years after this incident, and Mustafa and Salih were able to finish their education in the capital. Celaleddin passed away in 1528–29, while

---

[4] On the tensions between the Ottomans and the Anatolian principalities, see Feridun M. Emecen, *İlk Osmanlılar ve Batı Anadolu Beylikler Dünyası* (Istanbul: Kitabevi, 2001); Hasan Basri Karadeniz, *Osmanlılar ile Beylikler Arasında Anadolu'da Meşruiyet Mücadelesi (XIV.–XVI. Yüzyıllar)* (Istanbul: Yeditepe, 2008). On mechanisms of annexation, see Halil İnalcık, "Ottoman Methods of Conquest," *StIsl* 2 (1954): 103–29.

[5] Information about Celaleddin is encountered only in two Ottoman biographical dictionaries: Mecdi Efendi, *Terceme-yi Şaḳā'iḳ-ı nuʿmāniyye* (Istanbul: Tabhane-yi Amire, 1853), 466; Müstakimzâde, *Tuḥfetü'l-ḫaṭṭāṭīn*, 152.

[6] İsmail Hakkı Uzunçarşılı, *Osmanlı Devletinin İlmiye Teşkilâtı* (Ankara: Türk Tarih Kurumu, 1965), 66–67. Also see the chart on the transfer from madrasa appointments to judgeships in Halil İnalcık, *The Ottoman Empire: The Classical Age 1300–1600* (New York: Praeger, 1973), 171.

[7] Uzunçarşılı, "Celâl zâde Mustafa ve Salih Çelebiler," 422. Salih received a madrasa education like his father and brother and subsequently climbed through the ranks of the Ottoman scholarly and legal hierarchy. He became known as an author of religious works, a translator, and a historian. The brothers remained close and spent their retirement in the same Istanbul neighborhood. For a concise account of his career and output, see *ibid.*, 422–41.

[8] *Mevahib*, 305b–306a.

living in his native Tosya[9] or, according to another report, in Amasya.[10] Celaleddin had a third son, Ataullah, also known as Atai, who must have died at a relatively young age because he is not mentioned in the majority of the sources from the period.[11]

Other than these scattered details, we do not have any information about Mustafa's forefathers. Celaleddin had a modest career; the positions he held as lecturer and judge were relatively unimpressive. Vulçitrin was one of the lowest appointments in the Balkan provinces,[12] and Sarajevo was a relatively small city when he served there. It is difficult to ascertain the family's social and economic background. Did Celaleddin come from a peasant family? This is not altogether impossible, but it would be difficult for agriculturalists to send a son to study in the capital. A scholarly background is also unlikely, given that the biographical dictionaries, which always reflect an acute concern with social and family background, do not mention any such ties for either Celaleddin or Mustafa. Celaleddin's forefathers were most probably mid-level merchants, shopkeepers, or perhaps artisans. It is true that these professions were transferred from father to son; however, in the presence of an elder son taking over the family business, younger sons were allowed (or obliged) to pursue opportunities elsewhere. Celaleddin's tenure at a minor madrasa and his low- to mid-level judgeships show that he did not necessarily enjoy the support of influential acquaintances, powerful figures from his own province, or elders of the religious orders (tarikat) through whose intercessions he might have obtained better positions. His name survives in the historical record mostly because his sons Mustafa and Salih adopted it as their patronymic.

Even though Celaleddin had a modest career, his relocation from Tosya to Istanbul and his career in Ottoman service created opportunities for his sons Mustafa and Salih. Thus, although Mustafa usually presents himself as a self-made man who rose to prominence solely through individual merit, he began his life with a crucial advantage, thanks to his father. Freeborn Muslims could enter the Ottoman ruling elite, the 'askeri class,

[9] Mecdi, Terceme-yi Şakā'ık, 466.
[10] Hüseyin Hüsameddin, Nişancılar Durağı. Mehmet Şakir Yılmaz agrees with the Amasya connection and relates it to Mustafa's rise in the bureaucratic career, as will be discussed later. See Yılmaz, "'Koca Nişancı' of Kanuni: Celalzade Mustafa Çelebi, Bureaucracy and 'Kanun' in the Reign of Süleyman the Magnificent, 1520–1566" (PhD diss., Bilkent University, 2006), 26–27.
[11] Uzunçarşılı, "Celâl zâde Mustafa ve Salih Çelebiler," 392. A letter from Salih to Atai suggests that the third brother was alive around late 1544, when Salih was given the Aleppo judgeship. See Salih, Münşe'āt, ms. SK, Kadızade Mehmed 557, 16b–18b.
[12] Uzunçarşılı, İlmiye Teşkilatı, 92n2.

after a madrasa education and also through descent from a father with *'askeri* status. (This particular background would become an important element of Mustafa's identity later in his life, when he would extol the virtues of freeborn Muslims over the limitations of the sultan's slaves.) The word *'askeri* implies a military form of service. At the time Mustafa and Salih joined the ruling elite, however, it encompassed madrasa teachers, judges, members of the sultan's palace household, and holders of various military-administrative positions. Next to freeborn Muslims, the ruling elite included many individuals who were enslaved as children through the practice of *devşirme* and educated in the palace household. Whereas freeborn Muslims mostly served as teachers and legal professionals, the slaves, whose owner was the sultan himself, mostly became soldiers and palace functionaries, and some of them eventually rose to important positions as governors-general and viziers. Especially after the middle of the fifteenth century, Ottoman sultans began to rely more on individuals from a slave background to create a non-aristocratic ruling elite. As a whole, the members of the ruling elite were distinguished from the subject population by the fact that they did not pay taxes, received stipends and land grants from the sultan for their services, and depended on special regulations and a special jurisdiction.[13] Socialization within the elite, patronage, and personal relationships played an important role in securing appointments. The relatively small size of the Ottoman scholarly and legal establishment in this period allowed individuals to know each other, study under the same masters, and have common acquaintances. For instance, Celaleddin studied together with Tacizade Cafer (d. 1515), one of the most influential early Ottoman prose masters and a chancellor under Selim I. Even though Cafer fell from favor and was executed on Selim's orders in 1515, it is very likely that Celaleddin had other influential acquaintances willing to help his sons receive a good madrasa education and find employment.[14]

The Education of a Muslim Boy

In the absence of a formal system of primary education, children's education in Ottoman lands, until the second half of the nineteenth

---

[13] The most concise description of the *'askeri* status is in Fleischer, *Mustafa Âli*, 5–7. Also see Colin Imber, *The Ottoman Empire, 1300–1650: The Structure of Power* (Basingstoke, Hampshire: Palgrave Macmillan, 2002), 128–42, for the recruitment and employment of the sultan's slaves.

[14] Yılmaz, "Koca Nişancı," 31–32.

century,[15] was basically left to local communities, religious orders, guilds, and families. Mosques, churches, and synagogues served as schools, where the children of parents who could afford the related fees and the cost of the necessary equipment learned the basics of reading religious texts. The level and quality of education depended on the family's status and wealth. In urban centers, well-to-do families could provide tutors for their children. Muslim religious orders and Christian monasteries reproduced their institutions and cultures through the instruction of members and acolytes. On the more practical side, education was part of the family business. The crucial skills of numeracy and bookkeeping, for instance, could best be learned either in one's own family or by working in a commercial enterprise. Receiving an education in the religious sciences might also begin as a family business, through the efforts of educated individuals who desired to transfer the family legacy to the future generations.[16] Celaleddin was probably the first teacher of his sons, introducing them to reading and writing; then, the brothers might have been sent to a mosque school, where they would be instructed on how to read the Quran and receive some rudimentary knowledge about Quran interpretation, Arabic grammar, the sayings of Prophet Muhammad, and the basics of Islamic law.[17] Ottoman territories were not much different than the rest of the Eurasian world, where elementary education was secured through multiple channels and in view of different objectives.[18]

[15] Two pioneering works about nineteenth-century Ottoman education that are best read in tandem are Benjamin C. Fortna, *Imperial Classroom: Islam, the State, and Education in the Late Ottoman Empire* (Oxford: Oxford University Press, 2002); Selçuk Akşin Somel, *The Modernization of Public Education in the Ottoman Empire, 1839–1908: Islamization, Autocracy, and Discipline* (Leiden: Brill, 2001).

[16] For useful studies on Islamic education, see Jonathan Berkey, *The Transmission of Knowledge in Medieval Cairo: A Social History of Islamic Education* (Princeton, NJ: Princeton University Press, 1992); Nelly Hanna, "Literacy and the 'Great Divide' in the Islamic World, 1300–1800," *Journal of Global History* 2 (2007): 175–93; Francis Robinson, "Education," in *Islamic Cultures and Societies to the End of the Eighteenth Century*, ed. Robert Irwin, vol. 4 in *The New Cambridge History of Islam*, ed. Michael Cook (Cambridge: Cambridge University Press, 2010), 497–531.

[17] This was the curriculum for a "children's school," as described in the endowment deed of the Süleymaniye Mosque, opened in 1557. See Ziya Kazıcı, *Osmanlı'da Eğitim-Öğretim* (Istanbul: Bilge, 2004), 87. For the mosque schools, see Hasan Akgündüz, *Klasik Dönem Osmanlı Medrese Sistemi: Amaç-Yapı-İşleyiş* (Istanbul: Ulusal, 1997), 200–210. Mustafa Âli, who attended a mosque school in the late 1540s/early 1550s, learned the basics of Arabic grammar there (Fleischer, *Mustafa Âli*, 21).

[18] For a comparison with early modern Europe, see Hilde de Ridder-Symoens, "Training and Professionalization," in *Power Elites and State Building*, ed. Wolfgang Reinhard, Theme D in *The Origins of the Modern State in Europe, 13th to 18th Centuries*, eds. Wim

Following basic education, a student's next step was to enroll in a madrasa, either in his native town or city or in another urban center, where he would be sent on the recommendation of his first teachers or on the basis of family connections. The Ottoman madrasas, beneficiaries of imperial and individual patronage, consisted of various strata. They were roughly classified with reference to the daily stipend their teachers received: madrasas of twenty (where a teacher received twenty *akçe*s a day) were followed by those of thirty, forty, and outer and inner fifty. Provincial madrasas, like those in the Balkans that Mustafa and Salih probably attended before moving to Istanbul, basically functioned as preparatory schools. Graduation from an inner-fifty madrasa, located at the time of Mustafa's adolescence in Edirne, Bursa, and Istanbul, allowed students to proceed to the next and highest level of the Ottoman madrasa system of the time: the eight madrasas established by Mehmed II after the conquest of Istanbul, called Sahn-ı Seman. After receiving a diploma from a Sahn-ı Seman teacher, the fresh graduate had to be designated, by the sultan's order and through the patronage of a prominent legal authority or a religious scholar, as an "attendant" (*mülazım*). This status made the graduate eligible, when available, for a teaching position at one of the lower-level madrasas or a judgeship at a small town.[19]

Around the time Mustafa was a student, the Ottoman madrasas did not have meticulously prepared and centrally determined curricula. Education, which became somehow more sophisticated as the student progressed through the layers of madrasas, involved the study of various Islamic sciences, such as Quranic exegesis and the analysis of Muhammad's sayings, and various aspects of Islamic law; philosophy and rhetoric were other major topics. A student could also concentrate on a wide variety of subjects ranging from mathematics and geometry to astrology,[20] but these often depended on the students' curiosity and the

Blockmans and Jean-Philippe Genet (Oxford: European Science Foundation, Clarendon Press, 1996), 149–72.

[19] This summary description of the Ottoman madrasa system is taken from Fleischer, *Mustafa Âli*, 25–26. Mustafa's brother Salih proceeded through this system and became an attendant under the patronage of Süleyman's personal preacher (*hoca*) Hayreddin Efendi in 1523–24 (TSMA, D. 9555, 3a).

[20] For lists of subjects and works studied in the madrasas, see Uzunçarşılı, *İlmiye Teşkilâtı*, 19–43; Mustafa Bilge, *İlk Osmanlı Medreseleri* (Istanbul: Edebiyat Fakültesi, 1984), 40–64; Câhid Baltacı, *XV–XVI. Asırlar Osmanlı Medreseleri: Teşkilât, Tarih* (Istanbul: İrfan Matbaası, 1976), 35–43. Cevat İzgi (*Osmanlı Medreselerinde İlim*, vol. 1, *Riyazî İlimler*, vol. 2, *Tabiî İlimler* [Istanbul: İz, 1997]) mentions a wide variety of subjects, from physics to zoology, from algebra to astronomy. It is quite likely that

teachers' ability. The intellectual capacities and level of knowledge of particular teachers, especially in the higher levels of the madrasa system, often shaped the formation of particular students. The student–teacher relationship was a crucial part of the education. Students graduated not only from an institution, but also from a particular teacher. The student–teacher bond could represent the beginning of a lifelong relationship, and teachers often vouched for their students and supported them throughout their careers.

Beyond providing an education, the upper-level madrasa was an important locale of socialization. Many students shared the same hostels and rooms, attended classes together, roamed the streets of the city, studied together, and wrote poetry and commented on each other's poems. This was the time when they made their first steps into urban and cultural life.[21] Not all madrasa students reached the ranks of the ruling elite, and not every successful graduate received a satisfactory appointment, but, in principle, a madrasa education paved the way to becoming a judge or a lecturer. With the increase in bureaucratic positions after the last decades of the fifteenth century, and especially in the first decades of the sixteenth, a considerable percentage of madrasa graduates became secretaries working for the imperial council or the treasury.[22] Next to his father's social and professional status, Mustafa's veritable entry into the ruling elite was realized through his madrasa education. Mustafa and his brother probably attended the first layers of the madrasa system in the Balkans,[23] but they received the best part of their education in the capital and became acquainted with prominent Ottoman scholars and administrators. Mustafa's teachers remain anonymous, but his brother Salih studied in Edirne and/or Istanbul with Kemalpaşazade Ahmed (1468/69–1534), one of the most accomplished scholars of the period, and a future chief jurisconsult.[24]

---

many of these were either not part of the core teaching or were only taught through the intermediary of encyclopedic works summarizing various topics, especially in natural sciences.

[21] Mustafa Âli's reminiscences of his madrasa days are in Fleischer, *Mustafa Âli*, 28–32.

[22] Fleischer, *Mustafa Âli*, 19–20. Colin Imber provides a concise account of the career paths open to the madrasa graduates in *The Structure of Power*, 229–31. Also see Uzunçarşılı, *İlmiye Teşkilatı*, 45–46 and 87–88.

[23] For various Balkan madrasas see Bilge, *İlk Osmanlı Medreseleri*, 168, 169, 175, 200–203, 205–07.

[24] Uzunçarşılı, "Celâl zâde Mustafa ve Salih Çelebiler," 422–23; Mustafa Kılıç, "Kemal Paşa-Zâdenin (İbn Kemal) Talebeleri," *Belleten* 58, no. 221 (1994): 55–70.

What was the particular use of a madrasa education for Mustafa, the future bureaucrat? In terms of particular bureaucratic skills, such as the mastery of epistolary literature or the Ottoman *kanun*, the body of customary/dynastic law, a madrasa graduate did not learn much, at least at the beginning of the sixteenth century. (Elements of the Sharia, on the other hand, figured prominently in the curriculum.) Madrasa education rather provided the future teachers, bureaucrats, and judges with a sound educational and intellectual basis on which hands-on professional learning could be built during their later career. Being a madrasa graduate, like his descent from a freeborn Muslim family, would become another identity marker for Mustafa. For the rest of his life, true to the neo-Platonic formation he received in the madrasa, he would associate the perfect application of divine law and the securing of political order with piety and reason and believe that, in the management of the empire, the pen was mightier than the sword.

The World that Selim Made: The Ottomans Join Early Modern Eurasia

Mustafa's family relocated from Sarajevo to Istanbul around 1510, during a time of intense political troubles. Succession struggles among princes, an endemic Ottoman problem, were exacerbated by the rise of Shah Ismail around the turn of the century and the rebellions of his followers in Anatolia in 1511–12. The Ottomans had, from the very beginning, opposed the partition of their lands among princes, and favored what Cemal Kafadar calls "unigeniture":[25] following the sultan's death, and sometimes before, princes fought among themselves for succession, and only one of them became sultan. Thus, rather than dividing territories among the members of the ruling family according to a common Turko-Mongol practice, the Ottomans were able to secure the reign of only one member of the dynasty. This ensured the preservation of the domains, but also legitimized civil war as the path to succession.[26]

---

[25] Cemal Kafadar, *Between Two Worlds: The Construction of the Ottoman State* (Berkeley: University of California Press, 1995), 136–38.

[26] See Halil İnalcık, "The Ottoman Succession and its Relation to the Turkish Concept of Sovereignty," in *The Middle East and the Balkans under the Ottoman Empire: Essays on Economy and Society* (Bloomington: Indiana University Press, 1993), 37–69; cf. Joseph Fletcher, "Turco-Mongolian Monarchic Tradition in the Ottoman Empire," *Harvard Ukrainian Studies* 3–4 (1979–80): 236–51.

FIGURE 2. Selim I is presented with the head of the Mamluk sultan Qansuh al-Ghawri (*Hünernāme*, vol. 1, TSMK, Hazine 1523, 211b).

In 1509, Selim, an Ottoman prince, was the provincial governor (*san-cakbeyi*) of Trabzon, on the southeastern corner of the Black Sea. He was concerned that his father and the majority of the elite favored his brother, Ahmed, as the successor to the Ottoman throne, which amounted to an eventual death sentence for him. Selim left Trabzon, crossed over to the Crimea to join his father-in-law (who was the khan of Crimea) and his son (the future sultan Süleyman, the provincial governor of Caffa), and then moved to the Balkans, where he gathered an army. He could not prevail over his father's forces in a fateful encounter near Istanbul in the summer of 1511, but he was able to secure the support of the janissary corps and the military elements in the Balkan provinces. He had already established a martial reputation for having fought against the Georgians and Ismail's supporters during his governorate in Trabzon. His nearly self-destructive campaign against his father further solidified his image as a warrior prince: he was widely seen, against his more gentlemanly brothers Korkud and Ahmed, as the man who could meet the considerable military challenges created by pro-Ismail rebellions in Anatolia and Ismail's move from Iran and Eastern Anatolia to the west. Selim thus came to the throne in May 1512. From then until January 1514, he waged incessant warfare against his brothers and their sons, finally emerging as the sole victor in early 1514.[27]

The march of Shah Ismail Safavi (r. 1501–24) to power in the lands of the Akkoyunlu Turkmen confederation prepared the necessary background for Selim's rise to power as well. Ismail, as the leader of the Safavid religious order and the self-styled representative (or incarnation) of Twelver Shiism's messianic Hidden Imam, led a politico-religious movement that created a powerful vortex for various groups in the Middle East, including many in Ottoman territories. The relations between the Ottoman political center and the nomadic communities in Anatolia had always been strained, and the nomads resisted, to the extent of their abilities, Ottoman attempts at taxation, sedentarization, and deportation. Moreover, in various parts of Southern and Eastern Anatolia, Ottoman conquest was relatively recent, and the Ottomans did not have time to co-opt or assimilate the local power holders. Ismail, willingly or

---

[27] For Selim's rise to power, the classical study is Çağatay Uluçay, "Yavuz Sultan Selim Nasıl Padişah Oldu?" *Tarih Dergisi* 6, no. 9 (March 1954): 53–90; *Tarih Dergisi* 7, no. 10 (September 1954): 117–42; *Tarih Dergisi* 8, nos. 11–12 (September 1955): 185–200. For a more recent study that discusses the contemporary and modern literature about the issue, see Erdem Çıpa, "The Centrality of the Periphery: The Rise to Power of Selim I, 1481–1512" (PhD diss., Harvard University, 2007).

unwillingly, started a powerful movement that resembled a social revolution and pulled in not only nomads, but also townsmen and disgruntled *tımar* holders as well.[28] Since Timur's (r. 1370–1405) invasion of Anatolia in 1402, the death of Bayezid I (r. 1389–1402) in captivity, and the partition of the Ottoman realm among surviving princes, this was the first genuinely existential threat encountered by the Ottoman polity.

Under Bayezid II, the Ottoman establishment had already tried to formulate a coherent military as well as ideological/theological answer against the Safavids.[29] Selim, on the other hand, turned it into his main focus. He sought the support of religious scholars, who sanctioned his activities against the Safavids through legal opinions (*fetva*) that described the latter as apostates and unbelievers and ascribed to the Ottoman sultan the duty to fight.[30] As soon as he exterminated his dynastic rivals, Selim marched against Ismail's followers in Anatolia and massacred thousands of them. He then marched further east and defeated Ismail's troops at the Battle of Çaldıran in August 1514. The victory at Çaldıran, secured by the supremacy of Ottoman gunpowder weapons over the Safavid cavalry and light infantry, probably stopped an eventual Safavid takeover of Anatolia. Because both rulers survived what was expected to be a final and fatal encounter, however, Çaldıran also signifies the first step in the institutionalization of the Ottoman-Safavid religious and political

---

[28] John E. Woods, *The Aqquyunlu: Clan, Confederation, Empire*, revised and expanded edition (Salt Lake City: University of Utah Press, 1999), 163–72; Adel Allouche, *The Origins and Development of the Ottoman-Ṣafavid Conflict (906–962/1500–1555)* (Berlin: Klaus Schwarz, 1983), 65–99; Andrew Newman, *Safavid Iran: Rebirth of a Persian Empire* (London: I.B. Tauris, 2006), 13–20. Colin Paul Mitchell brings together the political events of the time with the religious and intellectual climate in his *The Practice of Politics in Safavid Iran: Power, Religion and Rhetoric* (London: I.B. Tauris, 2009), 19–46. For the impact of the Safavids on the Anatolian tribes, see Hanna Sohrweide, "Der Sieg der Ṣafawiden in Persien und seine Rickwürkungen auf die Schiiten Anatoliens im 16. Jahrhundert," *Der Islam* 41 (1965), esp. 138–64; Faruk Sümer, *Safevi Devletinin Kuruluşu ve Gelişmesinde Anadolu Türklerinin Rolü: Şah İsmail ve Halefleri ile Anadolu Türkleri* (Ankara: Selçuklu Tarih ve Medeniyeti Enstitüsü Yayınları, Güven Matbaası, 1976), passim; Rıza Yıldırım, "Turkomans between Two Empires: The Origins of the Qizilbash Identity in Anatolia (1447–1514)" (PhD diss., Bilkent University, February 2008), 245–415.

[29] Feridun Emecen, "Osmanlı Devleti'nin 'Şark Meselesi'nin Ortaya Çıkışı: İlk Münasebetler ve İç Yansımaları," *Tarihten Günümüze Türk-İran İlişkileri Sempozyumu* (Ankara: Türk Tarih Kurumu, 2003), 33–48.

[30] For a detailed analysis of these legal opinions, see İsmail Safa Üstün, "Heresy and Legitimacy in the Ottoman Empire in the Sixteenth Century" (PhD diss., University of Manchester, 1991), 35–59.

competition. In his next attempts at securing Ottoman domination in the region and preempting another Safavid push eastward, Selim destroyed the principality of Dulkadir in 1515 and overran the Mamluks of Egypt and Syria in 1516–17, bringing the Holy Cities of Mecca and Medina under Ottoman sovereignty. Thanks to his swift conquests, he was thus able to almost double the empire's territory and population in the scope of a few years.[31]

Selim's takeover of Egypt and Syria has aptly been called "the beginning of the sixteenth century world war." His capture of parts of the Arabian Peninsula and the Red Sea coast pitted the Ottomans against the Portuguese in the Indian Ocean, further contributing to their emergence as global actors in early modern Eurasia.[32] Selim's role in preparing the political, religious, and cultural agenda of the sixteenth century, however, has not received enough recognition.[33] By rising to the challenges posed by Ismail and his supporters, Selim started a period of intense military, cultural, and religious competition. Ottoman imperial ideology began to revolve increasingly around notions of messianism, universal monarchy, the caliphate, and the ultimate politico-religious leadership of the ruler over his subjects.[34] Such universalist ideologies had been popular among the Ottoman elite since the conquest of Constantinople in 1453,[35] but their popularity had somehow decreased under Bayezid II,

---

[31] Allouche, *Ottoman-Ṣafavid Conflict*, 104–30; for a documentary history of the Ottoman-Safavid conflict in this period, see Jean-Louis Bacqué-Grammont, *Les Ottomans, les Safavides et leurs voisins: contribution à l'histoire des relations internationales dans l'Orient islamique de 1514 à 1524* (Istanbul: Nederlands Historisch-Archaeologisch Instituut te Istanbul, 1987), 50–274. For a concise account of Selim's reign, see Caroline Finkel, *Osman's Dream: The Story of the Ottoman Empire, 1300–1923* (New York: Basic Books, 2006), 102–14 and Halil İnalcık, "Selīm I," *EI 2*; for a detailed study and analysis of the Ottoman conquest of Egypt and Syria from the perspective of both sides, see Benjamin Lellouch, *Les Ottomans en Égypte: Historiens et conquérants au XVIe siècle* (Paris: Peeters, 2006), 1–36 passim.

[32] Andrew Hess, "The Ottoman Conquest of Egypt (1517) and the Beginning of the Sixteenth-Century World War," *IJMES* 4, no. 1 (January 1973): 55–76; Casale, *The Ottoman Age of Exploration*, 25–31.

[33] For a rare treatment of these issues, see Snjezana Buzov, "The Lawgiver and His Lawmakers: The Role of Legal Discourse in the Formation of Ottoman Imperial Culture" (PhD diss., University of Chicago, 2005), 17–23.

[34] Cornell Fleischer, "The Lawgiver as Messiah: The Making of the Imperial Image in the Reign of Süleymân," in *Soliman le magnifique et son temps: Actes du Colloque de Paris. Galeries Nationales du Grand Palais, 7–10 Mars 1990*, ed. Gilles Veinstein (Paris: La Documentation Française, 1992), 160–64.

[35] See Kaya Şahin, "Constantinople and the End Time: The Ottoman Conquest as a Portent of the Last Hour," *JEMH* 14, no. 4 (2010): 317–54.

whereas Selim revived them to an unprecedented extent. In the coming decades, the new ideological arsenal would be utilized not only against the Safavids, but the Habsburgs as well.

Selim's conquests did not solely produce new political and ideological stakes. They also led to the emergence of new problems on the administrative front. The quick conquest of large territories in Eastern Anatolia, Syria, and Egypt did not mean that the Ottomans had control over them. Most of these areas had been under the rule of various Muslim powers for several centuries, and local laws, customs, and rules were developed enough to require a careful work of harmonization and adaptation on the part of the Ottomans. Moreover, in predominantly Muslim areas of the Middle East, the Ottomans had always suffered from being a Muslim dynasty with a less than stellar pedigree, and the simple act of conquering never brought them the comforts of legitimacy. The persistence of local and tribal identities and the survival of figures from the old dynasties further complicated the task. For these reasons, a new administrative apparatus was increasingly needed to make the Ottoman presence durable in the newly conquered areas and to ensure the extraction of resources necessary for the Ottoman military machine.

Selim was the first ruler to actively steer the Ottoman enterprise toward a process of early modern Eurasian empire building. He deployed large armies fortified with gunpowder weapons and instigated a process of territorial expansion. He explained and defended this expansion with reference to ideologies that attributed the Ottoman sultan a function of political and spiritual guidance and a world-historical role in a fight between the forces of good and evil. He promoted sultanic authority, tried to curtail the power of the Ottoman elite and especially the prominent pashas, and created an environment that was conducive to the rise of secretaries as record keepers and the rulers' trusted assistants. The generation of Süleyman and Mustafa inherited these challenges, problems, and opportunities, and members of this generation spent their lives in a world whose foundations were laid by Selim.

A Wise Career Choice at a Favorable Moment

Mustafa entered Ottoman service as a secretary of the imperial council in the spring of 1516,[36] while he was a *danişmend*, an advanced madrasa

---

[36] Since Mustafa claims that he (or the case for his appointment) was personally presented to the sultan, the date of his appointment must have been between the beginning of AH 922

student. He was, by his own admission, particularly supported by Piri Mehmed Pasha and Seydi Bey.[37] Piri Mehmed was the third vizier at the time and would advance to the rank of grand vizier in early 1518, also serving Süleyman in this capacity until 1523.[38] Seydi Bey served as treasurer (*defterdar*) under Selim and chancellor under Süleyman. It has been argued that his recruitment was a reflection of Mustafa's ties to a group of individuals hailing from Amasya, all members of the Halveti religious order.[39] In the absence of strict regulations for the recruitment of madrasa graduates into the scribal service, patronage and personal guarantees were crucial factors for potential candidates.[40] It is thus possible that Mustafa, as the son of a retired judge, benefited from his father's friends and acquaintances. Finally, it is quite likely that, in front of the daunting administrative challenges in the aftermath of Selim's Eastern conquests, Piri Mehmed simply asked madrasa teachers to recommend skilled pupils. For instance, another future chancellor, Ramazanzade Mehmed, was also hired by Piri Mehmed a year after Mustafa, while he was also an advanced madrasa student.[41]

Mustafa's own account of his entry into Ottoman service, composed toward the end of his life, is highly romanticized. At the same time, it is quite revealing about his thoughts on bureaucratic identity and merit. In the introduction of his work on Selim, Mustafa briefly revisits, with a nostalgic tone, his last years in the madrasa. He presents himself as a young man who devoted himself to what might be translated as the literary arts and Islamic sciences (*tahṣīl-i fünūn-ı ādāb ve tekmīl-i 'ulūm-ı ma'ārif-iktisāba ṭālib ve rāġıb*). Toward the end of his education, he says, he began to seek a position suitable for a young man from a distinguished background. Mustafa does not explain what he means by the "distinguished sons (*ebnā-yı cins*)," but he obviously implies freeborn Muslims from families like his own. It is not clear whether he developed this particular social identity early in his life or later, but it is important

(February 5, 1516) and Selim's departure to confront the Mamluks on 4 Cumaziyelevvel 922/June 5, 1516 (İsmail Hami Danişmend, *İzahlı Osmanlı Tarihi Kronolojisi*, vol. 2, *M.1513–1573, H. 919–981* [Istanbul: Türkiye Yayınevi, 1948], 24; hereafter İOTK 2). Mustafa corroborates the date of AH 922 in *Mevahib*, 87b.

[37] *Selimname*, 21b.

[38] For a laudatory account of Piri Mehmed's life and career, see Yusuf Küçükdağ, *Vezîr-i Âzam Pîrî Mehmed Paşa (1463?–1532)* (Konya: n.p., 1994).

[39] Yılmaz, "Koca Nişancı," 30.

[40] The first regulations to that effect were promulgated under Süleyman (Uzunçarşılı, *İlmiye Teşkilatı*, 45–46).

[41] Yılmaz, "Koca Nişancı," 34.

to note that he thus establishes an important difference between himself and those members of the ruling elite from a slave background. As for his professional options in the mid-1510s, Mustafa informs his readers that the teaching profession is financially insecure (*ḥall-i ʿavāidi meşkūk*), condemning its practitioners to poverty and want (*fakr ve iḥtiyāca enīs*). The legal profession (*każā*), on the other hand, is presented through a play of words as prone to chance and accident (*maḥż-ı każā*).[42] Becoming a secretary offers a solution out of this financial and moral conundrum.[43] Moreover, it provides the satisfaction of working with pen and paper, which chases away anxiety and sadness (*fevāid-i ṣemerāt-ı kalem dāfiʿ-i envāʿ-ı humūm ve elemdir*). Only the secretarial path offers *rāḥat* and *ḥużūr*, material well-being and peace of mind.[44]

Mustafa's idealization of the bureaucratic career, which amounts to a repudiation of the professions exercised by his father, brother, and many of his acquaintances, is a reflection of his anxieties about promoting the secretaries as the most valuable servants of the empire. Mustafa entered the Ottoman scribal service at a time when it was about to become a prominent section of the Ottoman central administration even though, in terms of numbers, the secretaries never surpassed the military men or the religious scholars and judges. In 1515, a year before Mustafa entered the service, there were a total of thirty-six secretaries working for the treasury and the imperial council. On the other hand, in the last decades of the fifteenth century, scribal units had become relatively separate from the sultan's own household, and treasury and imperial council secretaries were on their way to constitute two separate groups within the scribal service.[45] These developments led to a new administrative mentality and professional identity, as will be discussed in Chapter 7. It suffices to say here that they are typical of early modern empire formation and were observed between the late fifteenth and mid-sixteenth centuries in various

---

[42] Mustafa's moral qualms about the legal profession were shared by other madrasa graduates in the sixteenth and seventeenth centuries: Aslı Niyazioğlu, "On Altıncı Yüzyıl Sonunda Osmanlı'da Kadılık Kabusu ve Nîhânî'nin Rüyası," *JTS* 31, no. 2 (2007): 133–43.

[43] Cornell Fleischer (*Mustafa Âli*, 221n15), while discussing a list of secretaries from 1527, shows that the sons of judges who entered the scribal service received higher stipends and enjoyed a particular prestige.

[44] *Selimname*, 21a–b. For *ḥużūr* as a prominent individual and communal ideal under Süleyman, see Buzov, "The Lawgiver and His Lawmakers," 11, 180–87.

[45] For these processes, the best study is still Cornell Fleischer, "Preliminaries to the Study of Ottoman Bureaucracy," *JTS* 10 (1986): 137–39. Also see Yılmaz, "Koca Nişancı," 11–13.

Eurasian polities that underwent a process of expansion as well as internal consolidation. These developments were accompanied by an increase of the ruler's and the court's political power, new attempts at ideological legitimacy, and new levels of institutionalization.[46] Without neglecting the particularities of the Ottoman experience, and after recognizing differences among various cases (e.g., the Safavids suffered more than the Ottomans the challenges of reining in semiautonomous military figures), it can be argued that Mustafa found himself at the beginning stages of a typically early modern bureaucratic development, which was characterized by a slow but determined transition "from ad hoc to routine."[47]

Some of Mustafa's late-life reminiscences provide a few clues about the atmosphere of the Ottoman scribal service in this period. At the end of 1517, Selim invited Piri Mehmed to join him in Damascus, together with a group of secretaries which, probably due to his relative inexperience at the time, did not include Mustafa. Piri Mehmed, appointed grand vizier in January 1518, was given the task of guarding the Ottoman-Safavid border and, more importantly, supervising the activities of the Ottoman land surveyors in the area.[48] The detailed survey registers (tahrir) of Diyarbekir (1518) and Malatya (1519) show the level of intense administrative activity and the Ottoman urge to create a viable presence in Eastern Anatolia.[49] The workload increased following the pasha's return to Edirne at the end of 1518. Selim's dismissal of his other viziers and his reliance on Piri Mehmed did not facilitate the process either; the pasha had to ask the sultan to appoint to the vizierate Çoban Mustafa Pasha, the governor-general (beylerbeyi) of Rumeli, to assist him.[50] According to Mustafa's testimony, Piri Mehmed was so busy that, after leaving the palace at the end of a full work day, he would continue working in his

---

[46] Cf., among others, Klaus Michael Röhrborn, *Provinzen und Zentralgewalt Persiens im 16. und 17. Jahrhundert* (Berlin: Walter de Gruyter, 1966); Howell A. Lloyd, *The State, France and the Sixteenth Century* (London: Allen & Unwin, 1983), 48–83; David Loades, *Tudor Government: Structures of Authority in the Sixteenth Century* (Oxford: Blackwell, 1997), 17–79; Muzaffar Alam and Sanjay Subrahmanyam, "Introduction," in *The Mughal State 1526–1750* (Delhi: Oxford University Press, 1998), 1–71; Kenneth H. Marcus, *The Politics of Power: Elites of an Early Modern State in Germany* (Mainz: Philipp von Zabern, 2000), 37–74.

[47] Cf. Ellen E. Kittell, *From Ad Hoc to Routine: A Case Study in Medieval Bureaucracy* (Philadelphia: University of Pennsylvania Press, 1991).

[48] *Selimname*, 209a.

[49] M. Mehdi İlhan, *Amid (Diyarbakır): 1518 Tarihli Defter-i Mufassal* (Ankara: Türk Tarih Kurumu, 2000); Ersin Gülsoy, *Malatya Divriği ve Darende Sancaklarının İlk Tahriri (1519)* (Erzurum: Fenomen, 2009).

[50] *Selimname*, 212a–b.

mansion through the night. He would attend the imperial council meeting the next morning where, until noon, he would present to the sultan his work from the previous night. These long nights in the pasha's mansion were often interrupted, as Mustafa remembers, by palace gatekeepers sent by the sultan to inquire about various matters.[51]

Mustafa, writing in the mid-1560s, presents Piri Mehmed and Seydi as two officials who shouldered the heavy burden of managing the realm; more importantly, they taught the young secretary skills that were not imparted by his madrasa education.[52] Piri Mehmed must have trusted the young man, because he chose him to testify for a prominent religious leader accused by the sultan of supporting pretenders to the throne. Following the day's imperial council meeting, Piri Mehmed brought Mustafa into the sultan's presence. Braving Selim's famously harsh temperament, Mustafa defended the sheikh's reputation to the best of his knowledge, and his determination left a positive impression on the sultan.[53] Another anecdote shows that the embryonic bureaucratic apparatus was already careful about the language and style of its documents and also gives clues about Mustafa's privileged place in the scribal service. Accordingly, Selim began to ask for Mustafa when he needed to write secret dispatches. The young secretary, already imbued with a sense of scribal pride, would correct some expressions in drafts prepared by the sultan, which irritated Selim. Mustafa would then appease the sultan by telling him that only the new versions were worthy of a world conqueror such as Selim.[54]

It is possible that Mustafa amplified his role in these anecdotes, told many years later from a position of power. On the other hand, it seems that he did enjoy the care and attention of two important mentors and was given the opportunity to distinguish himself among his peers, to the extent of personally helping the sultan compose his correspondence. His fortune also depended on the fact that he lived in a period that was formative for the Ottoman scribal service. In this environment, at the

---

[51] *Ibid.*, 40a.

[52] *Ibid.*, 22a. Mustafa often mentioned Seydi Bey as his master and teacher, lauding his knowledge of Ottoman law and chancery procedure (Uzunçarşılı, "Celâl zâde Mustafa ve Salih Çelebiler," 393n8).

[53] The anecdote is taken from Mustafa Âli. Cf. Fleischer, *Mustafa Âli*, 392n6, and Yılmaz, "Koca Nişancı," 36–37. According to Yılmaz, this anecdote establishes Mustafa's connection to the Amasya circles because the accused, Gümüşlüoğlu Mehmed, was a prominent Halveti leader from Amasya. Mustafa gives a full account of the sheikh's troubles in *Selimname*, 215b–217a, without mentioning his role in Mehmed's release.

[54] Beyani, *Tezkire-yi şu'arā-yı Beyānī*, 92b.

very beginning of a phase of bureaucratic development, merit was quickly awarded, and a young and relatively inexperienced secretary could play an important role in the administration. If he had chosen an academic or legal career, he might have received a position as a junior lecturer or the judge of a small town. After a few years in the scribal service, on the other hand, he had become the close collaborator of the grand vizier Piri Mehmed and the occasional helper of the sultan. From this privileged and elitist vantage point, Mustafa would observe and record the political and ideological developments of the era, and play an ever-growing role in the management of the empire and the creation of a new imperial discourse.

The Perils of the Sultanate: Süleyman Comes to Power

The accession of a new sultan always meant changes within the Ottoman ruling elite. The new sultan promoted his household members and clients, whereas the viziers and household members of the previous sultan presented a challenge. The sultan needed the knowhow of his father's grand vizier and viziers; at the same time, he needed to establish his authority. Orientalist clichés of Ottoman absolutism and Oriental despotism notwithstanding, every sultan had to negotiate his position vis-à-vis the high-ranking members of the Ottoman ruling elite. The first years of every reign were thus characterized by particularly intense factional struggles in the highest administrative and palace circles.

Süleyman's first years on the throne were no exception. His uneventful accession in the absence of other contenders has traditionally been interpreted as a positive event. However, it also meant that he had not established a martial reputation by fighting his way to the throne. Second, his father's swift victories over the Safavids and the Mamluks, coupled with his tight control over the members of the 'askeri class, constituted a seemingly insurmountable legacy. Third, the persistence of the Safavid problem and Selim's failure to organize any military campaigns against the European Christians imposed an ambitious military and political agenda. Finally, Eastern Anatolia, Syria, and Egypt had been conquered, but lasting Ottoman control had not yet been established.[55] Just as Mustafa had entered the secretarial profession at a time when its sphere of action and

---

[55] For the challenges that awaited Süleyman both inside and outside the Ottoman realm, see Buzov, "The Lawgiver and His Lawmakers," 23–29; Ebru Turan, "The Sultan's Favorite: İbrahim Pasha and the Making of the Ottoman Universal Sovereignty in the Reign of Sultan Süleyman" (PhD diss., University of Chicago, 2007), 16–71 passim.

responsibilities were increasing, Süleyman came to the throne in an environment that required considerable dedication to imperial consolidation, both administratively and ideologically. His contemporaries in Eurasia, such as Charles V (king of Spain, 1515–55; Holy Roman Emperor, 1520–55), the Safavid ruler Shah Tahmasb (r. 1524–76), the Mughal Humayun (r. 1530–40, 1555–56), Henry VIII (r. 1509–47), and Francis I (r. 1515–47) were faced with similar agendas. Süleyman would spend most of his political and military career fighting against Charles and Tahmasb, countering their universalist political and religious claims, and establishing an administrative structure tailored to the requirements of the era.

Mustafa's *Tabakat* presents an insider's view of the tensions at the beginning of Süleyman's reign. Compared with other contemporary Ottoman works, *Tabakat*'s passages on Süleyman's early years are strikingly candid in their description of the sultan's inexperience, the struggles at the court, the hardships of long military campaigns, and the tensions that plagued the higher echelons of the Ottoman administration. One of the chief architects of sixteenth-century Ottoman imperialism thus offers, out of his self-ascribed duty as historian and bureaucrat, one of the most original narratives on this particular period. He clearly identifies with Piri Mehmed's faction and expresses his unbound sympathy for this fellow madrasa graduate and freeborn Muslim. Piri Mehmed's rival is Ahmed Pasha, the governor-general of Rumeli under Selim and an administrator with a military and slave background. Beyond Mustafa's sympathy for Piri Mehmed, the rivalry is also presented as an opposition between two stereotypes: the talented and rational administrator who serves the dynasty and the realm out of a sense of duty, and the impetuous and ambitious military man who yearns for more power and glory, acts against the realm's interests, and eventually brings about his own destruction.[56]

Mustafa was very likely present in Süleyman's ceremonial sitting on the throne on September 30, 1520, the submission ritual the next day, and Selim's burial, all of which he vividly describes for his readers. In passages that amalgamate the gravity of the funeral with elation for the enthronement, he compares Süleyman's accession to the rise of the sun, the king of all stars, from the East.[57] After providing a few anecdotes about how the new sultan tries to redress injustices throughout his realm, Mustafa

---

[56] For various negative portrayals of Ahmed Pasha, see *Tabakat*, 27b, 47a, 83a, 86a, 88a, 110b.

[57] *Selimname*, 218b; *Tabakat*, 25a–27a.

FIGURE 3. Süleyman's enthronement (detail from *Hünernāme*, vol. 2, TSMK, Hazine 1524, 26a).

discusses two issues that required the sultan's immediate attention: a rebellion in Syria, and the refusal, on the part of the king of Hungary, to renew the Ottoman-Hungarian armistice of March 1519.[58] Janbardi al-Ghazali was an old Mamluk commander who had changed sides and joined the Ottomans following their victory over the Mamluk sultan Qansuh al-Ghawri at Marj Dabik in 1516. He was subsequently appointed the governor-general of Damascus, in the hopes that he would remain loyal. (The policy of using ex-Mamluks in Ottoman service extended to others such as Khayr Bak, who was named the governor of Egypt.) A number of Italian sources and intelligence reports by Ottoman officials in Mosul and Diyarbekir suggest that Janbardi considered himself a semiautonomous ruler and established relations with Ismail, Selim's arch-rival.[59] After Selim's death, Janbardi severed his ties with the Ottoman capital and rebelled in November 1520, with the support of his fellow Mamluks. The rebellion and the Ottoman response, in Mustafa's account, illustrate the new sultan's inexperience and Piri Mehmed's weight in the management of the realm. The sultan was utterly surprised by these developments, but the grand vizier quickly organized a military response by sending Ferhad Pasha against Janbardi.[60] Following Janbardi's defeat, he ordered Ferhad Pasha to identify the *tımar* holders in the region (some of whom were members of the Mamluk military class) to determine Janbardi's supporters.[61] A letter from Piri Mehmed to Süleyman portrays the nature of the relationship between the sultan and his grand vizier in these early days. In the letter, after summarizing the misdeeds of some *tımar* holders and listing their names, the pasha merely asks the sultan to give his formal approval for the measures that he planned.[62] The usual ceremonial formulae used to address the sultan, which would

---

[58] This refusal was probably due to the king's conviction that he had a better position vis-à-vis the Ottomans following Selim's death and Süleyman's coronation, the latter being perceived as relatively weak and inexperienced in Europe. See Turan, "The Sultan's Favorite," 30–31.

[59] Bacqué-Grammont, *Les Ottomans, les Safavides et leurs voisins*, 274–93.

[60] For a detailed account, by Mustafa, of Janbardi's background and his entry into Ottoman service, followed by his rebellion and the Ottoman victory, see *Tabakat*, 28b–40a; also see Hüseyin Gazi Yurdaydın, *Kanunî'nin Cülûsu ve İlk Seferleri* (Ankara: Türk Tarih Kurumu, 1961), 6–14; *İOTK 2*, 65–67; Adnan Bakhit, *The Ottoman Province of Damascus in the Sixteenth Century* (Beirut: Librairie du Liban, 1982), 19–34. Turan's discussion of the Janbardi affair through the testimonies of contemporary Italian sources (Turan, "The Sultan's Favorite," 37–52) illuminates Janbardi's activities in a larger context beyond Mustafa's Ottoman-centric narrative.

[61] Küçükdağ, *Vezîr-i Âzam Pîrî Mehmed Paşa*, 54.

[62] The letter (TSMA E. 5013) is reproduced in *ibid.*, 255, Document 5.

become even more elaborate under Mustafa's supervision in the decades to come, are conspicuously absent.

The Hungarian challenge, on the other hand, was met with a large-scale military campaign that took Süleyman to the Balkans and resulted in the capture of Belgrade. The Hungarians had been the major rival of the Ottomans in the Balkans and Central Europe since the middle of the fifteenth century. Both Bayezid II and Selim I had preferred to manage Ottoman-Hungarian relations relatively peacefully, with a series of treaties.[63] According to Mustafa, Süleyman initially wanted to renew his father's agreement with the king of Hungary and sent an envoy upon his coronation. The king, however, delayed the Ottoman envoy and proved, by this act, his unwillingness to renew the ceasefire.[64] It is possible that the Ottoman offer for peace was not entirely sincere; the king's refusal provided the sultan with the excuses he needed to start a campaign. Süleyman's first campaign has been described as the first step of a conscious policy toward Hungary, or the first phase of Ottoman imperialism's claims to universal monarchy, but these arguments, first proposed by sixteenth-century Ottoman historians themselves, were formulated ex post facto, in the light of later developments in Ottoman imperial ideology.[65] In reality, the dynamics behind the campaign were of a humbler nature. Süleyman had yet to prove his worth on the battlefield and assert his authority over the members of his own ruling class; moreover, there were expectations in various circles in Istanbul that the new sultan should compensate for his father's failure to act on the European front.[66]

Mustafa had witnessed Selim's conquests in Syria and Egypt from afar, as a secretary in Istanbul. Süleyman's first campaign was his first as well, and he left Istanbul on May 20, 1521, traveling with the army. Because he spent the campaign as a secretary assisting Piri Mehmed, he

---

[63] Turan, "The Sultan's Favorite," 27–30.

[64] *Tabakat*, 31b. For other contemporary Ottoman interpretations of the motives behind the campaign, see Yurdaydın, *Kanunî'nin Cülûsu ve İlk Seferleri*, 15–16.

[65] M. Tayyib Gökbilgin, "Kanunî Sultan Süleyman'ın Macaristan ve Avrupa Siyasetinin Sebep ve Âmilleri, Geçirdiği Safhalar," in *Kanunî Armağanı*, ed. Uluğ İğdemir (Ankara: Türk Tarih Kurumu, 1970), 5–7; Pál Fodor, "Ottoman Policy Towards Hungary, 1520–1541," *Acta Orientalia Academiae Scientiarum Hungaricae* 45, nos. 2–3 (1991): 285–91; Turan, "The Sultan's Favorite," 75–78. For a discussion of the ad hoc aspects of Ottoman policies in Central Europe, see Rhoads Murphey, "Süleyman I and the Conquest of Hungary: Ottoman Manifest Destiny or a Delayed Reaction to Charles V's Universalist Vision," *JEMH* 5, no. 3 (2001): 197–221, passim.

[66] Turan, "The Sultan's Favorite," 72–75.

narrates the campaign from the viewpoint of the grand vizier. He discloses many unsavory incidents that are not encountered in other contemporary works and shows that the conquest of Belgrade, far from being the main objective of the campaign, was an almost unintended consequence. The general direction of the campaign was Central Europe, but the specific target would be determined at a council meeting in Sofia at the end of June. The tensions among the sultan's administrators, already brewing under the surface, came out into the open on that occasion. Mustafa, either present in the meeting as the grand vizier's secretary or on the basis of Piri Mehmed's testimony, informs his readers that the grand vizier proposed to besiege Belgrade. His nemesis Ahmed Pasha, on the other hand, advocated a more ambitious plan: to capture Böğürdelen (Šabac) and then march to the Hungarian capital, Buda. Piri Mehmed was concerned that the Hungarians would use Belgrade, fifty miles to the east of Böğürdelen, to attack the Ottoman army from the rear. However, Ahmed's suggestion, perhaps due to its ambitiousness, carried the day. The council meeting in Sofia was also the first instance in which Ahmed's military skills and ambitions began to ingratiate him with the sultan at Piri Mehmed's expense. The latter was far from surrendering to his rival. The grand vizier pressured the sultan for permission to besiege Belgrade and was given one thousand janissaries.[67] Leaving the sultan, with Mustafa in tow, Piri Mehmed marched to Smederevo, where he was met by ten thousand light infantrymen from the Anadolu governorate. After ordering for the transport of the fortress' cannons to Belgrade via the Danube, Piri Mehmed and his men reached Belgrade on July 9th.[68]

Even though he besieged Belgrade and took the nearby fortress of Zemun, Piri Mehmed's troubles continued. The sultan had captured Böğürdelen on July 7th and began crossing the Sava into Hungary, ordering Piri Mehmed to join him. Although Mustafa sees Ahmed Pasha's hand in this order[69] and bemoans the sultan's failure to congratulate Piri Mehmed about Zemun, it is likely that the sultan needed all his effectives if he were to face the king of Hungary in open battle. Piri Mehmed contested the sultan's orders, writing to him directly and also asking for

---

[67] Unlike Mustafa, contemporary Ottoman historians state that Süleyman ordered Piri Mehmed to besiege Belgrade. See Kemalpaşazade Ahmed, *Tevārīḫ-i Āl-i ʿOsmān, X. Defter*, ed. Şerafettin Severcan (Ankara: Türk Tarih Kurumu, 1996), 77–78, 92; Lütfi Paşa, *Tevārīḫ-i Āl-i ʿOsmān*, ed. Âlî Bey (Istanbul: Matbaa-yı Âmire, 1922–23), 298–300; Yurdaydın, *Kanunî'nin Cülûsu ve İlk Seferleri*, 26.

[68] *Tabakat*, 46a–47b.

[69] *Ibid.*, 54b.

the intercession of the sultan's preacher Hayreddin.[70] In yet another indication of factional rivalries, Piri Mehmed's son-in-law and the second vizier Mustafa Pasha supported the grand vizier's case.[71] Piri Mehmed finally received a much-awaited dispatch from Süleyman, informing him that the sultan was coming to Belgrade. Although Mustafa presents this as the sultan's choice of the more reasonable alternative, the historian and grand vizier (1539–41) Lütfi Pasha, who wrote his work around the middle of the sixteenth century, argues that the sultan received intelligence reports about the king of Hungary's reluctance to face him in an open battle. Rather than returning empty-handed, he thus decided to go back to Belgrade.[72] Indeed, King Louis II's counterattack abilities were seriously hampered by tensions among his barons and prelates.[73]

The sultan's arrival with the main army in early August changed the nature of the siege and sealed Belgrade's fate. Piri Mehmed was humiliated once more when his sector was transferred to Mustafa Pasha's command, and he was relegated to a less important sector. Ottoman forces breached the city's defenses the following week, but the fortress held until the end of August, when it surrendered to the sultan. Heavy artillery fire, the frenetic activity of the Ottoman sappers, and waves of general attacks had finally exhausted the defenders' resources. After supervising the repair of the city walls and sending raiders into Hungarian territory, the sultan left Belgrade after the middle of September, reaching Istanbul around the middle of October 1521.[74] The capture of Belgrade may have been an unintended consequence of the campaign, but the sultan could now say that he had been successful where his illustrious predecessor, Mehmed II, had failed in 1456, only three years after capturing Constantinople.[75] Mustafa remarks with particular glee that cannons, left behind by Mehmed II during his retreat, were now recovered.[76] Strategically, the capture of Belgrade and Böğürdelen meant that the southern

---

[70] Two of these letters are reproduced in Küçükdağ, *Vezîr-i Âzam Pîrî Mehmed Paşa*, 258 (TSMA E. 6142, from the pasha to the sultan) and 259 (TSMA E. 6551, from the pasha to the sultan's preacher).

[71] *Tabakat*, 56a.

[72] Lütfi Paşa, *Tevārīḫ-i Āl-i 'Osmān*, 300.

[73] Pál Engel, *The Realm of St. Stephen: A History of Medieval Hungary, 895–1526*, trans. Tamás Pálosfalvi (London: I.B. Tauris, 2001), 367.

[74] The siege's second stage, the fortress' surrender and the army's return are vividly described in *Tabakat*, 58b–65a.

[75] For Mehmed II's failed siege, see Feridun Dirimtekin, "Belgrad'ın İki Muhasarası," *İstanbul Enstitüsü Dergisi* 2 (1956): 51–76.

[76] *Tabakat*, 48a–49a.

defenses of the Hungarian kingdom were breached and that the next invasion army could utilize these fortresses as forward bases. Indeed, the loss of Belgrade (Nándorfehérvár in Hungarian) has been called "the beginning of the end of the medieval Hungarian kingdom."[77] Also, "[w]ith the capture of Belgrade in 1521 Suleyman secured the Danube waterway and completed the communications, transport and defence requirements of the sub-Danubian and broader Black Sea region of his empire,"[78] which allowed the economic integration of the empire's diverse areas.

Mustafa was obviously very much affected by his baptism of fire. Many years later, he remembered, next to his frustration at Piri Mehmed's decreasing fortunes, the difficult terrain between Smederevo and Belgrade, the sight of Belgrade's imposing walls and towers, and sundry details about the siege. He once helped soldiers under enemy fire by relaying an order by Piri Mehmed; he closely watched the melee that followed the Ottomans' breach of the city walls; he saw women and children take shelter in the city's churches and watched slaves being sold in the army camp. Despite his pasha's problems and his first exposure to the violence of a siege, there is a tone of unsuppressed enthusiasm, glorification, and self-congratulation in Mustafa's account: he took pride in the achievement and felt that he was a part of it. The secretary's transformation into a chronicler of Süleyman's achievements was probably motivated by what he saw at the siege of Belgrade. As for his pasha, his position was considerably weakened after Belgrade. His nemesis Ahmed Pasha was given the rank of vizier as a reward for his leadership throughout the campaign, a fact that is utterly unacknowledged by Mustafa.[79] The frictions between Piri Mehmed and Ahmed would continue to grow in the next military campaign and culminate in an unexpected denouement.

---

[77] For the negative consequences of these conquests for the defense of Hungary, see Ferenc Szakály, "Nándorfehérvár, 1521: The Beginning of the End of the Medieval Hungarian Kingdom," in *Hungarian-Ottoman Military and Diplomatic Relations in the Age of Süleyman the Magnificent*, eds. Géza Dávid and Pál Fodor (Budapest: Loránd Eötvös University, 1994), 47–76.

[78] Rhoads Murphey, "Ottoman Expansion, 1451–1556 II. Dynastic Interest and International Power Status," in *Early Modern Military History, 1450–1815*, ed. Geoff Mortimer (Basingstoke, Hampshire: Palgrave Macmillan, 2004), 65–66.

[79] Halil İnalcık, "Aḥmad Pasha Khā'īn," *EI 2*. Mustafa's account again differs from most of his contemporaries. Also see Turan, "The Sultan's Favorite," 85–86, 89. Ahmed's increased prominence was noted by the Venetian observer Marco Minio as well (*ibid.*, 92–93).

Süleyman Proves Himself: The Capture of Rhodes

The Order of Hospitallers, established in the immediate aftermath of Jerusalem's capture by the Crusaders in 1099, had relocated to the island of Rhodes in 1306. Between 1306 and 1522, it established an uneasy symbiosis with the Venetians, the Mamluks, the Byzantines, Anatolian Turko-Muslim principalities, the Ottomans, the kingdom of Cyprus, and myriad European/Catholic, Orthodox, and Muslim potentates, soldiers of fortune, corsairs, and merchants who competed with each other and cohabited in the Eastern Mediterranean world. Very much like other actors in the area, the Hospitallers exhibited a mixture of zealous religious rhetoric and political pragmatism and mitigated their predatory military activities with tactical peace treaties and other diplomatic overtures.[80] The expansion of Ottoman naval capabilities under Mehmed II and Bayezid II created increasing challenges for the Hospitallers. Their intervention in Ottoman succession struggles and sheltering of the defeated Ottoman prince Cem in 1482 gave them a temporary respite. Selim's victory over the Mamluks destroyed a major power that represented a counterweight against the Ottomans. Moreover, Rhodes' position at a strategic location that could upset the communications between Alexandria and Constantinople became particularly bothersome for the Ottomans.[81] The island was living on borrowed time when Süleyman came to the throne. With the conquest of the island, Süleyman would "secure the sea routes between the Anatolian provinces, and link Istanbul with the main centres of commerce in the southern Mediterranean."[82]

The capture of Belgrade and Rhodes enhanced Süleyman's image in similar ways. Both the fortress of Belgrade and the fortifications of Rhodes presented a difficult task to any besieging army. Süleyman's victories were thus particularly impressive in military terms. Second, fighting against

---

[80] See Anthony Luttrell, "The Hospitallers at Rhodes, 1306–1421" and Ettore Rossi, "The Hospitallers at Rhodes, 1421–1523," in *A History of the Crusades*, ed. Kenneth M. Setton, vol. 3, *The Fourteenth and Fifteenth Centuries*, ed. Harry W. Hazard (Madison: The University of Wisconsin Press, 1975), 278–313 and 314–39; Nicolas Vatin, *Rhodes et l'ordre de Saint-Jean-de-Jérusalem* (Paris: Éditions CNRS, 2000).

[81] Palmira Brummett, "The Overrated Adversary: Rhodes and Ottoman Naval Power," *The Historical Journal* 36, no. 3 (1993): 517–41; Nicolas Vatin, *L'Ordre de Saint-Jean-de-Jérusalem, l'empire ottoman et la Méditerranée orientale entre les deux sièges de Rhodes (1480–1522)* (Paris: Peeters, 1994). Also see Vatin, "The Hospitallers at Rhodes and the Ottoman Turks," in *Crusading in the Fifteenth Century. Message and Impact*, ed. Norman Housley (London: Palgrave-Macmillan, 2004), 148–62.

[82] Murphey, "Ottoman Expansion, 1451–1556," 66.

Christian forces helped Süleyman establish his image as a sultan dedicated to *ghaza*. Finally, Mehmed II's forces, albeit not under the personal command of the sultan himself, had not been able to subdue Rhodes in 1480. By capturing Rhodes, Süleyman once again emerged successful where the conqueror of Constantinople had failed. Mustafa, in his *Tabakat*, emphasizes all three issues and adds that the Hospitallers disrupted trade and travel in the Mediterranean, attacking pilgrims and merchants.[83] The international situation was also suitable. Venice, which had at best a checkered relationship with the Hospitallers, had signed a comprehensive treaty with the Ottomans in December 1521. The papacy, the usual ally and supporter of the Hospitallers, suffered from Leo X's death earlier that year and his successor Adrian VI's inability to organize help. Charles, the recently elected Holy Roman Emperor, and Francis I, both self-styled defenders of Christians against Muslims, were locked in an intense military and political struggle over the control of northern Italy and could not come to the help of the distant island.[84]

Mustafa's account of the campaign is once again torn between two different attitudes. On the one hand, he wants to promote Piri Mehmed and downplay Ahmed Pasha's contributions, whereas other contemporary Ottoman sources refer to Piri Mehmed's mistakes and Ahmed's good management of the campaign.[85] On the other hand, he desires to amplify the sultan's role. Indeed, there is a subtle change of tone in the narrative, and the figure of the Ottoman sultan comes to the forefront, despite Mustafa's references to factional struggles. The decision to attack Rhodes, for instance, is now solely attributed to the sultan's own perseverance and farsightedness.[86] The ever-curious Mustafa, the storyteller, also describes for his readers the extensive campaign preparations, the various stages of the difficult siege, the heated debates at the war council,

---

[83] *Tabakat*, 65a–67a.

[84] Turan, "The Sultan's Favorite," 95; Kenneth M. Setton, *The Papacy and the Levant, 1204–1571*, vol. 3, *The Sixteenth Century to the Reign of Julius III* (Philadelphia: American Philosophical Society, 1976–1984), 200–205 (hereafter *The Papacy and the Levant 3*); Richard Bonney, *The European Dynastic States, 1494–1660* (Oxford: Oxford University Press, 1991), 100–101; Şerafettin Turan, "Rodos'un Zaptından Malta Muhasarasına," *Kanunî Armağanı*, 54–56, 62–64. For the Ottoman-Venetian treaty see Mahmut Şakiroğlu, "1521 Tarihli Osmanlı-Venedik Andlaşmasının Aslî Metni," *İÜEF Tarih Enstitüsü Dergisi* 12 (1982): 387–404.

[85] See Turan, "The Sultan's Favorite," 98–99, 102–3. Another major source, Matrakçı Nasuh's *Süleymānnāme*, corroborates Mustafa's version (quoted in Yurdaydın, *Kanunî'nin Cülûsu ve İlk Seferleri*, 42).

[86] *Tabakat*, 67a.

the temerity of the defenders, the physical characteristics of the island, and the impressive fortifications. Mustafa participated in the campaign as a secretary of the imperial council and left Istanbul in advance, with the naval units commanded by the vizier Mustafa Pasha, Piri Mehmed's son-in-law and supporter. This was Mustafa's first sea voyage, and he was clearly impressed by the navy's departure, in early June 1522, amidst the shouts and prayers of the onlookers, the thunder of cannons and small guns, and the clouds of gunpowder smoke that enveloped the ships. After stopping in Gallipoli and then Chios for reinforcements and provisions, the navy set sail toward Rhodes, while the sultan marched overland in the same direction. Mustafa's detailed account tells us about how the navy approached Rhodes, crossed the bay across the main fortress in a daring maneuver, began the preliminary landings under cannon fire, and secured a beachhead. The first landing party also realized crucial infrastructural work such as the building of tunnels, trenches, and roads for the safe transport and circulation of men and materiel under enemy fire.[87]

Mustafa's enthusiastic tone subsides, however, when news of Ahmed Pasha's promotion to the general military command of the campaign arrives. He argues that the reason behind the promotion was Ahmed Pasha's slandering of Mustafa Pasha, the initial commander of the campaign.[88] The genuine difficulties of the siege add to Mustafa's bitterness, and his tendency to accuse Ahmed Pasha for the reversals suffered by the Ottomans becomes especially pronounced. To the benefit of modern readers, on the other hand, his partisanship motivates Mustafa to candidly discuss the campaign's problems. Thus, in the first phase of the campaign, the Ottoman tactic relied on shelling the fortifications and then organizing infantry attacks against the walls, which resulted in heavy casualties and demoralized the soldiery. The defenders were able to observe the positions of Ottoman siege guns from their towers and direct their fire accordingly, to deadly effect. These issues were discussed in a tense military council meeting on August 11th, which saw yet another heated discussion between Piri Mehmed and Ahmed. From the middle of August to the last week of September, the attackers tried various methods, such as filling the moats with sand and rocks, sending soldiers with crowbars and pickaxes to dismantle the walls' foundations, digging tunnels under the walls and detonating charges, attacking the walls with the

---

[87] *Ibid.*, 69b–72b, 78a–82b.
[88] *Ibid.*, 83a.

infantry, and concentrating cannon fire on different sections of the walls, all to no avail. These constant reversals led to yet another tense imperial council meeting at the end of the month. The pashas explained the situation to an angry Süleyman, who exhorted them to apply themselves for the sake of Allah and motivate their men; the sultan was especially frustrated by the lack of advances in the sectors commanded by Piri Mehmed and Mustafa Pashas, a detail that Mustafa eschews.[89] The only hope, he remarks, was the deterioration of the situation inside the fortress. This hope was supported by the testimonies of deserters, such as the artillery-man who admitted that the commander of the musketeers was dead and that there was an atmosphere of despair in the fortress. In October, while the autumn rains made life in the army camp miserable, the Ottomans began to infiltrate parts of the walls and towers. On November 1st, in an imperial council meeting, a difficult decision was taken: contrary to Ottoman military practice, the army and the sultan would spend the winter on the island.

After four general offensives the following week, the Ottomans finally occupied the outer walls, and the defenders retreated to the citadel. The last handful of defenders proposed to surrender on December 10th, but the Ottomans were informed by an escapee that this was a ploy. In fact, on the 14th, a few ships carrying reinforcements entered the port and landed their men. The Ottomans answered this move with a major attack against the citadel on the night of the 17th and the following day. The Grand Master of the Hospitallers, Philippe Villiers de L'Isle-Adam, finally asked for surrender. The offer was promptly accepted by the sultan and, in an imperial council meeting on the 20th, the Hospitaller leaders were granted an audience. The Grand Master was given permission to leave the island with his ship and was ordered to release the Muslim prisoners as a gesture of good will. On December 24th, Piri Mehmed, Ahmed, and the commander of the janissaries entered the citadel, followed by Süleyman five days later. The Grand Master, after a final visit to the sultan, left the island on the January 1, 1523. Süleyman attended the Friday prayer in the newly converted cathedral of St. John and soon after crossed over to the mainland.[90]

The long and exhausting campaign dealt the coup de grace to Piri Mehmed's position as grand vizier. His lack of military skills was particularly exposed, whereas Ahmed, despite Mustafa's claims to the contrary,

[89] Küçükdağ, *Vezîr-i Âzam Pîrî Mehmed Paşa*, 93–95.
[90] *Tabakat*, 85a–104a.

distinguished himself by carrying a very difficult campaign to a successful end. Piri Mehmed's standing was further weakened by the departure of his son-in-law Mustafa Pasha to replace the deceased governor of Egypt, Khayr Bak. Ahmed could now expect to be nominated grand vizier, on the basis of his valor in Süleyman's first two military ventures. The new sultan, who benefited from these victories to strengthen his own authority and image, had different plans for the future.

Reshuffling at the Top: İbrahim Becomes Grand Vizier

Between February and June 1523, tensions in the highest echelons of the Ottoman administration came further to the fore. This was partly due to the sultan's request to investigate the matter of families force-fully relocated from Egypt to Istanbul after the Ottoman conquest. The investigation was directed against Piri Mehmed, and he was accused of having allowed, in exchange for bribes, some of these families to return to Egypt. The official charged with the investigation, Fenarizade Muhyiddin Çelebi, who was then the military judge (*kadı'asker*) for Rumeli, found the accusations legitimate. Piri Mehmed was dismissed from the grand vizierate and sent into retirement.[91] Mustafa saw the hand of Ahmed Pasha, and his vying for the grand vizierate, behind these accusations. He presents the whole affair as a conspiracy against Piri Mehmed (he goes so far as to state that all those who conspired against the pasha were dead within a year[92]) and particularly vituperates the military judge as a peon of anti-Piri Mehmed forces. However, the near-simultaneous dismissal of another vizier, Ferhad Pasha, and his embarrassing demotion to the rank of provincial governor, shows that the sultan's intention was to radically change the composition of the imperial council and assert his own power at the expense of the viziers he had inherited from his father.

The most telling illustration of this intention was the appointment, on June 23, 1524, of the sultan's head of the Privy Chamber to the grand vizierate. The sultan's longtime companion and confidant, İbrahim Ağa, now became İbrahim Pasha, and his authority was further augmented by

---

[91] *Ibid.*, 109b–110a; Küçükdağ, *Vezîr-i Âzam Pîrî Mehmed Paşa*, 108.

[92] *Tabakat*, 110a. Indeed, Muhyiddin died of natural causes approximately a year after the incident. Ferhad Pasha, whom Mustafa did not like and possibly saw as anti-Piri, was executed in November 1524, and Ahmed Pasha was executed in August 1523. In his *Selimname* (214b–216a), written toward the end of his life, Mustafa accuses Ferhad Pasha of having oppressed innocent Muslims in Central Anatolia in 1519 under the pretext that they supported a pretender to the throne.

his simultaneous appointment as governor-general of Rumeli.[93] This was Süleyman's ultimate assertion of his own authority at the expense of any notions of merit or hierarchy that may have existed in 1523. The sultan's decision led to new tensions inside the ruling elite and the capital city, and many contemporaries openly stated that they found İbrahim inexperienced and unworthy. With the dismissal of Piri Mehmed, it was Ahmed Pasha who, on the basis of his military and political experience and his recent service to the sultan, expected to become grand vizier. Mustafa corroborates this information but argues that Ahmed was not suitable for the position. Displaying once again his bureaucratic bias, Mustafa defines the grand vizierate as a purely political and administrative office that supports the dual institutions of the sultanate and the caliphate; the duty of a grand vizier is thus to follow the Sharia (whatever Mustafa may attribute to this particular concept) and implement justice. Ahmed Pasha, according to Mustafa, did not respect the Sharia enough, was not a learned man, and had an impetuous character, traits that effectively disqualified him. The sultan, says Mustafa, was aware of Ahmed's shortcomings, and this is why he decided to send him to Egypt as governor-general.[94] Sent away to Egypt in the first days of August 1523, Ahmed would subsequently rebel and would be defeated only thanks to the collaboration of some of his own men, in the spring–summer of 1524. These events, together with Mustafa's damning portrayal of the pasha, would earn him the nickname of ha'in, or traitor, in Ottoman historiography. On the other hand, some of his contemporaries viewed Ahmed as a victim of power struggles around the palace, an opinion that is utterly lacking in Mustafa's account.[95] Contemporary reactions and debates notwithstanding, Ahmed's execution decisively resolved the last few years' tensions in the imperial council and allowed Süleyman to finally have control over his own men.

For Mustafa, Piri Mehmed's fall and İbrahim's rise opened a new period of opportunities. Although the realities of patronage often entailed

[93] For a detailed account of İbrahim's rise to the grand vizierate and the initial reactions from within the ruling elite, see Turan, "The Sultan's Favorite," 179–88, 203–10; Turan, "Voices of Opposition in the Reign of Sultan Süleyman: The Case of İbrahim Pasha (1523–1536)," in Studies on Istanbul and Beyond, ed. Robert G. Ousterhout (Philadelphia: University of Pennsylvania Museum of Archaeology and Anthropology, 2007), 23–35.

[94] Tabakat, 110a–b.

[95] Mustafa's strongly anti-Ahmed account of these events is in Tabakat, 112a–115a. For an alternative interpretation, see Turan, "The Sultan's Favorite," 193–98.

the demotion of a patron's protégés and associates after their protector's downfall, Mustafa's professional fortunes did not decline in 1523. It is possible that his association with Piri Mehmed was not as obvious as he re-imagined and presented it later in his life. A junior secretary would not be seen as a particularly dangerous figure to be eliminated. It is also likely that, having proven his worth as a secretary in the past few years, and given the scarcity of similarly talented individuals, his service was needed in the palace and the imperial council. İbrahim's rise ended Mustafa's problem of potentially conflicting loyalties. In his account of the Belgrade and Rhodes campaigns, Mustafa had to balance his loyalty to Piri Mehmed and his loyalty to the sultan. As the lifelong companion and confidant of the sultan, however, İbrahim could now be portrayed as the sultan's ideal collaborator. Even though some Ottoman sources assert that İbrahim was among those who conspired against Piri Mehmed, Mustafa, who heavily edited his work after İbrahim's death in 1536, is oblivious to the criticisms directed against the new grand vizier.[96] As a political survivor, he is unbridled in his praise for İbrahim, whom he describes as the sultan's servant since childhood and an individual endowed with particularly impressive mental faculties. Moreover, with the eclipse of the old regime's men, Mustafa observes, the working environment in the imperial council improved considerably, and İbrahim assumed his new duties enthusiastically.[97] For the sultan, İbrahim, and Mustafa, the new ruler's true reign had begun.

Later in his life, Mustafa would tell the poet and biographer Beyani of his first days working with İbrahim. In Beyani's account of Mustafa's reminiscences, the grand vizier is presented as an inexperienced but well-intentioned administrator. He did not know much about the affairs of the realm. Moreover, because of the previous problems in the imperial council, the requests of many petitioners had been left unanswered, and there was a tremendous amount of work to do. İbrahim asked for a knowledgeable secretary to help him, and this secretary turned out to be Mustafa. The secretary and the grand vizier agreed on a method. On Mustafa's sign and guidance, issues or petitions that pertained to the application of the Sharia would be referred to a military judge, and matters related to the imperial treasury would be sent to a treasurer. Affairs that fell under the purview of the grand vizierate, on the other

---

[96] *Tabakat*, 110a–111a. For references to İbrahim's actions against Piri Mehmed see *İOTK* 2, 95–6; and Turan, "The Sultan's Favorite," 101–2.

[97] *Tabakat*, 110b–111b.

hand, would be handled by Mustafa. The secretary would "grab [his] pen, and the pasha would decree: 'Let an order be written!,'"[98] after which Mustafa would compose the necessary document in the correct style. This was the beginning of a collaboration that would continue uninterruptedly for the next thirteen years, until the pasha's execution in 1536.

[98] Beyani, *Tezkire-yi şu'arā-yı Beyānī*, 92b–93a.

2

The Secretary's Progress (1523–1534)

Mustafa spent this decade as a senior secretary, and then as chief secretary, in the proximity of İbrahim and Süleyman. As a close collaborator of the grand vizier, he witnessed the articulation of an imperial ideology based on universal monarchy, the administrative and fiscal reconstruction of Egypt, the pacification of Anatolian rebellions, the end of the Hungarian kingdom, the emergence of the Ottoman–Habsburg frontier in Central Europe, and the diplomatic negotiations with various powers. He had learned from Piri Mehmed the technical aspects of the scribal profession. With İbrahim, he began to discover the more active role a bureaucrat could play in administering and promoting the empire. He became one of the voices of the sultan in this period through the dispatches he wrote and was trusted with tasks that were not given to his superiors in the scribal service, such as the composition of various important letters and documents. Thanks to his proximity to İbrahim, he became acquainted with a group of poets and historians and established lifelong friendships with some of them. He tried his hand at writing history and composed campaign narratives (*fethname*), the circulation of which played a crucial role in the construction of Süleyman's image as an accomplished conqueror.

Presenting the Sultan and the Grand Vizier to the Ottoman Public

Unlike Mustafa, who welcomed İbrahim's grand vizierate as a fresh beginning, various individuals and factions in the palace circles and the capital were less ready to acknowledge him. The pasha's wedding, his inspection voyage to Egypt, his actions during the Hungarian campaign of 1526, and his dispatch against the pro-Safavid rebels in 1527 were all meant to build his reputation and help him become better acquainted in the practical matters of Ottoman governance. The first step was the pasha's wedding ceremony in May 1524.

Weddings, royal entries, processions, and festivals were privileged occasions for the assertion of royal or civic authority throughout the early modern world. The new Renaissance monarchies created and disseminated carefully crafted images of royalty through literature and portraiture and in semipublic or public activities such as hunts, public appearances, processions, entries, and weddings.[1] The latter were designed as microcosms that represented the variety of a realm's cultural and political ideals and included elaborate processions of soldiers and artisans, mock battles, sportive games, and public feasts. The proliferation of public rituals in early modern Europe has been studied by Edward Muir, who associates this development with the impact of the Reformation and the birth of a new theory of representation.[2] Frances Yates and Roy Strong, on the other hand, have established links between early modern political ideas (justice, peace, religious renewal and reform, universal monarchy) and the emergence of new political symbolisms around sovereigns. Strong further argues that "the art of festival was harnessed to the emergent modern state as an instrument of rule."[3]

---

[1] The following works are particularly useful in adopting a pan-European comparative perspective and analyzing the politics of image making in the early modern period: Frances A. Yates, *Astraea: The Imperial Theme in the Sixteenth Century* (London: Kegan Paul, 1975); Allen Ellenius, ed., *Iconography, Propaganda, and Legitimation* (Oxford: Clarendon Press; New York: Oxford University Press, 1998).

[2] Edward Muir, *Ritual in Early Modern Europe*, 2nd ed. (Cambridge: Cambridge University Press, 2005), 9.

[3] Roy C. Strong, *Art and Power: Renaissance Festivals, 1450–1650* (Berkeley: University of California Press, 1984), 19. Also see Ralph E. Giesey, "Models of Rulership in French Royal Ceremonial," in *Rites of Power: Symbolism, Ritual and Politics since the Middle Ages*, ed. Sean Wilentz (Philadelphia: University of Pennsylvania Press, 1985), 41–64; Sydney Anglo, *Spectacle, Pageantry, and Early Tudor Policy*, 2nd edition (Oxford: Clarendon Press; New York: Oxford University Press, 1987); Alison Cole, *Virtue and Magnificence: Art of the Italian Renaissance Courts* (New York: H.N. Abrams, 1995). For an expansion in ceremoniality and the ceremonial display of power relations within the Ottoman ruling elite, see Konrad Dilger, *Untersuchungen zur Geschichte des osmanischen Hofzeremoniells im 15. und 16. Jahrhundert* (Munich: Rudolf Trofenik, 1967); Rhoads Murphey, *Exploring Ottoman Sovereignty: Tradition, Image and Practice in the Ottoman Imperial Household, 1400–1800* (London: Continuum, 2008). Unlike Murphey, I believe that innovation and context (i.e., developments in early modern Eurasia) were more important than "tradition" in the emergence of new ceremonies.

These new ceremonies have been usually evaluated as purely European phenomena and linked to the artistic culture of the Renaissance and the patronage of the early modern monarchies. The emergent early modern Islamic empires, however, also felt the urge to use public ceremonies to create ideological and cultural links between sovereigns and subjects. The ongoing polarization around the definition of Sunni and Shiite Islams, and the identification of Ottoman and Safavid dynasties with the defense of Sunnism and Shiism, gave a particular poignancy to these public rituals, as shown, in the Safavid case, by Babak Rahimi.[4] Mughal architecture and portraiture, the emperors' audiences, and other public ceremonies served a similar purpose.[5] Süleyman's reign represents, among other things, an increased participation in a typically early modern Eurasian imperial culture of presenting the ruler to the subjects through highly elaborate public rituals.[6] Indeed, between 1521 and 1528, notes Gülru Necipoğlu, Italian visitors to Istanbul noticed an increase in the pomp and ceremonialism around the sultan. Moreover, "[the] extensions of palace ceremonial into the larger urban fabric of Istanbul were displays of imperial power that turned the iconic sultan, accompanied by thousands of richly dressed and hierarchically ordered courtiers, administrators, and slave soldiers, into a showpiece for the populace."[7] İbrahim's wedding gave Süleyman and his grand vizier the opportunity to assert the pasha's new role and the sultan's grandeur vis-a-vis the ruling elite and the population of Istanbul. There had been similar Ottoman ceremonies involving the sultan's participation, notably under Mehmed II, but they were surpassed, in terms of length, participation, financial cost, and ideological significance, by the wedding.

İbrahim was married in October 1523 to Muhsine Hatun, a member of the family that had initially purchased him as a slave boy, in an ultimate show of his promotion and change of status. The bride's large family had connections to the Ottoman administration. Also, thanks to its ties to the

---

[4] Babak Rahimi, "The Rebound Theater State: The Politics of the Safavid Camel Sacrifice Rituals, 1598–1695 C.E.," *IrSt* 37, no. 3 (September 2004): 451–78.

[5] Ebba Koch, *Mughal Art and Imperial Ideology: Collected Essays* (New Delhi and New York: Oxford University Press, 2001); Annemarie Schimmel, *The Empire of the Great Mughals: History, Art and Culture*, trans. Corinne Attwood, ed. Burzine K. Waghmar (London: Reaktion: 2004).

[6] Christine Woodhead, "Perspectives on Süleyman," in *Süleyman the Magnificent and His Age*, 164–90.

[7] Gülru Necipoğlu, *Architecture, Ceremonial, and Power: The Topkapi Palace in the Fifteenth and Sixteenth Centuries* (New York: Architectural History Foundation; Cambridge, MA: MIT Press, 1991), 15, 20.

Mevlevi order, and through the endowments controlled by the order, it maintained close relations with various sections of Istanbul's population, the support of which Süleyman and İbrahim vied for.[8] The celebration took place at the end of May 1524. It is likely that preparations had begun shortly after news of Ahmed Pasha's defeat and execution in Egypt in February–March 1524.[9] In the wake of the formidable adversary's defeat, the celebrations were suffused with a new sense of confidence that elevated İbrahim, Süleyman, and the empire itself to an unprecedented level of political and cultural assertiveness. After receiving the visit of various groups, such as janissaries, palace troops, and elders of religious orders, and feasting them over a few days, the sultan relocated from the palace to the Byzantine Hippodrome, the center of public celebrations. Exhibitions of tents, expensive clothes, garments, bejeweled weapons, and other war booty, taken from the Safavids and the Mamluks and brought from pillaged Tabriz and Cairo, displayed the empire's might and established a link between the victories of Selim and Süleyman. A public debate by scholars on the caliphate further enhanced the political message of the event.[10] Entertainment was not shunned either. The city's inhabitants watched artists parading animals and monsters made of colored cut paper, soldiers organizing mock fights on wooden horses, strong men breaking apart iron chains, janissaries climbing on long poles, and an artist dressed as a stork and walking on long sticks. There were wrestling matches, races, and archery contests. The members of the ruling elite and the population of Istanbul were feasted throughout. While the scholars and administrators were served pastries, pies, choice meats and sweet drinks, the spectators at the Hippodrome were offered whole camels and cows roasted on spits.[11]

Contemporary Ottoman sources present short glimpses of the wedding. Mustafa, on the other hand, was well aware of the event's ideological and cultural significance and left behind a detailed narrative of

---

[8] It was usually assumed that İbrahim had married Süleyman's sister, until the bride's identity was established by Turan, "The Sultan's Favorite," 210–20; also see Turan, "The Marriage of İbrahim Pasha (ca. 1495–1536). The Rise of Sultan Süleyman's Favorite to the Grand Vizierate and the Politics of the Elites in the Early Sixteenth-Century Ottoman Empire," *Turcica* 41 (2009): 3–36.

[9] Lellouch, *Les Ottomans en Égypte*, 59–60; *Tabakat*, 114b–115a.

[10] The scholars debated a Quranic verse (38:26): "*Yā Dāvud inna ja'alnāka khalīfatan fī al-arḍ*" (O David! We did indeed make thee a vicegerent [caliph] on earth).

[11] *Tabakat*, 116a–121a.

the festivities, summarized in the preceding paragraph. The ceremonies, which publicly feted İbrahim's unprecedented rise to power, symbolically opened a new era in Ottoman history. Moreover, as Mustafa suggests, they were meant to establish a special relationship between the sultan and his subjects.[12] The scholarly discussion on the caliphate, for instance, was one of the first occasions when Süleyman openly and publicly assumed this particular mantle. The term *caliphate* does not fit a simple description, and Ottoman political writers of the fifteenth and sixteenth centuries attributed various meanings to it, from a contract between man and God to a form of supreme rulership.[13] During Süleyman's early years, at a period when the sultan and the new grand vizier intended to devise an ambitious political program, the concept was utilized to emphasize the God-given nature of the sultan's mandate and his claims to rule over both the temporal and the spiritual realms.

An Ottoman Grand Vizier in Action: The Egyptian Inspection

Ottoman grand viziers usually managed the affairs of government from the capital, leaving it on occasions such as hunting or military campaigns. Inspecting the provinces was the duty of officials such as military judges and treasurers. Investigations were also pursued through correspondence with local officials, to whom the necessary authority might be delegated for that particular occasion. İbrahim's voyage to Egypt included two interrelated objectives: the construction of the pasha's reputation and the pacification of a tumultuous province that had been rocked by recent rebellions.[14] Even though it remained limited to Syria, Janbardi al-Ghazali's rebellion in 1520 had shown that the Mamluk military element in the region was restless and difficult to control. The first Ottoman governor of Egypt, Khayr Bak (1517–22), was a Mamluk officer who switched sides and joined Ottoman service in 1517, and he had ruled the province

---

[12] *Ibid.*, 121a.

[13] For these debates, see Hüseyin Yılmaz, "The Sultan and the Sultanate: Envisioning Rulership in the Age of Süleyman the Lawgiver (1520–1566)" (PhD diss., Harvard University, 2004), 135–219 passim, especially 176–84. About the pragmatic uses of the concept by the Ottomans, see Colin Imber, "Süleymân as Caliph of the Muslims: Ebû's-Su'ûd's Formulation of Ottoman Dynastic Ideology," in *Soliman le Magnifique et son temps*, 179–84; Imber, *Ebu's-su'ud: The Islamic Legal Tradition* (Stanford: Stanford University Press, 1997), 103–11.

[14] Here I am following Turan's interpretation, formulated in the light of contemporary Ottoman and Venetian sources ("The Sultan's Favorite," 223–33).

through alliances with the Mamluks and the Arab tribes.[15] Following his death, when Çoban Mustafa Pasha became governor, various Mamluk elements rebelled and were suppressed with great difficulty, only after the pasha convinced some of their tribal allies to support the Ottoman side by giving them tax incentives.[16] Ahmed Pasha's rebellion nearly destroyed whatever Ottoman administration there was in the area, and the governorate's treasury had been looted during the troubles. Ottoman administrators sent to Egypt following Ahmed's defeat failed to pacify the province.[17] Beyond the restlessness of the Mamluk survivors, Ottoman attempts at imposing financial and judicial control over Egypt after 1517 had alienated large sections of the Egyptian society, and created economic distress and general mistrust.[18]

Mustafa, writing later in his life, sees the crisis through the lens of an Ottoman administrator and interprets the inspection as an attempt at establishing lasting control through administrative reforms.[19] As someone who played an important role during the grand vizier's voyage, his narrative is skewed toward emphasizing its successes.[20] Mustafa's eyewitness account is a firsthand testimony about how Ottoman officials attempted to secure public order through a mixture of violence, legal regulation, and public acts of charity. The members of the traveling party, duly recorded by Mustafa, included the treasurer of Rumeli İskender Çelebi, a commander of the palace troops named Hayreddin, the chief pursuivant (çavuşbaşı) Sofioğlu Mehmed, thirty pursuivants, some treasury secretaries, and five hundred janissaries, the latter to join the ships at Gallipoli. The treasurer İskender worked closely with İbrahim in financial matters and played a similar role to Mustafa in assisting the pasha. The command of the fleet was given to the promising naval commander and geographer, Piri Reis. As a whole, the travelers represented the best financial, bureaucratic, and military talent available to the Ottoman administration of the time.

---

[15] On Khayr Bak see P.M. Holt, "Khā'ir Beg," *EI 2*; Lellouch, *Les Ottomans en Égypte*, 39–53; Michael Winter, *Egyptian Society under Ottoman Rule, 1517–1798* (London: Routledge, 1992), 12–13.

[16] For an account of this rebellion, see *Tabakat*, 104a–109b. The details of the narrative suggest that Mustafa saw reports and talked to Mustafa Pasha about the incident. Cf. Lellouch, *Les Ottomans en Égypte*, 53–56, 66–71; Winter, *Egyptian Society under Ottoman Rule*, 14–15, 83–87.

[17] Lellouch, *Les Ottomans en Égypte*, 60–62.

[18] Winter, *Egyptian Society under Ottoman Rule*, 10–12.

[19] *Tabakat*, 121a.

[20] For alternative views, see Turan, "The Sultan's Favorite," 225–29.

İbrahim and his associates left the capital on September 30, 1524. The late departure date, well outside the Ottoman campaign season, indicates the urgency attributed to the visit. Indeed, harsh weather made progress difficult. After waiting at Kızılada (currently known as Büyükada) for the strong winds to subside, the party proceeded to Gallipoli, then to Chios and ultimately Rhodes. They left for Egypt on November 7, hoping to reach their destination after a five-day journey, but the strong southeast winds forced the travelers to return to the island. After recuperating on the island, İbrahim decided to follow the longer but safer land route, to the relief of Mustafa, whose account conveys a genuine sense of fear inspired by gigantic waves and howling winds on the open sea. The travelers crossed over to Anatolia on November 28. After securing mounts and pack animals from the provincial governors in the area and following an arduous and restless march through Southern Anatolia, İbrahim and his company reached Aleppo in January 1525, almost three months after their departure. The pasha used this opportunity to further secure his reputation as a promoter of justice and administrative efficiency, as told by Mustafa. He listened to the complaints of the inhabitants in Aleppo and Damascus, chastised the Ottoman governors-general for various mistakes, and worked to redeem their past mistakes. Mustafa's description of the pasha's actions in these cities shows an image-conscious Ottoman grand vizier with a particular talent in public relations and a flair for theatrical displays of magnanimity. Promoting his own role, Mustafa also mentions his collaboration with the grand vizier and describes meetings with local governors as well as individual conversations with İbrahim.[21]

Leaving Damascus in early February 1525, and after an eventful journey through the desert, the pasha reached Cairo on April 2. He immediately set out to secure control of the province through a mixture of violence and charity. A tribal lord from Upper Egypt, recorded by Mustafa as Ömeroğlu Ali, was invited to Cairo and then executed, followed by the public hanging of another tribal chief, whom Mustafa calls Bakaroğlu.[22] The pasha's violent methods, says Mustafa, earned him the moniker of *mushattit al-shaml* (scatterer of families/tribes) among the locals, which implies that he also engaged in a certain level of demographical engineering. After proving that he would not refrain from using violence, the

---

[21] *Tabakat*, 121b–124b.

[22] These were Ali ibn Umar and Ahmad ibn Baqar, who had been important political actors in post-Ottoman Egypt. See Winter, *Egyptian Society under Ottoman Rule*, 83–87.

pasha sent letters to various local leaders and informed them he was there to fulfill the sultan's wish to apply the Sharia. Very much like Aleppo and Damascus, local inhabitants were also invited, through public criers, to voice their complaints. İbrahim released funds for the repair of major Cairene mosques, paid the debts of imprisoned debtors, and organized a stipend system for the city's orphans. Mustafa, by his own account, played an important role in these activities, preparing lists that included the names and addresses of creditors and the amount they were due or recording the names and ages of the city's orphans. According to Mustafa, the pasha confided in him that he engaged in all these activities to serve the sultan well and increase his popularity.[23] However, İbrahim wanted to leave a larger impact on Egypt, and his next step was to lay down the grounds for a viable Ottoman administration. He asked to see previous land and tax registers and studied the law codes of the last two Mamluk sultans as well as the previous Ottoman governors. Did they indeed find documents or use oral testimonies?[24] It is possible that Mustafa tries to portray the Mamluk-Ottoman transition as a smooth process by arguing that Ottoman legislation was issued in the light of previous practices.[25] In any case, the grand vizier prepared, with the help of the secretaries and treasurers in his company, a new Egyptian law and tax code, meant to establish control both over the Mamluks and the finances of the province.[26] Through provisions favorable to merchants and commercial activity in Egypt and the Red Sea region, the pasha hoped to create a counterpoint to increased Portuguese activity around the Arabian peninsula.[27]

Next to its legal content, the law code is distinguished by its long preamble written in a sophisticated prose, a feature that is rarely encountered in previous Ottoman *kanunname*s. The preamble clearly shows

---

[23] *Tabakat*, 124b–126b, 127b–128b.

[24] Lellouch (*Les Ottomans en Égypte*, 65–66) argues, on the basis of an Ottoman land survey from 1527–28, that surveyors had to use oral testimonies because the archives of the previous regime could not be located. Michael Winter, on the other hand (*Egyptian Society under Ottoman Rule*, 16–17), finds an element of continuity between Mamluk and Ottoman legislation.

[25] Cf. Reem Meshal, "Antagonistic Sharī'as and the Construction of Orthodoxy in Sixteenth-Century Ottoman Cairo," *Journal of Islamic Studies*, 21, no. 2 (2010): 194.

[26] Lellouch, *Les Ottomans en Égypte*, 64–65. For a discussion of the "Ottomanization" of the Egyptian legal system in the sixteenth century also see Meshal, "Antagonistic Sharī'as," which provides a strong counterpoint to approaches that portray the Ottoman presence in Egypt as more benign and minimally intrusive.

[27] Casale, *The Ottoman Age of Exploration*, 40–41.

that the Egyptian expedition was attributed a function that went beyond a simple administrative reorganization.[28] It is the first official document that displays the specific ideological tenets of Ottoman sovereignty under Süleyman and İbrahim. It develops a new "political theology" as an answer to the ideological challenges of early modern Eurasia and, as such, constitutes a valuable contribution to the debates of the time. It describes the Ottoman ruler as a divinely ordained sultan and caliph who presides over the Ottoman realm with perfect justice and as a ruler who reigns over both spiritual and temporal realms. This idea is supported with references to a range of sources that extend from a mainstream reading of Sunni Muslim political theory to astrology and apocalypticism. İbrahim is described as the ideal grand vizier whose unconditional devotion to the sultan and moral and intellectual capacities make him the perfect instrument of the ruler's will.

The secretive aura around the preamble's composition (the text was written far from the capital and the writing process involved only İbrahim Pasha and Mustafa, if we believe the latter) shows that, rather than conferring with other high officials, Süleyman and İbrahim realized a fait accompli through what Snjezana Buzov calls "the young Süleyman's manifesto." The sultan inquired about the finished product and wanted to read it before it was publicized. He gave it his approval only after the draft was sent to Istanbul with a special messenger.[29] The preamble signifies the dawn of a new era in which the global and world-historical program it outlines would be put into action. It also marks the beginning of İbrahim's genuine political career.[30] Finally, it symbolizes the rise to prominence of Mustafa and his participation in the political experimentations of this period. Next to his close collaboration with İbrahim throughout the voyage, Mustafa lent his composition skills and administrative knowledge to the preparation of this crucial text. His first major contribution to Ottoman imperial ideology was also his first attempt at endowing this new

---

[28] For a detailed analysis of the preamble, see Buzov, "The Lawgiver and His Lawmakers," 29–45; for an English translation, see *ibid.*, 197–232. In comparison, the preamble of the law code for Tripoli of Syria (Trablus-Şam) from 1519 is much less elaborate. Moreover, its composition in Arabic reflects the desire to appeal to the local population, whereas the Egyptian preamble is written in a flowery high Ottoman, the trademark of Mustafa's style. See Rifaat Abou-El-Haj, "Aspects of the Legitimization of Ottoman Rule as Reflected in the Preambles of Two Early Liva Kanunnameler," *Turcica* 21–23 (1991): 371–83.

[29] *Tabakat*, 127a.

[30] Turan, "The Sultan's Favorite," 239.

ideology with a sophisticated linguistic expression and complex political, historical, and theological arguments.

The idealistic tone of the preamble was soon contrasted by developments in the capital, which necessitated the pasha's quick return. It is difficult to establish whether these were a specific response to the preamble itself or a general reaction to the pasha's absence and the sultan's long stay in Edirne during this time. It is also possible that anti-İbrahim factions in Istanbul had hoped the pasha would stay in Egypt as governor and became agitated when they heard he would eventually return to the capital.[31] On March 25, 1525, at night, some janissaries and armed youth looted the houses of Ayas Pasha and the treasurer Abdüsselam Çelebi; some Jewish households were also pillaged in the melee.[32] The next day, the looters attacked İbrahim's mansion. The sultan's violent reaction to these troubles shows that, far from being a random mob, the looters had connections to members of the Ottoman administration. As a result, the commander of the janissaries, the senior imperial council secretary Haydar and the chamberlain (*kethüda*) of Mustafa Pasha, Bali, were executed.[33] The sultan sent a pursuivant to Egypt, informing the pasha of the recent developments and recalling him to the capital. İbrahim appointed the governor-general of Damascus Süleyman as the new governor of Egypt and left Cairo on June 14, carrying the annual tax yield of the province with himself. He reached the capital on September 16, almost a year after his departure for Egypt.[34]

Soon after returning to the capital, in recognition of his contributions, Mustafa was given the title of *re'isülküttab*, chief secretary. It is not certain whether he was the first Ottoman official to carry this title.[35] Regardless, his promotion meant a redefinition of the position, and its endowment with specific duties that would help accommodate the new working

---

[31] Uzunçarşılı notes that the imperial council did not convene in the pasha's absence (*Osmanlı Devletinin Merkez ve Bahriye Teşkilâtı* [Ankara: Türk Tarih Kurumu, 1948], 6). This and Süleyman's residence in Edirne during the Egyptian voyage created tensions in Istanbul and led to the revolt. See Turan, "The Sultan's Favorite," 233–39.

[32] The date of the rebellion is taken from *İOTK* 2, 106. Mustafa, who gives the date of the rebellion as 23 Receb 931 (May 16, 1525), may be confusing the date when the rebellion occurred with the date when the news of the rebellion reached İbrahim in Egypt.

[33] *Tabakat*, 129a–129b.

[34] *Ibid.*, 129a–130a.

[35] Jean Deny ("Re'îs ül Küttāb," *EI2*) claims that Mustafa was the first secretary to hold this title, but Halil İnalcık ("Reis-ül-Küttâb," *İA*, vol. 9, 671) argues that it was used before Mustafa's appointment. The eighteenth-century bureaucrat Ahmed Resmi (*Ḥalîfetü'r-rü'esâ*, 4), a chief secretary himself, saw Mustafa, rather than his immediate predecessor Haydar, as the first individual worthy of the title.

relationship between the sultan and İbrahim. This relationship widened the executive authority of the grand vizier, as already seen in İbrahim's appointment of a governor-general for Egypt, a power usually exercised by the sultan. It also required a closer collaboration between the sultan and the grand vizier, as well as a careful monitoring and regulation of the activities of the grand vizierate. Mustafa, as the trusted bureaucrat of the "new regime," was supposed to fulfill this role. His new duties entailed the preparation and presentation of the memoranda and reports from the grand vizier to the sultan. He was also asked to be present in audiences granted by the sultan to the grand vizier and by the grand vizier to foreign ambassadors and to supervise the preparation of diplomatic treaties. The secretaries under the chief secretary began to assume a series of important tasks such as the renewal of appointment diplomas for governors and judges, the preparation of the sultan's dispatches, or the supervision of the correspondence between the sultan and the viziers. In terms of the history of the Ottoman bureaucracy, Mustafa's appointment as chief secretary represents the first stages of a process toward a more formal bureaucracy with better defined positions and functions. In a reflection of these trends, İskender Çelebi, İbrahim's other trusted advisor and collaborator, was made chief treasurer (*başdefterdar*) around the same time.

The Downfall of the Hungarian Kingdom

Süleyman's second Hungarian campaign is the first military venture organized without the presence of major political and military figures inherited from the previous regime, such as Piri Mehmed, Ferhad, or Ahmed Pashas. The campaign's success, in the contemporary sources, is thus attributed to the sultan, who is hailed as the architect of a tremendous victory over the century-long rivals of the Ottomans. On the ideological front, the campaign constitutes the first practical step of the ambitious political program outlined in the Egyptian preamble. Before the campaign, İbrahim pompously informed the Venetian *bailo* in Istanbul that, according to the prophecies of an ancient book he and Süleyman had read in their childhood, under his grand vizierate, the sultan would conquer many lands, eventually capture Rome and establish the dominance of a single religion.[36] The Ottoman–Hungarian rivalry, especially after the fall of Constantinople, had included a critical apocalyptic element. The

---

[36] Cornell Fleischer, "Shadows of Shadows: Prophecy and Politics in 1530s Istanbul," *IJTS* 13, no. 1–2 (2007): 55.

FIGURE 4. The Battle of Mohacs from an Ottoman perspective (*Hünernāme*, vol. 2, TSMK, Hazine 1524, 257a).

conquest of Constantinople motivated the Ottomans to conflate dynastic ideology with apocalyptic/messianic speculations. Thus, under Mehmed II, battles with European Christians were seen, among other things, as signs of tribulations preceding the End Time. An eventual Ottoman conquest of Rome or another major European Christian capital, referred to as the "Red Apple (*Kızıl Elma*)," was expected to happen in the near future.[37] Ottoman apocalyptic speculations corresponded with various prophecies about Turks that circulated in Europe. Because Hungary was the major European Christian rival of the Ottomans until 1526, these prophecies were particularly popular in the Hungarian lands.[38] Although the sultan's previous Hungarian campaign did not give primacy to these speculations, his second campaign pushed them to the fore.

Mustafa, together with many other Ottomans, indeed saw this campaign through the lens of Ottoman claims to messianic kingship and universal monarchy. In this regard, his account differs from his narratives on the capture of Belgrade and Rhodes. While describing Süleyman's departure for the campaign, for instance, Mustafa calls the sultan "the messiah of the End Time (*mehdī-yi āḫiru'z-zamān*)" and "the master of the auspicious conjunction (*ṣāḥib-ḳırān*)" (i.e. an individual born under a conjunction of Saturn and Jupiter).[39] *Ṣāḥib-ḳırān*, a term often encountered in early modern Ottoman as well as Safavid and Mughal political thought, emerged within a sophisticated cultural context that was influenced by the Mongol/Timurid political/military legacy, astrology, Islamic apocalypticism, and various prophecies. There was a resurgence of messianic expectations all over the Islamic world in the period following the Mongol invasions. In Iran, Eastern Anatolia, and Mesopotamia, in the fourteenth and fifteenth centuries, there were a series of religious movements that dabbled in messianism and the science of letters and suggested the abolition of confessional boundaries and the creation of a new, universal religion. The belief that the End Time was near was an important

---

[37] Şahin, "Constantinople and the End Time"; for the focus of Ottoman apocalyptic speculations on Hungary see Turan, "The Sultan's Favorite," 324–35.

[38] Kenneth M. Setton, *Western Hostility to Islam and Prophecies of Turkish Doom* (Philadelphia: American Philosophical Society, 1992); Yoko Miyamoto, "The Influence of Medieval Prophecies on Views of the Turk: Islam and Apocalypticism in the Sixteenth Century," *JTS* 17 (1993): 125–45; Pál Fodor, "The View of the Turk in Hungary: The Apocalyptic Tradition and the Legend of the Red Apple in Ottoman-Hungarian Context," in *Les traditions apocalyptiques au tournant de la chute de Constantinople*, eds. Benjamin Lellouch and Stéphane Yérasimos (Paris: Harmattan; Istanbul: Institut français d'études anatoliennes Georges-Dumézil, 2000), 99–131.

[39] *Tabakat*, 134b, 135a.

element in most of these new religious discourses.[40] The concept of *ṣāḥib-ḳırān*, an amalgamation of these various themes, represented universalist notions of politico-religious leadership in the post-Mongol and early modern Islamic world.[41] First used by Timur to enhance his political claims, the epithet was widely applied to Süleyman in the first decade of his reign. With its powerful messianic overtones, it represented Ottoman claims to universal monarchy and world conquest.[42] It also established a privileged link between past glory and the Ottoman present, as the earlier holders of the title were generally accepted to be such world conquerors as Alexander the Great, Chinggis Khan, and Timur. Mustafa believed that Selim I had come close to this distinction, only to be stalled by his death at a relatively young age and his failure to fight with European Christians.[43] By deploying this particular title against the Hungarians and by subsequently using it against Habsburg claims to universal monarchy, the Ottomans brought together two separate halves of early modern Eurasian political thinking.

Beyond his remarks on the campaign's ideological issues, Mustafa is silent about the developments in Central Europe in 1521–26 and the campaign's international background. Ottoman–Hungarian hostilities

---

[40] For this environment, see Shahzad Bashir, "Deciphering the Cosmos from Creation to Apocalypse: The Hurufiyya Movement and Medieval Islamic Esotericism," in *Imagining the End: Visions of Apocalypse from the Ancient Middle East to Modern America*, ed. Abbas Amanat (London: I.B. Tauris, 2002), 168–84; Bashir, *Messianic Hopes and Mystical Visions. The Nurbakhshiya between Medieval and Modern Islam* (Columbia, SC: South Carolina University Press, 2003); Mohammad Ahmad Masad, "The Medieval Islamic Apocalyptic Tradition: Divination, Prophecy and the End of Time in the 13th Century Mediterranean" (PhD diss., Washington University at St. Louis, 2008); İlker Evrim Binbaş, "Sharaf al-Dīn 'Ali Yazdī (*ca.* 770s–858/*ca.* 1370s–1454): Prophecy, Politics, and Historiography in Late Medieval Islamic History" (PhD diss., University of Chicago, 2009).

[41] For a discussion of the emergence and subsequent uses of this crucial concept, see Ahmed Azfar Moin, "Islam and the Millennium: Sacred Kingship and Popular Imagination in Early Modern India and Iran" (PhD diss., University of Michigan, 2010), 30–56, 85–92, 138–43, etc. For the uses of the Timurid legacy in the Mughal context, also see Lisa Balabanlılar, *Imperial Identity in the Mughal Empire: Memory and Dynastic Politics in Early Modern South and Central Asia* (London: I.B. Tauris, 2011), 7–17 and passim.

[42] For the meaning and specific uses of this term in the Ottoman context, see Fleischer, *Mustafa Âli*, 162–63, 165–69; Fleischer, "The Lawgiver as Messiah," 279–81; Barbara Flemming, "Sāhib-kırān und Mahdī: Türkische Endzeiterwartungen im ersten Jahrzehnt der Regierung Süleymāns," in *Between the Danube and the Caucasus*, ed. György Kara (Budapest: Akadémiai Kiadó, 1987), 43–62; Flemming, "Public Opinion under Sultan Süleymân," in *Süleymân the Second and His Time*, eds. Halil İnalcık and Cemal Kafadar (Istanbul: Isis, 1993), especially 52–53.

[43] *Tabakat*, 20b–21a; 41b.

had continued after the capture of Belgrade. While the Hungarians tried to muster the necessary financial and military resources to capture the fortresses they had lost, Ottoman governors in the area continued to harass Hungarian border defenses.[44] Ottoman preparations for a large-scale campaign in Hungary had continued since December 1524, but the campaign was delayed by İbrahim's activities in Egypt. Unlike Mustafa, contemporary historians such as Kemalpaşazade Ahmed and Lütfi Pasha mention the international environment. Lütfi Pasha explains the campaign by the sultan's reaction to news of a general attack against the Ottomans under the leadership of the Hungarians. The Hungarians indeed asked for the help of various European powers against an imminent Ottoman onslaught following the fall of Belgrade, but the tensions between France, the Habsburgs, Venice, and the Papacy over the control of Italy made it nearly impossible to organize a concerted attack. Kemalpaşazade Ahmed, on the other hand, refers to Francis I's plea for help from the Ottomans following his captivity after the Battle of Pavia in 1525 and portrays the king of Hungary as an ally of Charles V.[45] The Ottoman campaign against Hungary can thus be construed as the first stage of the Ottoman–Habsburg rivalry and a constituent part of an "Ottoman grand strategy" in Europe, which brought together universalist ideological arguments and a cross-continent political and geostrategic competition with the Habsburgs.[46]

Süleyman and İbrahim left the capital on April 23, 1526, at the date fixed by astrologers as a propitious time for the campaign's beginning. İbrahim, who also carried the title of the governor-general of Rumeli, marched with his own troops ahead of the sultan and the main body of

[44] András Kubinyi, "The Battle of Szávaszentdemeter-Nagyolazsi (1523): Ottoman Advance and Hungarian Defence on the Eve of Mohács," in *Ottomans, Hungarians, and Habsburgs in Central Europe: The Military Confines in the Era of Ottoman Conquest*, eds. Géza Dávid and Pál Fodor (Leiden: Brill, 2000), 71–115.

[45] Lütfi Paşa, *Tevārīḫ-i Āl-i ʿOsmān*, 319–21; Kemalpaşazade Ahmed, *Tevārīḫ-i Āl-i ʿOsmān*, 218–220. Cf. Gökbilgin, "Kanunî Sultan Süleyman," 9–12; Géza Perjés, *The Fall of the Medieval Kingdom of Hungary: Mohács 1526-Buda 1541*, trans. Márió D. Fenyö (Boulder, CO: Social Science Monographs; Highland Lakes, NJ: Atlantic Research and Publications, 1989), 9–10, 104–117; *The Papacy and the Levant 3*, 229–48; Turan, "The Sultan's Favorite," 254–322 passim.

[46] I am borrowing the concept from Gábor Ágoston, "Information, Ideology, and Limits of Imperial Policy: Ottoman Grand Strategy in the Context of Ottoman-Habsburg Rivalry," in *Early Modern Ottomans*, 76–78. Murphey ("Süleyman I and the Conquest of Hungary") explains the campaign as a reaction against Habsburg expansionism while Fodor ("Ottoman Policy towards Hungary") sees it as yet another step in a conscious Ottoman policy of annexing Hungary.

the army. Mustafa, whose account gives unique details about İbrahim's activities, was most likely in the pasha's company. There were legitimate doubts about the pasha's military abilities in the capital and in the army[47]; hence, Süleyman and İbrahim carefully designated relatively manageable tasks for the pasha. As commander of the experienced Rumeli troops, he did not have to show much military initiative. During the first phase of the campaign, İbrahim's main task was to secure the advance of the Ottoman army by scouting the area and building roads and bridges. The campaign's second phase started after the army began crossing the Drava in the vicinity of Osijek, on August 20, 1526. Various intelligence reports, summarized by Mustafa, informed the Ottomans that the Hungarian army lay in wait in an area called Mohacs; the same reports also told that the Hungarian army was fortified with cannons and carts and was assisted by a fleet on the Danube. Mustafa's enthusiastic account does not include the obvious feelings of apprehension on the eve of battle. Rather, he describes an army camp full of cantors, storytellers, and Quran reciters. Experienced frontier warriors play their lutes and sing heroic songs, and public criers exhort soldiers to prepare for the following day. After the morning prayer, on August 29, the army became ready for battle while the sultan, İbrahim, other prominent figures, and Mustafa took position on a nearby hill to observe the developments. Mustafa observed the Hungarian army in awe, likening it to the nearby Danube, spreading in every direction and slowly moving.[48]

On the hill, the battle tactics were revised for the last time. On the advice of Bali Bey, an experienced military man who had fought the Hungarians many times in the past, the Ottomans allowed the Hungarian heavy cavalry to attack.[49] The Hungarian attack was met by musket and cannon fire. After a diversionary retreat, the Rumeli cavalry units surrounded the attacking Hungarians and determined the battle's outcome.[50] The Hungarian army and its noblemen officers were decimated, and Louis II lost his life while trying to leave the battlefield. Following celebrations the next day, the sultan began his advance toward Buda, the capital city, which he entered nearly two weeks later, on

---

[47] Turan, "The Sultan's Favorite," 241–42.

[48] *Tabakat*, 132a–145b.

[49] Cf. a report from Bali Bey to the sultan about the Hungarians' military capabilities, TSMA E. 6146/2. Mustafa probably saw this report.

[50] For a detailed reconstruction of the battle see Perjés, *Mohács 1526-Buda 1541*, 251–57; Feridun Emecen, "'Büyük Türk'e Pannonia Düzlüklerini Açan Savaş Mohaç 1526," in *Muhteşem Süleyman*, ed. Özlem Kumrular (Istanbul: Kitap, 2007), 45–92.

September 10. Mustafa was very much impressed by this wealthy city and by the king's treasury and weapons, which were discovered in the citadel. He walked through the king's palace, admiring the paintings and ornaments. He closely observed Süleyman and İbrahim, who enjoyed their stay at the king's palace, organized celebrations, and even used the king's hunting lodge. The symbolic takeover of the Hungarian king's domain was thus complete, after his death on the battlefield.[51] After spending ten days in the Hungarian capital, the sultan ordered the construction of a bridge from Buda to the other side of the Danube, toward Pest, where he stayed for a few days. He met anti-Habsburg Hungarian nobles in the city, and, presumably, the name of John Szapolyai was mentioned as a candidate to the Hungarian throne.[52] The aim of the sultan was not to annex the Hungarian territories at this time. Moreover, attacks by the remaining Hungarian forces, Buda's distance from the Ottoman territory, food shortages, and the arrival of the cold season created an unsuitable environment. Perhaps more importantly, the Ottomans were already looking for an ally to place on the vacant Hungarian throne.[53]

The sultan and the grand vizier began their journey back to Istanbul on September 24. The army followed a double-pronged route, with İbrahim going to the northeast, following the river Tisza, and the sultan following the Danube. The last phase of the campaign, as told by Mustafa, served the purpose of exterminating the last pockets of Hungarian resistance. Moreover, since the sultan had prohibited the looting of Buda and Pest, the janissaries had not been able to gather any material benefits. This had caused tensions in the army, as a result of which some janissaries burned a number of churches in Pest to voice their frustration. İbrahim, aware of the tensions, offered the city of Szeged to the janissaries and the rest of his men. The sultan and the part of the army under his command also proceeded in the same fashion, taking various fortresses and allowing soldiers to loot Hungarian cities on the way back to Istanbul.[54] The two branches met around October 7 at Peterwardein, where Mustafa was able to see with his own eyes the tremendous quantity of looted goods and the large numbers of captives. The atmosphere of elation quickly subsided after the army crossed the Drava toward Istanbul. There, messengers informed the sultan of rebellions in Anatolia. At

[51] *Tabakat*, 146b–152a.
[52] *İOTK* 2, 118–19.
[53] Fodor, "Ottoman Policy towards Hungary," 291–93.
[54] *Tabakat*, 152b–155b.

Belgrade, a few days later, more messengers arrived with dire news, and the sultan ordered a forced march, at the end of which he reached Edirne on October 29. Istanbul was finally reached on November 14, and the sultan began to monitor the situation in Anatolia.[55]

Süleyman's second Hungarian campaign, during which he had defeated a king, finally gave him a prestige equal to that of his father. Its outcome provided a concrete support to Ottoman claims of universal monarchy and divinely anointed sovereignty, because such a major victory over a Christian kingdom could only be achieved, as it was widely argued by various Ottoman sources, with the direct intervention of God. İbrahim's first military campaign established his martial prowess, at least in theory. Mustafa, on the other hand, further solidified his position as one of the chief propagandists of the new imperial project. His long account in *Tabakat* was composed soon after the campaign and independently circulated. The account purges unsavory incidents such as the burning of the churches in Pest, or the execution of undisciplined soldiers on the sultan's orders, and focuses on what were, for Mustafa, the positive aspects of the campaign.[56] Moreover, on the way back to the capital, he was given the task of composing the sultan's letter to his governors, judges, and other officials, the *fethname*.[57] The "letter of victory" informs its audience of the campaign's basic events and developments. Toward the end, in a language heavy with Quranic references and Islamic metaphors, it describes the sultan's achievement as an unparalleled and unprecedented victory. Finally, it orders the officials to share this information with the subjects and organize celebrations.

While Mustafa's letter of victory circulated throughout the empire, and rebels in Anatolia attacked towns and scoured the countryside claiming supreme political and religious authority for their leaders, on November 11, 1526, John Szapolyai, a prominent Hungarian nobleman and the duke (*voivode*) of Transylvania, was elected the new king of Hungary. Louis II had died without leaving a male heir, and many pro-German courtiers and noblemen perished together with him, which facilitated Szapolyai's election. The anti-Habsburg League of Cognac, established in 1526 by Pope Clement VII, Francis I, Venice, and the dukes of Bavaria, quickly

---

[55] *Ibid.*, 156a.

[56] Yılmaz, "Koca Nişancı," 62.

[57] The text, preserved in Feridun Ahmed Bey, *Mecmū'a-yı Münşe'āt-ı Ferīdūn Bey* (Istanbul: Daru't-tıbaati'l Âmire, 1848–1857), 1: 546–551, does not include its author's name. I agree with Yılmaz ("Koca Nişancı," 61) that, on the basis of stylistic and linguistic features, it was written by Mustafa.

recognized John's new title. In this regard, the Ottomans were not alone in conceiving of John's kingship as a barrier in front of Habsburg designs to control Central Europe.[58] Charles V's brother Ferdinand was the last in a long line of Habsburgs pursuing a claim to the Hungarian throne. His sister Maria was the deceased king's wife, and his own wife Anna was Louis' sister, which made him a powerful contender. He controlled Austria and Bohemia in agreement with his brother after the latter was elected emperor, and Hungary was of crucial importance, strategically and economically, for the defense of his dominions in Central Europe. In the summer of 1527, spurred by his brother's recent victory over the League of Cognac that resulted in the Sack of Rome, Ferdinand entered Hungary with his German troops, occupied Buda, and had himself crowned the king of Hungary in early November 1527.[59] This was the first step of a military and ideological enmity that would transform much of Hungary into a costly battle zone between the Ottomans and the Habsburgs.[60]

Both the Habsburgs and the Ottomans underwent processes of territorial consolidation in the first two decades of the sixteenth century, the Habsburgs mostly through inheritance and family alliances and the Ottomans through military conquest. Their respective imperial enterprises continued to expand beyond the first decades of the sixteenth century and clashed around competing military, political, and economic objectives in Central Europe and the Mediterranean. Charles V and Süleyman entertained similar dreams of unifying spiritual and political authority under a single mantle. The Habsburgs revived late medieval ideas of universal empire and redefined them within the fold of "true" (i.e., Catholic) Christianity, whereas the Ottomans brought together the Chinggisid/Timurid/messianic notion of ṣāḥib-ḳırān with a claim to the caliphate and the leadership of "true" (i.e., Sunni) Islam.[61] Both sides

---

[58] *The Papacy and the Levant 3*, 251–52.

[59] Paula Sutter Fichtner, *The Habsburg Monarchy, 1490–1848: Attributes of Empire* (New York: Palgrave Macmillan, 2003), 11–16; *The Papacy and the Levant 3*, 252.

[60] For Habsburg attempts at incorporating Hungary into their domains, see Péter Sahin-Tóth, "A Difficult Apprenticeship. The Integration of Hungary into the Habsburg Monarchy in the 16th Century," in *The World of Emperor Charles V*, eds. Wim Blockmans and Nicolette Mout (Amsterdam: Royal Netherlands Academy of Sciences, 2004), 247–63; Teréz Oborni, "Die Herrschaft Ferdinands I. in Ungarn," *Kaiser Ferdinand I. Aspekte eines Herrscherlebens*, eds. Martina Fuchs and Alfred Kohler (Münster: Aschendorff, 2003), 147–65.

[61] For Habsburg ideas of universal monarchy, among the rich literature on the subject, I find the following especially useful: John M. Headley, "The Habsburg World Empire and

appealed to European, Mediterranean, and Middle Eastern audiences to recognize Charles V or Süleyman as the sole legitimate emperor. They skillfully used each other's aggressive policies as tools of legitimization against their other rivals, such as France, the Protestant princes and cities, and the Safavids. The messianic and apocalyptic dimensions of the rivalry abated around the middle of the sixteenth century, but, for two decades, the Ottoman–Habsburg conflict represented one of the liveliest scenes of ideological competition in early modern Eurasia.[62] Mustafa was present during this time in the vicinity of the sultan, and he became one of the most prominent chroniclers of this rivalry.

A Clash of Political Theologies: Rebellions in Anatolia and a Heresy Trial in Istanbul

While Süleyman was in Hungary, a series of rebellions broke out in Anatolia. These rebellions belonged to what might be called the Ottomans' "Eastern Question" and presented various challenges that were vital for Süleyman to address. Very much like the last Hungarian campaign, these rebellions were related to debates on political theology in early modern Eurasia. Ottoman-centric studies usually explain them with the influence of pro-Safavid groups inside the Ottoman realm and the activities of

the Revival of Ghibellinism," *Medieval and Renaissance Studies* 7 (1975): 93–127; Franz Bosbach, "The European Debate on Universal Monarchy," in *Theories of Empire, 1450–1800*, ed. David Armitage (Aldershot: Ashgate, 1998): 81–98; Juan Carlos d'Amico, *Charles Quint, maître du monde: entre mythe et réalité* (Caen: Presses Universitaires de Caen, 2004). For a general discussion of the concept in the early modern world, see Anthony Pagden, "Monarchia Universalis," chap. 3 in *Lords of All the World: Ideologies of Empire in Spain, Britain and France c. 1500–c. 1800* (New Haven: Yale University Press, 1995), 29–62. Pagden illustrates very well how claims to establish a universal empire always went hand in hand with ecumenical religious arguments in Europe, which was also the case for the Ottomans.

[62] For concise descriptions of the rivalry, see John Elliott, "Ottoman-Habsburg Rivalry: The European Perspective," in *Süleymân the Second and His Time*, 153–162; Gábor Ágoston, "Ideologie, Propaganda und politischer Pragmatismus: Die Auseinandersetzung der osmanischen und habsburgischen Grossmächte und die mitteleuropäische Konfrontation," in *Kaiser Ferdinand I. – Ein mitteleuropäischer Herrscher*, eds. Martina Fuchs et. al. (Münster: Aschendorff, 2005), 207–33; Ágoston, "Information, Ideology, and Limits of Imperial Policy," 93–100. For a discussion of the respective imperial ideologies, see Turan, "The Sultan's Favorite," 254–355 passim; Krstić, *Contested Conversions*, 75–97. The Ottoman threat was indeed seen as an apocalyptic challenge against Habsburg claims to universal monarchy: Franz Bosbach, "*Imperium Turcorum* oder *Christianorum Monarchia* – Die Osmanen in der heilsgeschichtlichen Deutung Mercurino Gattinaras," in *Das Osmanische Reich und die Habsburgermonarchie*, eds. Marlene Kurz et. al. (Vienna: R. Oldenbourg, 2005), 167–80.

Safavid missionaries and "spies."[63] It is true that, for many Ottoman subjects in Anatolia, the Safavids represented a tribal political ideal that granted more autonomy to individuals and communities. In the same vein, the Safavid political theology continued to exert a powerful attraction over many Anatolian Muslims. In this sense, it is possible to interpret these rebellions, which were partly fueled by universalist claims to an alternative political and spiritual leadership, as extensions of the social and religious upheavals that accompanied the Safavids' rise to power. At the same time, however, they were reactions to long-standing Ottoman attempts at establishing fiscal and military control in Central and Eastern Anatolia. These consisted of increasing the number of *timar* grants at the expense of local landed interests, imposing taxes and other regulations on nomadic tribes, and curtailing the power of tribal aristocracies.[64]

Mustafa wrote about these rebellions most probably during his retirement, a few decades after they happened, and he portrays them alongside the Sunni–Shiite division, remarking that the rebels killed *Sunni* Muslims. Reports from various Ottoman officials in Anatolia, which he quotes in his work, show that the rebellions compounded popular dissent with latitudinarian beliefs. The first revolt broke out in the province of Bozok, during the visit of Ottoman tax assessors. In August 1526, a tribal chief named Musa Bey killed the Bozok provincial governor, together with a judge and a secretary who were charged with surveying the area for the assessment of taxes. He was soon joined by a group of antinomian preachers and their supporters under the leadership of Baba Zünnun. The rebels, whose ranks grew with every passing day, defeated the forces of two Ottoman governors-general, killing both officials on the

---

[63] İsmail Hakkı Uzunçarşılı, *Osmanlı Tarihi*, vol. 2, *İstanbul'un Fethinden Kanunî Sultan Süleyman'ın Ölümüne Kadar* (Ankara: Türk Tarih Kurumu, 1943), 345–47; Remzi Kılıç, *Kânunî Devri Osmanlı-İran Münâsebetleri* (Istanbul: I.Q., 2006), 145–50. A more objective study is Sohrweide, "Der Sieg der Safawiden in Persien," 170–86. For a discussion of the "fifth column" mentality, see Walter Posch, "Der Fall Alkâs Mîrzâ und der Persienfeldzug von 1548–1549: ein gescheitertes osmanisches Projekt zur Niederwerfung des safavidischen Persiens" (PhD dissertation, Bamberg University, 1999), 170–74.

[64] For the tension between the Ottoman political center and the nomads, see Rudi Paul Lindner, *Nomads and Ottomans in Medieval Anatolia* (Bloomington: Research Institute for Inner Asian Studies, Indiana University, 1983); Yıldırım, "Turkomans between Two Empires," 34–62 (for a theoretical discussion of the issue) and 63–149 (for the Ottoman case). My understanding of the reasons behind the rebellions is based, next to Mustafa's own account, on Jean-Louis Bacqué-Grammont, "Un rapport inédit sur la révolte anatolienne de 1527," *StIsl* 62 (1985): 156–160.

battlefield. They were finally overwhelmed by a large force from Damascus and Diyarbekir in late September. Various nomadic tribes in Adana soon rose, however, and captured a few towns in the area, where they attacked and looted marketplaces and killed Ottoman officials. After the Adana rebels were defeated, Bozok witnessed another revolt, under the leadership of the aforementioned Baba Zünnun's son. At this stage, the rebellions' religious dimension was intensified by the participation of Kalender, the sheikh of Hacı Bektaş, the prominent figure of the Bektaşi order. Kalender, very much like Süleyman, presented himself as the rightful sultan and caliph, posing a direct challenge against the sultan's ideological claims.[65] Mustafa describes the rebels' activities as being against both Sharia and *kanun* and accuses them of disrupting the order of the realm. However, he was no doubt aware, like others within the Ottoman ruling elite, that the rebels' political claims were uncomfortably similar to those of the Ottoman political center. The importance attributed to the rebellions is further proven by the sultan's dispatch of İbrahim to Anatolia. Mustafa left the capital on April 30, 1527, with the pasha and a contingent of janissaries.

Rather than abating after the pasha's arrival, the rebellions were strengthened by the participation of disgruntled local elements in the province of Dulkadir, including members of the old princely family. The reorganization of the area, which was conquered by Selim in 1515, had left indigenous tribal leaders and members of the military class destitute and, in the absence of new land grants, these formed a potentially dangerous group in a state of constant agitation. The son of the last Dulkadir ruler, Şehsuvaroğlu Ali Bey, had ruled over his ancestral lands as an Ottoman governor but was executed in 1522 for not following the instructions of the palace and harboring plans of independence.[66] İbrahim had already encountered this problem on his way back from Egypt, when the military men whose land grants had been revoked had planned to attack him and loot the revenues of the Egyptian treasury he carried in his caravan.[67] İbrahim's initial attempts to subdue the rebels were

---

[65] For the details of the rebellions see *Tabakat*, 159a–165a.

[66] Mustafa narrates the Ali Bey affair in *Tabakat*, 67b–68b, 77a–78a. Also see Alaaddin Aköz and İbrahim Solak, "Dulkadirli Beyliğinin Osmanlı Devletine İlhakı ve Sonrasında Çıkan İsyanlar," *Türk Dünyası Araştırmaları* 153 (November–December 2004): 41–50. For later Ottoman attempts at incorporating the old military class of the area after these rebellions, see Aköz and Solak, "Dulkadirli Eyâletine Ait Bir Kânûnnâme (1533–1546)," *Kırgızistan "Manas" Üniversitesi Sosyal Bilimler Dergisi* 9 (2004): 9–29.

[67] *Tabakat*, 130a.

unsuccessful. Two governors-general he ordered against the rebels were defeated. One of the governors-general was killed on the battlefield, and the rebels obtained significant quantities of weapons from the defeated Ottoman forces. Changing his approach, İbrahim moved to Elbistan. There, he was informed that, against his force of five thousand, the rebels fielded thirty thousand fighters. He immediately organized a meeting with the notables of the area, held audiences with tribal leaders, distributed gifts and new *tımar*s. As a result of these activities, says Mustafa, rebel forces dwindled to a few thousand and were then defeated by a contingent sent by İbrahim. The pasha was truly relieved when he heard the news and ordered celebrations with martial music in Elbistan. He then launched an investigation into the performance of Ottoman administrators against the rebels because, according to Mustafa, İbrahim was worried that these defeats would have negative consequences in the future, for they made Ottoman soldiers appear weak and vulnerable. The infuriated pasha particularly insisted on finding out how the mighty Ottoman forces had been routed by naked dervishes, runaway Turkish peasants, and rabble-rousers (*"bir bölük çıplak 'ışıklar, çiftbozañ Türkler, münāfıklar"*). After several days of interrogations, İbrahim and his retinue left the area on July 25, reaching the capital on August 11.[68] The issue of political theology would soon re-emerge, not in the Anatolian countryside this time, but in the capital.

In this period, Ottoman administrators were intensely preoccupied with alternative political theologies offered by Bektaşis, Safavids, scholars, and mystics. A dervish claiming both spiritual and worldly authority might be seen as a potential ally of the Ottoman sultan in the fifteenth century[69]; however, similar figures became suspect in the eyes of the political center in the sixteenth century. For instance, an important mystic such as İbrahim Gülşeni, a prominent participant in debates on new political theologies and a typical product of the more tolerant religious and political environment of the fifteenth century, was regarded with suspicion by both the Mamluk sultans and the Ottomans when he lived in Cairo in the first decades of the sixteenth century.[70] In an age when

---

[68] *Ibid.*, 165b–170b. The lively account of the Ottoman officials' interrogation is in 168b–170b.

[69] See Halil İnalcık, "Dervish and Sultan: An Analysis of the Otman Baba Vilayetnamesi," *The Middle East and the Balkans under the Ottoman Empire: Essays on Economy and Society* (Bloomington: Indiana University Turkish Studies, 1993), 19–36.

[70] See Side Emre, "İbrahim-i Gülşeni (ca. 1442–1534): Itinerant Saint and Cairene Ruler" (PhD diss., University of Chicago, 2009).

religion was radically politicized and became a constituent part of imperial ideologies, matters of doctrine ceased to be limited to scholarly circles and produced wider repercussions, drawing both larger numbers of
followers and the scrutiny of political authorities. The first decades of
Süleyman's rule witnessed attempts by the political center to create an
"official" version of doctrine and the circulation of alternative political theologies and criticisms.[71] The political center presented the sultan
as, alternatively, the caliph of Sunni Islam, a messianic conqueror with
a claim to universal sovereignty, and the renewer of Islam (mujaddid).
At the same time, various scholars and mystics offered alternative messianic figures, debated the possibility of a universal religion that would
unite Islam and Christianity, or described the powers that be as corrupt and waited for the dawn of universal renewal or the coming of the
End Time.[72] The conflation of all these factors at a critical juncture prepared the reaction of the Ottoman palace against a scholar named Molla
Kabız. Especially in the aftermath of the Anatolian rebellions, which had
a crucial religious dimension, the Ottoman elite was particularly sensitive
to the political implications of what it perceived as deviance. Mustafa,
whose account of the Kabız affair immediately follows his narrative of
the Anatolian rebellions, obviously saw a connection between the two
events.

Some of Kabız' religious ideas, revolving around the supremacy of
Jesus over Muhammad, were already quite widespread in various circles
of Ottoman society, especially among recent converts.[73] Kabız' demise
was precipitated when he started publicizing his ideas. His preaching
had gained him a certain following in Istanbul. Some scholars noticed his
growing influence but were unable to prevail over him in religious debates.
They sought a last refuge in Ottoman authorities, reporting Kabız to the
imperial council.[74] Although Mustafa downplays Kabız' scholarly abilities by describing him as a vagrant and a drunkard, Kabız was in reality a
relatively prestigious scholar who knew the Quran and the Islamic tradition well and who skillfully utilized the Quran and Muhammad's sayings

---

[71] For a discussion of this politicized version of Sunni Islam and its function in Ottoman
official ideology, see Ahmet Yaşar Ocak, Osmanlı Toplumunda Zındıklar ve Mülhidler
(15.–17. Yüzyıllar) (Istanbul: Tarih Vakfı, 1998), 93–96; about the Ottoman doctrinal
reaction to the challenges of the age, also see Üstün, "Heresy and Legitimacy."

[72] Flemming, "Public Opinion under Sultan Süleymân"; Fleischer, "The Lawgiver and the
Messiah"; Ocak, Zındıklar ve Mülhidler, 230–43, 248–50, 270–304.

[73] Ocak, Zındıklar ve Mülhidler, 228–30.

[74] Ibid., 233.

to support his arguments on the supremacy of Jesus over Muhammad. The affair must have had widespread repercussions in Istanbul because the sultan felt the need to personally watch Kabız' trial from behind a latticed window.

Kabız was brought to an imperial council meeting on November 3, 1527. İbrahim ordered the two military judges of Anadolu and Rumeli to interrogate him but, on this first day, they failed to refute the scholar's arguments. The judges began to claim that he had to be executed on the basis of customary law ('örf), but İbrahim, aware of the ideological stakes in the trial, insisted on a condemnation on the basis of the Sharia, which would be seen as less arbitrary and more authoritative by the followers of the debates. The judges failed to find a justification on the basis of the Sharia and, as a result, Kabız was released from the imperial council. Süleyman summoned the pasha immediately after the meeting. As the pasha told Mustafa later, the sultan, in an angry tone, asked him why he had not given the task to the mufti of Istanbul, Kemalpaşazade Ahmed, and the city's chief judge, Sa'dullah. Realizing his mistake, the pasha quickly sent a pursuivant after Kabız and had him imprisoned. In another session, the next day, Kabız was interrogated by Ahmed on theological issues but refused to recant his beliefs, as a result of which the chief judge ordered his execution on the basis of the Sharia.[75]

Although Mustafa omits the details of Kabız' arguments during his trial, it is possible to reconstruct these on the basis of three pamphlets composed in Arabic by Kemalpaşazade Ahmed after the affair, in an attempt at publicizing the official position.[76] Despite serving a multireligious empire, Ottoman scholars were not in a position of comparing Christian and Muslim theologies in a sophisticated manner, as shown by the inability of the judges to refute Kabız' claims. Even though Mustafa gives his readers the impression that Kemalpaşazade Ahmed rose to the challenge, Ahmet Yaşar Ocak shows that the mufti's riposte remained within the confines of Islamic theology and consisted of a critique of Kabız' use of Islamic arguments to prove the supremacy of Jesus over Muhammad. The most potent danger posed by the ideas of Kabız was the casting of doubt over the Sharia and the tradition of Muhammad (*sunna*) as the latest (and most perfect) manifestations of divine will. Because such an argument seriously undermined the basis of Ottoman

---

[75] Mustafa's account of the incident is in *Tabakat*, 172b–175b.
[76] Üstün, "Heresy and Legitimacy," 77–99; Ocak, *Zındıklar ve Mülhidler*, 231, 235–38.

law and imperial ideology, Kabız had to be sacrificed for the sake of the *raison d'état*, but by using the authority of Islamic law.

Who Is the "Master of the Auspicious Conjunction"? Süleyman versus Ferdinand of Austria

Ferdinand's election by pro-Habsburg Hungarian nobles and his occupation of Buda led to frenetic diplomatic activities by the other king-elect, John Szapolyai. John's Hungarian possessions suffered constant attacks from Ottoman frontier forces as well as incursions by Ferdinand. The latter was initially unable to muster the necessary forces to overrun John's domains, however, because most of the Habsburg resources were mobilized in Italy against the French. Szapolyai was somehow comforted by the fact that anti-Habsburg actors in Europe, especially Venice, did not desire a major Habsburg presence in Central Europe at this particular juncture. In a letter to Szapolyai in February 1527, which reached the king in the summer of the same year, Francis I, the king of France, expressed his delight at Szapolyai's coronation, and a formal convention would be signed between the two in October 1528. However, these sympathies did not translate into concrete military and financial support. Szapolyai was unable to stop Ferdinand from invading his domains in the summer and fall of 1527, and had to take refuge in Poland in March 1528. In April 1528, Szapolyai sent a letter to the princes and estates of the German Empire, protesting Ferdinand's occupation of his domains and accusing the emperor of not fighting against the Ottomans. He also appealed to Pope Clement VII and the College of Cardinals, to no avail. The Ottomans emerged in this context as the only international power to offer tangible help to Szapolyai. Toward the end of 1527, Szapolyai had sent Jerome Laski to Istanbul. In an audience with İbrahim, Laski was told that the Ottomans would recognize Szapolyai as the King of Hungary and end the practice of calling him the voivode of Transylvania. On February 29, 1528, with a treaty, the Ottomans guaranteed to provide help against Ferdinand. Ferdinand's envoys, who reached Istanbul at the end of May 1528, had a different reception. In audiences with İbrahim, the ideological rivalry manifested itself when the envoys insisted on referring to Ferdinand as the king of Hungary, to the pasha's displeasure. İbrahim informed them that various European Christian rulers such as the kings of Poland and France, the Papacy, the Venetians, and Szapolyai had obeyed the sultan, inviting Ferdinand to follow their example. The request to return a number of fortresses taken from the Hungarians in the last decade did not facilitate the negotiations either, and the envoys were released after being told that the sultan would soon come to meet Ferdinand in person.[77]

Before departing for the campaign that would eventually culminate in the siege of Vienna, Süleyman and İbrahim reached another crucial agreement about their political and military collaboration. One day, after the viziers had left the imperial council meeting, Mustafa was personally summoned by the sultan. Süleyman explained to him that the Ottoman realm had become extensive and required the management of a great variety of issues. Thus, the sultan needed to appoint a helper and endow him with some of his powers. He then asked the chief secretary to prepare a draft and present it to the sultan the next day.[78] After working on the text of a diploma (berat) through the night, Mustafa read his version to the sultan the next morning. Süleyman approved of the text, ordering his chief secretary to prepare an official copy with the sultan's signature. After the official copy was finished, on March 28, 1529, a ceremony was organized to the pasha's honor and the diploma was publicly read to a gathering of the janissaries and the palace troops. In addition, the pasha's annual stipend, together with the number of banners he carried, was increased, setting him further apart from the other viziers.[79]

The diploma announced a new title for the pasha, one that had not been given to any Ottoman grand vizier before him: ser'asker (i.e., commander-in-chief). It also ordered the sultan's servants and subjects to obey him. The pasha was granted the authority to appoint governors-general, provincial governors, and other holders of land grants. As mentioned previously, the pasha had already exercised this power by nominating a governor for Egypt or by distributing land grants during the pacification campaign against the Anatolian rebels, but the diploma formalized his executive power and regularized it by making him responsible for these appointments. Finally, the diploma allowed the pasha to punish anybody found guilty of oppressing the subjects or straying from the Sharia or kanun.[80] Whereas earlier examples of devolution had mostly been de facto arrangements, the power sharing between İbrahim

---

[77] İOTK 2, 127–28; The Papacy and the Levant 3, 251–54, 312–24; Fodor, "Ottoman Policy Towards Hungary," 297–98; Gökbilgin, "Kanunî Sultan Süleyman," 16–18.

[78] Tabakat, 179a.

[79] Ibid., 179a–b.

[80] For the text of the decree, see Tabakat, 180a–181b. For a slightly different version, see Feridun Ahmed, Mecmū'a-yı Münşe'āt, 1: 480–83. A Turkish transliteration that collates the two versions is in Yılmaz, "Koca Nişancı," 234–46.

and the sultan was made official. Mustafa's claim that the affairs of the empire required the new position is probably genuine, because the growth of the Ottoman realm, the increased ideological competition, and the attempts at enhancing the power of the Ottoman political center required increased levels of administrative/bureaucratic supervision. On the ideological front, because Ferdinand of Austria called himself the "surrogate" and commander-in-chief of the Holy Roman Emperor (*Sacre Caesareae et Catholicae Maiestratis in Imperio Locumtenens generalis*, a title that the Ottoman translators rendered as *ser-leşker*), it is probable that the pasha's new title was meant to match those employed by Ferdinand.[81] Mustafa's secret composition of the diploma, on the other hand, shows the privileged position he occupied in the Ottoman bureaucracy. He had become both İbrahim's trusted helper and the sultan's reliable secretary. His nominal superior, the chancellor, was often bypassed on his behalf, especially when a particularly important document with an obvious ideological argument was being composed. The pasha's empowerment also meant his empowerment, because increased administrative powers for the pasha meant that Mustafa would play an even larger role in his everyday relationship with İbrahim. With the pasha's new mandate, the scene was now set for new struggles.

Musing about the situation in Hungary between 1526 and 1529, Mustafa laments the fact that John Szapolyai is not a worthy adversary for Ferdinand of Austria. Ferdinand, he informs his readers, is the brother of the king of Spain (this is how he calls Charles V to minimize his imperial claims) and the lord of the German and Bohemian lands, whereas Szapolyai is the legitimate king of Hungary. Ignoring the fact that Ferdinand was also elected by an assembly of (albeit pro-Habsburg) nobles, Mustafa portrays him as a usurper. More importantly, he claims that, after his capture of Buda in 1527, Ferdinand began to refer to himself as *ṣāḥib-ḳırān*, the use of which was Süleyman's exclusive right. Strategically speaking, the Ottomans were genuinely concerned by a counterattack on Ferdinand's part and his eventual capture of all of Hungary, which he could then use as a base against the Ottomans.[82]

---

[81] This title was used in a letter sent to the sultan in July 1529. Quoted in Jean-Louis Bacqué-Grammont, "Sur deux lettres de Ferdinand Ier à İbrâhîm Paşa," *Turcica* 19 (1987): 170 (for the Ottoman translation of the title), 180n15 (for the use of the title in another letter).

[82] *Tabakat*, 183a–b. *İOTK* 2 (129–30) presents the campaign as part of a policy to annex Hungary in the long run (cf. Fodor, "Ottoman Policy Towards Hungary," 296), whereas Lütfi Paşa (*Tevārīḫ-i Āl-i ʿOs̱mān*, 332–35) talks about the necessity to help Szapolyai.

From its very beginning, Süleyman's third Hungarian campaign was hampered by the elements. Torrential rains delayed the departure from the capital for two days. After an arduous march on muddy roads, two idle weeks were spent in Edirne waiting for the arrival of the Anadolu troops, and five more days were lost because of hard rains, which meant that the sultan had not advanced much by the end of May 1529. The first week of June saw the overflowing of the Maritsa in the vicinity of Philippopolis, when the bridges over the river were destroyed and the army camp was flooded. It was still raining when Sofia was reached by the middle of June. Süleyman arrived in the plain of Mohacs on August 18 for the rendezvous with John Szapolyai. In this highly symbolic meeting place, the Ottoman-supported king of Hungary was made to kiss the hand of the sultan in an elaborate ceremony of submission. The joint armies then marched on to Buda and reached it on September 3. Mustafa likened the city to an islet lost amidst the waves of Ottoman soldiers. Indeed, following a general attack on the 8th, the defenders surrendered with a mutual agreement. When a "German" soldier, according to Mustafa, stabbed a janissary while leaving the city, the fate of the defenders was sealed. Despite the agreement, the janissaries, always eager for booty, attacked the soldiers and their families while they were leaving the city and enslaved many women and children. On September 11, another imperial council meeting was summoned, and that is where, according to Mustafa, the decision to march toward Vienna was made. On the 14th, John Szapolyai was crowned with the crown of St. Stephen, captured by Ottoman forces a few weeks earlier, and he was placed on the throne of the Arpads in Buda.[83] In terms of political competition and symbolism, one of the campaign's objectives was thus realized by early September. To supervise Szapolyai's activities, the Ottomans left behind a long-time resident of Istanbul, Alvise Gritti. He was the illegitimate son of the doge of Venice Andrea Gritti (served btw. 1523–38), İbrahim's confidant, and one of the key actors of Ottoman diplomacy on the European front.[84] Gritti would represent the empire's interests in Hungary, serve the king as an advisor thanks to his

---

[83] *Tabakat*, 183b–188a; İOTK 2, 131–33.

[84] For this curious figure, see Turan, "The Sultan's Favorite," 280–316; Robert Finlay, "'I am the Servant of the Turkish Sultan:' Venice, the Ottoman Empire, and Christendom, 1523–1534," chap. 10 in *Venice Besieged: Politics and Diplomacy during the Italian Wars, 1494–1534* (Aldershot: Ashgate Variorum, 2008); Özlem Kumrular, "Osmanlı Sarayında ve Avrupa Siyasi Sahnesinde Venedikli Bir Sınır Diplomatı: 'Mir-i Venedik Oğlu' Alvise Gritti," *TTYY* 6 (Fall 2007–Winter 2008): 39–59.

tremendous grasp of European politics and diplomacy, and establish a system of supply for the Ottoman troops.[85]

Why did the sultan and his notables decide to attack Vienna despite the fact that the campaign season was about to end? This may be partly explained by the need to challenge Ferdinand to open battle or directly question his political claims and authority by attacking his capital. Mustafa does not explain why this stage of the campaign was organized despite the coming of autumn, but he provides detailed observations on logistic difficulties. After Buda, the Ottoman army proceeded relatively uneventfully toward Vienna, passing by Habsburg fortresses abandoned or destroyed by their defenders. The last Habsburg fortress on the Hungarian frontier, Esztergrad, surrendered September 22, and raiding parties were sent in all directions. Mustafa, who calls the region the "German realm," was very much impressed by what he saw. This land had never been blessed by Islam, he says, and hence was one of the major centers of Christianity. Despite its wealth, however, it was a very inhospitable place. The valleys, forests, and hills delayed the advance of the Ottoman army and created many logistic difficulties. These difficulties would only increase in Vienna.

Ottoman scouts reached the city's vicinity on September 24, and the main body of the army followed on the 27th. İbrahim led the army, while Süleyman and his palace troops took position behind him, and the doomed siege began. Mustafa, in an apologetic tone, enumerates various reasons for the failure: Vienna's northern location and its cold weather, the early onset of winter, the constant rain and hail, the distress of the Ottoman soldiers who felt isolated in the middle of an enemy territory, and the strength of the city's fortifications. Although apologetic European historians emphasize the city's small garrison and the unrepaired state of its fortifications to magnify the achievement of the Habsburg defenders, a Venetian informant who left the city in mid-September concurs with Mustafa's assessments on the city's defenses.[86] Moreover, the campaigns of the Ottoman army were generally modeled on the tactic of leaving the capital by early spring, fighting during the summer, and ending the campaign before the onset of autumn, when the cold

---

[85] Perjés, *Mohács 1526-Buda 1541*, 128; Ferenc Szakály, *Lodovico Gritti in Hungary 1529–1534: A Historical Insight into the Beginnings of Turco-Habsburgian Rivalry*, translated by Dániel Székely (Budapest: Akadémiai Kiadoó, 1995), 49–55.
[86] *The Papacy and the Levant 3*, 325–26.

weather created discomfort and the muddy roads made the movements of the army (of its heavy artillery, especially) difficult.[87]

The siege of Vienna opened with skirmishes between the defenders, who organized various sorties, and the Ottoman infantry. The absence of large-caliber siege guns, which had not been brought with the army, further hampered the Ottomans' military capabilities. On October 5, in a change of tactic, provincial cavalrymen (*sipahis*) were ordered to dig underneath the city walls, and raiders were distributed ladders to climb them; palace troops and Anadolu contingents were instructed to gather wood to fill the ditches. Two days later, when an Ottoman contingent chasing a Habsburg force almost entered the city, the defendants sealed all the gates. On the 10th, explosive charges were detonated at two different locations and the Ottomans attacked the breaches, but they were met with musket and cannon fire and repulsed. The harshness of the weather was making itself felt more and more, and it was decided to lift the siege after the failure of the last Ottoman assault on October 14. Mustafa explains this decision with the sultan's compassion and pity vis-à-vis his soldiers. Another incident that he notes, the distribution of a thousand *akçe*s per person to the janissary corps, a typical attempt at appeasing the soldiery, shows that unrest in the army was the main reason behind the lifting of the siege. Mustafa finds solace in the idea that Ottoman raiders had sown seeds of terror in the "German realm" and that they had taken many captives. If the German realm were not fortified with all these towers and castles, he says, its whole population would have been carried away by the Ottoman raiders.[88]

Süleyman's third campaign in Central Europe produced mixed results. Szapolyai's reinstitution as the king of Hungary and Buda's recovery from Ferdinand were important achievements. A possible attack by Ferdinand was prevented by this campaign, and the dispatch of Ottoman raiders deep into Habsburg territory served the Ottoman propaganda well. On the other hand, the so-called usurper of the title *ṣāḥib-ḳırān*, Ferdinand, did not face the Ottoman army in an open battle, which meant that he

---

[87] The difficulty of staging and pursuing a campaign during autumn and winter is well illustrated (albeit for a slightly later period) by Gilles Veinstein, "L'hivernage en campagne: talon d'Achille du système militaire ottomane classique. A propos des *sipāhī* de Roumélie en 1559–1560," *StIsl* 58 (1993): 109–148; also see Rhoads Murphey, *Ottoman Warfare, 1500–1700* (New Brunswick: Rutgers University Press, 1999), especially the section entitled "Physical barriers and environmental constraints," 20–25.

[88] *Tabakat*, 188a–192b. For the siege also see *İOTK* 2, 135–39.

was not defeated and thus divested of his ideological claims. His flight from Vienna to Prague was duly noted by the Ottomans, but he was able to preserve his capital city.[89] On the international front, the campaign led to a rapprochement between Charles V and Pope Clement VII, who signed the Treaty of Barcelona at the end of June 1529, voicing their determination to collaborate in protecting Christians from the Ottomans. Francis I, without any hopes of receiving papal support against Charles, signed the Treaty of Cambrai with the emperor in August 1529. Venice, after receiving news of the Ottoman retreat from Vienna, entered into a pact, at the end of December, and pledged to ally with Charles, Ferdinand, the Papacy, and other pro-imperial Italian powers against any Christian ruler or power threatening the peace of the peninsula. The Ottoman envoy Yunus Bey, who reached Venice in mid-December, tried to present the Ottoman campaign as a success, but was not able to prevent the Venetians from entering into an agreement with the imperialists. The new balance of forces culminated in Charles' coronation, by the hand of the pope, as the Holy Roman Emperor in Bologna on February 24, 1530.[90]

The Ottoman answer to the ambiguities of the campaign's outcome and Charles' coronation was an elaborate display of imperial grandeur, staged on the occasion of the circumcision of princes Mustafa, Mehmed, and Selim in June–July 1530. The celebrations were similar in content to İbrahim's wedding. Through well-organized processions, public acts of charity, the display of war booty, and the performances of artists and entertainers from all parts of the empire, they served to project the image of a powerful empire and a glorious sultan ruling over different realms. Süleyman's need to present himself as a ruler of rulers is apparent in his public appearances in the company of surviving members of Muslim dynasties defeated by the Ottomans. The inhabitants of Istanbul could thus watch their sultan surrounded on his right by his grand vizier and viziers and on his left by the son of the penultimate Mamluk sultan Qansuh al-Ghawri, two descendants of the Akkoyunlu dynasty, and a member of the Dulkadir family. Venetian observers paid particular attention to the pomp of the ceremonies and noted the special place occupied by İbrahim in them, whom, they wrote back home, looked like a "second emperor."[91] Mustafa, who narrates these ceremonies in great detail,

---

[89] For a similar assessment of the campaign's outcome see Perjés, *Mohács 1526-Buda 1541*, 130–31.

[90] *The Papacy and the Levant 3*, 327–37.

[91] *Ibid.*, 342–43.

describes İbrahim as the true representative of the sultan. The pasha acted in a role similar to a godfather, by supervising every detail of the princes' circumcision and thus assuming another highly symbolic mantle.[92] As Mustafa emphatically remarks, around this time, the sultan and İbrahim managed well the affairs of the Ottoman realm; they were friends and collaborators.[93] This remark is particularly meaningful at this juncture, because the relationship between Süleyman and İbrahim would become strained soon, and the tensions would culminate in the pasha's execution in 1536.

Who Is the Last Roman Emperor? Süleyman versus Charles V

The failure of the Ottoman siege of Vienna, John Szapolyai's reinstitution as the king of Hungary, and Charles' coronation as the Holy Roman Emperor meant that the Hungarian question had become a cornerstone of the Ottoman–Habsburg rivalry. Charles V, despite his anti-Ottoman posture, informed his brother Ferdinand, in a letter sent from Bologna in January 1530, that he desired to negotiate a truce with the Ottomans.[94] However, the negotiations of a delegation in Istanbul in October–November 1530 did not produce the desired outcome. The Ottomans insisted on Ferdinand's renunciation of all claims over the throne of Hungary, whereas the Habsburg envoys asked for their recognition.[95] At the end of December 1530, Habsburg forces laid siege to Buda for nearly two months. The city was relieved by Ottoman forces in the area, and this short-lived affair gave Mustafa the opportunity to complain once again about Szapolyai's lack of military capabilities. It is interesting, on the other hand, that he calls the king a "friend of the holy warriors (mücāhid)" and explains the Ottoman alliance with him as part of an elaborate plan to defeat the Habsburgs.[96]

This plan was put into action in the spring of 1532. When he talks about the preparations for a new military campaign, Mustafa first of all emphasizes that Ferdinand constantly attacked Szapolyai's lands. Moreover, Ottomans received news of an imminent attack by Ferdinand, from land and sea, into Ottoman territory, if we are to believe Mustafa.[97] On

---

[92] The account of these ceremonies is found in *Tabakat*, 194a–202a.
[93] Ibid., 207a.
[94] *The Papacy and the Levant 3*, 348.
[95] *İOTK* 2, 141–43.
[96] *Tabakat*, 202a–203b; *İOTK* 2, 143–44.
[97] *Tabakat*, 207a–b.

the other side, Charles V, who was busy renegotiating with the Protestants in 1531–32, had heard the news of an impending Ottoman attack against Hungary and possibly his German possessions. This forced him to sign the Peace of Nuremberg (1532) with the Lutherans, his first detailed political and religious concession to the Protestant camp, in return for which the Protestants pledged military and financial help against the Ottomans.[98] On the ideological front, the Ottomans were preoccupied this time not by Ferdinand, but by his brother "Karlos" (i.e., Charles V). As Mustafa saw it, following his coronation, Charles V had succeeded in becoming the leader of almost all Christians, and his possession of a special, bejeweled crown symbolized his claim to universal sovereignty. Mustafa states that the crown entitled Charles to rule over the German lands as well, not fully realizing that many German princes were alarmed as much as the Ottomans by Charles' coronation. He continues by saying that the emperor received monetary and military assistance from many other European rulers and nominated his brother Ferdinand as his *locum tenens* (*ḳā'im-i maḳām*) for the Bohemian and Austrian lands.[99] The Ottomans were now intent on contesting Charles' titles on the battlefield. Indeed, during the campaign, İbrahim would tell Habsburg envoys that there could be only one true monarch in the world, either the emperor or the sultan.[100]

The ideological dimension determined the tenor of the "German" (*Alamān*) campaign from the very beginning. Mustafa's narrative shows that the campaign was conceived as a show of force and a long procession through Southeastern and Central Europe, rather than a campaign with specific military objectives.[101] Leaving the capital toward the end of April 1532, the sultan and the army proceeded at a leisurely pace. The city of Nish was reached in the middle of June, where Ferdinand's envoys waited for the sultan. The envoys, true to the campaign's general characteristics, were received amidst elaborate ceremonies, but were unable to convince

---

[98] Stephen A. Fischer-Galati, *Ottoman Imperialism and German Protestantism, 1521–1555* (Cambridge, MA: Harvard University Press, 1959), 50–56.

[99] *Tabakat*, 209b–210a. Similar arguments are repeated in Bostan Çelebi, *Süleymānnāme*, ms. SK, Ayasofya 3317, 129b.

[100] Robert Finlay, "Prophecy and Politics in Istanbul: Charles V, Sultan Süleyman, and the Habsburg Embassy of 1533–1534," *JEMH* 2, no. 1 (1998): 12.

[101] Ágoston, "Information, Ideology, and Limits of Imperial Policy," 100–101. For the symbolic nature of the campaign also see Murphey, "Süleyman I and the Conquest of Hungary," 214–16; Özlem Kumrular, "Campaña de Alemania: Rito, arte y demostración," in *L'Empire ottoman dans l'Europe de la Renaissance...*, eds. Alain Servantie et. al. (Leuven: Leuven University Press, 2005), 191–214.

the Ottomans to end the campaign.[102] In clear defiance of Charles' imperial title, Süleyman entered Belgrade coiffed with an elaborate crown, which was manufactured in Venice and was meant to imitate and surpass the papal tiara and the imperial crown.[103] After passing through Belgrade and crossing the Sava, a French delegation arrived in the Ottoman army camp. On July 7, after the army was ordered to take battle positions, the Habsburg and French ambassadors were brought to the sultan's tent. Unlike the Habsburg envoys, the French diplomats were admitted into the imperial tent, where they kissed the sultan's hand amidst the fanfare of musical instruments and the clamor of cannon and musket fire. The sultan, says Mustafa, agreed to provide naval support to the French in the western Mediterranean, after which the French envoys were allowed to return to their king. The Habsburg envoys, however, were detained in the army camp.

It appears that Süleyman and İbrahim had genuine hopes for these diplomatic negotiations, because they sacrificed an important section of the campaign time for them. The decision to take military action was made only after it became apparent that negotiations with Ferdinand's envoys would remain fruitless. A fleet was prepared on the Danube, and raiders were sent into Habsburg territory, while the army resumed its march on July 9 to the northwest, reaching Osijek on the 17th. There, in a missive to Ferdinand, Süleyman informed him that his true enemy was the king of Spain (i.e., Charles V). The sultan invited the emperor to fight with him to finally resolve their enmity.[104] In the next three weeks, the Ottoman army, with the provincial governor of Semendire as scout, followed by İbrahim Pasha and then the sultan himself, continued to progress through the western Hungarian countryside, capturing or receiving the submission of a large number of small and medium-sized fortresses. The Ottoman advance displayed the features of an expedition that was a combination of punitive action and show of power: although the fortresses that refused to surrender were attacked and looted, those which surrendered were left untouched. According to Mustafa, the foremost aim of this campaign was not to take fortresses, but to upset the machinations of Charles and Ferdinand against the Ottomans.

---

[102] *The Papacy and the Levant 3*, 363–64.

[103] Gülru Necipoğlu, "Sülemân the Magnificent and the Representation of Power in the Context of Ottoman-Habsburg-Papal Rivalry," *Art Bulletin* 71, no. 3 (1989): 401–27, especially 407–09.

[104] *The Papacy and the Levant 3*, 364–65.

FIGURE 5. Süleyman receives French diplomats (Ârifi, *Süleymānnāme*, TSMK, Hazine 1517, 346a).

Mustafa's description of the "German" campaign is distinguished by the author's particular enthusiasm, even though the campaign lacked striking military feats that could be compared with the capture of Belgrade or the victory at Mohacs. Mustafa arrogantly remarks that Charles V, despite his pretension to the title of *ṣāḥib-ḳırān* and his title of Caesar, was afraid of challenging Süleyman directly. The Ottoman soldiers thus had no mercy for the subjects of this pretender, who were overwhelmed by the Ottoman army and scattered into every direction, like the Biblical supporters of the Pharaoh. During the day, the smoke coming from the burning churches shadowed the light of the sun; at night, the light coming from the torches of the Ottoman soldiers shone brighter than the moon. The Ottoman army, like a wide sea, expanded into every direction and covered the face of the earth. Because the enemy refused to challenge the Ottoman army, says Mustafa, the best option was to march into his heartland and force him to fight. Hence, until September 11, the Ottomans advanced and reached the vicinity of Graz. Mustafa says that, at this ancient seat of Ferdinand's ancestors, it became apparent that neither Ferdinand nor Charles would challenge the Ottoman army in an open battle. After looting and burning down the environs of the city, the Ottoman army began its return journey. Of course, Charles, during this time, was in Vienna, with a fairly large army, and it is highly likely that the Ottomans were aware of the emperor's presence. Neither side, it appears, wanted to engage in a potentially fatal encounter, preferring to wage an intense propaganda war instead. Although the campaign did not yield any tangible results, Süleyman was careful to represent it as a major victory. On the return voyage, around the middle of October, an imperial council meeting was organized in Belgrade. Süleyman distributed gifts to the governors-general and other commanders; messengers were sent to various Ottoman governors in the east with the news that the campaign had been a successful one. After reaching Istanbul on November 22, 1532, the sultan immediately ordered a five-day long celebration.[105]

The results of the campaign were at best mixed. The campaign provided a quick reaction to Charles' coronation as emperor and forestalled any major Habsburg attack in Central Europe. However, it failed to fulfill its ideological objectives. The lackluster performance of the last two campaigns resulted, contrary to Ottoman expectations, in the enhancement of the Habsburg position in European politics. The most tangible result

---

[105] This summary of the campaign is provided on the basis of *Tabakat*, 209b–237a. Cf. *İOTK 2*, 144–55.

of the German campaign was the peace accord concluded at the end of June 1533 in Istanbul. The accord is, at first sight, an admission of defeat for Ferdinand, who agreed on paper to be the equal not of the Ottoman sultan but of the grand vizier. He also relinquished, again on paper and temporarily, his claims over the Hungarian throne. On the other hand, the portion of Western Hungary that was under Ferdinand's occupation was left to him. The treaty thus formalized the stalemate that was reached in Central Europe between the two sides. The negotiations between the Habsburg envoys and İbrahim are otherwise interesting in shedding light over the specifics of the Ottoman–Habsburg rivalry and the image of the pasha. During the negotiations, the pasha presented himself as an all-powerful official whose decrees carried the same power as the sultan's. At other times, he contested the titles that Charles V used in a letter he addressed to the sultan, such as the king of Jerusalem, the duke of Athens, and the lord of Tripoli. The pasha mockingly told the Habsburg envoys that Charles was an impostor, because all these territories lay under the control of the Ottoman sultan. He was amused by the inability of Charles to end the Protestant problem and offered to bring the pope and Martin Luther together in a council. As for Ferdinand, he said, he was not wealthier or more powerful than an Ottoman provincial governor.[106]

Mustafa participated in some of the meetings with the ambassadors. He was presented to the Habsburg envoys as the sultan's private secretary and described as a bureaucrat who supervised the sultan's correspondence and presided over the official matters. The Habsburg ambassadors believed that there was a tension between İbrahim and Mustafa: in their reports, they remarked that İbrahim was much more amicable when Mustafa was absent, whereas his attitude became haughtier and more demeaning in the presence of the chief secretary.[107] The impressions of the Habsburg ambassadors show that, at that time, Mustafa had reached a position whereby he represented the office of the sultan himself, rather than İbrahim. He was, in a sense, the link tying İbrahim to

---

[106] İbrahim reiterated these arguments in a letter sent to the emperor In July 1533: Jean-Louis Bacqué-Grammont, "Une lettre d'İbrâhîm Paşa à Charles Quint," in *Comité international d'études pré-ottomanes et ottomanes, 6th Symposium, Cambridge, 1st–4th July 1984*, eds. Bacqué-Grammont and E.J. van Donzel (Istanbul: Divit, 1987), 65–88.

[107] For the negotiations see *The Papacy and the Levant 3*, 370–88; cf. *İOTK 2*, 156–58; Ralf C. Müller, "Der umworbene 'Erbfeind': Habsburgische Diplomatie an der Hohen Pforte vom Regierungsantritt Maximilians I. bis zum 'Langen Türkenkrieg' – ein Entwurf," in *Das Osmanische Reich und die Habsburgermonarchie*, 262–67.

the sultan and the rest of the Ottoman ruling elite, and the pasha was careful to behave in a way that would please Mustafa and the edifice he represented. Despite his overwhelming power, İbrahim was thus obliged to constantly negotiate his image and his activities vis-à-vis the sultan and the elite, especially after the unimpressive outcome of the last two campaigns against the Habsburgs. He had played an important role in the preparation and management of these campaigns and in the ideological speculations that were formulated around them. The failure of the campaigns had a negative impact on his stature. Because preparations for a campaign against the Safavids had begun during the negotiations with the Habsburgs, the pasha was criticized in certain circles for his eagerness to make peace with the Christians.[108] İbrahim probably hoped that refocusing the Ottoman imperial policy on the Safavid heresy might restore his reputation. The outcome would be quite different than his expectations.

---

[108] Finlay, "Prophecy and Politics," 24–29.

3

The Empire and Its Chancellor (1534–1553)

In 1534, in the middle of a difficult campaign against the Safavids, Mustafa was finally appointed *nişancı,* following his mentor Seydi Bey's death. During the previous decade he had already assumed responsibilities beyond his position as chief secretary. His new title made a de facto position official. In documents from the first decade of Süleyman's reign, he was usually called "Mustafa son of Celal" or Mustafa Çelebi (a title similar to "gentleman," utilized by members of the learned professions). After his promotion, he became "His Eminence Mustafa" and began to use his father's name as a patronymic. The son of the judge from the provinces now became Hazret-i Mustafa Çelebi Efendi Celalzade[1] or, in its shorter version, Celalzade Mustafa Çelebi. Between 1534 and 1557, the date of his retirement, he would hold considerable authority as the new empire's chief bureaucrat. He came to represent the ideal secretary in the eyes of his colleagues and, as seen in the dream narrative of an anonymous secretary, was securely anchored in their subconscious minds as a figure of power, on a similar level with the sultan, the grand vizier, and the imperial princes.[2]

The two decades between his appointment as chancellor and the early 1550s saw Mustafa write letters on behalf of the sultan, supervise the distribution of *timars,* contribute to the sultan's legislation (*kanun*), and

[1] BOA, KK 1764, 211, recorded on December 9, 1534.

[2] The anonymous secretary saw Mustafa in two separate dreams. See Cornell H. Fleischer, "Secretaries' Dreams: Augury and Angst in the Ottoman Scribal Service," in *Armagan: Festschrift für Andreas Tietze,* ed. Ingeborg Baldauf (Prague: Enigma, 1994), 83–84. For other contemporary testimonies on the recognition Mustafa enjoyed, see n4 above.

preside over the further development of the Ottoman scribal service. He continued to participate in the sultan's campaigns and remained, through his "letters of victory" and other diplomatic writings, one of the most prominent voices of Ottoman imperialism. These two decades witnessed the opening of an eastern front with the Safavids and an active political and military articulation of Ottoman imperialism against both the Safavids and the Habsburgs. Ideological competition with the Habsburgs had been the main cultural and religious challenge in the first decades of Süleyman's reign. After the mid-1530s, the Ottomans had to fight, both militarily and ideologically, on two separate fronts, against the Habsburgs and the Safavids.

Süleyman's First Eastern Campaign: Sunni Triumphalism versus Logistical Problems

Following the Battle of Çaldıran (1514), Selim and Ismail focused their energies on different objectives. Selim consolidated his domain by his capture of the Dulkadir and Mamluk lands, whereas Ismail faced another set of typically early modern Eurasian problems: the vicissitudes of concurrent empire building and competition over the Timurid legacy in and around Central Asia and the rise of the Uzbeks; the incursions of the Portuguese in Hormuz; tensions among the tribal military elements, on the one hand, and between the tribes and the sedentary populations, on the other. From 1514 until his death in 1524, Ismail increased his diplomatic activities and communicated with various European Christian powers, such as the Hospitallers of Rhodes, Venice, the Papacy, and eventually Charles V, in the hopes of collaborating against the Ottomans. Selim, whose religious propaganda against Ismail intensified after Çaldıran, knew that three years of campaigning had depleted his financial and human resources. Moreover, Ismail's supporters were numerous in Eastern Anatolia, and the main Ottoman task was to consolidate the newly acquired areas. Mustafa, who heard his mentor Piri Mehmed narrate the post-Çaldıran events, conveys to his readers the preoccupations of the Ottoman officials in this period.[3] For instance, in 1519, a man named Celal rebelled, proclaiming himself as the messiah. The rebellion was quelled, but rumors circulated about how Selim's nephew Murad, who had crossed over to the Safavids in the early 1510s

---

[3] *Selimname*, 206b–216a passim. Cf. Bacqué-Grammont, *Les ottomans, les safavides et leurs voisins*, 235–71.

and passed away in Iran, was alive and would come back at the head of an army.[4]

Süleyman, in the words of Jean-Louis Bacqué-Grammont, inherited from his father a policy of "relentless confrontation" with the Safavids, but was able to formulate his own policy of military "disengagement" with the assistance of Piri Mehmed.[5] One of his first acts of justice upon his accession was to lift the anti-Safavid commercial blockade imposed by Selim and restitute their confiscated merchandise to various traders. At the same time, the Ottoman-Safavid frontier was closely watched by both sides, as shown by the intense spying activity. Ismail sent a letter to the new sultan in September 1523, expressing his condolences about Selim's passing away three years ago and congratulating the sultan about his capture of Rhodes, but these openings were met with a haughty indifference.[6] Süleyman needed to focus on campaigns in Europe to establish his reputation and assert his control over the ruling elite. Moreover, the locus of Ottoman claims to universal sovereignty was seen as the European front in these early years. This has been interpreted as the absence of any persistent ideological problems in Ottoman-Safavid relations and as an indication that the Safavids were only a minor concern for the Ottomans.[7] To the contrary, the Safavid threat continued to loom in the minds of Ottoman administrators, the majority of whom had come of age during the troubles of Bayezid II's last years in power. The rebellions of Janbardi al-Ghazali in Syria in 1520, Ahmed Pasha in Egypt in 1524, and various Anatolian latitudinarians and tribal elements in 1526–27 were all evaluated as partly or wholly stemming from Safavid interference. The struggles with the Hungarians and then the Habsburgs kept alive the pressing importance of concepts such as ṣāḥib-ḳırān, or concerns about the function of religion in the definition of sovereignty and imperial policy. In the meantime, the "East," which Mustafa would later call the "Sharia-abrogating and

---

[4] My account is based on Roger Savory, *Iran under the Safavids* (Cambridge: Cambridge University Press, 1980), 45–49; Allouche, *Ottoman-Safavid Conflict*, 123–30; Colin Paul Mitchell, "The Sword and the Pen: Diplomacy in Early Safavid Iran, 1501–1555" (PhD diss., University of Toronto, 2002), 119–30; Newman, *Safavid Iran*, 20–25.

[5] This policy is analyzed in Bacqué-Grammont, *Les Ottomans, les Safavides et leurs voisins*, 294–368; Bacqué-Grammont, "The Eastern Policy of Süleymân the Magnificent," *Süleymân the Second and His Time*, 249–58.

[6] Details of this Safavid mission are found in Bacqué-Grammont, *Les ottomans, les safavides et leurs voisins*, 369–78; for a discussion of Ismail's letter significance, see Mitchell, *The Practice of Politics*, 57–58.

[7] This argument receives its best articulation in Rhoads Murphey, "Süleyman's Eastern Policy," in *Süleymân the Second and His Time*, 259–78.

sedition-full Orient,"[8] remained a relatively unknown land, difficult to administer and hostile to the Ottomans, populated by individuals and communities who harbored alternative ideas about politics and religion.

Süleyman's activities on the European front were facilitated by the relative absence of aggression displayed by Ismail in the last years of his reign and, especially, by the troubles encountered by his son Tahmasb, who came to the throne in 1524, when he was ten years old. The period between 1524 and 1533, often characterized as an interregnum by Safavid historians, witnessed severe tensions among different tribal confederations vying for power after the death of the charismatic spiritual leader and military commander Ismail. Whereas the tribal aristocracies, which had underwritten Ismail's rise to power, demanded more power and autonomy, the sedentary elements inside the Safavid realm were laying the foundations for a bureaucratic and scholarly establishment and debating the questions of doctrine and their role in politics. The remaining energies were devoted to fending off Uzbek attacks from the east.[9] The most concrete Ottoman challenge directed against the Safavids after Tahmasb came to power took the form of a threatening letter, a *tehdid-name*. The letter was composed by Mustafa and sent to the shah in the second half of 1525. It is considerably simpler in style than Mustafa's later writings and uses various colloquialisms, for instance, while threatening the shah about the imminent arrival of the Ottoman army and the fate that supposedly awaits him. The letter reminds the shah of his father's defeat by the power of Ottoman firearms in 1514, informs him that Süleyman is the conqueror of Belgrade and Rhodes, and chastises him for not having submitted to the Ottoman sultan like so many other rulers. Despite the relative simplicity of its style, through its references to the Ottoman sultan as caliph and *ṣāḥib-ḳırān*, its characterization of the Safavids as misguided (the term Mustafa uses is *ḍalālet*) and heretical (Tahmasb is said to wear the headgear of *ilḥād*), and its use of a Quranic verse on the caliphate (the same verse publicly discussed by religious scholars at İbrahim's wedding), this first letter from Süleyman to Tahmasb firmly locates the Ottoman-Safavid rivalry within the political theologies of early modern Eurasia.[10]

---

[8] *Tabakat*, 247b. The expression is *Şarḳ-ı şer-farḳ ve fitne-ġarḳ*.

[9] Sümer, *Safevî Devletinin Kuruluşu ve Gelişmesinde Anadolu Türklerinin Rolü*, 57–61, 85–109 passim; Savory, *Iran under the Safavids*, 50–57; Allouche, *Ottoman-Ṣafavid Conflict*, 130–38; Mitchell, "The Sword and the Pen," 182–217; Newman, *Safavid Iran*, 26–27.

[10] Feridun Ahmed, *Mecmū'a-yı Münşe'āt*, 1: 541–43.

During this time, the Ottoman–Safavid frontier in Eastern Anatolia and Iraq remained a highly fluid zone. Constant skirmishes occurred, intelligence peddlers traveled between the two sides, fortresses changed hands, allegiances were quickly shifted and restored, and commercial activity took place despite the tensions. Both the Ottomans and the Safavids relied on various tribal aristocracies, the majority of whom were Kurds, to help establish a military and political presence in the area.[11] The policy of entering into alliances with tribes was not limited to the frontier. The Ottomans strived to receive the support of Arab tribes in Egypt and Syria, and İbrahim Pasha quelled the Anatolian rebellions in 1527 through a careful policy of tribal diplomacy.[12] As seen earlier, Tahmasb, during the first decade and a half of his rule, lived in an environment characterized by tribal warfare and competition. The symbiotic relationship between the Safavid political center and the tribes was vital for the dynasty's survival; in this period, the tribes constituted its main military force against the Ottomans and the Uzbeks. Concurrently, various tribal groups fought to obtain high military and administrative positions and resented the intervention of the political center in their affairs. These tensions gave the Ottomans the "official" reasons for a campaign against the Safavids. Mustafa informs us that a man named Zülfikar, a prominent fighter, became the lord of Irak-ı Arab, which corresponds to the territory of today's Iraq. He sent a letter of submission to Süleyman, offering the lands under his control to the sultan. Tahmasb, alarmed by the news, laid siege to Baghdad. Zülfikar was able to resist the first attacks but was then betrayed by some of his men.[13] Indeed, Zülfikar was a prominent member of the Mawsillu tribal group, a major component of the Safavids' tribal base. He captured Baghdad in May 1528 by killing his

---

[11] For the Ottoman tribal policy, see Tom Sinclair, "The Ottoman Arrangements for the Tribal Principalities of the Lake Van Region of the Sixteenth Century," in *Ottoman Borderlands: Issues, Personalities and Political Changes*, eds. Kemal H. Karpat and Robert W. Zens (Madison: The University of Wisconsin Press/Center of Turkish Studies, 2003), 119–43; for the Ottoman-Safavid frontier in Iraq, see Rudi Matthee, "The Safavid-Ottoman Frontier: Iraq-i Arab as seen by the Safavids," in *ibid.*, 157–73. Both articles survey the area from the first decades of the sixteenth to the mid-eighteenth century. For two near-contemporary narratives by local Kurdish lords, see Şeref Han, *Şerefname*, trans. Mehmet Emin Bozarslan, 2 vols. (Istanbul: Ant, 1971); İsmet Parmaksızoğlu, "Kuzey Irak'ta Osmanlı Hâkimiyetinin Kuruluşu ve Memun Bey'in Hatıraları," *Belleten* 37, no. 146 (1973): 191–230. The most detailed analysis of the frontier is Posch, "Der Fall Alkâs Mîrzâ," 31–130. The Kurdish areas are discussed in *ibid.*, 50–74.

[12] Murphey, "Süleyman's Eastern Policy," 273–74.

[13] *Tabakat*, 242a–b.

uncle and, because he thus eliminated an ally of Shah Tahmasb, he contacted Süleyman in the summer of 1529 to receive support. Tahmasb recaptured Baghdad in June 1529, after Zülfikar was assassinated by his own brothers or relatives.[14] Mustafa uses this incident to explain that the Ottomans merely reclaimed what had become rightfully theirs through Zülfikar's pledge, but he conveniently omits any dates for the incident, as there is a five-year gap between it and the eastern campaign.

Mustafa, together with other Ottoman and Safavid sources, offers a second reason for the Ottoman campaign, one that also stems from the challenges of accommodating the tribal/military elements. At the center of these developments stands a military commander and administrator named Ulame, who had started his career as an Ottoman provincial cavalryman in Teke, an area populated by Turcoman tribes. After joining the pro-Ismail rebels around 1510, Ulame left Anatolia for Iran, where he became a member of the Takalu tribal aristocracy. He served Ismail in various capacities and was given the governorate of Azerbaijan in 1528–29. His desire to become a vizier was not realized, however, and he defected to the Ottomans toward the end of 1531. Ulame, in several accounts, is described as a skilled political actor who knew how to succeed in highly factional environments. After crossing to the Ottoman side through the supervision of Şeref, the Kurdish lord of Bitlis, he was able to convince Ottoman authorities that Şeref harbored Safavid sympathies and was about to defect. He obtained the newly minted title of governor-general of Bitlis and was sent to lay siege to the city. Şeref was forced to take refuge with Tahmasb. Ulame's forces reached the city in the summer of 1532 but retreated to Diyarbekir when news of an imminent attack by Şeref and Tahmasb arrived. The alliance between a prominent Kurdish lord and the shah caused legitimate concern among the Ottomans. According to some sources, Ulame used this as a pretext to convince İbrahim for a large-scale campaign. Ulame further promised that he personally knew many Safavid commanders and governors, and that these would side with the Ottomans in the case of an eventual invasion.[15]

---

[14] Kılıç, *Osmanlı-İran Münâsebetleri*, 152–53; Allouche, *Ottoman-Safavid Conflict*, 137.

[15] *Tabakat*, 242b–243a. Mustafa does not provide many details about Ulame's activities, which are discussed in Fahrettin Kırzıoğlu, *Osmanlı'nın Kafkas-Elleri'ni Fethi (1451–1590)* (Ankara: Sevinç Matbaası, 1976), 128–30; Kılıç, *Osmanlı-İran Münâsebetleri*, 154–58; Sinclair, "Tribal Principalities," 122–23; Mitchell, "The Pen and the Sword," 218–19. For near-contemporary testimonies about Ulame's role before the campaign, see Bostan Çelebi, *Süleymânnâme*, 128b, 130b–132a, 143b–144b; Lütfi Paşa, *Tevârīḫ-i Āl-i ʿOṣmān*, 341–42; Eskandar Beg Monshi, *The History of Shah ʿAbbas the Great*

Süleyman's first eastern campaign was thus orchestrated primarily by İbrahim. Ottoman sources called it *sefer-i 'Iraḳeyn*, the "Two Iraqs" campaign, since the purported aim was to conquer both the "Arab" Iraq and the "Persian" Iraq (Irak-ı Acem, approximately encompassing the territory of today's Western Iran). İbrahim probably expected that a successful campaign, assisted as per Ulame's promises by the massive defection of Safavid commanders and administrators, would help repair his reputation. Signing a peace treaty with Ferdinand, the latter's admission on paper of the Ottomans' superiority, and John Szapolyai's survival might have been construed as important successes for a less ambitious imperialist policy. The Vienna and German campaigns were seen as reversals, however, and a new objective was needed. Victory over the Safavids would mean the resuscitation of the Ottoman claims to universal sovereignty, this time within a more Islamicized fold. As Mustafa states, the campaign indeed targeted "Ismail's sedition" and thus included, like the previous European campaigns, a religio-political dimension.[16]

Mustafa's reminiscences of the campaign represent some of the most personal sections in his *Tabakat*. Compared with near-contemporary Ottoman accounts, where the campaign is narrated as a succession of military actions, Mustafa's narrative is dominated by his bitter observations on human folly and ineptitude, on the one hand, and a discourse of Sunni triumphalism, on the other.[17] Writing late in his life, he is torn between the unsavory elements of the campaign, such as the growing distance between İbrahim Pasha and the sultan, or the Ottoman inability to hold on to Tabriz and what he sees as its achievements, such as the capture of Baghdad. Moreover, he distances himself from İbrahim, who would be executed after the campaign. The confident, indeed buoyant tone of İbrahim's letters to Süleyman, composed by Mustafa in the spring of 1534, is not reproduced in *Tabakat*.[18] Like Mustafa's narrative of the Belgrade and Rhodes campaigns, the sections on the eastern campaign are

---

(Tārīḫ-e 'ālamārā-ye 'Abbāsī), trans. Roger M. Savory (Boulder, CO: Westview Press, 1978), 1: 110; Şah Tahmasb-ı Safevî, *Tezkire*, trans. Hicabi Kırlangıç (Istanbul: Anka, 2001), 29–33.

[16] *Tabakat*, 243a. For a similar, religious, justification of the campaign, see Bostan Çelebi, *Süleymānnāme*, 144a–b, where Bostan mentions the requirements of the caliphate and refers to Selim's struggles with the Safavid "heresy."

[17] Cf. Bostan Çelebi, *Süleymānnāme*, 145a–167b; Lütfi Paşa, *Tevārīḫ-i Āl-i 'Oṣmān*, 344–55.

[18] For two letters informing the sultan of castles captured, Kurdish lords co-opted, and Safavid administrators attracted to the Ottoman side, see M. Tayyib Gökbilgin, "Arz

filled with conspiracies, factional struggles, bad decisions, and strategic and logistical problems.

Mustafa's narrative begins with İbrahim's departure from Istanbul and his travel to Aleppo, where he would make the necessary preparations for a spring offensive. During his journey, the pasha dispatched letters to Ottoman governors in the east to ascertain the military and political situation inside the Safavid lands, the conditions in Baghdad, and the activities and loyalties of the Kurdish tribal lords in the area. Aleppo was reached on a particularly cold day, on November 30, 1533, where the pasha learned that Tahmasb had left Azerbaijan in the direction of Khurasan. Mustafa, the close observer of these developments, reports that İbrahim planned, while in Aleppo, to take a series of castles on the Ottoman-Safavid border (Adilcevaz, Erciş, Van, and Genc) and establish a defensive perimeter and then march against Baghdad.[19] However, these plans were upset by the emergence of a faction under the leadership of the chief treasurer İskender Çelebi. The treasurer, like Mustafa, had been İbrahim's trusted collaborator in the past decade but, according to Mustafa, he had used his position – unlike Mustafa, obviously – to amass a considerable fortune. His personal wealth supposedly attracted İbrahim's ire, as a result of which the chief treasurer associated with a group of ex-Safavid renegades to mislead İbrahim. Mustafa says the treasurer's plan was to convince the pasha to attack Tabriz, as a result of which he would either be forced to surrender to Tahmasb or suffer such a shameful defeat as to become discredited in the sultan's eyes. He also blames İbrahim for having fallen prey to these conspiracies because of his vanity, despite the warnings of his trusted advisors. This is the reason why the grand vizier abandoned his plans to attack Baghdad and decided to take the shah's capital city instead. These lines probably reflect Mustafa's personal and professional jealousies and his mistrust of the ex-Safavids who joined the Ottomans during the campaign. They are also meant to legitimize the subsequent Ottoman failure to control Tabriz, by attributing the grandiose and unrealized military objectives of the campaign to İbrahim and a group of conspirators.[20]

ve Raporlarına Göre İbrahim Paşa'nın Irakeyn Seferindeki İlk Tedbirleri ve Fütuhatı," *Belleten* 21, nos. 81–84 (1957): 466–76.

[19] *Tabakat*, 243b–247b; cf. Kırzıoğlu, *Osmanlı'nın Kafkas-Elleri'ni Fethi*, 130–34; Gökbilgin, "Arz ve Raporlarına Göre," 463–65.

[20] *Tabakat*, 247b–248b; cf. Kılıç, *Osmanlı-İran Münâsebetleri*, 171–73; Uzunçarşılı, *Osmanlı Tarihi* 2: 353–54.

Mustafa's excuses are not supported by the documentary evidence, which shows that both Süleyman and İbrahim indeed harbored great expectations. A letter sent from the grand vizier to the sultan in April 1534, composed by Mustafa himself, describes the situation inside the Safavid realm as very favorable to the Ottomans and requests the sultan to leave Istanbul in the middle of May. (The sultan would eventually depart from the capital on June 10, 1534.) The tone of the letter suggests that the sultan and the grand vizier had agreed to conduct this new stage of the campaign together.[21] Mustafa, on the other hand, presents the letter as an admission of the pasha's weakness and remarks that the pasha's power depended on the sultan. His real or perceived weakness notwithstanding, İbrahim behaved like a commander in chief and continued his march on to Tabriz, which he reached around the middle of July. Once there, he instituted various new governorates in Western Iran and appointed Ulame and his associates to these positions while, in reality, these areas had not yet entered under Ottoman control. A list of appointments and appointees sent in a letter from the pasha to the sultan lists Ulame himself, a certain Veli Can (the new provincial governor of Maragha), Şah Ali (the new provincial governor of Ardabil), Üveys Bey, and so forth. The same letter refers to various local lords and fortresses that had submitted to the pasha. More importantly, it is a lively testimony to the level of hubris that existed in the grand vizier's camp in the early stages of the campaign.[22]

Mustafa was thrilled by the quick capture of Tabriz and what he presents as the city's restitution to the fold of Sunni Islam. On the other hand, he continues to narrate other conspiracies. He reports, for instance, that some of the ex-Safavids in the Ottoman camp, together with the shah's supporters in Tabriz, contacted Tahmasb and described the pasha's position as vulnerable. Their plan was to direct the pasha's forces toward Ardabil while Tahmasb would march to Tabriz. An imminent disaster was apparently averted when a captured Safavid commander revealed Tahmasb's presence near Tabriz.[23] In reality, the shah was able to muster only seven thousand cavalrymen, a force that could not measure up to the Ottoman forces under the pasha, whose effectives reached fifty thousand. Tahmasb's military capabilities were genuinely hampered by defections from his camp and the atmosphere of confusion that seems to have reigned

---

[21] Gökbilgin, "Arz ve Raporlarına Göre," 452–53, 466. The letter is in TSMA E. 11997.
[22] *Ibid.*, 470–76.
[23] *Tabakat*, 248b–254a.

among the Safavids in front of the major Ottoman offensive.[24] He thus resorted to the tactic that was the most suitable for the cavalry-heavy Safavid forces, a form of guerilla warfare.[25]

Süleyman reached Tabriz on September 28, 1534, three and a half months after his departure from Istanbul. A week later, the army was ordered to move forward in pursuit of Tahmasb who, after finding out about the sultan's arrival, had begun to retreat from the city's vicinity. According to Mustafa's dramatic account, the Ottoman army was met with almost no resistance. The soldiers cruised past half-destroyed cities, seeing the occasional Safavid cavalrymen at a distance, and accepting the submission of various Safavid officials. The shah's forces were nowhere to be seen, and the winter began to be bitterly felt; it was decided, after almost a month, to fall back toward Baghdad. Mustafa compensates for the absence of military victory by stating that they had at least been able to chase the Safavids well into Iran; he also claims that this campaign proved the ideological superiority of the Ottomans over the Safavids. The latter pretended to have the support of the Shiite Twelve Imams; they also purported that their shah held the powers of sainthood (velāyet) and prophecy (kerāmet). Their retreat, on the other hand, clearly showed to Mustafa that only Süleyman displayed these faculties. As a final consolation, Mustafa argues that the real objective of the campaign was the capture of Baghdad, and that the failure to locate and exterminate the army of the shah should not be exaggerated.[26] The only true casualty at this stage was the treasurer İskender, who was dismissed from office on October 25.

The trek back to Baghdad was quite difficult. The weather was frigid, and the countryside so bare that enough firewood was not found. Strong winds uprooted tents, while floods and overflowing rivers carried away men, pack animals, and materiel. Baghdad's vicinity was reached on the November 22. The city's governor, who had previously sent a letter of submission, fled the city with his men, and İbrahim entered Baghdad on the 29th. The ancient seat of the Abbasid caliphs was now in Ottoman hands. Indeed, Mustafa presents the city's capture as a stage in the religious struggle between the Ottomans and the Safavids. The miraculous "discovery" of Abu Hanifa's tomb, for instance, receives a detailed

[24] Savory, *Iran under the Safavids*, 58; Eskandar Beg Monshi, *History of Shah 'Abbas the Great*, 110–13.
[25] Şah Tahmasb, *Tezkire*, 34–52 passim.
[26] *Tabakat*, 254a–257a.

description in *Tabakat*. Abu Hanifa is the founder of the Sunni Hanafi legal school of thought that constituted the "official" Ottoman creed in this period, and the discovery of his tomb provided a crucial support to Ottoman claims about the leadership of Sunni Islam. Mustafa even argues that the reason why Süleyman suffered so many hardships and traveled from such a long distance was to honor Abu Hanifa's tomb, which had previously been left in a land of heresy.[27]

Mustafa's personal enthusiasm was apparently shared by other members of the Ottoman elite and, indeed, the sultan himself. Süleyman's stay in Baghdad reflected a heightened sense of Sunni Ottoman triumphalism. Tombs belonging to prominent historical and religious figures were restored and were ceremonially visited on numerous occasions. Mosques were "Sunnified" through such acts as the inscription of the names of Abu Bakr, Umar, and Uthman on the walls. The Safavids saw the first three caliphs as usurpers who had denied Ali his legitimate right to lead the Muslims, and turned their public cursing and the eradication of their names into important political rituals. The Ottoman Sunnification of the mosques provided an Ottoman counter-ritual, meant to publicize and enhance an increasingly antagonistic Ottoman Sunnism. Moreover, Najaf and Karbala, the locations of the holiest Shiite shrines and tombs, passed under Ottoman control, turning the capture of Iraq into a signal event in the history of sixteenth-century Ottoman imperialism and Sunnism.[28] Other developments were not as auspicious. In February 1535, Tahmasb's forces recovered Tabriz, and the Ottoman garrison, under Ulame, fled to Van. Tahmasb continued his advance and besieged Van. On March 13, presumably due to these reversals, the treasurer İskender, whose presence in the campaign had been a source of various tensions, was executed. Süleyman left Baghdad in early April to meet Tahmasb's forces. While Tahmasb once again retreated, the Ottomans decided to march onto Tabriz a second time in the same campaign. The city was reached on July 1, and Süleyman made a triumphal entry into the city on the 4th. He visited the shah's palaces during his brief stay and made an explicit point in attending the Friday prayer in the main mosque, once more Sunnified for the occasion. On July 20, a contingent under

---

[27] *Ibid.*, 258b–259a.

[28] For another account that shows the Ottomans' fascination before this symbolic capital now in Ottoman hands, see Matrakçı Nasuh, *Beyān-ı menāzil-i sefer-i 'Irākeyn-i Sultān Süleymān Ḫān*, ed. Hüseyin G. Yurdaydın (Ankara: Türk Tarih Kurumu, 1976), 217–18, 242–49, etc. Nasuh carefully enumerates the tombs belonging to various ǧrominent individuals.

FIGURE 6. Baghdad after the Ottoman conquest. The restored tomb complex of
Abu Hanifa is depicted in the lower-right corner (*Hünernāme*, vol. 2, TSMK,
Hazine 1524, 283b).

İbrahim was sent against Tahmasb but returned empty-handed after a month. The sultan and the grand vizier left Tabriz on August 27 and reached Istanbul on the January 4, 1536.[29]

A Grand Vizier Dies, a Chancellor Rises

Like the two previous campaigns in Europe, the Two Iraqs campaign produced mixed results. Baghdad and most of Iraq entered Ottoman control. With the establishment of a governorate-general in Erzurum, in northeast Anatolia, the frontier defenses were strengthened. Various Kurdish lords, the Sunni rulers of Gilan on the Caspian Sea, and various Safavid commanders and administrators (including Tahmasb's brother Sam Mirza) pledged allegiance to the Ottomans, but most of these allegiances failed to be long-lived. The Sunni identity of the Ottoman enterprise was reasserted through highly symbolic acts such as the Sunnification of mosques, the "discovery" of tombs belonging to Sunni historical figures, and ceremonial Friday prayers with the sultan's participation. Moreover, the capture of important Shiite shrines allowed the Ottomans to claim, as Mustafa says, that the Twelve Imams had denied their support to Tahmasb. However, the immediate strategic gains were sometimes overshadowed by the ideological issues at stake. Although Ottoman sources call the campaign "Two Iraqs," only one of these (i.e., Iraq-i Arab) was captured. For Mustafa and others who attributed a major cultural and religious urgency to the Safavid problem, the failure of the Ottomans to locate and defeat Tahmasb was disheartening. Tahmasb's scorched earth and hit-and-run tactics were largely successful. Tabriz was captured twice by the Ottomans in the scope of a single campaign, but was lost soon after the sultan left the area. The same fate befell the fortress of Van, whose control was vital for the security of Tabriz. The financial costs of the campaign were simply staggering.[30] Perhaps the most significant outcome of the campaign for the Ottoman side was the fall of İbrahim Pasha.

When did the tensions between Süleyman and İbrahim emerge? The pasha's reputation had suffered after the European campaigns of 1529

[29] *Tabakat*, 272b–276b. The Safavid sources concur with Mustafa's account of the hardships during this stage of the campaign. See Eskandar Beg Monshi, *History of Shah 'Abbas the Great*, 113–15.

[30] This summary is based, next to Mustafa's writings, on Kırzıoğlu, *Osmanlı'nın Kafkas-Elleri'ni Fethi*, 141–59; Allouche, *Ottoman-Safavid Conflict*, 139–40; Mitchell, "The Pen and the Sword," 219–24; Kılıç, *Osmanlı-İran Münâsebetleri*, 235–38.

and 1532. He was eager to gain an impressive victory in the East and, as seen in his enthusiastic dispatches to the sultan in the campaign's early stages, he was confident of the outcome. The dismissal and execution of the chief treasurer İskender or the pasha's insistence on attacking Tabriz may have contributed to his unpopularity, as Mustafa suggests. His use of the title "sultan" is presented as another source of tension. According to this interpretation, under the negative influence of Ulame, who told the pasha that many Safavid commanders utilized this title, the pasha started to refer to himself as *ser'asker sultan*. In reality, the pasha had already used this title at least once before, in a letter to the doge of Venice.[31] It is likely that Süleyman did not initially object to the use of the title. As mentioned earlier, the title of *ser'asker* was influenced by Ferdinand's use of a similar title. By calling himself sultan, İbrahim continued to aspire to the status enjoyed by Ferdinand in the Habsburg domains. Unlike Ferdinand, however, he did not enjoy a dynastic lineage, which meant that he had to achieve his status through military prowess and political savvy. In this sense, the Two Iraqs campaign symbolizes the limits of the power-sharing agreement between the sultan and the grand vizier and represents the end of an interesting ideological and administrative experiment.

Mustafa, who rather awkwardly tries to legitimize the downfall of Süleyman's closest collaborator without blaming the sultan, offers a practical and moralistic explanation for the pasha's demise. He claims that İbrahim's personality underwent a negative change during the campaign. Although he used to be respectful of the Sharia, he strayed during the Two Iraqs campaign by causing unnecessary bloodshed. Also, by listening to unworthy individuals and following every rumor and gossip, he spent his time in vain. Due to this laxity and the resulting waste of time, the Ottoman army was not able to reach its goal and capture the shah. After this analysis, Mustafa reminisces about the first days of his collaboration with the pasha. At the beginning, the pasha was an extremely cautious and attentive individual. He always consulted worthy advisors, did not act on a whim, and respected *kanun* and Sharia. In fact, he was so pious and so respectful of Islam that, whenever he was presented with a Quran, he held the holy book in his hands and pressed it against his chest, never putting it down. During the Two Iraqs campaign, on the other hand, his arrogance overwhelmed his piety. He refused to accept the Qurans that

---

[31] M. Tayyib Gökbilgin, "Venedik Devlet Arşivindeki Türkçe Belgeler Kolleksiyonu ve Bizimle İlgili Diğer Belgeler," *Belgeler* 5–8, nos. 9–12 (1968–71): 54.

a group of calligraphers, in Baghdad, desired to present him. This could only result in the execution of the pasha, which happened on the night of March 14/15, 1536. The sultan did not promote another member of his own household this time and simply appointed Ayas Pasha, the second vizier, to the grand vizierate.[32]

In the decades following the pasha's execution, the atmosphere of ideological and cultural experimentation that characterized the first decade and a half of Süleyman's rule began to change, and the gaze of Ottoman imperialism began to turn inward. İbrahim's imperialist policies, based on a mixture of diplomacy and warfare in Europe and an insistent pursuit of claims to universal monarchy, were not abandoned altogether. His legacy continued in the form of a new alliance with France, an ambitious naval policy in the Mediterranean, and the intensification of the Ottoman–Habsburg rivalry over Central Europe. In the next two decades after his death, however, the Ottoman establishment increasingly centered its claims to legitimacy on legality (both *kanun* and Sharia) and relinquished the apocalyptic and messianic overtones that characterized the Ottoman–Habsburg ideological rivalry. The sultan was increasingly presented as the guarantor of peace and justice for his subjects, and his claim to being the caliph of all Muslims was revised to imply the leadership of Sunni Islam only.[33] As for Mustafa, he survived the demise of the second grand vizier with whom he closely collaborated. When his old mentor and current *nişancı* Seydi Bey passed away in Baghdad, he took his place on December 5, 1534.[34] With this appointment, Mustafa's bureaucratic career reached its peak. His tenure as chancellor would allow him to codify various ad hoc administrative practices into relatively well-defined and systematic procedures.[35] He would also play an active role in the

---

[32] *Tabakat,* 274b–275a; 277a–278b. Modern apologists of Süleyman follow Mustafa's narrative, sometimes adding that tensions between İbrahim and Süleyman's wife Hürrem, another *bête noire* of nationalist Ottoman historians, played a role in the pasha's execution. See Uzunçarşılı, *Osmanlı Tarihi 2:* 357–59; Kılıç, *Osmanlı-İran Münâsebetleri,* 238–41; *İOTK 2,* 184–89.

[33] For a discussion of the growth of this conservative approach in the Ottoman mentality in the second half of the reign of Süleyman, see Fleischer, "The Lawgiver as Messiah," 167–69, 171–74; Gülru Necipoğlu, "A *Kânûn* for the State, a Canon for the Arts: Conceptualizing the Classical Synthesis of Ottoman Arts and Architecture," in *Soliman le magnifique et son temps,* 195–216. For a very detailed and perceptive analysis of this sea change in legal culture and mentality see Buzov, "The Lawgiver and His Lawmakers," 123–189.

[34] *Tabakat,* 259b–260b.

[35] Halil İnalcık, "State, Sovereignty and Law during the Reign of Süleymân," in *Süleymân the Second and His Time,* 78–79, 81–82.

promulgation of sultanic law and in the association of legality with sultanic legitimacy and efficient government.

Filling İbrahim's Void: New Ventures on the European Front

One of İbrahim's last diplomatic acts was to devise a more active Ottoman naval policy in the Mediterranean and negotiate a higher level of collaboration between the Ottomans and the French. Andrea Doria, the famous Genoese admiral, had joined the service of Charles V in 1528 after working for the Papacy and then France. During Süleyman's German campaign, Doria captured Coroni, Patras, and Lepanto, thus creating a new front for the Ottoman–Habsburg rivalry. The Ottoman response was to invite Hayreddin Barbarossa (?1466–1546) to the capital. A merchant turned corsair and self-made ruler on the Maghribi coast in the first decades of the sixteenth century, Hayreddin had emerged as an important figure in Western Mediterranean politics, helping the Morisco rebels in Spain, competing and collaborating with the local Arab dynasties, and interacting with other corsairs, magnates, and merchants in the complex world of the "Ibero-African frontier."[36] An initial contact with Selim in 1519 had not resulted in long-term collaboration, and Hayreddin's interests coincided with Ottoman imperial policy only in the early 1530s. Attacks by Doria and the Hospitallers had exposed the weakness of the Ottoman naval forces in the Eastern Mediterranean, whereas the increasing encroachments of the Habsurgs motivated Hayreddin to seek Ottoman protection.[37]

After an audience with the sultan, Hayreddin traveled to Aleppo where, in April 1534, İbrahim appointed him the governor-general of the Mediterranean islands, the provincial governor of Gallipoli, and the admiral of the Ottoman fleet.[38] Hayreddin sailed from Istanbul in May 1534 and captured Tunis from Mulay Hasan, of the Hafsid dynasty, in August 1534. Ottoman imperialism now had a new beachhead at the

---

[36] For a concise account of Hayreddin's life and career, see Aldo Galotta, "Khayral-Dīn (Khidîr) Pasha, Barbarossa," *EI* 2. I borrow the term "Ibero-African frontier" from Andrew Hess, whose *The Forgotten Frontier: A History of the Sixteenth-Century Ibero-African Frontier* (Chicago: University of Chicago Press, 1978) remains the best account of the area.

[37] For the Ottoman naval consolidation after 1534 see Murphey, "Süleyman I and the Conquest of Hungary," 206–08.

[38] İdris Bostan, "Cezâyir-i Bahr-i Sefîd Eyaletinin Kuruluşu," *Tarih Dergisi* 38 (2003): 61–78; *Tabakat*, 245a–246a.

expense of a local Muslim dynasty. Charles was quick to act, however. With Mulay Hasan in tow, who had taken refuge with the emperor after the loss of Tunis, Charles took La Goletta on July 14, 1535, and Tunis on July 21 from Hayreddin, who fled to safety. After his first uncontested victory over Ottoman forces, the emperor paraded throughout Italy, from Naples to Rome, organizing processions and celebrations on the way. Victory at Tunis would become one of his most cherished laurels in his fight against the Ottomans and his claim to be the protector of Christianity.[39]

İbrahim's other contribution came in the form of an Ottoman–French alliance. Ottoman–French relations underwent a critical transformation in the sixteenth century. The French, in their bid to control northern Italy and expand French possessions to the south, north, and east, had been struggling from the last decade of the fifteenth century onward, most notably with the Habsburgs. Francis I, very much like Charles, Süleyman, and Tahmasb, inherited a set of ambitious political projects from his predecessors and spent his relatively long rule seeking conquest abroad and consolidation and institutionalization inside his domains.[40] These monarchs were also united by their aspirations to universalist political titles that placed religious and political authority under a single mantle. In the antagonistic world of early modern imperialism, Francis, like the German Protestants, considered the Ottomans a necessary evil and made various openings to them following his captivity at the Battle of Pavia in 1525. French diplomatic missions were sent to Istanbul, and a French embassy was received with great pomp during the German campaign of 1532. The haphazard diplomatic activity produced a tangible outcome during the Two Iraqs campaign, when the French envoy Jean de la Fôret traveled to the east. As a result, in February 1536, an important commercial and political document was drafted. The document gave French merchants considerable privileges and motivated European traders to seek the protection of the French king while traveling in Ottoman territory. Another outcome was the relative eclipse of Venetian commercial power in the eastern Mediterranean. This was the first formal document establishing an Ottoman–French alliance against the Habsburgs and their various allies, particularly Venice.[41]

---

[39] Uzunçarşılı, *Osmanlı Tarihi*, 2: 371–73; İOTK 2, 160–62, 168, 175; *The Papacy and the Levant 3*, 394–400.

[40] Robert J. Knecht, *The Rise and Fall of Renaissance France, 1483–1610* (London: Fontana Press, 1996), 41–80, 93–121, 139–180; Bonney, *European Dynastic States*, 80–109.

[41] *The Papacy and the Levant 3*, 400–401. For a French and Italian text of the document see Ernest Charrière, *Négociations de la France dans le Levant...* (Paris: Imprimerie

The military campaign of 1537 was a reflection of these diplomatic issues. The initial plan was for the French to attack Liguria and Lombardy, while the Ottoman navy would raid southern Italy and the sultan would march to Avlonya (Vlorë) in Albania, across from the region of Apulia in the Italian peninsula. The Ottoman show of force was also aimed at preventing a rapprochement between Venice and the Habsburgs.[42] Indeed, Ottoman–Venetian relations had been deteriorating since the late 1520s. The murder of Alvise Gritti in Transylvania in 1534 and the execution of İbrahim in 1536 eliminated the two most important interlocutors of the Venetians in the Ottoman camp. The Ottomans had been pressuring the Venetians to side more openly against the emperor, and this request was repeated in late 1536–early 1537, when the Ottoman envoy Yunus Bey asked the Senate to support Francis I.[43] Beyond these diplomatic reasons, as Rhoads Murphey suggests, Ottoman control in Albania was relatively weak, and the local population often supported raids by the Ottomans' Christian rivals.[44]

Mustafa's account gives a glimpse of Süleyman's efforts at replacing the void left by İbrahim and illustrates the symbolic aspects of the campaign. For the first time in a military venture, Süleyman was accompanied by two of his sons, Mehmed and Selim. Elaborate greeting and submission ceremonies were organized in Edirne and Skopje, and the sultan organized hunts throughout the campaign to assert his presence.[45] The Ottoman army reached Avlonya on July 14. While the navy attacked the Italian coast, the sultan received the famously unruly Albanian tribal leaders in the area and renewed alliances. French failure to attack Piedmont in a coordinated fashion (the French would enter Piedmont in October 1537) severely undermined the intended show of force. Süleyman sent his navy to the Venetian island of Corfu toward the end of summer and marched over land toward a location closer to the island. However, the unexpected arrival of cold weather and the strong winds in the area

nationale, 1848), 1: 283–94. For a Turkish nationalist interpretation that refuses that the Ottomans granted any "capitulations" to a European Christian power see *İOTK 2*, 182–184. For Ottoman-French relations in this period see Christine Isom-Verhaaren, "Ottoman-French Interaction, 1480–1580: A Sixteenth-Century Encounter" (PhD diss., The University of Chicago, 1997). This work was recently published in a shortened version as *Allies with the Infidel: The Ottoman and French Alliance in the Sixteenth Century* (London: I. B. Tauris, 2011).

[42] *Tabakat*, 284b–285a; Lütfi Paşa, *Tevārīḫ-i Āl-i ʿOs̱mān*, 358, 360–61.

[43] *The Papacy and the Levant 3*, 401–11, 422–30.

[44] Murphey, "Süleyman I and the Conquest of Hungary."

[45] *Tabakat*, 285a–287a.

hampered naval operations. The sultan decided to leave the region on the September 12 and returned to Istanbul on November 22.[46] For the Ottomans, other than the pacification of various Albanian clans, the campaign did not produce any tangible benefits and represented yet another costly venture organized for the sake of imperial claims. Moreover, the attempts at pressuring Venice pushed the Serenissima to ally with the Papacy in mid-September 1537, and the arrival of the Ottoman army near Italy motivated the creation of the Holy League in February 1538, with the participation of Venice, the Papacy, the Hospitallers (who had relocated to Malta in 1530 thanks to Charles), and Charles. The League's treaty stipulated that, after the defeat of the Ottomans, Charles would become the emperor of Constantinople.[47] The signing of the Treaty of Nice between Charles and Francis in the summer of 1538 rendered the Apulia campaign even more fruitless for the Ottoman side.

Mustafa found solace in the exploits of the Ottoman army in Karaboğdan (a region that corresponds to today's Northern Romania and Moldavia) in the summer of 1538 and Hayreddin Barbarossa's victory over the navy of the Holy League. In these sections of his work, Mustafa's analytical skills recede on behalf of imperial propaganda, which was reconfigured, after İbrahim's execution, to present Süleyman as the sole guiding intellect behind the Ottoman imperial enterprise. In his account of the campaign, whose first draft was circulated among the literati after the return to Istanbul, Mustafa portrays the sultan as stepping in and assuming all the responsibilities: he analyzes the international situation, sends orders to all the commanders in his realm with specific instructions, and takes necessary measures for the protection of his subjects during his absence from the capital. Mustafa's description of the sultan's departure ceremony includes the unfurling, in the palace courtyard, of seven banners, symbolizing the rule of the sultan over seven climes, and four horsetail standards (*tuğ*), showing that Süleyman controlled the four corners of the world. The long section then proceeds with the sultan's march through the decorated streets of the city in the company of his sons Mehmed and Selim, and the farewell of religious scholars and dervishes at the city gates, who are said to have prayed for the perpetuation of the sultan's good fortune (*devlet*) and the victory of the army of Islam over the infidels.[48]

---

[46] *Ibid.*, 285a–291a.
[47] *The Papacy and the Levant 3*, 433–34.
[48] *Tabakat*, 299b–302b.

Mustafa provides a mixture of historical and political arguments to explain the reasons behind the campaign. He remarks that this kingdom had become an Ottoman tributary during Mehmed II's reign and that Bayezid II had conquered two important cities in the area, Kilia and Akkerman. The rulers of the area had always been reluctant to pay their yearly tributes, and Ottoman campaigns against them had failed to produce any results. To aggravate the situation, the present king, whom Mustafa calls Petr, refused to submit to the Ottomans, harmed Muslims, and thus deserved a punishment. Mustafa's standard explanation overlooks the specific reasons behind the campaign. King Petru Raresh had a tense relationship with the Ottoman ally John Szapolyai, and had been coveted by Ferdinand after 1535, as a proxy to be utilized against the Ottomans. He had also been implicated in the assassination of Alvise Gritti, the Ottoman diplomat and factotum extraordinaire. In a show of pan-European diplomatic entanglements, the Polish kingdom, an occasional ally of the Ottomans, had been agitating for the removal of Petru and offered help to the Ottoman sultan. From a strategic point of view, the Ottoman campaign was a reaction to the Peace of Nagyvárad between Ferdinand and Szapolyai, signed in February 1538.[49]

The campaign was conceived as a two-pronged operation, destined to upset Habsburg plans in East-Central Europe and the Mediterranean. The day before the sultan's departure with the army, on July 8, 1538, Hayreddin sailed with the navy. On July 26, an envoy from Petru arrived. Mustafa drafted a letter to Petru, inviting him to personally come and submit to the sultan. The army then resumed its march, reaching the shores of the river Prut on September 1. Ottoman progress into Karaboğdan was relatively smooth, because Petru had been attacked by Polish forces and was busy defending his northern frontier. After looting and burning Ciubarciu and dispatching a Wallachian contingent to loot Jassy, the sultan reached Sucsava on September 15. In Petru's absence, the inhabitants of the king's fortified city surrendered, and the royal treasury was captured. Stefan Lacusta, who had spent years in the Ottoman court, was nominated as the new ruler of a smaller Karaboğdan, whereas the Ottomans annexed an area in the southeast. Stefan's coronation took place in the Ottoman imperial council. He swore on the Bible and the cross, was given a copy of the new treaty of submission, and was asked to wear a red skullcap with golden braids to symbolize his appointment

---

[49] Murphey, "Süleyman I and the Conquest of Hungary," 217–18.

by the Ottoman sultan. Thus the Ottoman campaign of Karaboğdan practically ended without engaging in any major battle.[50]

The victory at Karaboğdan was followed by other good news. On the October 17, on his way back to Edirne, the sultan was visited by Hayreddin's son, who informed him of his father's victory at Prevesa against the navy of the Holy League, under the command of Andrea Doria. Then, in late October, in Edirne, a message from Hadım Süleyman Pasha informed the sultan and the imperial council of his activities in the Indian Ocean.[51] This was an auspicious moment for Ottoman imperialism and, using these near-simultaneous "victories," Mustafa could convey to his readers the image of an empire fighting on land and sea and in distant lands to great success. The renewed feeling of imperial confidence manifested itself in the circumcision ceremony of princes Bayezid and Cihangir, organized a year later, between November 26 and December 8, 1539. The ceremony entailed the participation of numerous Ottoman governors-general and provincial governors, viziers, janissaries, members of the sultan's palace household, scholars, and other Ottoman officials, as well as the ambassadors of France, Austria, and Venice (the latter present in Istanbul for peace negotiations). Mustafa watched in awe while entertainers paraded exotic animals, model fortresses, still-life compositions showing flowers and fruits, and forest scenes with gazelles and exotic birds, all made of paper. Jugglers displayed their talents; shows with trained animals amazed the population of Istanbul. During the night, lanterns were lit in the Hippodrome, and mock fights were organized between fortresses made of paper. The cotton workers of the city paraded a detailed depiction of a garden made of pink cloth. Clowns, Mevlevi dervishes dancing on a platform, and Arabs beating drums succeeded each other while musicians and singers played and sung.[52]

Mustafa's enthusiastic tone, and the tenor of these celebrations, both hide the fact that the military ventures of the last two decades had culminated in a crisis for Ottoman imperialism, well summarized by Rhoads Murphey:

> It seems clear that from the 1530s onwards, the Ottomans increasingly –
> in Iran, Iraq, the Persian Gulf and the Red Sea on one side of their empire,

---

[50] For an account of the events of the campaign, see *Tabakat*, 291a–318b. Cf. Aurel Decei, "Un 'Fetih-nâme-i Karaboğdan' de Nasuh Matrakçı," in *Fuad Köprülü Armağanı/Mélanges Fuad Köprülü* (Istanbul: Osman Yalçın Matbaası, 1953), 113–24.

[51] For Hadım Süleyman's expedition of 1538 see Casale, *The Ottoman Age of Exploration*, 53–63.

[52] *Tabakat*, 337a–340b.

and in the wider Mediterranean world and the Danube basin on the other – began to face a guns versus guns in addition to the classical guns versus butter dilemma. They had to decide what parts of their empire required deployments in maximum strength, and where a minimal military presence would suffice to maintain the status quo.... Realistically..., by the mid-1530s the Ottoman empire had already reached the fullest extent that was manageable, sustainable and defendable.[53]

Mustafa would begin discussing the problematic relationship between imperial ambitions and economic cost only toward the end of his career, as discussed in the next chapter. In the late 1530s, however, Ottoman imperial propaganda, thanks to the efforts of men like Mustafa, continued to produce convenient fictions about the empire's might.

The Hungarian Question Comes Back with a Vengeance

The period following the circumcision was relatively peaceful. The Safavid and Habsburg frontiers remained calm, and a peace treaty was signed with the Venetians the following year, around October 1540. The treaty was concluded to the satisfaction of the Ottomans: the Venetians ceded a number of fortresses in the Morea and Dalmatia and recognized the loss of some Adriatic islands captured by Hayreddin in the last few years. They also agreed to pay a compensation of three hundred thousand ducats.[54] This atmosphere of relative peace was upset by events following the death of John Szapolyai in 1540 and the reopening of the Hungarian question.

In February 1538, Szapolyai had signed the Peace of Nagyvárad/ Grosswardein with Ferdinand of Austria. Accordingly, his rule would not be contested by the Habsburgs during his lifetime, but the throne of Hungary would pass to Ferdinand after his death, regardless of his leaving a male heir. Anti-Habsburg Hungarian nobles, informed of the treaty, forced Szapolyai into a marriage with the daughter of the Polish king Sigismund I (r. 1507–48), Isabella, in the expectation that the marriage would produce an heir to the Hungarian throne. They were rejoiced by the birth of a son, John Sigismund, but the sudden death of John Szapolyai two weeks later, in July 1540, upset their expectations. John Sigismund was soon elected as the new king of Hungary by the anti-Habsburg faction while Ferdinand sent his forces to lay siege to

---

[53] Murphey, "Ottoman Expansion, 1451–1556," 70.

[54] For a complete text of the peace treaty ('ahdname) of 1540 (a draft and the final version) see Hans Theunissen, "Ottoman-Venetian Diplomatics: the 'Ahd-names...," *Electronic Journal of Oriental Studies* 1, no. 2 (1998): 437–69.

Buda.[55] The Ottomans were now faced with the prospect of losing Central Hungary to the Habsburgs. They were further worried by an eventual Safavid attack in support of the Habsburgs, having received intelligence about an agreement between Tahmasb and Ferdinand. Hadım Süleyman Pasha was sent to the east with a few thousand janissaries and the troops of several governors-general, while Sofu Mehmed Pasha, the second vizier, was sent to rescue Buda from the Hungarians.[56]

Mustafa once again saw these events as an episode of the battle for supremacy over Central Europe and as part of the ideological competition between the Habsburgs and the Ottomans. According to him, the insistence of Charles V and Ferdinand about Hungary resulted from the fact that Charles had become the Caesar of the Christian world. He wanted to use the title of ṣāḥib-ḳırān, but his failure to control Hungary prevented him from doing so. Even though they were defeated many times, says Mustafa, the brothers did not relinquish this impossible dream and refused to recognize the Ottoman-appointed king of Hungary. They thus behaved foolishly and lost many of their ancestral domains to the Ottomans.[57] The sultan, who did not share Mustafa's nonchalance, judged the situation critical, as shown by his own departure for Buda on June 20, 1541. Forces previously sent under Mehmed Pasha had suffered important losses and failed to cut the supply routes of the besiegers. The news of the sultan's arrival changed the situation, and Ferdinand's forces began their retreat on the night of August 21.

Süleyman reached the city a few days later, on the 26th, in time to witness the execution of Habsburg captives. He then invited the regent George Martinuzzi, the dowager queen Isabella, and her son John Sigismund to his camp to discuss the issue of the Hungarian succession, as John Sigismund had not been recognized by the Ottomans as the new king of Hungary. It was eventually decided to appoint him the prince of Erdel (Transylvania), to come to the Hungarian throne upon reaching majority; in the meantime, the Ottomans would annex Central Hungary and occupy Buda immediately. Mustafa played an important role in the negotiations and was the Ottoman official who formally presented a copy of the treaty to the queen.[58] Ottoman soldiers then entered

---

[55] *The Papacy and the Levant 3*, 434–37; Perjés, *Mohács 1526-Buda 1541*, 152–62.

[56] Lütfi Paşa, *Tevārīḫ-i Āl-i 'Osmān*, 384–85.

[57] *Tabakat*, 341a–b.

[58] Peçevi İbrahim Efendi, *Tārīḫ-i Peçevī*, eds. Fahri Ç. Derin and Vahit Çabuk (Istanbul: Enderun Kitabevi, 1980), 232.

FIGURE 7. Queen Isabella and her son John Sigismund are received by Süleyman (detail from Ârifî, *Süleymānnāme*, TSMK, Hazine 1517, 441a).

Buda, banners were erected on the city walls, and the cathedral was turned into a mosque. Mustafa was there on September 2 when the sultan came to the city for the Friday prayer. After the appointment of a governor-general, Süleyman left Buda September 15.[59]

Whether the Ottoman annexation was the result of a long-term policy of incremental conquest, or the outcome of an Ottoman answer to Habsburg challenges, it did not resolve the Hungarian question.[60] Direct

[59] The details of the Ottoman annexation are in *Tabakat*, 342a–346a. Cf. Perjés, *Mohács 1526-Buda 1541*, 162–67.

[60] For differing interpretations see Fodor, "Ottoman Policy towards Hungary," 305–33; Murphey, "Süleyman I and the Conquest of Hungary," 218–19.

Ottoman presence in the region obviously alarmed the Habsburgs, who now would have to face a much stronger enemy than Szapolyai. Ferdinand dispatched various emissaries to Istanbul after the Ottoman annexation to be recognized king of Hungary; he also agreed to pay a tribute in return.[61] However, at the same time, he continued to pursue his objectives with military means. Thus, while Habsburg envoys were busy negotiating a settlement in Hungary during the autumn of 1542, news of the siege of Pest by a Habsburg force reached the capital. Süleyman, alarmed by the news of a possible attack by the Habsburgs and motivated by the king of France's offer of a joint campaign, had already given orders for the preparation of a navy. He reluctantly agreed to march against the Habsburgs despite the fact that it was very late for a campaign and left Istanbul on November 17, reaching Edirne nine days later. There, a messenger from Pest arrived to announce that the Habsburg force attacking the city had retreated. The sultan, relieved that he would not have to suffer the hardships of another winter campaign in Central Europe, decided to spend the winter in Edirne. Mustafa, together with the other officials, stayed in the city with the sultan. The weather was quite cold, and Mustafa lamented the fact that, despite its agreeable spring, the winter season in Edirne was too harsh for his taste. Eventually, the promise of assistance given to the French in their renewed war with the Habsburgs and the urge to respond to Habsburg attacks in Hungary pushed the sultan to leave Edirne on April 23, 1543, together with his son Bayezid. Hayreddin, who had already received orders to assist the French navy, sailed from Istanbul to the Mediterranean a month later, on his way to the siege of Nice.[62]

The sultan reached Belgrade, where he was joined by the forces of his governors-general, on June 4. The first major objective was the Habsburg fortress of Esztergom (Gran in German), which the sultan reached on July 25. Mustafa, the tireless observer, was very much impressed by the solid fortifications and describes the fortress as a major feat of engineering. He was also intrigued by a system of watermills that drew water from the Danube and accumulated it in a large pond inside the city. He had learned that the city was a major religious center for Christians and an abode for many Christian scholars. The main cathedral of the city, he says, was adorned with refined stained-glass windows and

---

[61] *İOTK* 2, 228, 231–32.

[62] *Tabakat*, 346b–354a. For Hayreddin's activities in the Mediterranean in 1543–44, see Isom-Verhaaren, "Ottoman-French Interaction," 239–288; Isom-Verhaaren, *Allies with the Infidel*, 114–40.

marble sculptures of Christian saints. His description of the Ottoman siege is similarly realistic. A river fleet on the Danube brought siege guns to the Ottoman camp, and the city was besieged both from land and river. Janissaries dug trenches and prepared fortified positions in front of the walls for the musketeers. After ten days of mutual cannon and musket fire and heavy casualties on both sides, the defenders surrendered on August 7. The next day, while an Ottoman martial band played music in front of the sultan's tent, the soldiers entered the city, broke the icons in the churches, and looted some properties. Mustafa notes that the Ottoman army was accompanied by Muslim settlers who took residence in the city. This must be the reason why Süleyman did not want the soldiers to remain in the city longer, so as to preserve some of the properties to be taken over by the settlers.[63]

After visiting the city and attending the Friday prayer in the newly converted cathedral, Süleyman ordered the army to march against Székesfehérvár (Stuhlweissenburg in German), the İstolni Belgrad of the Ottoman sources. Having reached the city on August 20, Mustafa remarks that it was located in the middle of marshes; these became impassable during winter, when they were flooded. Moreover, the city was the final resting place for many Hungarian kings; the presence of their tombs, according to Mustafa, gave the city's defenders a particular zeal, because they hoped for their successful intercession against the Ottoman army. The Ottomans realized that the city would not be taken without massive artillery fire, and the governor-general of Anadolu was sent to Buda to bring cannons from the citadel. Initial Ottoman attacks were pushed back, but the arrival of the artillery shifted the balance. Parts of the walls were destroyed, and the Ottoman soldiers were ordered to attack the breaches. Massive artillery barrages and close combats took place in the following days, and the lack of coordination among the Ottoman commanders cost many lives to the attackers. Finally, September 2, while the sultan looked on with his retinue and prayed, the Ottoman soldiers entered the outer city after a general attack.

The Ottoman infiltration was followed by massive skirmishes inside the city. Some of the defenders who wanted to escape to the citadel fell into the moat and drowned; corpses of dead soldiers piled up in the streets. The Ottomans were able to occupy the outer city that day; commanders and viziers, who entered the city in the wake of the troops, took residence in emptied churches and mansions. On September 3,

[63] *Tabakat,* 354b–364a.

the commander of the citadel asked for surrender; the keys of the city were offered to Süleyman the following day by a committee of commanders, priests, and notables. Mustafa entered the city before Süleyman and roamed its streets. During his visit of the cathedral, he mused, in front of the tombs of Hungarian kings, about the ruthlessness of time: all these rulers, some of whom had been ṣāḥib-ḳırāns, were now sleeping here, helpless and despondent. Mustafa admired the ornaments on the tombs, and he mentions the bejeweled crowns, the ornate crosses, and the daggers and swords that adorned the sepulchers of the kings and saints. He also notes that all these signs of a faith doomed to Hell were subsequently cleaned by the Ottoman soldiers when the cathedral was turned into a mosque.[64] Unlike other recent campaigns against the Habsburgs, the campaign of 1543 thus resulted in the Ottoman capture of two major cities. By the capture of these two cities, the Ottomans were able to secure further their newly annexed dominions in Hungary and establish a zone of control beyond Buda. This does not change the fact that Central Europe and the Hungarian front had turned into a veritable deadlock between the two powers.

Tabakat fails to record the events of the period between November 1543 and the spring of 1548. The work is mostly dedicated to Süleyman's achievements, and the sultan did not participate in any campaigns during this period. Developments in this period, however, were far from unimportant and indeed set the tone for the last years of Süleyman's reign and Mustafa's life. The first important event followed the passing away of Süleyman's son Mehmed the provincial governor of Manisa, in November 1543.[65] Ottoman princes served as provincial governors after puberty to gain political and military experience. They were usually sent to old princely cities in Anatolia taken from the Ottomans' first Muslim rivals, such as Manisa, Amasya, and Konya. These cities were not in close vicinity of Istanbul, but were not in the farthest confines of the empire either. Serving in Manisa was seen as more advantageous, because it was closer to Istanbul than the other governorships given to princes. The prince in Manisa, in theory, could reach the capital city before his brothers at the death of the sultan and become sultan.[66] In March 1544, Süleyman appointed his son Selim the provincial governor of Manisa.

---

[64] *Ibid.*, 365b–373a.

[65] For the prince's death, see *Tabakat*, 374b–379a; İOTK 2, 244–45.

[66] İsmail Hakkı Uzunçarşılı, *Osmanlı Devletinin Saray Teşkilâtı* (Ankara: Türk Tarih Kurumu, 1945), 117–30.

His son Bayezid was in Konya, and Mustafa was in Amasya. Selim's relocation to Manisa was seen as a sign that he was his father's favorite and led to tensions among the Ottoman princes.

The second important development of the period was the signing of a comprehensive truce between the sultan, Ferdinand, and Charles V. The Habsburg ambassador Gerard Weltwyck, the first envoy officially sent by Charles to the Ottomans, negotiated a one-year truce in August 1545 and returned the next year for more comprehensive negotiations. The negotiations revolved around the Hungarian question and, at the end, the Ottomans and the Habsburgs recognized each other's possessions in Hungary. Ferdinand accepted to pay a yearly tribute of thirty thousand ducats in return for his Hungarian lands, tacitly recognizing that the Ottomans, with their victory at Mohacs, had indeed inherited the Hungarian kingdom. The truce, signed in mid-June 1547, also stipulated that peace would prevail among the Ottomans, the Habsburgs, Venice, France, and the Papacy, giving the treaty a pan-European dimension. Mustafa played a prominent role in these negotiations, and he ratified the final version of the treaty in the name of the sultan. This was the first Ottoman-Habsburg agreement in which Charles V was included.[67] As for Charles V, the cessation of hostilities after the summer of 1545 had allowed him to focus on his European affairs. The pope, Paul III, had convoked the Council of Trent in March 1545, and Charles needed a respite from the Ottomans to pursue his cause against the Protestants, either through declarations of heresy at Trent or in the battlefield. The death of Martin Luther in February 1546, and of Francis I in March 1547, eliminated two of Charles' enemies. His astounding victory at the Battle of Mühlberg over the Lutheran princes of the Schmalkaldic League in April 1547 further consolidated his position as the chief political and religious leader of Christianity. Similarly, the truce gave Süleyman the opportunity to turn toward his other religio-political competitors: the Safavids. The defection of a Safavid prince in mid-1547 presented him with an unexpected but quite welcome pretext.

---

[67] The account of the events of 1544–48 is taken from İOTK 2, 245–54. For the peace negotiations and their importance within the European political context, see *The Papacy and the Levant 3*, 480–86; for the French position during the negotiations see Charrière, *Négociations*, 1: 580–620; for the text of the treaty, see Anton C. Schaendlinger and Claudia Römer, *Die Schreiben Süleymāns des Prächtigen an Karl V., Ferdinand I. und Maximilian II*, vol. 1, *Transkriptionen und Übersetzungen* (Vienna: Verlag der Österreichischen Akademie der Wissenschaften, 1983), 14–16 (transcription), 17–18 (German translation).

The Safavid Question Reemerges: The Alqas Mirza Affair

After the peace with the Habsburgs, Süleyman, who was now in his late fifties, decided to devote his time to more pleasant activities and relocated to Edirne to spend the winter. Mustafa, eager to emphasize that the Ottomans had imposed their supremacy to the Habsburgs, informs his readers that Süleyman had proven himself as the lord of various realms and a true *ṣāḥib-ḳirān*. In a passage heavy with ideological assertions, he states that Süleyman, by virtue of his exploits, had superseded the glory of all the legendary Persian kings. Thanks to divine support, he equaled the military successes of Muhammad and attained the stature of Solomon. Even the Caesar of the Christians had become one of his slaves.[68]

Between 1536 and 1547, Ottoman engagements in the European front had allowed Tahmasb to focus on the organization of his domain. Despite Uzbek attacks from the east, the shah was able to strengthen his position vis-à-vis the Turkoman tribes, and the Safavid bureaucracy and chancery, the crucial instruments of royal power in early modern Eurasia, continued to grow. Also in this period, a better defined doctrinal position around Twelver Shiism emerged, and this position was more and more voiced in the diplomatic documents produced by the Safavid scribal service. After the loss of Iraq and its Shiite shrines, Safavid Iran was increasingly defined as the abode of Shiism. While the Ottoman establishment began to relinquish its earlier claims of messianic kingship and universal monarchy on behalf of the caliphate of Sunni Islam and the perpetuation of law, justice, and order, the Safavid polity was going through a similar political and cultural process.[69] These developments, as discussed later, prepared the grounds for a new level of cultural, political, and religious debate and interaction between the Ottoman and the Safavid courts.

On the political and military front, during this eleven-year period, Ottoman governors-general in Erzurum continued to skirmish with Safavid forces while Tahmasb strengthened his position in the Caucasus by capturing, most notably, the territories of the Sunni Şirvanşah dynasty. His brother Alqas became the governor of Şirvan and started

---

[68] *Tabakat*, 380a–381a.

[69] An excellent analysis of these developments is in Mitchell, "The Pen and the Sword," 221–284; Mitchell, *The Practice of Politics*, 68–78, 88–103. Also see Kathryn Babayan, *Mystics, Monarchs, and Messiahs: Cultural Landscapes of Early Modern Iran* (Cambridge, MA: Center for Middle Eastern Studies of Harvard University, Harvard University Press, 2002), 295–348; Rula Jurdi Abisaab, *Converting Persia: Religion and Power in the Safavid Empire* (London: I. B. Tauris, 2004), esp. 7–53.

to build his own power base in the area. Tahmasb, mistrustful of his brother's motives, sent his troops to Şirvan and defeated Alqas' forces in March 1547, as a result of which Alqas sought refuge with the Ottoman sultan.[70] He arrived in Istanbul toward the end of summer 1547. In a letter addressed to Süleyman, who was in Edirne at the time, he told the Ottoman sultan of his misfortunes and demanded the help of the "Second Solomon." He also promised to turn Iran, following his conquest, into a possession of the Ottoman sultan.[71] Presented with this unexpected opportunity, the sultan moved from Edirne to Istanbul to see Alqas.

Mustafa's version of the Alqas Mirza affair was composed during his retirement and exhibits his deep anti-Safavid prejudices. After a short treatment of Alqas' defeat by his brother and his defection, Mustafa reviles the Safavids for being heretics and unbelievers and talks about the perils of brotherly enmity. He states that the unwelcome antagonism between brothers is a legacy that was left by Abel and Cain and the brothers of Joseph and that brotherly enmity is a typical Safavid practice. He, of course, refrains from referring to Ottoman succession struggles, which would result in the deaths of princes Mustafa and Bayezid in the next decade.[72] Mustafa's narrative of Alqas' reception in Istanbul manifests his mistrust of Alqas. If we are to believe Mustafa, Süleyman was wary of the Safavid prince from the beginning. This cautious remark is somehow belied by Alqas' treatment in the capital. Mustafa himself describes how the prince was welcomed in the imperial council with his retinue and given various presents and daily stipends for all his servants and assistants.[73]

Mustafa, who was present in the audience granted to Alqas, describes him as a manipulative individual who took refuge with the Ottomans

---

[70] For the developments on the Ottoman–Safavid border, see Kırzıoğlu, *Osmanlı'nın Kafkas-Elleri'ni Fethi*, 161–81. Posch gives a concise history of Şirvan and Alqas' activities there in "Der Fall Alkās Mīrzā," 89–104 and 104–130. Also see John R. Walsh, "The Revolt of Alqās Mīrzā," *WZKM* 68 (1976): 67–72; Cornell H. Fleischer, "Alqās Mīrzā Safawī," *Encyclopædia Iranica*, vol. 1, 907. For the Safavid perspective on the prince's defection, see Eskandar Beg Monshi, *History of Shah 'Abbas the Great*, 115–17; Şah Tahmasb, *Tezkire*, 52–56.

[71] Mitchell, "The Pen and the Sword," 314–19.

[72] *Tabakat*, 381a.

[73] For Alqas' reception in the capital, cf. Posch, "Der Fall Alkās Mīrzā," 208–23. Mustafa was not alone in his mistrust of Alqas: see Vladimir Minorsky, "Shaykh Bālī-efendi on the Safavids," *BSOAS* 20, nos. 1–3 (1957): 441–48. In a letter to the grand vizier, Bali Efendi, a prominent mystic who lived in the Balkans, expressed his discomfort at Ottoman support for Alqas, the scion of a wicked family.

for the sake of his personal interests. He adds that Alqas deserved to be taken off the face of the earth, but Süleyman nevertheless decided to show him mercy. Following this first meeting, Alqas was invited to the imperial council the following day. He had lunch with the council's members, and, in an afternoon meeting, he personally presented his case. He began with an account of what had transpired between him and his brother and then suggested a campaign against Tahmasb. Mustafa, who heard Alqas speak, thought that he wanted to incite the greed of the council members. Mustafa's suspicions notwithstanding, it was decided that such a campaign would be mutually beneficial to Alqas and the Ottomans. Campaign preparations began in the first months of 1548. Thanks to the inactivity of the Ottoman-Habsburg border, the Rumeli contingents were also included among the troops to take part in the campaign, showing the considerable scope of military preparations. Alqas was given a separate military contingent under the command of Ulame, who received the rank of governor-general of Erzurum. Mustafa refrains from repeating the criticisms he directed to Ulame during the Two Iraqs campaign and remarks that Ulame's knowledge of Safavid affairs was the reason behind this appointment. Alqas and Ulame were sent to the east in the middle of March, and Süleyman and the rest of the army left Istanbul on March 29, 1548.[74]

Mustafa's narrative of the campaign conveys the feeling that the Ottomans failed to achieve the expected success. The Ottoman army, which needed to carry its heavy artillery and ammunitions as well as provisions during long campaigns, was geared toward major field battles. The Safavids, on the other hand, preferred to attack isolated Ottoman scout forces and slow down the pace of Ottoman troop movements with hit-and-run attacks. Their scorched earth tactics created major problems of provisioning when the Ottomans tried to advance deep into Safavid territory. Mustafa decries the Safavid tactics as cowardly, but he also admits that they worked well. Moreover, just as it had happened during the Two Iraqs campaign, the Ottoman army had to rely on various local lords and Safavid renegades as guides in Iranian territory. The disparity between the objectives of the local lords and the Ottoman grand policy, crafted in Istanbul but unsuitable for the atomized world of the Ottoman-Safavid frontier, seriously hampered the campaign. Indeed, as it appears from Mustafa's account, this was not a major campaign but a series of

[74] *Tabakat*, 382a–384b.

loosely interconnected military operations extending over the whole of Eastern Anatolia, Western Iran, and parts of the Caucasus.

The initial plan, according to Mustafa, was to re-conquer Van from the Safavids, but Alqas convinced the sultan to attack Tabriz. The Ottomans entered Tabriz in the wake of the retreating Safavid cavalry on July 27. Once again, events in and around Tabriz led to the unraveling of the whole campaign. The sultan's plan, says Mustafa, had been to proclaim Alqas the shah of Iran. However, after the capture of Tabriz, Alqas and his retinue began to seek revenge on Tahmasb's subjects. This, says Mustafa, showed that he was not worthy of ruling Iran, that he did not have the necessary abilities, competence, and character. He was unable to control his men, who looted Tabriz and burned down Tahmasb's palace. Alqas then wanted to impose a summary tax on the city to raise funds and proposed to deport the city's merchants and artisans to the Ottoman side. These harsh measures were refused by Süleyman, who, according to Mustafa, instead ordered a tax amnesty for the city dwellers and the peasantry in the city's hinterland. At the same time, however, the artisans and merchants of the city were ordered to be sent to the Ottoman capital. The five days spent in the vicinity of Tabriz completely dashed the Ottoman hopes of installing Alqas on the Safavid throne. Hence Süleyman decided to leave Tabriz and help Ottoman forces who were previously sent to besiege Van. Very much like the Two Iraqs campaign, the grandiose objectives such as the institution of Alqas as the shah in Tabriz were, at an early stage of the campaign, abandoned, and the Ottoman army was forced to try and fight with an elusive enemy.

Following the arrival of the sultan on August 8 with the heavy artillery, the defenders of Van surrendered on the 24th. In anticipation of a Safavid counterattack, musketeers and artillerymen were ordered to garrison the city; to fortify the border, Van was made the seat of a new governorate-general.[75] While the Ottoman army was busy besieging Van, the Safavid cavalry roamed the Eastern Anatolian countryside and attacked the villages around Van and Adilcevaz, looting and massacring the population of Ahlat. An Ottoman force sent to repair and occupy the fortress of Kars was decimated by the Safavids. After a brief mop-up operation, the sultan decided to stay in the region for winter and traveled to Diyarbekir. Following the Ottoman army's move to the southwest,

---

[75] Tom Sinclair, "Administration and Fortification in the Van Region under Ottoman Rule in the Sixteenth Century," in *The Frontiers of the Ottoman World*, ed. A.G.S. Peacock (Oxford: Oxford University Press, 2009), 215.

the Safavid cavalry pillaged the countryside around Tercan and Erzincan, burned the crops, killed or chased the peasants, and carried away the livestock. The second vizier Kara Ahmed Pasha was sent to the north, but, after a few skirmishes, the Safavids retreated toward Georgia.[76] In Diyarbekir, most of the army units were sent to their winter encampments. Following the Eid in the first days of November, Süleyman moved to Aleppo to spend the winter in the company of his sons Cihangir and Bayezid. While still in Diyarbekir, Alqas had asked the sultan to attack Isfahan, Kashan and Qum, because his brother's treasury was apparently kept there. Süleyman, probably already suspicious about Alqas' usefulness, refused to give any Ottoman soldiers under his command but offered him funds instead. Alqas was granted an imperial edict allowing him to recruit soldiers from the Kurdish tribes and the peasantry in the region of Diyarbekir. After leaving Diyarbekir with his ragtag forces, Alqas attacked Isfahan, looting the treasury of his brothers Tahmasb and Bahram and capturing the latter's family members. Various valuable pieces from the treasuries of the shah and his brother were sent to Süleyman in Aleppo with Sayyid Azizullah, who served as vizier to Alqas.

While the sultan was in Aleppo, the final chapter of the Alqas Mirza affair unfolded. After looting various cities in central Iran, Alqas had retreated to the vicinity of Baghdad to spend the winter. There, given the reversals suffered during the campaign, the absence of support among the officials and subjects of the shah, and the growing dissatisfaction of the Ottomans, he sent a missive to his brother to ask for his pardon.[77] Apparently, the Ottoman grand vizier Rüstem already wanted to be rid of Alqas and prepared the conditions that forced him to leave the Ottomans.[78] Mustafa prefers a more dramatic explanation, which would become canonical among anti-Safavid Ottoman authors. According to the chancellor, Alqas wanted to visit the shrines of Hasan and Husayn, Ali's sons and the second and third Shiite imams, but was not allowed by the gatekeepers and custodians. Themselves Shiites, they accused him of having transformed himself into another Yazid, the early Umayyad caliph who had been an arch-enemy of Ali's sons. Realizing his mistake, Alqas, who supposedly had converted to Sunni Islam when he had

---

[76] *Tabakat*, 390a–395b. For detailed accounts of the campaign's first phase, see Kırzıoğlu, *Osmanlı'nın Kafkas-Elleri'ni Fethi*, 182–96 and Posch, "Der Fall Alḵās Mīrzā," 224–314.

[77] Walsh, "The Revolt of Alqās Mīrzā," 72–74; Posch, "Der Fall Alḵās Mīrzā," 387–93.

[78] Murphey, "Süleymân's Eastern Policy," 275–76.

arrived in Istanbul, reverted to his old faith. For Mustafa, the whole affair obviously showed once again that the Shiites/Safavids were not reliable.[79] As for Alqas, after spending the spring and summer of 1549 being pursued by both Ottoman and Safavid forces, he surrendered to his brother Tahmasb in early October 1549.

Alqas' flight meant the dissolution of any prospects for the Ottomans to gain leverage among the Safavid lords of Western Iran who, it was hoped, would join Alqas. The sultan did not want to return empty-handed, and a spring offensive against Georgia was ordered. Mustafa states that the Georgians had been enemies of the Turks since the eleventh century, when they had clashed with the Turkic tribes arriving in the Caucasus. The memories of these battles, he says, were still alive in the Oğuz epic cycle sung by bards in Anatolia. Moreover, the Georgians always played a double game by pitting Ottomans and Safavids against each other. Finally, during the last Hungarian campaign of the sultan, the governor of Erzurum, Musa Pasha, had fallen in a battle against the Georgians, and Süleyman had vowed to revenge his governor. The campaign, which had started with the hopes of placing a pro-Ottoman shah on the Safavid throne, was now turned into a punitive expedition against Georgia. Even this modest expedition was hampered by Süleyman's sudden illness, whose first symptoms were observed on June 23.

Mustafa was extremely worried when physicians could not determine the causes or nature of the sultan's ailment. After resting for a month, the sultan moved on August 1 to Karacadağ near Diyarbekir, a pasture famous for its salubrious climate. The task of campaigning was entrusted to the second vizier Ahmed, who left in the direction of Georgia on August 25. The pasha's forces captured a number of Georgian fortresses, and his dispatches, quoted by Mustafa, were apparently read in the sick sultan's presence. Ahmed returned to the sultan's camp on the October 24. The cold was making itself felt, and spending another winter in the region was pointless. Crossing Anatolia in the dead of winter, the sultan reached Istanbul on December 21, 1549.[80]

The years following Süleyman's eastern campaign witnessed the reopening of hostilities with the Habsburgs in Central Europe, around the question of Ferdinand's rights to sovereignty over Transylvania. As mentioned previously, after their annexation of Buda and Central

[79] *Tabakat*, 395b–401b.
[80] *Ibid.*, 401b–411a. Cf. Kırzıoğlu, *Osmanlı'nın Kafkas-Elleri'ni Fethi*, 196–205; Posch, "Der Fall Alḳās Mīrzā," 315–93, 401–31, 441–45.

Hungary, the Ottomans had appointed John Sigismund, the minor son of John Szapolyai, as the governor of Transylvania under the authority of the dowager queen Isabella and the regent George Martinuzzi. Martinuzzi continued to communicate with the Habsburgs, to the extent that, in 1550, Isabella asked for Ottoman help against an eventual takeover of the friar with Habsburg support. Probably convinced by Martinuzzi of the vulnerability of her position, however, Isabella signed, on July 19, 1551, the Treaty of Alba Iulia with Ferdinand. Similar to the Peace of Nagyvárad, the treaty transferred Transylvania and Szapolyai's dynastic rights in Hungary to Ferdinand, in return for the duchy of Oppel in Upper Silesia. The Ottomans answered the treaty by imprisoning the Habsburg envoy who had delivered the news and immediately ordering the Rumeli governor-general Sokollu Mehmed Pasha to Transylvania. In the summer of 1552, Ottoman forces annexed parts of Transylvania, which were turned into the governorate of Temeşvar.[81] Mustafa followed these campaigns from the capital and from Edirne, through dispatches and reports.[82] In his account of the hostilities, Mustafa sounds quite confident that the Ottoman forces will prevail against the Habsburgs. However, he misses the fact that the renewal of the hostilities with the Habsburgs created an opportunity for the Safavids. Indeed, the year following Süleyman's withdrawal, Tahmasb started to recover his losses in the region.[83] After the summer of 1552, in anticipation of a campaign against the Safavids in 1553, the Rumeli forces were ordered to go to Tokat in Central Anatolia and spend the winter there.[84] This was the first step of Süleyman's last campaign against the Safavids.

[81] Gökbilgin, "Kanunî Sultan Süleyman," 34–35; *The Papacy and the Levant 3*, 529–30; 4: 566–77, 584–85; *İOTK* 2, 262–78.
[82] *Tabakat*, 411b–424b.
[83] Kırzıoğlu, *Osmanlı'nın Kafkas-Elleri'ni Fethi*, 205–17; *İOTK* 2, 262–78.
[84] *Tabakat*, 424b.

4

Toward the End (1553–1567)

The last decade and a half of Mustafa's life and career displays a transition from the glory and pomp of earlier decades to a more austere and introspective mood. Ottoman "grand strategy," formulated in the early decades of Süleyman's rule, sent Ottoman armies to Central Europe, Azerbaijan, and Eastern Anatolia, but the resounding military and ideological victories that had been expected failed to materialize, creating a severe discrepancy between the reality of international politics and Ottoman imperial ideology. The Ottoman–French alliance against the Habsburgs continued willy-nilly, and Ottoman navies roamed the Mediterranean, winning a symbolically powerful victory at Djerba in the summer of 1560 but failing to take the island of Malta from the Hospitallers in 1565. Succession struggles resulted in the execution of two princes and exposed the weaknesses of the Ottoman dynastic system and Süleyman's declining authority. At the same time, this period witnessed two important events for the consolidation of the Ottoman Sunni identity. In 1555, after half a century of religious, political, and cultural tensions, frontier warfare, and devastating invasions, the Ottomans and the Safavids settled around the acknowledgment of each other's dynastic and religious identities. The construction of a mosque complex in Süleyman's name, started in 1553 and opened in 1557, provided the Ottomans with the supreme edifice of Ottoman imperial Sunnism.

Mustafa's retirement in 1557 signified the end of his bureaucratic career. Despite his nomination as the chief of palace notables, and a second tenure as chancellor in 1566–67, he ceased to play a role in the empire's management. As a result, he reinvented himself as a historian and a political writer. Mustafa had already established, at the time of his

123

retirement, a solid reputation as the empire's most skilled bureaucrat, and as the creator of a new style in Ottoman bureaucratic practice. His reputation as a historian, which would survive among the Ottoman literati of future generations, was an outcome of his activities during his retirement. The work of his life came full circle, in a sense: after contributing to the building of the empire, he wanted to leave to posterity a very personal account of the empire-building process. His unbridled imperialism, his dedication to Sunni Islam, and his promotion of bureaucratic merit, all products of a specific period and a particular cultural environment, were given an idealized, timeless expression in his works.

A Princely Demise: The Execution of Prince Mustafa

Süleyman's ultimate eastern campaign, which took place between 1553 and 1555, has two distinct phases. The first phase was directed against Süleyman's son Prince Mustafa and resulted in the latter's execution. As discussed previously in the case of Selim's march to power, the principle of "unigeniture" allowed the dynasty to keep the realm intact at the time of a new sultan's accession but, at the same time, created an environment conducive to factionalism and civil war. The practice of fratricide, already applied since the early decades of the polity and legalized by Mehmed II in the name of *raison d'état*, was seen as a necessary evil, even though it led to considerable unease among both the elite and the subject population.[1] In this particular case, Süleyman's old age and his illnesses, which led to rumors in European capitals – and, doubtlessly, in Istanbul – that he was near the end of his life, contributed to the crisis.[2] Four Ottoman princes were alive in 1553: Mustafa, whose mother was a concubine named Mahidevran/Gülbahar, and Selim, Bayezid, and Cihangir, all sons of Hürrem, the concubine Süleyman had freed and married in an exceptional show of personal love in 1534. Mustafa was near forty years of age, followed by Selim (thirty), Bayezid (twenty-eight), and

---

[1] For the earliest example of this practice, see Cemal Kafadar, "'Osmān Beg and His Uncle: Murder in the Family?," in *Studies in Ottoman History in Honour of Professor V.L. Ménage*, eds. Colin Heywood and Colin Imber (Istanbul: Isis, 1994), 157–64; *Between Two Worlds*, 105–09. For reactions to fratricide, see Imber, *The Structure of Power*, 108–09.

[2] There were reports that Süleyman suffered from gout, dysentery, and/or arthritis. See Alan Fisher, "The Life and Family of Süleymân I," in *Süleyman the Second and His Time*, 15–16; Metin Kunt, "Sultan Süleyman ve Nikris," in *Muhteşem Süleyman*, 93–99.

Cihangir (twenty-three). Cihangir, due to birth defects and related health problems, was generally seen as disqualified from the sultanate, whereas Selim was perceived as a relatively inactive and unimposing figure. The grand vizier Rüstem, his wife and the sultan's daughter Mihrimah, and Süleyman's wife Hürrem were rumored to prefer Bayezid as the successor, and Mustafa received the support, in Anatolia, of disgruntled *tımar* holders and various tribal elements, the perennial malcontents of Ottoman history.

Tensions reached their apogee when the sultan sent the grand vizier Rüstem, in early 1553, to Anatolia to either prepare for or command a campaign against the Safavids. After reaching Aksaray, halfway to the Eastern front, the grand vizier contacted the sultan with the news that Mustafa planned to kill him, assume the command of his forces (which included the palace contingents and janissaries, necessary allies for any contenders to the throne), march to Istanbul, and depose his father. The grand vizier's message also included allegations that the prince had contacted Tahmasb for an eventual alliance. It is possible that grand vizier invented the prince's alliance with Tahmasb, to motivate the sultan to act decisively. On the other hand, there are indications that the sympathies of the soldiery had begun to shift toward Mustafa, and the grand vizier found himself in a perilous situation.[3]

The chancellor, in his *Tabakat*, treads very carefully while narrating the events of the Prince Mustafa incident and positions himself as the defender of a necessary evil for the sake of preserving the empire. His attitude may be explained by his initial sympathy for Prince Bayezid, or the fact that, when he was writing this section of his work, Rüstem and other protagonists were still alive. Thus, without giving any clues about the contents of the messages sent by the grand vizier to the sultan, he informs his readers that Süleyman recalled Rüstem to the capital. The sultan had preferred to leave the command of the army to his pashas after 1549, but he was forced, due to the situation's gravity, to return to the field on August 28, 1553. His departure from Istanbul, in the company of his son Cihangir, included the usual pomp and circumstance, with the unfurling of the seven horsetail standards that symbolized the ailing sultan's claim

---

[3] Rüstem and Hürrem's anti-Mustafa position must have been common knowledge, because the Habsburg envoy, Ogier Ghiselin de Busbecq, knew about it: *Les lettres turques*, trans. and annotated by Dominique Arrighi (Paris: Honoré Champion, 2010), 72–80. The tense atmosphere is described in *İOTK* 2, 279–83; Şerafettin Turan, *Kanuni Süleyman Dönemi Taht Kavgaları*, revised second edition (Ankara: Bilgi, 1997), 22–36.

to rule over the seven climes. Nearly two weeks after his departure, Süleyman was joined by his son Bayezid for the Ramadan celebrations in the army camp, and Bayezid was then dispatched to Edirne to watch over the European front. Prince Selim joined his father on September 21. On October 5, near Ereğli, in Central Anatolia, the sultan was informed that Prince Mustafa had reached the vicinity of the army camp with his retinue and a force of five thousand. The following day, the sultan sent all his viziers to kiss his son's hand; the prince was then invited to come to the army camp and kiss the hand of his father. Immediately after the prince entered the tent of the imperial council, he was strangled by four executioners. Simultaneously, his chief of the stables and an *ağa* in his retinue were beheaded in front of the tent. The rest of the affair, as told by the chancellor, unfolded in a surprisingly cold-blooded manner. The imperial treasurer was sent to the unfortunate prince's camp to expropriate his belongings. The prince's retinue was dispersed through the distribution of land grants and provincial governorships. His corpse was exhibited in front of the imperial council tent, and was subsequently sent for the funeral prayer to the nearby town of Ereğli in the company of the military judges and other scholars. The body was then promptly sent to the old Ottoman capital Bursa for burial.[4]

Although the execution and burial took place relatively quickly, the affair created considerable unrest in the army camp and beyond, as contemporary poems lamenting the prince's execution show.[5] In an answer to the soldiers' reaction, the sultan quickly dismissed Rüstem from the grand vizierate. The third vizier, Haydar Pasha, suspected of being a Mustafa sympathizer, was also dismissed, and the second vizier Kara Ahmed was appointed grand vizier.[6] The chancellor, who witnessed the unrest in the army camp and heard the angry rumors, does not share the view that Rüstem was behind the prince's execution. As customary, he blames the rumors on those who were unaware of the genuine reasons behind the execution and on those who reflected on the situation without recourse to reason. On the other hand, his unease is apparent in his justification of the execution, which sounds somehow forced and contrived. He states that the execution was due, first of all, to the inscrutable will of God. Süleyman, who always respected the commandments of God and the

---

[4] *Tabakat*, 431b–437a.
[5] For these reactions see *İOTK* 2, 283–87; Ş. Turan, *Taht Kavgaları*, 36–42. Two elegies, by Yahya Bey and Sani, respectively, are in *ibid.*, 159–65.
[6] *Tabakat*, 436b–437a.

Sharia, treated his children the way he would treat any of his subjects, and the prince's punishment was a result of his misdeeds. The chancellor then tries to devalue the prince's reputation, saying that, although he had distinguished himself in the battlefield against the Safavids, he was indebted to his father's help and munificence for his success. According to the chancellor, the prince did not have the necessary attributes for the sultanate either. Even though he had not personally acted against the precepts of justice, he had given liberties to his men, who had mistreated the inhabitants of Amasya, where the prince served as the provincial governor.[7]

After the execution of his son, Süleyman turned his attention to the Safavids. Since the end of the campaign season had already been reached, various units were sent to their winter quarters while the sultan decided to spend the cold season in Aleppo. He entered the city on November 8, amidst the sound of the cannons fired from the citadel and the cheers of scholars, dervishes, and city notables. While spending the winter in Aleppo, Prince Cihangir passed away of natural causes. Mustafa remarks that the prince had a very severe illness that resisted every treatment, drug, and prayer, but there were other opinions, ignored by Mustafa, according to which Cihangir died as a result of his distress at his brother's execution.[8] Süleyman thus lost two sons in the scope of a few months. The next Ottoman sultan would now be determined by the competition between the two remaining sons, Bayezid and Selim.

Toward the First Ottoman–Safavid Settlement: A War of Letters

Süleyman's last campaign against the Safavids took place in a gloomy atmosphere, and Mustafa's impressions of this last military excursion against the Safavids bear the marks of fatigue and war weariness. In a long poem that forms the prelude to his campaign narrative, he states that campaigns serve the enemy more than the Ottomans, because they lead to a considerable human cost. Moreover, they create exceptional situations in which it is impossible to apply the Sharia and provide justice. Finally, campaigns take their toll on the subjects and the realm by sowing destruction and squandering precious resources. The best instrument with which to fight the enemy, according to Mustafa, is alertness and caution.[9]

---

[7] *Ibid.*, 437a–438a.
[8] *Ibid.*, 438b–439b; İOTK 2, 287.
[9] *Tabakat*, 426a–b.

These late-life ruminations of the chancellor constitute a sharp departure from his enthusiastic and unconditional endorsement of earlier Ottoman military ventures and represent a new level of thinking that became more and more prevalent during Süleyman's last years on the throne. As a result of the gunpowder revolution, military expenditures and the destructive capacities of armies had radically increased in the early modern period.[10] After the 1530s, the Ottoman ruling elite found itself irretrievably committed to constant warfare in Central Europe, the Mediterranean, and the East. These wars of attrition did not lead to expansion and the gain of new revenue sources. Although he does not discuss these issues directly, Mustafa's portrayals of various Ottoman campaigns include, sometimes implicitly and sometimes explicitly, the logistical problems related to provisioning, campaigning in winter, and the management of large armies with heavy baggage trains. However, he usually compensates for these difficulties with reference to the successes of Ottoman imperialism. Around the last eastern campaign, on the other hand, at a moment when the optimism of the earlier periods is on the wane, the chancellor finally develops a more sober assessment of early modern warfare. It is significant that he uses this as a pretext to defend a model of imperialism based on justice, good government, and reason, rather than unbridled militarism.

In strategic terms, Süleyman's last campaign against the Safavids was an answer to the recent Safavid military resurgence in the east. In 1552, benefiting from the Ottoman forces' presence in Hungary, Safavid forces attacked the region of Van, Erciş, and Adilcevaz. The town of Ahlat surrendered, and the members of the Ottoman garrison were executed. In Erciş, the Kurdish fortress commander, an Ottoman ally, was killed by townsmen who then invited the Safavid forces in. The governor-general of Erzurum, İskender, was unable to withstand the waves of Safavid attacks. More importantly, both Ottoman and Safavid sources suggest that the Safavids enjoyed the support of various local groups that were supposedly subjects of the Ottoman sultan. The Safavids legitimized their activities by referring to the harassment policy of İskender against them, whereas Mustafa, predictably enough, presents Tahmasb as the eternal enemy of the Ottomans, as someone who eagerly awaits the propitious moment to attack the lands and subjects of the sultan. According to Mustafa, this is

---

[10] For an excellent discussion of this issue, see John Landers, *The Field and the Forge. Population, Production, and Power in the Pre-industrial West* (Oxford: Oxford University Press, 2003), 10, 282–308, 334–54, 355–76.

why the sultan shunned Tahmasb's diplomatic openings in the spring of 1553 and decided to give a military answer instead.[11]

After overseeing the execution of his son and spending the winter in Aleppo, Süleyman departed on April 9, 1554 for Diyarbekir, where governors-general and their forces joined him. The Prince Mustafa incident obviously continued to create tensions among the soldiery, so much so that the sultan felt the need to address his officers in person. The chancellor remarks that the sultan aimed to raise the troops' morale, but he does not comment on why the morale was low in the army. On May 15, commanders and officers of various units were invited to an imperial council meeting. The sultan sat on a throne and, from this exalted position, reminded them that the Ottoman army was in the East to fulfill the sacred duty of holy war and that they were bound to serve the sultan. This declaration was followed by the distribution of gifts. The commanders publicly declared that they were faithful to the sultan and would follow him wherever he saw fit to go.[12] After this gathering, Süleyman gave the order to proceed toward Erzurum. From the middle of May to the end of June, the Ottoman army, whose effectives were considerably increased by the participation of various contingents on the road, marched to Erzurum and then to Nahçıvan. Nahçıvan was reached on June 29, but the sultan soon fell back on Kars on July 5.[13]

The quick retreat from Nahçıvan was partly due to logistical difficulties, namely, the delay in the arrival of necessary provisions and the successful scorched earth tactics applied by the Safavids.[14] Another reason was, in all likelihood, the aging sultan's desire to reach a satisfactory conclusion to his enmity with the Safavids by using the presence of the Ottoman army in the region as leverage. Indeed, the same day the sultan came to Kars, a letter, written by Mustafa, was sent to the Safavids. Before reproducing the letter in *Tabakat*, Mustafa engages in a bitter anti-Shiite polemic.[15] He offers his readers his own version of Islamic history and Sunni–Shiite relations from an intensely Sunni-centric point of view. He accuses the Safavids of illicit religious practices and defends the Ottomans by arguing that they were compelled to fight by Tahmasb's actions. The

---

[11] *Tabakat*, 426b–433b passim. Cf. Mitchell, "The Sword and the Pen," 322. For the Safavid perspective see Eskandar Beg Monshi, *History of Shah 'Abbas the Great*, 124–29; Şah Tahmasb, *Tezkire*, 73–75.

[12] *Tabakat*, 446a–449a.

[13] *Ibid.*, 449a–457a.

[14] Kırzıoğlu, *Osmanlı'nın Kafkas-Elleri'ni Fethi*, 218–19.

[15] *Tabakat*, 457a–458b.

letter to the shah bears the marks of Mustafa's profound anti-Shiite senti-
ments. Similar to his "letter of threats" of 1524, Mustafa brings together
religious arguments (the Safavid "heresy," the Quranic injunction to fight
the heretics with the sword, etc.) with accusations of cowardice and chides
Tahmasb for failing to appear on the battlefield. It ends with a final warning: in case the shah does not provide an immediate answer, the Ottoman
army will advance and lay waste to Nahçıvan.[16] Despite its antagonistic
tone, however, this letter is the first step in what might be called semifor-
mal negotiations between the Ottomans and the Safavids.

Without waiting for the shah's answer, the Ottoman army marched
on to Nahçıvan on July 10. Once again, the Ottomans advanced without encountering any serious resistance from the Safavids. Burning and
looting the countryside and the towns they came across, they reached
Yerevan on July 18 and destroyed the gardens in the vicinity of the city.
In Nahçıvan, they burned down the palaces belonging to the shah and
his sons, destroyed royal gardens, and cut down the poplar woods sur-
rounding the palaces. The inhabitants of the region were enslaved and
sold in the army market. Mustafa justifies these extreme measures by saying that they were meant to reciprocate what the shah and his men had
done to the Ottoman subjects in the previous years.[17] It is also obvious
that the Ottoman soldiers were ordered to behave particularly harshly to
bring the shah to the battlefield or convince him to sue for peace. After
three weeks of pillaging, Süleyman, on the pretext of the holy month of
Ramadan, ordered the army back to Erzurum. The expected letter from
the shah reached the Ottomans at the end of the first week of Ramadan
(around the end of the first week of August 1554). Written in a subdued tone, it addressed the grand vizier Ahmed Pasha from the part of
Safavid grandees. Mixed with its threats of a counterattack, the letter also
stated that, in case the Ottomans were willing to reach an agreement, the
Safavids would follow suit.

The Ottoman side answered this letter with two different missives. A
letter written from the mouth of the grand vizier repeated the contents
of the letter sent from Süleyman to Tahmasb, whereas a second document, signed by the Ottoman viziers, stated that the Ottomans had not
asked for peace, but would not reject Safavid demands for the sultan's
clemency. According to Mustafa, the shah was genuinely concerned that
the Ottomans would attack the spiritual center of the Safavid order, the

[16] *Ibid.*, 459a–460b.
[17] *Ibid.*, 460b–463b.

city of Ardabil, as it had been stated in the preceding letters. For this reason he addressed another letter, this time to the governor-general of Erzurum, Ayas Pasha. Mustafa does not reproduce the shah's letter due to its powerful Shiite polemic against the Ottomans,[18] but instead records Ayas' reply to the shah, in which the pasha reassures the shah that, contrary to his expectations, the Ottomans have enough provisions to spend the winter in the region and attack Ardabil.[19] To exert more pressure on the shah, the Ottoman army resumed its activities on August 9, but the Safavid forces were nowhere to be seen. The most serious harm during this stage of the campaign was caused by a fire that was started by sparks flying from the field kitchens. Following the celebration of the Eid, on September 3, the grand vizier Ahmed was dispatched to Georgia after it was heard that the shah attacked Ottoman fortresses in the area. However, when the pasha reached the region, Tahmasb had already retreated. Finally, on September 26, an envoy of Tahmasb brought a letter asking for peace. The envoy was greeted by the pashas, and a feast was given in his honor. He was then taken to the sultan, who personally asserted that the Ottomans were favorable to a peace agreement with the Safavids and would cease their military operations. This was the end of the Nahçıvan campaign, which was fought more on the written page than the battlefield.[20]

The Amasya Settlement: Mutual Recognition or War Weariness?

After this preliminary agreement for peace, Süleyman decided to spend the winter in Amasya, to preserve a military presence in the region before the realization of a conclusive peace treaty. The army left Erzurum on September 28, 1554, and arrived at Amasya on October 30. To comfort his readers about the sultan's majesty, Mustafa informs them that the sultan was expected in this city by the ambassadors of the Habsburgs, France, Venice, and Poland. He then summarizes the recent activities of the Ottoman navy in the Mediterranean and the Indian Ocean and gives a concise account of recent French successes against the Habsburgs in

---

[18] For an analysis of this letter, see Mitchell, *The Practice of Politics*, 81–87.

[19] For the texts of these letters, see *Tabakat*, 465a–470a.

[20] *Ibid.*, 470a–472b. For another account of the campaign with an emphasis on Ottoman successes, see Kırzıoğlu, *Osmanlı'nın Kafkas-Elleri'ni Fethi*, 219–39. Eskandar Monshi (*History of Shah 'Abbas the Great*, 129–30) mentions the success of the Safavids' scorched earth tactics and guerilla warfare.

the ongoing Italian War of 1551–59. On the basis of a letter from Henri II (r. 1547–59) to Süleyman, Mustafa describes French territorial gains in the north and proudly provides an account of the Battle of Renty (August 12, 1554), where French forces under Henri Duke de Guise (on whom Mustafa bestows the title of chief vizier) defeated Charles V. The chancellor informs his readers that, when Henri's father Francis was a captive, Süleyman graciously agreed to help him and has been helping Henri himself by sending his navy to his assistance. Imperialist propaganda aside, Mustafa's discussion of the practical aspects of the French–Ottoman alliance immediately after the cessation of the hostilities with the Safavids is a precious testimony about the dynamics of the Ottomans' position between East and West. It is also obvious that news of French victories against the imperial forces gave the Ottomans considerable leverage vis-à-vis Ogier Ghiselin de Busbecq, who anxiously awaited in Amasya to renew the truce between the Ottomans and Ferdinand.[21]

Despite the pressing concerns of the European front, Mustafa's narrative shows that a settlement with the Safavids was seen as a more important item on the diplomatic agenda. Mustafa tells us how Süleyman spent the winter hunting in the vicinity of Amasya and lauds the region's gardens and spas, but he also remarks that everyone awaited the arrival of spring. He claims that the Safavids were preoccupied by the sultan's presence in the area and were worried about an Ottoman attack against major urban centers such as Tabriz, Isfahan, and Ardabil. However, these belligerent arguments are belied by Mustafa's own record of the events of 1554 and the Ottomans' desire to reach an understanding with the Safavids while keeping an air of haughtiness for appearances' sake. Finally, in early spring, the governor-general of Erzurum informed Amasya that a Safavid delegation had arrived. Süleyman immediately sent a dispatch to the governor, ordering him to treat the Safavid envoys well and send them to Amasya with an escort. The delegation was headed by Tahmasb's chief courtier (eşik ağası başı), Kamal al-Din Farrukhzada. Tahmasb was aware that the Ottomans were amenable to peace and was confident of his political and military position.[22]

Unlike their treatment of previous Safavid ambassadors, the Ottomans were very careful this time in welcoming the delegation. A mansion was designated in Amasya as their residence, and they were assisted by palace

---

[21] The accounts of these episodes are found in *Tabakat*, 474b–483b. For the Ottoman–French alliance, also see Charrière, *Négociations* 2: 135–328.

[22] Mitchell, "The Sword and the Pen," 352–53.

servants. The sultan personally sent provisions from the imperial kitchens and fodder from the imperial stables. After an initial meeting with the viziers, the ambassadors were invited by Süleyman to an imperial council meeting on May 21, 1555. Mustafa, who attended the meeting, mentions its friendly atmosphere. This is corroborated by the Habsburg ambassador Busbecq, who did not enjoy such a friendly reception and began to despair of his chances of obtaining a truce.[23] In the morning, the ambassadors met with the viziers and presented, according to Mustafa, the apologies of the shah. This was followed by a long and amicable dialogue. The lunch itself was carefully organized as an elaborate feast; for instance, the ambassadors were offered a choice selection of game as their meat course. After lunch, the gifts of the shah to the sultan were brought to the imperial council. Mustafa says that, at the sight of the gifts of the shah, the winter cold that had existed between the Ottomans and the Safavids suddenly turned to spring. Süleyman came to the imperial council meeting soon afterward, and he was given the letter of the shah, after which the council meeting ended.[24]

Mustafa, who was among the first Ottoman officials to read the letter, had mixed feelings. Despite the earlier atmosphere of friendly conversation in the imperial council, he was upset about the letter's Shiite overtones. He admits that he liked the Safavid chancery's style. However, the letter's references to Ali and the first three caliphs were, according to the chancellor, unsuitable for such a document. The sultans, busy with state matters, might not be well-versed in various sciences, says the chancellor. However, the secretaries (erbāb-ı imlā ve inşā') have to be knowledgeable, and the responsibility of ignoring the legitimacy of the first three caliphs belongs to them. Mustafa here enters into a monologue and tells his readers that Ali had always submitted to the authority of the first three caliphs in his lifetime. Books of history as well as various traditions showed that the first four caliphs acted together on a variety of matters and enjoyed a close relationship. Hence, the claims of the Safavids that the first three caliphs had usurped the entitlement of Ali to the caliphate after the death of Muhammad were not substantiated by historical evidence. Mustafa then engages in a long diatribe against the Shiites and offers various anti-Shiite anecdotes.[25]

---

[23] Busbecq, *Les lettres turques*, 120–22.
[24] *Tabakat*, 484a–487a.
[25] Mustafa's criticisms are in *Ibid.*, 487a–488a, and his anti-Shiite outburst is in 488a–491a.

Interestingly enough, although the chancellor used to call the Safavids heretics and unbelievers before, he now seems to acknowledge, with the rest of the Ottoman establishment, that they are Twelver Shiites. This time, he feels the need to create a pro-Sunni and anti-Shiite discourse, rather than claiming that the Ottomans represent Islam and the Muslims as a whole. Tahmasb's letter itself, reproduced by Mustafa, shows another dimension of the rapprochement between the two sides. The letter was written by the members of the Safavid chancery who, very much like their Ottoman counterparts, had developed a powerful form of expression to defend the dynasty they served. Beyond its assertion of the Safavids' Twelver Shiite identity, it is highly conciliatory in political matters. It repeats Süleyman's titles by closely following the style of the Ottoman chancery created by Mustafa and recognizes his supremacy over different realms. Written from the mouth of the shah, it advocates for peace among Muslims (i.e., between Sunni Ottomans and Shiite Safavids). It also asks the Ottoman sultan to grant Safavid subjects the right to visit the two Holy Cities and the Shiite shrines of Iraq for pilgrimage.[26]

The Ottoman answer, composed either by Mustafa or under his super-vision, is milder in tone than the previous Ottoman missives. After repeat-ing the now standard Ottoman claims that respect for Ali does not necessarily imply the cursing of the first three caliphs, the letter asserts Süleyman's caliphate and supremacy over the world. More importantly, it assures the Safavids that, barring a Safavid attack, the Ottomans will not attack Safavid territory. Finally, the Safavids are given permission to visit the Holy Cities and the Shiite shrines without any hindrance on the part of the Ottomans. On June 1, this document was presented to the Safavid ambassadors together with various gifts; the sultan also informed the Ottoman governors in Eastern Anatolia of the end of the hostilities. Süleyman then left Amasya on June 21, ending his third and last campaign against the Safavids. One of his most tangible gains, on the ideological front, was the Safavid promise to end the ritual cursing of the first three Sunni caliphs.[27] Busbecq, able to obtain only a precarious

---

[26] The letter is in *ibid.*, 491a–494b. C.P. Mitchell provides an excellent analysis of the letter's stylistic characteristics as well as religio-political contents in "The Pen and the Sword," 354–59.

[27] *Tabakat*, 494b–497a. Süleyman's letter to the shah is in 495a–496b. For the negotia-tions, also see Kırzıoğlu, *Osmanlı'nın Kafkas-Elleri'ni Fethi*, 241–44; İOTK 2, 293–95; Mitchell, "The Pen and the Sword," 352–59 passim. For analyses of the correspon-dence from an Ottoman-centric point of view, see A. Ekber Diyanet, *İlk Osmanlı-İran Anlaşması (1555 Amasya Musalahası)* (Istanbul: Edebiyat Fakültesi, 1971); Remzi Kılıç,

six-month truce between Süleyman and Ferdinand, had already left Amasya the day following the Ottoman-Safavid settlement, on June 2.

The Ottoman–Safavid negotiations thus produced the first official peace settlement since the beginning of the hostilities in the first decade of the sixteenth century. The half century of warfare between the two sides had not produced the desired outcome. Ismail's grandiose designs to expand into Anatolia thanks to the support of the Turcoman tribes presented a tremendous challenge to the Ottomans. Although the Ottomans were able to counterattack under Selim and Süleyman, conquering a large swath of territory in the east, and quelling pro-Safavid rebellions, they were not able to eradicate the Safavid politico-religious movement as they wished. The campaigns of 1533–35 and 1548–49 resulted, at best, in the containment of Safavid expansion through the creation of governorates-general at Erzurum, Van, Baghdad, and eventually Basra. However, Ottoman control over Eastern Anatolia and Iraq outside fortified places relied on a tenuous alliance with the local Kurdish aristocracy. Plans to use the Sunni ruling class of Şirvan against the Safavids or organize joint campaigns with the Uzbeks did not produce long-lasting outcomes either. More importantly, the local Alevi/Shiite populations clearly preferred Safavid rule to the Ottomans, and Ottoman attempts at persecuting Safavid sympathizers in the frontier regions did not help gain hearts and minds to the Ottoman cause.

Both the Safavids and the Ottomans had to wage war on two fronts in this period, the former against the Uzbeks and the latter against the Habsburgs. The settlement of 1555 was the belated recognition that neither side could realize the ambitious imperialist projects of the earlier decades. It is also crucial in its inclusion of an element of religious recognition. The Ottomans recognized the Safavids as Twelver Shiites (i.e., the representatives of a time-honored Muslim confession), rather than accusing them of heresy and unbelief. The Safavids, in their demand for the right to pilgrimage, accepted the Ottomans as the protectors of the Two Holy Cities, one of the tenets of Ottoman imperial Sunnism. The settlement also indicates that both sides adopted a politicized version of Sunnism and Shiism as the main identity marker of the empires, relinquishing earlier messianic and latitudinarian dimensions and espousing a more conservative religious rhetoric. The settlement was reached only

XVI. ve XVII. Yüzyıllarda Osmanlı-İran Siyasi Antlaşmaları (Istanbul: Tez, 2001), 71–76.

a few months before the religious Peace of Augsburg, which was signed between Charles V (his brother Ferdinand signed it in the name of the emperor) and Lutheran princes on September 25, 1555.[28]

The settlements at Amasya and Augsburg exhibit both fundamental differences and interesting parallels. For instance, the peace constitutes the foundations for the principle of *Cuius regio, eius religio*, while the Amasya settlement does not address the state of Alevis and Shiites who live under Ottoman rule, or the Sunnis under Safavid rule, whose numbers had been dwindling under Safavid attempts at forced conversion. Moreover, given the presence of large Christian communities in Ottoman and Safavid territories, the principle of a single confession is not relevant, because the main question is the *primacy* of Sunnism or Shiism as Muslim confessions in the midst of multi-religious empires. Finally, issues such as the rights of cities or religious freedom, found at the heart of the negotiations between the emperor and his subjects, are not encountered in the Ottoman–Safavid case, in which the outcome of the negotiations was determined not through discussions in a Diet, but by what might be called two rival and fairly similar establishments. On the other hand, both settlements are outcomes of half a century of intense propaganda and warfare and signify the defeat of earlier claims of universal sovereignty under the leadership of a single ruler bringing together religious and spiritual leadership. Finally, they represent a reluctant but nevertheless formal recognition of the other side's creed as both a legitimate religious discourse and a political identity and introduce a level of territorialization whereby specific areas, be they cities, principalities, or imperial entities, would be characterized, among other identity markers, by the prominence or domination of a religious confession.

Mustafa's Last Years in Ottoman Service

The Ottoman–Safavid settlement was the last major event in which Mustafa played a role. The period between mid-1555 and his retirement in 1557 was, in terms of his administrative responsibilities, relatively uneventful. As a result of his advanced age and the increased professionalization of the Ottoman scribal service, he had already relinquished

---

[28] For articles on various aspects of the Peace of Augsburg see Heinz Schilling and Heribert Smolinsky, *Der Augsburger Religionsfrieden 1555. Wissenschaftliches Symposium aus Anlass des 450. Jahrestages des Friedensschlusses, Augsburg, 21. bis 25. September 2005* (Münster: Aschendorff; Gütersloh: Gütersloher Verlagshaus, 2007).

various responsibilities to the chief secretary Abdurrahman Efendi, who hailed from Tosya like Mustafa and had been appointed to this position in November 1553.[29] A glimpse into the register that records the treasury's activities during the last campaign shows that the regular chancery business was conducted mostly through the chief secretary. Mustafa continued to fulfill an important role in the sultan's retinue but intervened only on important occasions, such as the Ottoman–Safavid negotiations.[30] A few events preoccupied Mustafa, however, and he subsequently recorded these in his *Tabakat*. The first one of these is a rebellion in the empire's European provinces, the second is the return of Rüstem Pasha to the grand vizierate, and the third is the building and opening of the Süleymaniye Mosque as the most articulate cultural statement of Ottoman imperial Sunnism.

The rebellion in Rumeli started almost immediately after the Amasya settlement. A man claimed that he was the recently executed Prince Mustafa and that he had escaped unscathed from his father's army camp. He gathered land grant holders around him in Niğbolu and Silistre, executed some Ottoman judges in the area, and proclaimed his sultanate. To the chancellor's disgust, he apparently imitated the Ottoman system of rule and appointed a grand vizier and other officials. Süleyman learned of the developments while he was near Istanbul, on his way back from Amasya. He immediately dispatched the third vizier Sokollu Mehmed Pasha, the previous governor-general of Rumeli, with some household troops and janissaries. Mustafa, who saw the reports received about the rebellion, remarks that the rebels had been able to recruit men from among the "Simavna mystics," meaning the latitudinarian religious communities of the Balkans that had supported the massive uprising of Sheikh Bedreddin in 1413. In this sense, the rebellion was a typical Ottoman phenomenon: alienated low-ranking members of the military class united with various mystical/religious groups with their own non- or anti-Ottoman political theologies.

According to Mustafa's account, Prince Bayezid, who had been sent to Edirne before the 1553–55 campaign, took the necessary measures by sending his forces against the rebels and also contacting the "grand vizier" of the pretender. The pretender was caught and sent to Istanbul where, after being interrogated, he was hanged before the arrival of Süleyman

---

[29] Yılmaz, "Koca Nişancı," 134–35.
[30] See BOA, KK 1766. Abdurrahman Çelebi is regularly mentioned in the register through his reception of funds and materials such as ink and paper necessary for the chancery.

on July 31, 1555.[31] Although the rebellion was quelled relatively rapidly, it left an important legacy by souring the relationship between Prince Bayezid and Süleyman. The sultan believed that his son could have moved against the rebels earlier and found it suspicious that he had established communications with some of the rebel leaders. He wanted to punish his son but was prevented by his wife Hürrem.[32] The allegations against the prince were widespread in Istanbul, and they are also recorded by the Habsburg ambassador Busbecq, who goes so far as to suggest that the revolt had been started by Bayezid himself in the hopes of creating a crisis and coming to the throne while his father was in Anatolia.[33] The chancellor explains to his readers that an earlier victory was hampered by the fact that the army was in campaign and various units were scattered throughout the empire, thus deflecting any criticisms from Prince Bayezid.

The other important development was the restoration of Rüstem Pasha to the grand vizierate in September 1555, following the execution of the grand vizier Ahmed Pasha.[34] Rüstem was a particularly powerful figure during the last decades of Süleyman's rule. As the husband of Mihrimah, Süleyman and Hürrem's daughter, he had a considerable influence on the aging sultan. However, the reactions created by the execution of Prince Mustafa were so overwhelming and extensive that Süleyman was obliged to dismiss his grand vizier in the summer of 1553. After his dismissal, Rüstem was confined to his mansion in Üsküdar. In the period between his dismissal and his reappointment, he continued to exert his influence on the members of the Ottoman ruling elite, whom he had supported in their careers; moreover, he always had a powerful ally in the person of the sultan's wife, Hürrem. The continuing prestige of the pasha is shown by the fact that the Habsburg ambassador Busbecq, who reached Istanbul after the pasha's dismissal, found it necessary to visit him, in the expectation that the pasha would soon rise to power. Mustafa's account shows that he too desired to have a good relationship with the powerful Rüstem.

Mustafa, probably writing while Rüstem is still alive, portrays the executed grand vizier, Ahmed Pasha, as an administrator who did not have the necessary skills to manage the realm and as one who abrogated both the Sharia and *kanun*. The chancellor does not give specific details about the pasha's mistakes, but implies that, contrary to the chancellor's

---

[31] *Tabakat*, 497b–500a; İOTK 2, 296–98; Ş. Turan, *Taht Kavgaları*, 44–46.

[32] Ş. Turan, *Taht Kavgaları*, 47–49.

[33] Busbecq, *Les lettres turques*, 142–50.

[34] İOTK 2, 298–299.

notions of good government and bureaucratic merit, the pasha misman-
aged the Nahçıvan campaign, did not accept counsel, and acted on his
own initiative. His anti-Safavid bias pushes the chancellor to argue that it
might have been possible to win a victory against the Safavids were it not
for the errors of Ahmed Pasha. He does not mention the allegations that
Ahmed Pasha was executed because of his failure during the revolt of the
pretender and on the suspicion that he had lent his tacit support to the
revolt and hence to Prince Bayezid.[35] Rather than addressing the tensions
of the day, and probably for fear of seeming to side with any particular
faction, Mustafa criticizes the executed grand vizier through references
to general bureaucratic ideals.[36] His presentation of Rüstem, in contrast,
focuses on piety and hard work. Even though the pasha was famous for
his clientelism, Mustafa describes him as a man who refrained from gossip
and calumny, liked to listen to Quran recitations, did not swear in public,
followed the Sharia, and patronized public works.[37] The portrait Mustafa
provides is that of a hard-working and pious bureaucrat who treats all
Ottoman subjects equally and whose activities contribute to the perpetuation of the order of the universe (*niẓām-ı ʿālem*). These praises for Rüstem
were written during Mustafa's retirement, perhaps in the hope of returning to his position as chancellor, but more likely to evade the pasha's
anger and secure good careers for his two sons, Mahmud and Hüseyin.[38]

The Construction of the Süleymaniye Mosque: The Epitome of Ottoman Imperial Sunnism

The Ottomanization of Istanbul had existed as a political, cultural, and
administrative project for slightly more than a century at the time the
Süleymaniye was built. Already under Mehmed II, the Ottomans introduced conscious policies to repopulate their new capital, turn it into a
vibrant economic hub, and also appropriate and transform the cultural
heritage of the Byzantine Empire.[39] Especially under Süleyman, Istanbul,
very much like the sultan's claim to providing justice or representing

---

[35] Ş. Turan, *Taht Kavgaları*, 49.
[36] *Tabakat*, 500a–502a.
[37] *Ibid.*, 502a–503a.
[38] His son Mahmud would eventually serve in the financial branch of the scribal service in
the last decades of the sixteenth century. See Yılmaz, "Koca Nişancı," 152, 163–64.
[39] Çiğdem Kafescioğlu, *Constantinopolis/Istanbul: Cultural Encounter, Imperial Vision,
and the Construction of the Ottoman Capital* (College Park: Pennsylvania State University Press, 2009), esp. 16–142.

FIGURE 8. The Süleymaniye Mosque dominates the city's skyline (from Melchior Lorck, *Prospect of Constantinople*, Leiden University Library, ms. BPL 1758, sheet 10).

FIGURE 8 (*continued*)

Sunni Islam, became a dynastic identity marker. During the correspondence of 1554 with the Ottomans, for instance, the Safavids used Istanbul as a metonymy for the Ottoman dynasty itself.[40] Süleyman's reign symbolizes, among other things, the construction and promotion of Istanbul as the imperial and dynastic center par excellence.[41] The city's fortunes in the sixteenth century were very similar to other important dynastic centers such as London and Paris. Although the inhabitants had to struggle with plagues, fires, high prices, and various crimes, the cities were being radically transformed through royal/imperial as well as individual (official and nonofficial) patronage and under the impact of global economic trends and the rise of new social classes. Istanbul, in this sense, is the bellwether of a process of early modern imperial urbanity that predates and foretells the subsequent rise of Vienna, Madrid, Isfahan, and Agra.

The Süleymaniye complex meets different needs: the ideal of a Sunni Muslim empire, the claim of civilizational superiority over the Safavids and the European Christians, and the urge to leave a cultural legacy that represents the whole imperial edifice. As Gülru Necipoğlu argues, the complex was Süleyman's ultimate ideological testimony. The idea had emerged after the 1547 peace treaty with the Habsburgs, when the Ottomans claimed they were finally able to prove their supremacy over Charles V. The reassertion of the empire's Sunni identity in the Amasya settlement of 1555 in a sense completed the missing half of the picture, because it meant, at least for the Ottoman elite, the reception of religious/doctrinal concessions from the Safavids and the recognition of the Ottomans as the legitimate protectors of the Two Holy Cities.[42] The cultural and ideological significance of the edifice is best understood by looking at Mustafa's treatment of the event. The story of the building, in *Tabakat*, is prefaced by a detailed praise of Süleyman. The chancellor provides a list of the realms that are under his dominion and presents the sultan as the most powerful ruler in human history, whose achievements surpassed those of King Solomon and Alexander the Great. Curiously

---

[40] Mitchell, *The Practice of Politics*, 81.

[41] For the physical expansion of the city in the sixteenth century, see Selma Özkoçak, "The Urban Development of Ottoman Istanbul in the Sixteenth Century" (PhD diss., School of Oriental and African Studies, University of London, 1997). The new city became a commercial and cultural hub and exhibited a lively cultural and social life, as told by, among others, Robert Mantran, *Istanbul au siècle de Soliman le Magnifique*, revised second edition (Paris: Hachette, 1994).

[42] Gülru Necipoğlu, *The Age of Sinan: Architectural Culture in the Ottoman Empire* (Princeton: Princeton University Press, 2005), 207–08.

ignoring Selim, Mustafa argues that Süleyman is the sole ruler to bring together so many military achievements with the title of Servant of the Two Holy Cities. Indeed, he says, comparing Süleyman to past rulers is meaningless, because it is an endeavor akin to comparing the sun to the moon, or an emerald to a rough stone.[43]

Beyond his emphasis on the sultan's achievements, Mustafa's preface reflects a state of mind that prevailed in the sultan's circle in the past two decades of his rule. In this period, the enthusiasm of the earlier period left its place to a more pronounced austerity, and references to law, order, just government and piety became more frequent. In the words of Cornell Fleischer, "[t]he excitement, polyphony, eclecticism, innovation, and universalist dreams of the first three decades were replaced . . . with a new gravity of tone and a formalizing impulse to establish consistency of imperial style."[44] Mustafa, as seen previously, does not refrain from referring to Süleyman's majesty, but combines it with the sultan's piety and humility. He informs his readers that the sultan never became arrogant, that he was always aware that the divine support he perpetually enjoyed was a result of his thanking and praising God. Mustafa waxes poetic in these passages and talks about the transitory nature of the world. At first sight, he says, gardens look full of blossoms and nightingales sing among the trees. However, in the blink of an eye, all this beauty is destroyed. The aroma of the flowers, after lingering in the air, disappears after a few days; the songs of the nightingales are silenced. The day, once profiting from the light of the sun, is suddenly overcome by the shadows of the night. Those who listen to their reason know that, while they still have power and riches, they have to engage in good works, because these ensure a second life for their patrons by carrying their name to posterity. Süleyman is aware of these realities, according to Mustafa, and also wants to emulate the example of his ancestors who left mosques bearing their names.[45]

Mustafa's narrative of the construction and opening of the mosque complex displays the same emphasis on Sunni Muslim piety. After the plans of the building are approved by the sultan and the foundations are dug, a propitious time and date for the beginning of the construction are designated. On July 8, 1550, the sultan parades from the palace to the construction site in the company of various palace servants, officials, and

---

[43] *Tabakat*, 517a–518a.
[44] Fleischer, "The Lawgiver as Messiah," 171; also see Necipoğlu, "A Kânûn for the State, a Canon for the Arts."
[45] *Tabakat*, 518a–519a.

scholars. After a group prayer and the ritual butchering of sheep and rams, on the designated hour, the first stone is placed by the chief jurisconsult Ebussu'ud, who would also compose the inscription that still stands over the mosque's portal.[46] The dome of the mosque itself is put into place after years of toil, on August 16, 1556.[47] (The mosque was opened to the public in June 1557). Mustafa's detailed description of the mosque complex, which forms the last pages of his *Tabakat*, is a paean to Ottoman Sunnism and summarizes very well the state of mind of a pious member of the Ottoman elite. He weaves together his admiration of the craftsmanship and the rare materials used in the construction with his emphasis on the function of the mosque as a privileged locus of worship and his focus on the components of the mosque complex as instruments of the sultanic will in catering to the souls and bodies of the Muslim subjects. From its gate inscribed with the Sunni profession of faith to its ornamented Quran copies, from its special platform for the Quran reciters to the big candles and candleholders that facilitate the reading of the Holy Word, the mosque is, for Mustafa, the highest example of devotion to God. The complex itself, in the chancellor's narrative, is a microcosm that reflects the paternalistic relationship between the Ottoman sultan and his subjects.

Mustafa first emphasizes that the complex houses four madrasas and a special institution for the study of Muhammad's sayings (*dārü'l-ḥadīs*). A *dārü'l-ḳırā'at* is also instituted to teach the mosque's reciters the most correct way to read the Quran because, says Mustafa, the sultan is extremely keen on ensuring that the Quran is correctly recited. Next to these learning institutions, the complex includes an elementary school to teach children, particularly orphans, the reading and recitation of the Quran. Other components include a bathhouse (because the cleansing of the human body of its animal essence is a rule of Islam, remarks Mustafa), a soup kitchen, and a guesthouse. Visitors can profit from these services for up to three days; poor students, orphans, and widows are allowed to eat at the soup kitchen. Finally, a hospital serves patients from morning until the afternoon.[48] Both the physical complex and Mustafa's account reflect a holistic look at politics, religion, and everyday life. The mosque is the coronation of Süleyman's achievements, the culmination of a political and cultural project to which Mustafa contributed considerably. It is the

---

[46] For the inscription see Cevdet Çulpan, "İstanbul Süleymaniye Camii Kitabesi," in *Kanuni Armağanı*, 291–99; Imber, *Ebu's-su'ud*, 74–76.

[47] *Tabakat*, 519a–521a.

[48] *Ibid.*, 521a–527a. Cf. Necipoğlu, *The Age of Sinan*, 208–22.

supreme expression of Ottoman imperial Sunnism and constitutes a universe unto itself within which a Muslim individual can learn, pray, clean his body, eat, and receive medical treatment. In this sense, the description of the complex is a suitable final chapter for *Tabakat*. The work opens up with the author's description of springtime and his emphasis on the liveliness and dynamism of Süleyman's first years on the throne. After decades of struggles, when old age strikes, Süleyman, Mustafa, and the Ottoman elite find a convenient refuge in the reassertion, within a sophisticated synthesis, of Sunni Islam and the new empire.

Mustafa retired from his position as chancellor in the fall of 1557. His fellow bureaucrat and historian Mustafa Âli notes that, according to some rumors, Rüstem had promised to appoint his son Mahmud in his place, thus convincing him to retire. Âli, however, ignores the fact that Mustafa's son Mahmud was either a low-ranking secretary of the imperial council at the time or a member of the corps of palace notables (*müteferrika*) and was obviously not qualified for the post of chancellor. Indeed, a career bureaucrat and treasurer, Eğri Abdizade Mehmed Çelebi, became Mustafa's successor. The appreciation given to Mustafa by the sultan was shown by Süleyman's instructions that he keep his actual pay, 300,000 *akçes*, as his retirement stipend. In another sign of sultanic favor, he was made the chief of the corps of palace notables, *müteferrika başı*.[49] The *müteferrika* included retired palace officials as well as sons of high-ranking officials, including the children of the Khan of Crimea. Because they attended the Friday prayer with the sultan and visited him on other ceremonial occasions, this new position continued to give Mustafa access to the palace and the sultan, albeit limited.[50] Even though he probably retired due to his advancing age, Mustafa responded to his retirement by writing a melancholic diptych: '*Aceb mi göklere ağsa fiğānum / Elümdeñ uçdı şāhīn-i nişānum* (Is it any wonder that my lament rises to the skies?/ The hawk of my *nişān* flew from my hand).[51]

---

[49] For the *müteferrika*, see Uzunçarşılı, *Saray Teşkilâtı*, 428–31.

[50] For the details of Mustafa's retirement, see Uzunçarşılı, "Celâl zâde Mustafa ve Salih Çelebiler," 398; *İOTK 2*, 451–52; Yılmaz, "Koca Nişancı," 151–52. Yılmaz (152n450) establishes that Mustafa's retirement stipend was considerably larger than those of other bureaucrats and surpassed those of a few ex-grand viziers. Although Yılmaz gives Mustafa's date of retirement as October 1556, a register (TSMA, D. 10151) listing the members of the *müteferrika* corps for AH 964 (November 4, 1556–October 23, 1557) does not include Mustafa, which points to a retirement date after October 1557.

[51] Mustafa Âli, *Künhü'l-Ahbâr'ın Tezkire Kısmı*, ed. Mustafa İsen (Ankara: Atatürk Kültür, Dil ve Tarih Yüksek Kurumu, 1994), 278.

The End of the Süleymanic Era

Mustafa did not record his immediate reactions to the political developments between 1557 and 1567, even though the composition of his *Tabakat* and *Selimname* was partly influenced, as discussed later, by the war between Selim and Bayezid, the two remaining princes, in the second half of 1558. Already around the rebellion of a pretender in 1555, there were suspicions that Bayezid was preparing to stage a coup and come to the throne. The French envoy de la Vigne reported in 1557 that the situation was exacerbated by Süleyman's ongoing illness and that the viziers were worried about the princes' potential reactions to the situation.[52] Hürrem was the only one able to manage the tensions between her sons and, after she died in May 1558, the last barrier in front of armed confrontation disappeared. In September, Süleyman changed his sons' appointments, ordering Selim from Manisa to Konya and Bayezid from Kütahya to Amasya, further away from Istanbul. This meant that Bayezid lost his advantageous strategic location, because Kütahya is closer to Istanbul than Manisa. Bayezid was reluctant to relocate and wrote to his father, asking for higher stipends for himself and his own men and complaining about the relocation. The period between September 1558 and May 1559 saw Bayezid gathering soldiers and preparing for a final encounter with his brother. On May 30, 1559, around Konya, Bayezid's recruits lost their battle with Selim's forces. The latter included new recruits as well as the men of various governors-general, ordered by Süleyman to help the obedient son against the rebellious one. The sultan himself crossed over to Anatolia on June 5, in anticipation of a campaign against Bayezid.[53]

Bayezid was now faced with the wrath of his father and the disapproval of the military and scholarly establishment. Indeed, Süleyman had obtained fatwas from the chief jurisconsult and had them approved by an impressive number of active and retired judges and scholars, thus creating a powerful legal consensus against his son.[54] Bayezid left Amasya in early July 1559 and reached Qazvin, Tahmasb's new capital city, in October. There is no doubt that the Bayezid incident brought to mind the Alqas

---

[52] *The Papacy and the Levant*, vol. 4, *The Sixteenth Century from Julius III to Pius V* (hereafter *The Papacy and the Levant 4*), 699.

[53] *İOTK* 2, 309–13; Ş. Turan, *Taht Kavgaları*, 50–104; Busbecq, *Les lettres turques*, 228–43.

[54] See Ş. Turan, *Taht Kavgaları*, 180–82.

Mirza affair.[55] Rather than using this opportunity to organize an invasion of Ottoman territory, however, Tahmasb utilized Bayezid as leverage to ensure the continuation of peace between the Ottomans and the Safavids. He was even able to obtain a letter from Prince Selim, the heir apparent, to the effect that the Ottoman–Safavid peace would be observed until the Day of Judgment. The affair finally ended on a violent note in July 1562, with the strangling of Bayezid by an Ottoman executioner working for his brother Selim.[56] These years finally gave Tahmasb the respite he had not been able to find since his coming to the throne as a child. While his chancery issued new decrees about public morality and piety, the Safavid establishment entered a new period of consolidation.[57]

The fight between the princes and Bayezid's captivity in Iran had important repercussions for the empire and for Mustafa. On the international front, as seen in the reports of French diplomats and the writings of Busbecq, the Ottomans were mostly immobilized by the Bayezid affair during a period extending from mid-1558 to mid-1562.[58] It has been argued that the recruitment of armies by the princes allowed individuals and groups outside the Ottoman military class to become acquainted with firearms and military knowhow in general, thus contributing to new levels of banditry. The Ottoman palace began to station janissaries in Anatolian fortresses after the Bayezid affair, and the practice of sending princes out to governorships was limited to the eldest prince.[59] For Mustafa, even though he does not discuss it openly, the Bayezid affair had far-reaching consequences as well. During the period when Bayezid seemed to be a

---

[55] Tahmasb, in his memoirs, discusses the incident in comparison with the Alqas Mirza affair (*Tezkire*, 83–86).

[56] Busbecq, *Les lettres turques*, 260–65, 266–74, 338–43; İOTK 2, 313–18, 322–28; Ş. Turan, *Taht Kavgaları*, 105–36. For the correspondence between the Ottomans and the Safavids, also see Mitchell, *The Practice of Politics*, 125–37; Mitchell, "Am I My Brother's Keeper? Negotiating Corporate Sovereignty and Divine Absolutism in Sixteenth-Century Turco-Iranian Politics," in Mitchell, ed., *New Perspectives on Safavid Iran: Empire and Society* (New York: Routledge, 2011), 41–52. For the transliteration of the correspondence on the basis of an Ottoman collection of miscellany, see İsa Şevik, "Şah Tahmasb (1524–1576) ile Osmanlı Sarayı Arasında Teati Edilen Mektupları İçeren 'Münşe'āt-ı 'Atīk'in Edisyon Kritiği ve Değerlendirilmesi" (MA thesis, Dokuz Eylül Üniversitesi, 2008), 100–223.

[57] Mitchell, *The Practice of Politics*, 105–20; Newman, *Safavid Iran*, 31–32.

[58] For the extreme caution adopted by the Ottoman administrators, see *Négociations* 2: 549–53, 607–08; Busbecq, *Les lettres turques*, 274–75, states that the Ottomans would preserve the status quo in Central Europe as long as Bayezid remained alive.

[59] Ş. Turan, *Taht Kavgaları*, 137–53.

better candidate than Selim for the Ottoman throne, between 1555 and Bayezid's rebellion, Mustafa maintained good relations with the prince. His brother Salih, through Mustafa's intercession, translated a collection of historical anecdotes and moral tales from Persian into Ottoman Turkish for the prince. Salih had been appointed to a teaching post on the request of the prince in late 1558, a short while before the breaking out of the hostilities between the latter and his brother.[60] For these reasons, Mustafa would later feel the need to ingratiate himself with Prince Selim.

The period after 1555 was, compared with the imperialist struggles of the earlier decades, considerably less eventful. Charles V, like Süleyman, had been struggling with various illnesses and had become increasingly withdrawn and melancholic.[61] Spurred by the necessity to secure his son's transition to power, he abdicated on January 16, 1556, leaving the Spanish crown to Philip II (r. 1556–98). His brother Ferdinand, elected King of the Romans already in 1531, was formally given the title of Holy Roman Emperor in a Diet on May 3, 1558, but his territorial possessions and his authority as emperor were considerably less than those of his brother. The tenure of the anti-Habsburg Paul IV between May 1555 and August 1559 disrupted the alliance between the Habsburgs and the Papacy. The Ottomans followed the developments very closely, thanks to the Venetians who supplied them with news.[62] There are signs that they wanted to develop a new policy together with France following Charles' abdication,[63] but were prevented from doing so by the Bayezid affair and developments inside France. Financial problems in Spain, coupled with Protestant activities in both Habsburg and French territory, forced both sides to end the Italian war of 1551–59 with the Treaty of Cateau-Cambrésis. Henri II of France died soon after, in July 1559, and was succeeded by the fifteen-year-old Francis II, who passed away in 1560. The ten-year old Charles IX (r. 1560–74) and his retinue had to concentrate on their own wars of religion at the expense of any pan-European

---

[60] Uzunçarşılı, "Celâl zâde Mustafa ve Salih Çelebiler," 425. Salih frequently corresponded with the prince and members of his retinue and developed a relationship that went beyond simple patronage. See idem., Münşe'āt, 83a–90a.

[61] M.J. Rodríguez-Salgado, The Changing Face of Empire: Charles V, Philip II and Habsburg Authority, 1551–1559 (Cambridge: Cambridge University Press, 1988), 73–77.

[62] The Papacy and the Levant 4, 646–47.

[63] For the frenetic diplomatic activity between the Ottomans and the French see Négociations 2: 374–404, 452–70, 508–29, 541–53, 578–90.

policies and alliances with the Ottomans. Ferdinand, who had been struggling with the Ottomans for nearly forty years, passed away in July 1564,
succeeded by his son Maximilian. Two years before his death, he had
relinquished his rights over Transylvania and signed a six-year truce with
the Ottomans, and Maximilian renewed the treaty upon his accession.[64]
The new session of the Council of Trent, between 1561 and 1564, con-
vened comfortably in the absence of any pressing military threats from
Ottoman forces.

The Ottomans were more active in the sea, defeating the combined
forces of Philip II, Florence, Genoa, and the Hospitallers at Djerba in the
summer of 1560.[65] The Ottoman navy moved against the allies of Philip
II with an ambitious amphibious operation at Malta in May–September
1565 and captured the Genoese-controlled Chios in April 1566.[66] Rüstem
had died in July 1561, succeeded by Semiz Ali; Sokollu Mehmed came to
the empire's highest executive position in June 1565 and would remain
there until his assassination in 1579. Süleyman, old and sick, finally mus-
tered the energy to lead his army in yet another campaign in Central
Europe, in yet another episode of the Habsburg–Ottoman rivalry over
Hungary and Transylvania, a competition that had started as a major
case of imperialist contention but had been transformed into an endless
series of diplomatic negotiations and frontier warfare. The sultan died
there, during the siege of Szigetvar, on the night of September 6/7, 1566.

From Bureaucrat to Historian and Moralist: Mustafa in Retirement

Mustafa spent his retirement in the district of Eyüb, named after one of
Muhammad's earliest supporters, Abu Ayyub al-Ansari, who reputedly
died during the siege of Constantinople by a Muslim army in 674. His
tomb was "discovered" during the Ottoman siege of 1453 as a sign of
divine guidance and support, and a mosque was built soon after in situ.
The neighborhood, situated outside the walls of the old city, expanded
in the second half of the sixteenth century, and many members of the

---

[64] *The Papacy and the Levant* 4, 771, 844; İOTK 2, 328–29. A more detailed account of
this critical decade of transition is Rodríguez-Salgado, *The Changing Face of Empire*.

[65] For the victory at Djerba, see *The Papacy and the Levant* 4, 758–65; İOTK 2, 318–20.

[66] *The Papacy and the Levant* 4, 853–58, provides a very vivid account of the battles in
Malta, whereas İOTK 2, 330–40, gives, as usual, the Ottoman apologetic narrative. For
Chios, see *ibidem.*, 894–99; 340.

Ottoman elite relocated there and built mosques.[67] Mustafa's house over-looked the Golden Horn and was situated farther from the shoreline; it is likely that his was one of the first houses in that particular area, around which a neighborhood developed later. His brother Salih had already retired in 1550 and relocated to Eyüb.[68] The poet and biographer Âşık Çelebi notes that Mustafa had purchased the house of the poet Hayati when the latter became a dervish and decided to live in a dervish lodge, but he does not specify the date of the purchase. However, he says that during his retirement, the chancellor expanded his property and added a garden; he also had a mosque, a dervish lodge for the Halveti order, and a bathhouse built in the vicinity.[69] Mustafa created his oeuvre, so to speak, during this time. Already in 1551–52, while residing in Edirne with the sultan, he had translated Muin al-Din Haravi's (d. 1501–02) Persian Ma'ārij al-nubuvva fī madārij al-futuvva into Ottoman Turkish as Delā'il-i Nübüvvet-i Muḥammedī (Proofs of the Prophecy of Muham-mad, hereafter Delail).[70] Compared with his other works, all of which exhibit an acute attention to the political and cultural issues of the time, Delail appears to have been the outcome of a devotional act: Mustafa wanted to render into a relatively simple Ottoman Turkish, and in a shortened form, a popular work on Muhammad's life.[71]

Mustafa had worked on various independent campaign narratives since the late 1520s, and, in his retirement, he wove them together within a large survey of Süleyman's reign, which became his Tabakat. Mustafa continued to work on this project throughout his retirement. An extant table of contents alludes to an even more ambitious work, a general panorama of the Ottoman imperial edifice that would cover the empire's servants, its administrative divisions, cities, sources of wealth, and so forth, a project that he could not finish. However, thanks to his coverage of Süleyman's reign from its first days to the opening of the Süleymaniye Mosque, he was able to produce a voluminous history on the trajectories

[67] Halil İnalcık, "Istanbul," EI 2. In the neighborhood the chief architect Sinan built mosques for the treasurer Mahmud Çelebi (1541) and Zaloğlu Mahmud Pasha (ca. 1551).

[68] Uzunçarşılı, "Celâl zâde Mustafa ve Salih Çelebiler," 424.

[69] Âşık Çelebi, Meşā'irü'ş-şu'arā, 90b, 135a.

[70] Ms. SK, Fatih 4289.

[71] My interpretation of Mustafa's translation concurs with Gottfried Hagen, "Translations and Translators in a Multilingual Society: A Case Study of Persian-Ottoman Transla-tions, Late Fifteenth to Early Seventeenth Century," Eurasian Studies 2, no. 1 (2003): 95–134.

of Ottoman imperialism, written in a flowery prose and peppered with the chancellor's reminiscences and personal opinions. The second work of history he wrote during his retirement is his *Selimname*, which revisits the life and achievements of Selim I. The chancellor's self-attributed political and cultural mission is obvious in both works. Read together, they tell us how a political enterprise destined to ruin in the careless hands of a frail sultan (Bayezid II), warring princes, and Safavid heretics was rescued by Selim and carried to unprecedented heights by Süleyman. These works also tell us the author's response to the Prince Bayezid affair. *Tabakat* conveniently ends in mid-1557, a short while before the outbreak of the civil war, which would not be a suitable ending for such an auspicious reign. *Selimname*, on the other hand, severely criticizes those who believe that Selim had rebelled against his father Bayezid II (which would constitute a precedent for Prince Bayezid) and tries to prove that Selim was not a rebel.

Another work Mustafa composed during his retirement is a treatise on morals and politics: *Mevāhibu'l-ḥallāḳ fi merātibi'l-aḥlāḳ* (Gifts of the Creator on the Levels of Morality).[72] This is Mustafa's creative and selective rewriting of a Persian treatise, *Akhlāq-i Muḥsini*, by Husayn Vaiz Kashifi (d. 1504–05).[73] The translation is prefaced by a lengthy section on the ninety-nine names of Allah, another sign of the chancellor's Sunni Muslim devotion. Throughout his professional life, Mustafa had to address constantly the nature and function of counsel in the realm's management and had ample opportunities to reflect on the status of secretaries. Just as his works of history represent a particular version of sixteenth-century Ottoman history Mustafa wants to bequeath to posterity, *Mevahib* is meant to represent his political and sociocultural testament. Whereas Kashifi's original is dedicated to the Timurid ruler of Central Asia, Sultan Husayn Bayqara (r. 1469–1507) and follows the conventions of a mirror for princes, Mustafa, in his *Mevahib*, addresses a reading public that consists of fellow literati and secretaries and does not dedicate the work to any prince or ruler.

---

[72] The copy I use is ms. SK, Fatih 3521.

[73] For the Persian original, see Mulla Husayn Vaiz, *Akhlāq-i Muḥsinī* (Lucknow: Tij Kumar, 1972). A partial English translation of this work is *Akhlak-ı Muhsini, or, the Morals of the Beneficient*, translated by Henry George Keene (Hertford: Stephen Austin, 1850). For Kashifi's career and works, see Maria E. Subtelny, "Husayn Va'iz-i Kashifi: Polymath, Popularizer, and Preserver," *IrSt* 36, no. 4 (December 2003): 463–67; for this specific work, see Subtelny, "A Late Medieval Persian Summa on Ethics: Kashifi's Akhlaq-i Muhsini," *ibid.*, 601–14.

The only work Mustafa dedicated to a royal person is his *Cevāhiru'l-ahbār fi hasā'ili'l-ahyār* (Jewels of Reports on the Virtues of the Pious Men, hereafter *Cevahir*). This is a translation from Arabic into Ottoman Turkish of a vita of Prophet Joseph, completed in the spring of 1565 and offered to Prince Selim, the heir apparent.[74] In terms of the structural elements of his translation, Mustafa's endeavor is similar here to his *Delail*. Mustafa shortened the original text, translated some of the prose material in verse and vice versa, and aimed to produce a captivating, easily readable text, which he has succeeded in producing. *Cevahir*'s significance lies in the fact that it represents Mustafa's attempt at currying favor with Selim, probably to ensure his sons' future. In the introduction to the work, Mustafa underlines the importance of the secretaries for the management of the realm, reminds the reader of his long service to the dynasty, and suggests that his loyal service was one of the dynamics behind the glory of Selim I and Süleyman. By offering the prince a work on Joseph, Mustafa implies that, like the prophet, Selim had been the target of brotherly enmity, but was able to emerge victorious from his tribulations. Moreover, the introduction of the work provides clues about the image Mustafa wanted to leave posterity. Here, he informs the reader that he is past seventy years of age, and spends his time by reading the religious works of past and present scholars as well as works of history. Next, he states that he served the Ottoman sultans for more than forty years with his pen. During his service, he never abandoned the Sharia or led to the oppression of the subjects. By his services, he contributed to the perpetuation of Sunni Islam. Thanks to all these efforts, the Ottoman armies were victorious on all fronts and many fortresses and cities were added to the Ottoman realm; moreover, perfect order was established in the land. During his tenure, says Mustafa, he acquainted himself with scholars and knowledgeable men coming from a variety of places, such as Egypt, Syria, Northern Africa, Central Europe, India, Crimea, Iran, and Central Asia. By meeting these individuals, he learned about the affairs of the world; from his conversations with them, he drew many lessons about piety and became a better Muslim.[75]

During his retirement, Mustafa's house became a meeting place for poets and historians, as well as young and aspiring bureaucrats such as

---

[74] Ms. SK, Nuruosmaniye 2356. For the Arabic original, see Siraj al-Din Abi Khafs Umar, *Zahr al-qimam fi qissa Yūsuf ʿalayhi as-salām*, edited by Kamal al-Din Allam (Beirut: Dar al-kutub al-ilmiyya, 2003).

[75] *Cevahir*, 7a–8b.

FIGURE 9. Celalzade Mustafa in his old age (Âşık Çelebi, *Meşā'irü'ş-şu'arā*, Millet Kütüphanesi, Ali Emiri TR 772, 365a).

Mustafa Âli.[76] His already considerable reputation as an accomplished bureaucrat further increased with the composition of the previously mentioned works. Many aspiring literati eagerly anticipated the completion of Mustafa's historical works to gain privileged insight into the inner workings of Süleyman's administration. During his career he had befriended and patronized a considerable number of poets, whom he had first met during İbrahim's grand vizierate, and he continued to receive them in his mansion.[77] Some of the penniless poets were given burial ground in the courtyard of Mustafa's mosque, whereas others, such as the poet and biographer Âşık Çelebi, were given a copy of *Mevahib* to peruse.[78]

[76] See Fleischer, *Mustafa Âli*, 30–31.
[77] Some of these poets such as Kandi and Hayali are named in a register of gifts covering the period from May 1527 to December 1535–January 1536. See İsmail E. Erünsal, "Türk Edebiyatı Tarihinin Arşiv Kaynakları II: Kanunî Sultan Süleyman Devrine Ait Bir İn'âmât Defteri," *Osmanlı Araştırmaları* 4 (1984): 1–17.
[78] Âşık Çelebi, *Meşā'irü'ş-şu'arā*, 135a, 228b.

Qutb al-Din al-Nakhrawali, the envoy of the *sharīf* of Mecca to Istanbul, brought gifts and visited him on several occasions. Mustafa, whom the Arab diplomat describes as a unique historian and stylist and a generous man, gave him some crucial political advice. Before his departure from the capital, he presented the envoy with one hundred gold coins and some fine garments.[79]

Mustafa's years of reading and conversing with the Ottoman literati were interrupted with his second appointment as chancellor during the Szigetvar campaign in the summer of 1566. He had accompanied the sultan as head of the *müteferrika* corps and, as such, was present in the army camp when Süleyman died a few days before the fall of the fortress, on September 6/7, 1566. The passing away of the sultan had to be dissimulated for fear of a mutiny. Because the current chancellor also passed away during the campaign, the grand vizier Sokollu Mehmed appointed Mustafa to the vacant post. The chancellor's appointment was a sultanic prerogative, and Mehmed probably expected to give the impression that the sultan was still alive. Moreover, Mustafa was an ideal administrator to serve the new sultan during his transition period. When he entered the tent of the imperial council to receive his official appointment, Mustafa found out that Süleyman was dead, and he could not suppress his tears. The grand vizier sternly reminded him that the tragic news had to remain secret, and Mustafa left the tent with a contrived smile on his face. This final appointment ended with his own death in October 1567. He was buried in his mosque's courtyard, next to his brother Salih, who had passed away a few years earlier.[80]

---

[79] Richard Blackburn (ed. and trans.), *Journey to the Sublime Porte. The Arabic Memoir of a Sharifian Agent's Diplomatic Mission to the Imperial Court in the Era of Süleyman the Magnificent* (Beirut-Würzburg: Orient-Institut Berlin, Ergon Verlag, 2005), 177, 199–200, 204, 235.

[80] Uzunçarşılı, "Celâl zâde Mustafa ve Salih Çelebiler," 399, 425–26.

PART TWO

NARRATING, IMAGINING, AND MANAGING THE EMPIRE

5

Narrating the Empire

History Writing between Imperial Advocacy and Personal Testimony[1]

History writing preoccupied Ottomans from different social and cultural backgrounds throughout the empire's lifespan, and the product of their labors reached relatively large audiences. After the mid-fifteenth century, and particularly in the first half of the sixteenth century, there emerged an Ottoman "historical culture" that encompassed "habits of thought, languages, and media of communication, and patterns of social convention that embrace[d] elite and popular, narrative and non-narrative modes of discourse" about the distant and near-past of the empire.[2] History writing often dealt with contemporary issues, sometimes obliquely and sometimes quite openly, and thus constituted a privileged instrument for political commentary.[3] This historical culture is visible not only in works of history proper, but also in the increased references to history and

---

[1] This chapter is an expanded version of my "Imperialism, Bureaucratic Consciousness and the Historian's Craft: A Reading of Celālzāde Muṣṭafā's *Ṭabaḳātü'l-Memālik ve Derecātü'l-Mesālik*," in *Writing History at the Ottoman Court: Editing the Past, Fashioning the Future*, eds. Emine Fetvacı and Erdem Çıpa (Bloomington: Indiana University Press, 2013).

[2] Daniel Woolf, *The Social Circulation of the Past. English Historical Culture, 1500–1730* (Oxford: Oxford University Press, 2003), 9.

[3] For assessments that range from the fifteenth to the nineteenth century, see Kafadar, *Between Two Worlds*; Fleischer, *Mustafa Âli*; Gabriel Piterberg, *An Ottoman Tragedy: History and Historiography at Play* (Berkeley: University of California Press, 2003); Virginia Aksan, *An Ottoman Statesman in War and Peace: Ahmed Resmî Efendi 1700–1783* (Leiden: Brill, 1995); and Christoph Neumann, *Das indirekte Argument: ein Plädoyer für die Tanzīmāt vermittels der Historie: die geschichtliche Bedeutung von Aḥmed Cevdet Paşas Ta'rīḫ* (Munster: Lit, 1994).

historical precedent in law, poetry, administrative documents, and political debates.[4]

For the first two centuries of the Ottoman enterprise, the scarcity or irregularity of materials such as the land survey registers, court records (sicil), and chancery documents directed scholars to focus on historical works produced in Ottoman and adjacent territories. Works of history written inside the Ottoman realm by the sultans' subjects, although first produced a century or more after Osman's death (r. 1300?–26), have been studied to explain the "foundation" of an Ottoman "Empire."[5] These chronicle-based inquiries, whose apparent objective was to produce a coherent chronology of events and an exhaustive listing of historical actors, were often marred by their authors' Orientalist or Turkish nationalist mindsets. These mindsets have been the subject of a powerful critique from the 1980s onward. Going beyond the positivism of the earlier generations, the critical scholars have emphasized the narrative aspects of these early works and discussed the creation of a quasi-mythological aura around the early days of the Ottoman dynasty.[6] Thanks to these debates, fifteenth-century Ottoman historiography has remained, for a long time, a popular field of study, which led to the publication of a considerable number of critical editions, albeit of uneven quality. For instance, Âşıkpaşazade's popular Tevārīḫ-i Āl-i ʿOsmān saw many editions in the twentieth and twenty-first centuries. The Anonymous cycle and works by Ruhi, Neşri, Kıvami, and Tursun Bey have been published in critical editions. Even historical miscellany from the fifteenth century immediately attracts attention and is either published or used in analytical studies.

In contrast, sixteenth-century works of history, which range, in terms of the present discussion, from Kemalpaşazade Ahmed's Tevārīḫ-i Āl-i

---

[4] For the functions of history, time, and memory in Ottoman historiography, see Snjezana Buzov, "History," in Key Themes for the Study of Islam, ed. Jamal J. Elias (Oxford: Oneworld, 2010), 191–95, 197–99.

[5] For a thorough summary of the debate's earlier stages and a synthetic approach to early Ottoman sources, see Kafadar, Between Two Worlds. A compilation of articles that reflect various issues and positions of the debate's later phase is Elizabeth Zachariadou, ed., The Ottoman Emirate (1300–1389) (Rethymnon: Crete University Press, 2002). Rudi Paul Lindner's Explorations in Ottoman Prehistory (Ann Arbor: University of Michigan Press, 2007) is the most recent significant contribution.

[6] See Colin Heywood, Writing Ottoman History: Documents and Interpretations (Aldershot: Ashgate Variorum, 2002); Colin Imber, "The Ottoman Dynastic Myth," Turcica 19 (1989): 7–27; "Canon and Apocrypha in Early Ottoman History," in Studies in Ottoman History in Honour of Professor V.L. Ménage, 118–37; "The Legend of Osman Ghazi," in The Ottoman Emirate, 67–75; and Kafadar, Between Two Worlds. A concise account of these historiographical debates is Piterberg, An Ottoman Tragedy, 30–36.

'Osmān to Mustafa Âli's (1541–1600) *Künhü'l-aḫbār* and Selaniki's (d. 1600) *Tārīḫ*, have been overshadowed by the increasingly numerous, regular, and detailed chancery and treasury documents and court records from Süleyman's first decade onward. Positivistic trends in modern historical scholarship, ranging from a Rankean outlook to an Annales-style approach to longue durée economic history, led Ottoman scholars to concentrate on archival documents. Social historians, on the other hand, have found a treasure trove of evidence in the court records and their inscription of power relations at an intimate and immediate level.[7] Sixteenth-century histories have been studied mostly as repositories of chronological evidence or, in the case of illuminated manuscripts, as representatives of period art. The sudden increase in the number of historical works is usually interpreted in the context of an autocratic Ottoman central administration's control over the production of history. As a result, the overwhelming majority of sixteenth-century histories are hastily categorized as official or semiofficial works produced by the members of the ruling elite.

The present reading of Mustafa's corpus is influenced by works on Ottoman historiography as well as the rich literature that is associated with the linguistic turn and the New Historicism. Cemal Kafadar and Cornell Fleischer have already discussed, in the Ottoman case, the relationship between history writing and identity formation, both on individual and communal levels. They have also shown that works cast aside as highly partisan official/court histories or unreliable literary exercises often defy these hasty categorizations.[8] Gabriel Piterberg brought the insights provided by Kafadar and Fleischer together with lessons drawn from an open-minded assessment of debates on literary theory and historiography.[9] The New Historicism's emphasis on texts as interfaces where power relations manifest themselves, and as performative spaces where individuals build forms of social and political power through narrative, is particularly relevant in Mustafa's case.[10]

---

[7] Oktay Özel and Gökhan Çetinsaya, "Türkiye'de Osmanlı Tarihçiliğinin Son Çeyrek Yüzyılı: Bir Bilanço Denemesi," *Toplum ve Bilim* 91 (Winter 2001/2002): 8–38. References to other surveys of the state of the field, past and present, are provided in the article's extensive footnotes and bibliography.

[8] Kafadar, *Between Two Worlds*; Fleischer, *Mustafa Âli*.

[9] For Piterberg's description of Ottoman historiography from its beginnings to the first decades of the seventeenth century, see *An Ottoman Tragedy*, 30–45; for his "interpretive framework" see *ibid.*, 1–6, 50–68.

[10] See Claire Colebrook, *New Literary Histories: New Historicism and Contemporary Criticism* (Manchester: Manchester University Press, 1997); John Brannigan, *New Historicism and Cultural Materialism* (New York: St. Martin's Press, 1998).

Gabrielle M. Spiegel proposes to read texts within the context that produces their narrative, structural, and thematic aspects, rather than as
autonomous artifacts that exist in a phenomenological vacuum.[11] Frank
Ankersmit, on the other hand, reminds scholars to look for "the *juste
milieu* between the extravagances of the literary approach to historical writing and the narrow-mindedness of empiricists."[12] Approaching
Tabakat and *Selimname* as "narratives" produced within a specific historical and cultural context offers new opportunities to address the limitations of both literary extravagance and empiricist narrow-mindedness.
"Narrative" here refers to Hayden White's description, whereby every
narrative "has to do with the topics of law, legality, legitimacy, or,
more generally, authority." White continues by proposing that "[t]he
more historically self-conscious the writer of any form of historiography,
the more the question of the social system and the law that sustains it, the
authority of this law and its justification, and threats to the law occupy his
attention."[13]

Mustafa indeed writes as a deeply self-conscious bureaucrat and historian, and his narrative is meant to propose and protect a particular
social system that consists of the sultan, his associates (the most valuable of whom are, according to Mustafa, the bureaucrats), and a docile
population of tax-payers. The system is underwritten by the authority
of a law that consists of a harmonious synthesis between Sharia and
kanun. The bureaucrat-historian justifies the ruling elite's extraction of
resources and the obedience of the subjects through his insistence that
the sultan provides peace and justice, fights in the name of the empire,
and neutralizes threats to the system. These threats include the Habsburg
dreams of universal monarchy as well as the Safavid "heresy." Ottoman
subjects and officials themselves are under the constant threat of human
fallibility, personal ambition, disloyalty, the absence of piety, or the lack
of reason. Mustafa's works have already served, in this book, as highly

---

[11] I find, like Piterberg, the following essays by Spiegel particularly useful: "History, His-
toricism, and the Social Logic of the Text," in *The Past as Text: The Theory and Practice
of Medieval Historiography* (Baltimore: Johns Hopkins University Press, 1997), 3–28;
"Towards a Theory of the Middle Ground," in *ibid.*, 44–56. Also see idem., ed., see
Practicing History: New Directions in Historical Writing after the Linguistic Turn (New
York: Routledge, 2005).

[12] See Frank N. Ankersmit, "The Linguistic Turn: Literary Theory and Historical Theory," chap. 1 in *Historical Representation* (Stanford: Stanford University Press, 2001),
29–74.

[13] Hayden White, *The Content of the Form: Narrative Discourse and Historical Representation* (Baltimore: Johns Hopkins University Press, 1987), 13.

personal guides into the history of sixteenth-century Ottoman imperialism. In this chapter, they are discussed as multilayered textual reactions to their author's first-hand experience of imperial rivalries and religio-political tensions in early modern Eurasia.[14] *Tabakat* and *Selimname* hail the first half of the sixteenth century as an exceptional period that witnessed the establishment of a veritable "empire," with its distinct institutions, culture, and identity. They thus shift the focus of the debate on the empire's "foundation" from the fourteenth to the sixteenth century. Produced independently, without any direct patronage, they appeal to an elite audience of fellow literati, madrasa graduates, poets, historians, secretaries, and religious scholars, who can both recognize the message of the works and appreciate their literary style. Mustafa's works are representative of thematic, linguistic, political, and cultural trends that fully blossomed in the sixteenth century and are, in this regard, truly "Süleymanic."

Ottoman Historiography in the Sixteenth Century: Tropes and Trends

Ottoman history writing, which emerged in the first decades of the fifteenth century and expanded later on, had always been a conduit for a variety of political opinions. Stories reconstructing the origins of the Ottoman enterprise and describing the tribulations of the Ottoman dynasty often differed in tone and content, in a reflection of their authors' ideological positions and their audiences' needs and expectations. One of the major achievements, on the part of fifteenth-century Ottoman historians, was to promote history writing as the genre par excellence of historical and political debate. They wrote history in a variety of forms that included dynastic *tarih/tevarih*, event-based *fethnames/gazavatnames*, universal histories, and narratives about the reign of a single sultan. These works reflect a rich linguistic variety – Turkish, Arabic, Persian, Greek; works in Ottoman Turkish utilize different registers ranging from the colloquial to the sophisticated chancery prose

---

[14] The close relationship between imperial expansion and the need to produce historical justifications was not limited to the Ottomans. For parallel cases, see Peter A. Perdue, "The Qing Empire in Eurasian Time and Space: Lessons from the Galdan Campaigns," in *The Qing Formation*: 57–91; Arthur H. Williamson, "An Empire to End Empire: The Dynamic of Early Modern British Expansion," *Huntington Library Quarterly*, 68, nos. 1–2 (March 2005): 227–56; Sarah H. Beckjord, *Territories of History: Humanism, Rhetoric, and the Historical Imagination in the Early Chronicles of Spanish America* (University Park, Penn.: Pennsylvania State University Press, 2007).

(*inşa'*).[15] Sixteenth-century Ottoman historians thus inherited a significant number of forms and styles. Although the obsession of fifteenth-century historians with the polity's origins did not completely disappear, primacy was now given to the interpretation of the recent past and the immediate present.[16]

History writing became an especially lively field of political and cultural activity in the first decades of the sixteenth century. Reacting to developments such as Selim's march to power, the Habsburg and Safavid challenges, and Süleyman's military and ideological struggles, Ottoman subjects from different walks of life felt the need to state their positions, assert their identities, gain an audience, curry favor, or circulate criticism through the medium of history, and Süleyman's reign witnessed a "historiographical explosion."[17] This popularity continued to the end of the century and beyond, attracting viziers, poets, secretaries, judges, religious scholars, and others, and leading to the creation of universal histories, dynastic chronicles, accounts of Selim or Süleyman's reigns, and campaign narratives.[18] The majority of this corpus concentrates on either a particular sixteenth-century event or the reigns of Süleyman and Selim. Together with biographical dictionaries, sixteenth-century Ottoman historiography represents an acute realization about the overarching importance of the near-past and the present itself.

[15] The best account on fifteenth-century Ottoman historiography is Kafadar, *Between Two Worlds*, 90–117. For its themes, tropes, genres, and linguistic registers, also see Kaya Şahin, "Âşıkpaşa-zâde as Historian: An Analysis of the Tevârih-i Âl-i Osman [The History of the Ottoman House] of Âşıkpaşa-zâde" (MA thesis, Sabancı University, 2000), 12–31.

[16] For a concise analysis of sixteenth-century Ottoman historiography, see Fleischer, *Mustafa Âli*, 235–45. For a descriptive survey, see Abdülkadir Özcan, "Historiography in the Reign of Süleyman the Magnificent," in *The Ottoman Empire in the Reign of Süleyman the Magnificent*, ed. Tülay Duran (Istanbul: Historical Research Foundation, Istanbul Research Center, 1988), 165–222.

[17] Robert Mantran, "L'historiographie ottomane à l'époque de Soliman le Magnifique", in *Soliman le Magnifique et son temps*, 26–29. Mantran counts seventy-five authors and 119 works for 1520–1570.

[18] This lively panorama is reflected in Franz Babinger, *Die Geschichtsschreiber der Osmanen und ihre Werke* (Leipzig: Otto Harrassowitz, 1927); Bursalı Mehmet Tahir Efendi, *Osmanlı Müellifleri 1299–1915*, ed. İsmail Özen (Istanbul: Meral, 1975); M. Orhan Bayrak, "*Osmanlı Tarihi*" *Yazarları*, expanded second edition (Istanbul: Milenyum, 2002); Erhan Afyoncu, "Osmanlı Siyasî Tarihinin Ana Kaynakları: Kronikler," *Türkiye Araştırmaları Literatür Dergisi* 1, no. 2 (2003): 101–72. These works do not necessarily provide a definitive tabulation of sixteenth-century histories, some of which are still to be discovered and/or reassessed.

The Ottoman palace had been active in the patronage of historical works since the second half of the fifteenth century. With Süleyman's coronation, and especially after İbrahim Pasha's grand vizierate and the formulation of a new ideological agenda, the palace promoted and encouraged the composition and circulation of historical and literary works whose main concern was Süleyman's glory and his reign's exceptionality.[19] The proliferation of chronograms (poems that celebrate particular events and provide their date through the numerical value of the letters in the final verse) and campaign narratives (*fethname*) stem from these efforts and the Ottoman literati's answer to them.[20] The palace's wish to reach out to a wider audience is also illustrated in the emergence of new public ceremonies such as weddings, circumcisions, or the sultan's departures from and arrivals to Istanbul.[21] The composition of meticulous campaign diaries (*ruzname*) and the dispatch of letters to foreign rulers and Ottoman officials after military campaigns (also called *fethname*, these were shorter versions of the previously mentioned campaign narratives) further indicate a desire to create and propagate a historical record of recent events. This does not imply the creation of an "official" history but, rather, the emergence of the palace as an active supporter and consumer of historical writing. The Ottoman palace would eventually begin, later in the sixteenth century, to supervise the creation of historical works on a much larger scale, in the regnal form of *şehname* and *Süleymanname*. However, even in this case, the contents of the works were always negotiated through the respective ideas, convictions, and tastes of various

---

[19] New forms of patronage, authorship, and reading influenced poetic production in this period, and the politically charged atmosphere led to the use of politicized metaphors in poetry. See Walter G. Andrews, "Literary Art of the Golden Age: The Age of Süleymân," in *Süleymân the Second and His Time*, 353–68). For a more detailed analysis of "the voice of power and authority," see Andrews, *Poetry's Voice, Society's Song: Ottoman Lyric Poetry* (Seattle: University of Washington Press, 1985), 89–108. All poetic production was not the result of patronage, obviously. For a discussion of the relative autonomy of literary activity and the increasing levels of linguistic and artistic consciousness, see Sooyong Kim "Minding the Shop: Zati and the Making of Ottoman Poetry in the First Half of the Sixteenth Century" (PhD diss., University of Chicago, 2005), 6–55.

[20] For examples of these campaign narratives, see Özcan, "Historiography," 197–205; on their uses in this particular period, see Yılmaz, "Koca Nişancı," 187–88. For the *fethname* as genre, see Geoffrey Lewis, "The Utility of Ottoman Fethnâmes," in *Historians of the Middle East*, eds. Bernard Lewis and P. M. Holt (London: Oxford University Press, 1962), 192–96; Christine Woodhead, "The Ottoman Gazaname: Stylistic Influences on the Writing of Campaign Narratives," in *The Great Ottoman-Turkish Civilisation*, Vol. 3, *Philosophy, Science and Institutions*, ed. Kemal Çiçek (Ankara: Yeni Türkiye, 2000), 55–60.

[21] Woodhead, "Perspectives on Süleyman," 166–71.

factions around the sultan, which preempted the creation of a single "official" version that would reflect solely the sultan's views, whatever these might be.[22]

Another significant aspect of this period is the production of various works without specific patronage relations and the emergence of the historian as a semi-independent actor. Writing history enabled authors from different backgrounds to participate in debates concerning the nature of the Ottoman polity, the identity of the Ottoman sultan, or the meaning of true religion.[23] A look at the group of works on Selim, gathered under the generic name of *Selimname*s, reveals a variety of authors as well as ideological agendas and demonstrates the existence of an authorial initiative around issues deemed particularly important, such as Selim's accession to the throne.[24] Various phases of the Ottoman–Habsburg and Ottoman–Safavid struggles were similarly central to many historical works. The Safavid problem especially preoccupied many authors because it represented the crystallization of challenges to the Ottoman sultan's authority and the new relationship between religion and politics.[25] Even after the popularization of the political advice book (*nasihatname*) in the last decades of the sixteenth century as the privileged forum of

[22] The classical works for the study of the *şehname* literature are by Christine Woodhead: "An Experiment in Official Historiography: The Post of Şehnameci in the Ottoman Empire, c.1555–1605," *WZKM*, 75 (1983): 157–82; "Reading Ottoman *Şehnames*: Official Historiography in the Late Sixteenth Century," *StIsl*, 104–05 (2007): 67–80. Woodhead's emphasis on the works' official aspects has been shifted toward a multifaceted reading by Emine Fetvacı, "Viziers to Eunuchs: Transitions in Ottoman Manuscript Patronage, 1566–1617" (PhD diss., Harvard University, 2005), particularly 1–24; Fetvacı, "The Office of the Ottoman Court Historian," in *Studies on Istanbul and Beyond*, 7–21. Also see Fatma Sinem Eryılmaz, "The *Shehnameci*s of Sultan Süleyman: 'Arif and Eflatun and Their Dynastic Project" (PhD diss., University of Chicago, 2010); Baki Tezcan, "The Politics of Early Modern Ottoman Historiography," in *Early Modern Ottomans*, 169, 171–80.

[23] For the critical potential of historical works produced in highly politicized urban environments, see Flemming, "Public Opinion under Sultan Süleymân;" Turan, "Voices of Opposition," 23–35. The existence of a new public opinion in the sixteenth century is discussed by Turan, "The Sultan's Favorite," passim; Ralph Hattox, *Coffee and Coffeehouses: The Origins of a Social Beverage in the Medieval Near East* (Seattle, WA: University of Washington Press, 1985); Nelly Hanna, *In Praise of Books: A Cultural History of Cairo's Middle Class, Sixteenth to the Eighteenth Century* (Syracuse, NY: Syracuse University Press, 2003).

[24] A survey of the *Selimname* literature and a discussion of its evaluation in modern historiography is in Çıpa, "The Centrality of the Periphery," 73–127. A list of the existing *Selimname*s is in *ibid.*, 76–78.

[25] Colin Imber, "Ideals and Legitimation in Early Ottoman History," in *Süleyman the Magnificent and His Age*, 147–53; J.R. Walsh, "The Historiography of Ottoman-Safavid Relations in the Sixteenth and Seventeenth Centuries," in *Historians of the Middle East*, 197–211.

political debate, history writing preserved its characteristic as the genre par excellence of historical and political discussion.[26] Secretaries, whose numbers increased, became both producers and consumers of this historical material, but they were joined by many others living around the Ottoman palace, religious scholars, and some members of the urban middle classes.

Biographical dictionaries from the period testify to the rise of new social and professional groups and their level of self-consciousness. As Gabrielle Spiegel states in the case of thirteenth-century French historiography, "social groups most affected by changes in status tend to be the most conscious of alternative modes of discursive behavior, that they are, in other words, most sensitive to the power of language to register social transformations."[27] The new sociocultural groups in the Ottoman case similarly reacted to the realities of the time through texts, among other instruments. Mustafa belongs to a group of bureaucrat-historians whose works display an acute consciousness about bureaucratic function and its relation to historiography. These newly prominent servants of the dynasty believed that they contributed to the making of history through their service; they saw historiography as an extension of their service and as a means to present their own version of Ottoman history. Works by prominent bureaucrats such as Mustafa, Ramazanzade Mehmed (d. 1572), Feridun Ahmed Bey (d. 1583), or Mustafa Âli are far from being official histories. Rather, they reflect a new and self-conscious professional group's notions of history. Another distinguishing characteristic of the group is a close attention to language and style and the desire to promote history writing as both political and cultural statement.[28] Ottoman historical works of the sixteenth century thus bring together an understanding of history as a critical endeavor, a prestigious cultural activity, and a political tool. With his emphasis on the

---

[26] Douglas Howard's study of the Ottoman political advice literature ("Genre and Myth in the Ottoman Advice for Kings Literature," in *Early Modern Ottomans*) shows that there are striking parallels between sixteenth-century works of history and politics written by secretaries: a preoccupation with language (150); an obsession with lists (153, 155–56); an emphasis on order and disorder (161–63).

[27] Spiegel, "Social Change and Literary Language," in *The Past as Text*, 183.

[28] For a discussion on the language of a text as a special idiom, see J.G.A. Pocock, "Texts as Events: Reflections on the History of Political Thought," in *Politics of Discourse: The Literature and History of Seventeenth-Century England*, eds. Kevin Sharpe and Stephen N. Zwicker (Berkeley: University of California Press, 1987), 21–34; "The Concept of a Language and the *métier d'historien*: Some Considerations on Practice," in *The Languages of Political Theory in Early-Modern Europe*, ed. Anthony Pagden (Cambridge: Cambridge University Press, 1987): 19–38. For the nature of this historiographical "statement," see Fleischer, *Mustafa Âli*, 241.

FIGURE 10. The first pages of Celalzade Mustafa's *Ṭabaḳātü'l-memālik ve derecātü'l-mesālik* (ms. SK, Ayasofya 3296, 2a–b).

exceptionality of the period, his conflation of historical idiom and literary language, and his promotion of a bureaucratic mentality in the empire's management, Mustafa was among those who gave history writing one of its major directions in this period. He is indeed one of the architects of what has later been called the empire's "classical age," not only through his bureaucratic function, but also through his idealist historical imagination.

Introducing *Tabakat*

Tabakat is the most detailed historical account of Süleyman's reign written by a contemporary observer.[29] It has been granted an almost canonical status by Ottoman historians of the following generations, as well as

---

[29] For a comparison with Bostan, Matrakçı Nasuh, and a few other near-contemporary works, see *Tabakat*, 26–32; cf. Hüseyin Gazi Yurdaydın, "Bostan'ın Süleymannâmesi," *Belleten* 19, no. 74 (1955): 195–202.

modern scholars of the Ottoman Empire. Mustafa Âli, Peçevi (d. ca. 1649), Solakzade (d. 1657), and Karaçelebizade (d. 1658) extensively use it while narrating the reign of Süleyman and clearly see Mustafa as a prominent cultural figure to be emulated.[30] *Tabakat* is one of the main sources on Süleyman's reign in works as varied as Joseph von Hammer-Purgstall or İsmail Hakkı Uzunçarşılı's general surveys of Ottoman history, İsmail Hami Danişmend's chronological compendium, Fahreddin Kırzıoğlu's work on Ottoman activities in Eastern Anatolia and the Caucasus, and Walter Posch's monograph on the Safavid prince Alqas Mirza's revolt and the ensuing Ottoman campaign in 1548–49.[31]

Tabakat is an unfinished work. It was planned as a general panorama of the Ottoman enterprise, including a description of its administrative and military structure and the realm itself. The version that we have today was initially meant to be the last section (*tabaka*) of a work organized alongside 30 sections and 375 subsections. It starts with a concise treatment of Selim's rule, covers most of Süleyman's reign, and ends, somehow abruptly, with the completion of the Süleymaniye Mosque in 1557. It is written in a language that is often metaphor-laden, rich, and thick, and it reflects Mustafa's conviction that the first half of the sixteenth century represents an unprecedented era in Ottoman history. Accordingly, this era has to be recorded in a language that is worthy of its achievements; moreover, a correct account of it has to be produced and circulated by those few who have access to the inner workings of the Ottoman government. Mustafa follows precise historiographical, cultural, and political agendas to realize these objectives, and the result is a highly stylized, sultan-centric, but also quite personal view of Ottoman history written from the viewpoint of a career bureaucrat.

Mustafa's *Tabakat* strikes its readers, first of all, by its language, which both entices and deters them with its elaborate weaving of Turkish, Arabic, and Persian through the intermediary of the rhyming prose. This language is an outcome of Mustafa's exposure to a variety of texts that include collections of chancery writing, Persian works by Timurid historians, and, most importantly, Kemalpaşazade Ahmed's *Tevārīḫ-i Āl-i 'Osmān* and İdris Bitlisi's dynastic compendium in Persian, *Hasht*

---

[30] *Tabakat*, 32–35.
[31] Joseph von Hammer-Purgstall, *Geschichte des Osmanischen Reiches*, vol. 3, *Vom Regierungsantritte Suleiman des Ersten bis zum Tode Selim's II* (Pest: C. A. Hartleben, 1828); Uzunçarşılı, *Osmanlı Tarihi*, 2; İOTK 2; Kırzıoğlu, *Osmanlı'nın Kafkas Ellerini Fethi*; Posch, "Der Fall Alḳās Mīrzā."

Bahisht (The Eight Paradises, finished ca. 1512).[32] It represents a sophisticated attempt at emulating the linguistic style of revered cultural precedents and, at the same time, superseding them by thoroughly Ottomanizing the Timurid idiom and adapting it to the realities of the sixteenth century. Although *Tabakat* uses three distinct linguistic registers, classified by Petra Kappert as elaborate, middlebrow, and simple,[33] Mustafa's vivid descriptions often project themselves to the fore at the expense of other passages. A typical portrayal of Süleyman, for instance, calls him a sultan whose slaves and soldiers are as numerous as the stars and a world conqueror whose glory is comparable to ancient Persian kings.[34] This triumphalist language, which brings together poetic metaphors, historical themes, and religious references, is also used in developing a discourse of religious and intellectual superiority over the Mamluks, the Hungarians, the Safavids, and the Habsburgs.[35] Mustafa's insistence on developing and utilizing a highly literary language turns his historical production into a veritable work of art that conveys a profoundly aesthetic appraisal of sixteenth-century Ottoman history.

Although *Tabakat* is primarily concerned with Süleyman's rule and image, it is distinguished from most of the contemporary Ottoman historical works by offering its readers a theater-like succession of figures whose lives, personalities, and actions constitute positive and negative moral lessons. "Rebels" such as Janbardi al-Ghazali (d. 1521) and Şehsuvaroğlu Ali Bey (d. 1522), whom Mustafa knew only through official reports or the testimony of others, are described with regard to their poor political judgments, which led to their eventual demise.[36] Others whom he personally knew and respected, such as Kemalpaşazade Ahmed, or the

---

[32] For Bitlisi's importance in Ottoman historiography, see Sara Nur Yıldız, "Persian in the Service of the Sultan: Historical Writing in Persian under the Ottomans during the Fifteenth and Sixteenth Centuries," *Studies on Persianate Societies* 2 (2004): 153–55. Bitlisi's work is the most important conduit between Timurid and Ottoman historiographies. For Timurid historiography, see John E. Woods, "The Rise of Tīmūrid Historiography," *Journal of Near Eastern Studies* 46, no. 2 (April 1987): 81–108. Binbaş, "Sharaf al-Dīn 'Ali Yazdī," 175–220.

[33] *Tabakat*, 36–40. The elaborate register is utilized for describing the sultan, various grandees, and battle scenes. The middle register is used for ceremonies and celebrations, whereas the simple register is for the narration of mundane events such as the march of the campaigning army from one stop to the next.

[34] *Ibid.*, 132a–b.

[35] The Mamluks are presented as oppressors who stray from Islam and commit various sins (*ibid.*, 440b); armor-clad Hungarians are compared to wild animals and are said to be doomed to Hell (47b–48a), etc.

[36] *Ibid.*, 29b–41a passim; 67b–68b.

historian, soldier, and illustrator Matrakçı Nasuh (d. 1564), make brief but powerful appearances.[37] Mustafa's mentor Piri Mehmed, Süleyman's first grand vizier, dominates, together with the sultan, the early chapters of the work. Individuals against whom Mustafa harbors various grudges play negative roles in various dramatic sequences. Ahmed Pasha the "Traitor" (d. 1524), the political nemesis of Piri Mehmed, is portrayed as a veritable *bête noire* who acts out of pure self-interest, disrupts imperial council meetings, and schemes against other viziers.[38] This personal dimension is further enhanced by the narration of events to which Mustafa was privy, such as İbrahim Pasha's (d. 1536) travel to Egypt in 1524–25 or Molla Kabız' trial in 1527 for allegedly preaching Christianity's superiority over Islam. Finally, *Tabakat* is the repository of Mustafa's views on bureaucratic merit, the role of reason (*'akl*) in administration, and personal loyalty. The cultural artifact, which is meant to reflect the sixteenth-century *Zeitgeist*, is at the same time a vessel for Mustafa's selective remembering and creative narration of his personal and professional observations and experiences. This is not an autobiography, but, at times, it reads like Mustafa's memoirs. Defying the received wisdom that the Islamic literary tradition, before the nineteenth century, utterly lacks autobiographical elements, *Tabakat*'s author asserts himself through personal observations on the material landscape, anecdotes, and human portraits.[39]

Beyond the highly personal opinions and values that crisscross the text, Mustafa's endeavor as a historian is in itself impressive. Despite the existence of significant chronological gaps between individual chapters,[40] his methodical use of chronology within chapters, based on various campaign diaries and quite likely his personal notes, provides his readers with a solid temporal structure. He reproduces "documents," such as the diploma, dated 1529, that appointed İbrahim Pasha commander-in-chief and gave him quasi-sultanic prerogatives.[41] The official correspondence

[37] *Ibid.*, 174a–b; 197b–198a.
[38] From his first appearance in 24b to his execution in 115a, he plays an important role in the narrative as the antithesis of Piri Mehmed.
[39] For a discussion of the problem of autobiography and the Islamic written tradition in comparison with Renaissance Europe, see Stephen F. Dale, "Steppe Humanism: The Autobiographical Writings of Zahir al-Din Muhammad Babur, 1483–1530," *IJMES* 22, no. 1 (February 1990): 37–58.
[40] For instance, the narrative jumps from November 1527, the aforementioned "heresy" trial, to April 1529 (İbrahim's appointment as *ser'asker*), and then from November 1543 to the spring of 1548.
[41] *Tabakat*, 179b–182b.

between the Ottomans and the Safavids in the period leading to the accord of Amasya in 1555 is provided in the relevant chapter.[42] Various developments in Hungary, Crimea, and the Mediterranean in the early 1550s are presented on the basis of reports sent by Ottoman administrators and the khan of Crimea.[43] Mustafa's eye for detail is not limited to official matters and diplomatic issues and extends from descriptions of cities and fortresses to Ottoman siege technology and weaponry. The detailed metaphors, the personal opinions and observations, and the various forms of evidence culminate in a powerful, often ceremonious "effect of the Real"[44] that enthralls and at times overwhelms the reader.

Writing and Reading *Tabakat*

Tabakat was a work in progress for most of Mustafa's adult life, and its complex composition process consists of at least three different phases.[45] During the first phase, from the beginning of his secretarial career onward, Mustafa wrote a series of independent, campaign-based narratives. The second phase is represented by his unrealized plans for a structural analysis and definition of the empire as an administrative system and geographical entity. During the third phase, in his retirement, Mustafa edited/rewrote the earlier versions and composed new sections. Each phase is characterized by a different historiographical approach and a variety of political and cultural concerns. Due to its long process of composition and its inclusion of several textual layers, *Tabakat* is a repository of these different notions and approaches.

Four "mental tools," proposed by Elizabeth Clark for an analysis of the Patristic literature, are especially relevant for the present reading of *Tabakat*:

(1) an examination of "authorial function" that calls into question attributions of intention and context; (2) symptomatic and Derridean readings that attend to the gaps, absences, and aporias in texts; (3) ideology critique,

---

[42] *Ibid.*, 459a–460b, 465b–470a.

[43] *Ibid.*, 503b–516b.

[44] The concept was invented by Roland Barthes, who explained it as the creation of a powerful sense of verisimilitude through a concatenation of details. See Elizabeth A. Clark, *History, Theory, Text: Historians and the Linguistic Turn* (Cambridge, MA: Harvard University Press, 2004), 96–97.

[45] The work's structural aspects have been discussed before only by Kappert, in *Tabakat*, 16–26 and passim. My evaluation of *Tabakat* is a dialogue with and an elaboration on Kappert's excellent – and much overlooked – analysis.

especially helpful in unpacking the early Christian writers' representations of various "Others," including women; and (4) postcolonial discourse theory that helps to illuminate the ways in which Christianity and Empire intertwined.[46]

The "authorial function," in *Tabakat*, manifests itself as a bureaucratic view of Ottoman history that promotes bureaucratic ideals and defends the idea of an empire based on merit, law, and Sunni Islam. The historical narrative does not only present events, but narrates them through a moralistic perspective that is based on these larger themes. The most conspicuous absence in the text is the author's failure to recognize Ottoman reversals on the military and ideological fronts. Mustafa's representation of the empire's real or perceived enemies, such as the European Christians, the Mamluks, and the Safavids, produces a strong sense of alterity that is supported through cultural and religious arguments. Within this context, the empire is always intertwined with an overarching religious discourse and is legitimized with reference, variously, to the sultan's identity as a messianic conqueror or the caliph of Sunni Islam.

In his long introduction, composed some time after the 1540s and finished probably during his retirement, Mustafa proposes three historiographical objectives. The first objective is to hail Süleyman's unique and unprecedented achievements. No other ruler has ever conquered so many countries and captured so many fortresses, and, although the task of writing on Süleyman is a very arduous one, Mustafa decided to rise to the challenge.[47] The second objective is to portray the population and the "protected (i.e., Ottoman) realm" (*memālik-i maḥmiyye*) itself: learned men (*fużalā, 'ulemā*), the subject population (*re'āyā, berāyā*), the soldiery (*sipāh ve 'asker*), the fortresses (*ḳılā'*), the lands and regions (*memālik ve eḳālīm*), and the riches, merchandises, gems, possessions, and minerals (*ḥazāin, cihāz, cevāhir, emvāl, ma'ādin*) (i.e., the empire's overall wealth).[48] The third objective is to disclose the truth hidden behind various events of Süleyman's reign. All these objectives are directly related to Mustafa's assessment of previous historians' works: these are said to be similar to each other in content and style (i.e., devoid of originality), they fail to represent the realm itself, and their authors do not have access to the truth of the matter.[49]

---

[46] Clark, *History, Theory, Text*, 170.
[47] *Tabakat*, 7a–b.
[48] *Ibid.*, 9a.
[49] *Ibid.*, 8b–9a, 10a.

The First Objective: In Praise of Süleyman

In his own words, Mustafa first formed the idea of producing a historical record of Süleyman's activities while he was a secretary, before 1525. The first sections of what would become *Tabakat* were composed as individual campaign narratives. In tone and content, these were similar to *fethname*s and *ruzname*s. As chief secretary and then chancellor, Mustafa wrote *fethname*s after campaigns: he composed one each following Süleyman's victory at Mohacs in 1526, the "German" campaign of 1532–33, the "Two Iraqs" campaign of 1534–36, the Karaboğdan campaign of 1538, and the eastern campaign of 1548–49.[50] The corresponding campaign chapters in *Tabakat* rely on these earlier versions but considerably expand them.[51] The *fethname*s are distinguished by their elaborate introductions and conclusions, which praise the sultan in a highly metaphorical language. These texts were then used by Mustafa, as early as the 1530s, as constituent parts of a regnal history-in-progress, a *şehname*. This is shown by an anecdote, added probably during Mustafa's retirement. When he entered Tabriz with the Ottoman army in 1534, Mustafa sought the famous rhetoricians and historians of the city and presented sections of his *şehname* to them, apparently receiving high praises.[52]

In these earlier texts the sultan is the chief, indeed the only, actor in the narrative. Mustafa's claim to authority as a historian rests on his individual participation in the campaigns. Writing *fethname*s was Mustafa's duty, but his subsequent inclusion and reorganization in the form of a *şehname* was his own initiative. It is possible that he was encouraged by the sultan or the viziers. It is also very likely that the ambitious secretary wanted to distinguish himself and follow the ideal of the scholar/secretary as littérateur, an ideal that was represented in the previous generations by figures such as Kemalpaşazade Ahmed or Tacizade Cafer Çelebi.[53] By using the same flowery language in imperial correspondence, peace treaties, *ferman*s, and historical texts, Mustafa,

---

[50] Uzunçarşılı, "Celâl zâde Mustafa ve Salih Çelebiler," 408–09; Yılmaz, "Koca Nişancı," 105, 128; Gökbilgin, "Venedik Devlet Arşivindeki...," 111–13, etc...

[51] Although I see the same links between *fethname*s and some sections of *Tabakat*, I disagree with Yılmaz' argument ("Koca Nişancı," 189–92) that the whole work is an expanded *fethname*, since Mustafa considerably developed these shorter texts and added new chapters and sections.

[52] *Tabakat*, 250b. Distiches by Tabriz literati praising the work are quoted in 251a–b.

[53] On Cafer's life and works, see İsmail E. Erünsal, *The Life and Works of Tâcî-zâde Ca'fer Çelebi, with a critical edition of his Dîvân* (Istanbul: İstanbul Üniversitesi Edebiyat Fakültesi, 1983).

already early in his career, produced and propagated a form of expression that unified bureaucratic practice and history writing.[54] Soon, however, he began to feel the need to expand his vision of empire toward a more structural understanding of the realm. This would not necessarily render the *fethname*s redundant, but would lead Mustafa to conceive a larger and more ambitious historical project.

The Second Objective: The Empire as System

In the late 1530s, Mustafa developed the idea that he could write a panorama of the empire. Sehi Bey, who finished his biographical dictionary around the same time, praises Mustafa for his literary skills and remarks that he is writing a work called *Ṭabaḳātü'l-memālik*; this information is repeated by Latifi, who writes in the late 1540s.[55] These are the first references to the title of the work: *Ṭabaḳātü'l-memālik ve derecātü'l-mesālik* (i.e., the Echelons of the Dominions and the Hierarchies of Professional Paths). The choice of this particular title reflects Mustafa's desire to connect his work with the classical Islamic tradition of *al-mamalik wa al-masalik* (i.e., a geographical description of various realms and destinations/trajectories). In Mustafa's case, however, *memalik* refers to the lands under the control of the Ottoman dynasty, whereas *mesalik* denotes the various professional groups (professional paths) who serve the sultan both in his household and in the provinces of the empire.

The outline of this larger work survives in the form of a table of contents[56] and in a few scattered references. The projected work includes thirty sections and 375 subsections. The first twenty-nine sections describe the empire, whereas the last section is devoted to Süleyman's reign. The first section contains different professional groups whose salaries are paid by the central treasury and who serve the sultan, extending from the food tasters to gardeners and the palace troops. The second section enumerates the different governorates-general (*beylerbeylik*) and the Holy Cities; the third section lists the fortresses of the empire; the following sections are on the auxiliary troops (four and five), the fleet (six), and Istanbul (seven). Sections eight to twenty-nine are individual studies of the twenty *beylerbeylik* and the Holy Cities, and the last section is

---

[54] An analysis of the work's language is found in *Tabakat*, 36–40. For the close relationship between the language of bureaucratic practice and history writing, see Yılmaz, "Koca Nişancı," 174–82; Fleischer, *Mustafa Âli*, 236; Woodhead, "From Scribe to Litterateur."

[55] Sehi, *Teẕkire-yi Sehī* (Istanbul: Matbaa-yı Âmidî, 1907), 33; Latifi, *Teẕkiretü'ş-şuʿarā*, 336.

[56] *Tabakat*, 10b–20a.

about Süleyman's reign. Mustafa's plan is to provide his readers with a panorama of the empire and then explain, in the last section, the political and military processes that produced this panorama. Among these sections, only Mustafa's account of Süleyman's reign survives.

Probably after becoming chancellor, Mustafa developed the idea that an empire is the sum total of its various constituent parts (human, material, physical/geographical) and decided to use his considerable bureaucratic knowledge to describe them. The table of contents reflects Mustafa's desire to represent the world within hierarchically/ organizationally bound, recognizable, and also very bureaucratic categories. This elitist notion stems from the idea that every single part of the empire, from the smallest land grant holding to the corps of falconers in the palace, is tied together within a system in the middle of which sits the sultan, the ultimate lynchpin of a neo-Platonic universe.[57] The second phase of Mustafa's historical thinking represents an important departure from the first one, in the sense that the author's claim to historical authority is now based not only on his experiences as an eyewitness but on his knowledge as a bureaucrat. The main actor of history is not only the sultan, but the empire itself.

The desire to realize this feat survived until the end of Mustafa's life. In a number of manuscripts, reproduced on the basis of an original copy by Mustafa's son Hüseyin, the readers are told immediately after the table of contents that the first twenty-nine sections would have made the book too long and for this reason will be dealt with in another volume, which was never written.[58] While mentioning a plague outbreak in Egypt in 1523, for instance, the author inserts a comment informing his readers that he will provide more details on this event in the appropriate section on Egypt, which would be located in the unfinished part of the work.[59] The sheer size of such a volume would be sufficient to discourage the most zealous historian, of course, and Mustafa probably recognized this himself, especially as he became older and engaged in other writing projects. That he preferred to include the table of contents

---

[57] My understanding of neo-Platonism follows Olivier Leaman's description in *A Brief Introduction to Islamic Philosophy* (Malden, MA: Blackwell, 1999), 5: "[Neoplatonism] does trace the production and reproduction of everything back to a source – and a single source at that – and it establishes a rational structure behind the universe."

[58] *Tabakat*, 22, 46–50 (for a list of manuscripts with this particular information); Victor Ménage, Review of *Tabakat*, BSOAS 47, no. 1 (1984): 156.

[59] *Tabakat*, 109b.

in *Tabakat* nevertheless shows that he believed in the historiographical – and also cultural – value and vision it represented.[60]

The Third Objective: History as Personal Testimony

The third phase of *Tabakat*'s composition started during Mustafa's retirement, and it represents yet another historiographical step forward: the reign of the sultan is now conceived as a process that is not only made up of campaigns, but a series of other events as well.[61] More importantly, this is where Mustafa inserts himself, his own values and perspectives, within the story of Süleyman's reign. In the first two phases, the authority of the historian depends on his gaze as witness and his knowledge as bureaucrat; in the third phase, the historian's memory and personal opinion are introduced. Mustafa still claims the two earlier methods of authority, but actually recreates and thus memorializes the past. As Patrick Geary suggested in the case of medieval Europe around the year 1000, every act of memory has the particular purpose of influencing historical, collective, or group memory.[62] Especially in the hands of someone with Mustafa's career and reputation, the act of memorializing becomes a powerful tool.

An important dimension of Mustafa's work during his retirement is his editing and expansion of previous materials that existed as *fethname*s and *ruzname*s composed by him as well as others. For instance, in his chapter on the capture of Rhodes in 1522, he weaves together the march of the army to southwestern Anatolia under the command of the sultan and the progress of the Ottoman navy (with which he traveled) toward Rhodes, creating a powerful feeling of simultaneity. He adds more depth by inserting the news of a fortress captured from the Hungarians and by describing Ferhad Pasha's near-simultaneous punitive expedition in

---

[60] A similarly ambitious project was realized by the Mughal administrator Abu'l-fazl (1551–1602), a fellow bureaucrat and litterateur and, like Mustafa, very much a product of early modern Eurasian culture. See Abu al-Fazl ibn Mubarak, *The Āʾin-i Akbarī*, vol. 1, trans. H. Blochmann, ed. D.C. Phillott (New Delhi: Oriental Books Reprint Corporation, 1977), vol. 2, trans. H.S. Jarrett, ed. Jadunath Sarkar (Calcutta: Royal Asiatic Society of Bengal, 1949), vol. 3, trans. H.S. Jarrett, ed. Jadunath Sarkar (New Delhi: Oriental Books Reprint Corporation, 1978).

[61] In the introduction to his *Selimname*, a work that he finished toward the end of his life, Mustafa states that he worked on *Tabakat* during his retirement and presents it as a truthful account and detailed panorama of Süleyman's reign (*Selimname*, 23b).

[62] Patrick Geary, *Phantoms of Remembrance. Memory and Oblivion at the End of the First Millennium* (Princeton, NJ: Princeton University Press, 1994), 11–12, 25–26.

central Anatolia against Şehsuvaroğlu Ali Bey.[63] While talking about the Ottoman army's crossing of the Danube toward Moldavia, Mustafa reminds his readers that this is the same river the army had crossed on the way to Vienna in 1529, thus establishing narrative continuity between an earlier chapter and the current one.[64]

This third phase is further characterized by the insertion of highly personal passages into the existing *fethname* structure, transforming the impersonal campaign narratives into a background for Mustafa's opinions on various issues and individuals. In his chapters on the Belgrade (1521) and Rhodes (1522) campaigns, for instance, the driving dynamic of the narrative becomes the enmity between Piri Mehmed and Ahmed Pashas, an issue that could not be covered, for structural as well as political reasons, in a *fethname*.[65] Another typical example is the campaign against the Safavids in 1548–49, organized to put the renegade Safavid prince Alqas Mirza to the Safavid throne.[66] Mustafa presents a detailed historical background of the whole affair, describes Alqas' arrival in the sultan's palace, criticizes the Ottoman viziers for being misled by Alqas' empty promises, and tells anecdotes about God's punishment of those who leave the fold of Sunni Islam. These passages exist side by side with passages that were obviously composed earlier as parts of the campaign narratives, such as an elaborate description of Süleyman's departure from the capital, the visit of the Ottoman princes to the army camp, and the course of the military operations.

Authorial activity is not limited to these editorial additions, however. The composition of chapters focusing on events outside the sultan's campaigns endows *Tabakat* with a historiographical depth, richness of detail, and individual flair. The authorial "I," together with personal comments on events and individuals, gives the whole work an intense personal touch. For instance, Mustafa's accounts of his trip to Egypt in İbrahim Pasha's retinue in 1524–25, rebellions in Anatolia and İbrahim's campaign against the rebels in 1527, or the trial of Molla Kabız (also in 1527) provide the readers with previously uncirculated information.[67] Mustafa narrates these events on his own authority and emphasizes the

---

[63] The march of the army and navy is in *Tabakat*, 69b–84b passim, news from the Hungarian front in 76a–b, and the punitive expedition in 67b–68b, 77a–78a.

[64] *Ibid.*, 308a.

[65] The Belgrade campaign is in *ibid.*, 41a–65a, the pashas' disagreement in the imperial council meeting is in 46a–47a, and the Rhodes campaign is in 65a–104a.

[66] For the account of this campaign, see *ibid.*, 379b–411a.

[67] These accounts are found, respectively, in *ibid.*, 121a–130a; 157b–172a; 172b–175b.

challenges posed by troubles in Egypt, rebellions in Anatolia, or religious dissent in the capital. The dramatic tone of each chapter culminates in a positive denouement, when reason, hard work, careful management, extensive knowledge, and intense piety (represented by İbrahim Pasha and Kemalpaşazade Ahmed) lead to the expected solution. Indeed, the figure of the meritorious administrator who solves problems by the use of his mental faculties is yet another addition that emerges in the third phase of the work. Even though Mustafa does not credit himself with any specific achievements, his message to his readers is quite transparent.

An Unfinished or Interminable Work?

The poets, historians, secretaries, literati, and relatives who flocked to Mustafa's house in his retirement were probably the first readers and discussants of these additions and editions. The existence of three different groups of manuscripts suggests that Mustafa gave the work its final form around 1560. Copies were then produced by his two sons, Hüseyin and Mahmud, around 1560 and 1580, respectively.[68] One feature strikes the reader in this final form, however: although *Tabakat* is meant to be an account of Süleyman's reign, the last section of the extant version is on the building of the Süleymaniye Mosque. This abrupt ending begs a question: if Mustafa could find time to work on various other works during his retirement, why did he not finish his account of Süleyman? Petra Kappert associates this particular ending with Mustafa's belief that the construction of the Süleymaniye constitutes the culmination of Süleyman's reign.[69] Victor Ménage concurs, but finds it interesting that this event more or less coincides with Mustafa's retirement. In case he were dismissed by Rüstem Pasha, as rumor had it, he would prefer not to dwell on the conditions of his dismissal. A convenient ending would save Mustafa from embarrassment and, even more importantly, from the pasha's anger. Ménage points to another embarrassing incident: the fight between princes Bayezid and Selim after 1558, Bayezid's escape to Iran, and his execution there in 1561.[70] As mentioned previously, Mustafa's brother Salih enjoyed Bayezid's patronage, and the Celalzade family might have preferred to remain silent about the affair after the

---

[68] Kappert's discussion and presentation of the three groups is in *Tabakat*, 41–51, and Ménage's discussion is in Review, 156–57. Ménage briefly discusses the editorial strategies of Mustafa's two sons, showing that the personal and highly political nature of the work continued to be a matter of contention after Mustafa's death.

[69] *Tabakat*, 9–10.

[70] Ménage, Review, 156.

prince's execution. Mustafa was retired and had two sons who obviously expected to pursue successful careers, but this depended on the approval of the heir apparent and his entourage. In this environment, the construction of the Süleymaniye is indeed the best ending note for Süleyman's reign, because it saves Mustafa from wading into potentially dangerous waters.

Reassessing Selim: *Selimname* as Mustafa's Final Testimony

Even though they both promote, at first sight, the new Ottoman Empire, *Tabakat* and *Selimname* display several differences that are worthy of discussion. It is true that both works are written in Mustafa's metaphor-laden, flowery language and fit into the category of historical work as artistic achievement. Very much like *Tabakat*, *Selimname* is the product of a bureaucratic mentality that sees history writing as both an integral part of service to the dynasty and the assertion of a professional and cultural identity. In this regard, it is firmly anchored in sixteenth-century Ottoman historiography and the political and cultural debates of the era. Both *Tabakat* and *Selimname* are products of the author's intervention in ongoing debates. The contents of the intervention and the conclusions of the author are, however, quite different in *Selimname*.

The most obvious difference between the two works is the central figure of the narrative. The majority of *Tabakat* is built around Süleyman and his exploits, and Selim's short appearance at the beginning is only meant to reinforce his successor's achievements. *Tabakat* lauds Selim's determination to fight the Safavids, but also refers to his failure to fight against the European Christians.[71] His trade embargo against the Safavids leads to the unjust confiscation of numerous merchants' goods, an injustice that is remedied by Süleyman as soon as he comes to the throne.[72] In *Selimname*, on the other hand, Selim is portrayed as the sultan who saved the Ottoman enterprise from imminent destruction at the hands of a weak sultan (his father Bayezid), inept viziers, warring princes, and pro-Safavid rebels. *Tabakat* presents a plethora of characters next to the sultan and includes entire passages and indeed chapters on the activities of nondynastic actors. In *Selimname*, Selim is always at the center of the narrative. Piri Mehmed is granted a supporting role as a trusted advisor, but, unlike the Belgrade and Rhodes campaigns in *Tabakat*, he

---

[71] *Tabakat*, 24a.
[72] *Ibid.*, 27a–b.

FIGURE 11. The siege of Rhodes (Ârifi, *Süleymānnāme*, TSMK, Hazine 1517, 149a). Celalzade Mustafa's descriptions of battles are similar to miniatures in their concatenation of details.

never comes to the fore. He is mostly utilized as a static figure through whom Mustafa's bureaucratic ideals are promoted. The contrast between good and evil is somehow starker in *Selimname*. Anyone who stands in front of the force of nature that is Selim is crushed and cast aside, and this ruthlessness applies to his own brothers as well as enemy rulers. *Tabakat* is the product of a more analytical, polyvalent, and multi-faceted approach to history writing, whereas *Selimname* displays less variety.

Unlike *Tabakat*, *Selimname* is a finished work, completed during the last years of Mustafa's life. It consists of twenty-three chapters[73] and a long introduction, in which Mustafa engages in fatalist musings on life and death, explains his reasons behind the composition, remembers his first days in Ottoman service, and elaborates on his relationship with and attachment to Selim.[74] The first to twenty-second chapters, the section of the work devoted to Selim's career, open up with a study of Selim's character, proceed with a look into his governorship in Trabzon, provide a concise analysis of the rise of the Safavids and the state of the Ottoman polity at the turn of the sixteenth century, and then focus on the issue of Bayezid's succession and Selim's bid for power. After a concise account of Selim's crossing over to the Crimea, the face-off between him and his father in Çorlu, and his eventual succession to the throne, his struggles with and eventual defeat of his brothers is given extensive treatment in the fourteenth chapter. In general, *Selimname* displays a greater element of linearity compared with *Tabakat*. The account of Selim's political career and reign is provided without too many digressions, within a narrower focus. However, like *Tabakat*, the chapters are not of equal length. In an indication of the author's concerns and priorities, the fourteenth, fifteenth (the campaign against Ismail), and nineteenth (the campaign against the Mamluks) chapters occupy almost half of the text's length.

Another significant difference between the two works is the claim to authority. The historian's authority in *Tabakat* is supported by Mustafa being privy to the inner workings of government and his personal experiences, but he is unable to make such a claim for Selim's life and career. It is true that he was present in the last few years of Selim's reign as a secretary of the imperial council, but he was not present during the most

---

[73] The table of contents is in *Selimname*, 30b–33a. The twenty-third chapter (222a–495a), an independent collection of stories with moral and religious messages, is simply appended to the end of *Selimname*.

[74] The introduction is in *ibid.*, 2a–30b.

critical ventures of the sultan, such as his rush to power or his campaigns against Shah Ismail and the Mamluks. Mustafa's claim to veracity, for *Selimname*, is based on the idea that the secrets of the realm were known only by a select few. In this case, they are represented by two prominent administrators who served Selim in various capacities: Piri Mehmed and Seydi Bey. The authority of his old mentors, both idealized servants of the dynasty, thus helps Mustafa offer his readers a claim of exclusivity similar to the one he proposes for *Tabakat*: the trusted grand vizier and the talented secretary are aware of the secrets of government, but share it only with a select few. Mustafa once again presents his readers the prospect of welcoming them into the most intimate administrative circles. He positions himself as the bridge between Piri Mehmed's legacy and the readers of the late-sixteenth century through his reproduction of anecdotes from the pasha.[75] The pasha's testimonies, as shown by Celia Kerslake, allow Mustafa to include information that is not encountered in other contemporary works.[76]

Whereas the first thirteen chapters of the work have a simpler narrative content and flow, the events of Selim's struggles with his brothers and his reign are treated in a more detailed fashion, and these sections give clues about Mustafa's work as historian. He uses a number of *ruzname*s as well as official correspondence between Selim and other rulers to support his narrative with facts and documents.[77] The literary flavor is provided by Mustafa's lengthy descriptions of battles between the Ottomans and their enemies. The campaigns against Shah Ismail and the Mamluks are typical examples of Mustafa's historiographical approach, which brings together the rigorousness of chronology and official correspondence, the epic poetry of battle scenes, and the intimacy of Piri Mehmed's anecdotes. Despite the uneven quality of its chapters in terms of style and historical scholarship, and despite the existence of a number of factual and chronological mistakes, *Selimname* provides a streamlined narrative

---

[75] Piri Mehmed's testimony is used to report Selim's private conversations (39a–41b), the shortcomings of Bayezid II's viziers (51b–53a), Selim's Machiavellian attempts at tricking his brother Ahmed (94b–96a), troubles encountered during the campaign against Ismail (127a, 139a), or the situation at the Ottoman–Safavid border after the Ottoman conquest of Mamluk lands (208b–212a).

[76] Celia J. Kerslake, "The *Selim-nāme* of Celâlzâde Muṣṭafâ Çelebi as a Historical Source," *Turcica* 9–10, no. 2 (1978): 44.

[77] Kerslake determined (*ibid.*, 50–51), for instance, that the section on the campaign against Ismail (118b–154b) uses two *ruzname*s found in Feridun Bey. She also points out the importance of official correspondence reproduced by Mustafa, some of which exists uniquely in his text.

of Selim's rise to power and introduces the late-sixteenth-century readers and listeners to the issues and problems of a formative period.[78]

Selimname *as Political Intervention*

It has been demonstrated recently that works on Selim's reign, most of which carry the generic title of *Selimname*, represent a distinct corpus within the larger body of sixteenth-century Ottoman historiography. Many of these works share the task of making Selim's tumultuous succession palatable to the Ottoman public.[79] Mustafa's work can also be explained, at least in part, with his wish to leave to posterity an improved image of Selim. His references to previous *Selimname* writers such as Kemalpaşazade Ahmed, Edai, and İdris Bitlisi clearly establish his link with earlier works in the same tradition.[80] However, Mustafa once again endows his work with a highly personal tone and follows particular agendas that are worthy of closer scrutiny.

Mustafa's most apparent reason behind the work's composition is the need to correct information that has been circulating about Selim. Most of this information, according to Mustafa, is based on hearsay, whereas he, thanks to Piri Mehmed and Seydi Bey, has access to information that is known only by the grand vizier and the imperial council secretaries.[81] He then engages in a lengthy diatribe against those who spread lies about Selim's relationship with his father Bayezid and the encounter between the two at Çorlu in 1511.[82] Mustafa insists that Selim did not rebel against his father. His only intention was to visit him and pay obeisance, rather than forcing him to open battle. Mustafa attributes the skirmishes at Çorlu, after which Selim retreated, to the machinations of corrupt courtiers who supported Prince Ahmed for fear of Selim's eventual coronation and their punishment at his hands.[83] Mustafa's negative characterization of

---

[78] The limitations of a positivist approach are seen in Kerslake's otherwise pioneering study. Kerrslake gives herself the task of determining whether Mustafa's claim to provide superior information about Selim has any value, and she concludes by categorizing the work as "deficient or inaccurate in factual detail" ("*Selim-nāme*," 51). Mustafa's claim to truth here is an ideological and political one and has to be interpreted as such, rather than on the basis of his adherence to "fact."

[79] The state of *Selimname* studies is summarized in Çıpa, "The Centrality of the Periphery," 73–76. For a discussion about the treatment of various political issues in *Selimnames*, see *ibid.*, 92–119.

[80] His references to these authors are respectively in 33b–34b and 119b–120a.

[81] *Ibid.*, 24a.

[82] For the Çorlu incident the most up-to-date account is Çıpa, "The Centrality of the Periphery," 49–54. For a comparison of Mustafa's approach to this particular incident with other *Selimnames*, see *ibid.*, 100–106.

[83] *Selimname*, 25a–30b. The incident is then presented in a separate chapter in 76a–79b.

individuals who write and circulate anecdotes on Selim, and his references to the ignorance of the common people about Selim, show that he is concerned about intervening in ongoing debates.

The sense of urgency observed in the introduction of *Selimname* indicates that, beyond correcting the existing *Selimnames*, Mustafa is addressing more immediate issues. Why would it be so important to prove that Selim did not rebel against his father but came to the throne in a legitimate fashion, after gaining his father's acquiescence? An old and ailing sultan, his warring sons, the throne in the balance, tensions between a Bayezid and a Selim: these are tropes that resurfaced in Ottoman history in the late 1550s and early 1560s, with the tensions between princes Selim and Bayezid and the latter's open rebellion. It is quite clear that Mustafa is reacting to the aftermath of the Bayezid incident and the ensuing debates. The Bayezid incident, as suggested previously, already played an important role in the composition of *Tabakat*. Although Mustafa prefers to eschew this embarrassing incident in his account of Süleyman's reign, he returns to it obliquely and emphasizes that there is no precedent in recent history about filial rebellion. *Selimname*, then, is a statement of his support on behalf of Selim II.

Selimname, *Memory, Nostalgia*

The element of nostalgia is quite pervasive and widespread in *Selimname*. The pessimistic musings on the vanity of human life, the nostalgic references to young Mustafa's enthusiastic first days in Ottoman service, the vitriolic comments on Bayezid's corrupt viziers and inept courtiers, and the characterization of Selim's reign as a time of unbridled heroism and unlimited meritocracy not only serve the cause of restituting Selim's place in the Ottoman pantheon, but also represent Mustafa's disenchantment at the end of his life and his discontent with some recent developments, such as the creation of patronage networks under Rüstem Pasha and the relative eclipse of the bureaucratic element. In this sense, Mustafa's *Selimname* is a harbinger of more jaundiced assessments of Süleyman's last years in particular and the Ottoman polity in general. Here, he foretells various criticisms that would become more popular in the following decades, both in history writing and in political treatises.[84]

---

[84] For the uses of Selim's reign (in contrast to Süleyman) as an ideal period, see Cemal Kafadar, "The Myth of the Golden Age: Ottoman Historical Consciousness in the Post-Süleymânic Era," in *Süleyman the Second and His Time*, 46–8 passim. Cf. Christine Woodhead, "Murad III and the Historians: Representations of Ottoman Imperial Authority in Late-16th Century Historiography," in *Legitimizing the Order. The*

Mustafa's nostalgia consists of two aspects. The first one is highly personal and may be related to the state of mind of a pious individual who believes to be near the end of his life.[85] Over the length of several pages, Mustafa admits his sins and asks for forgiveness, considers the impending Day of Judgment, and wishes to pass away after saying the Muslim profession of faith one last time. Religious concerns were always at the fore of his works throughout his life, but this detailed manifestation of his search for atonement is unique. Mustafa also presents his work as an act of gratitude, because he feels indebted to Selim for having supported a youth from a relatively humble background such as himself.[86] He also admits having recently received a sign from Selim's spirit, which further motivated him to compose a work to laud the sultan.[87]

The second aspect of Mustafa's nostalgia is highly political and professional. As a secretary who witnessed the meteoric rise of the Ottoman bureaucratic corps and as a defender of bureaucratic merit, he presents Selim's rocky reign as a perfect era when worthy individuals received suitable positions and unworthy individuals were not allowed into Ottoman service.[88] The *kanun*, the bureaucrats' beloved instrument of justice, was applied spotlessly under Selim.[89] Indeed, victories against the Safavids and the Mamluks were achieved thanks to the presence of a vizier like Piri Mehmed and of a sultan who listened to good advice.[90] In several passages, Mustafa's insistent remarks on bureaucratic efficiency approach the critical tone of the late sixteenth century Ottoman political literature. There too, as shown by Douglas Howard, a group of bureaucrats engaged the challenges of the period through the lens of a small but cohesive professional group.[91] Similarly, Mustafa's *Selimname* is a personal and professional call to grant even more weight to secretaries in the realm's administration and a veiled criticism of the recent failures to do so. Through his re-envisioning of Selim's reign as an ideal period, Mustafa thus makes an unexpected contribution to the critical intellectual environment after 1550. When it comes to assessing the

---

Ottoman Rhetoric of State Power, eds. Hakan T. Karateke and Maurus Reinkowski, (Leiden and Boston: Brill, 2005), especially 86–89.

[85] *Selimname*, 4a–10a passim.

[86] *Ibid.*, 24b–31a.

[87] *Ibid.*, 24b.

[88] *Ibid.*, 21b–22a.

[89] *Ibid.*, 24a.

[90] *Ibid.*, 150b, 169b–171b.

[91] Howard, "Genre and Myth."

developments of the time, even Süleyman's trusted chancellor does not eschew a critical approach and engages in ongoing debates about the nature of the Ottoman enterprise, the Ottoman sultanate, and the best methods to ensure the enterprise's survival and expansion. Mustafa's motivations at the end of his life are best explained in comparison to late-medieval French historians:

> The search for a usable past, capable of redeeming a cause that has been lost, in ideological if not actual political terms, becomes a compelling task for those who feel the need to mask the failure of their enterprise, to dissimulate the malaise that accompanies a fall from social grace, a decline in political authority, and a sense of the irrelevance of values that had guided comportment and identified the once-prestigious possessors of power and authority as central players in the social game. . . . Ideology seeks to revive lost dreams of glory, to vindicate motives, and to mantle the discomfort that the contemplation of unwanted and adverse historical change germinates. Because failure is rooted in historical transformations, it is the past that becomes the repository of those dreams and desires, both because it can offer up a consoling image of what once was and is no longer, and because it contains within it the elements by which to reopen the contest and offer an alternative vision to a now unpalatable present.[92]

---

[92] Gabrielle M. Spiegel, *Romancing the Past: The Rise of Vernacular Prose Historiography in Thirteenth-Century France* (Berkeley: University of California Press, 1993), 1–2.

6

Imagining the Empire

The Sultan, the Realm, the Enemies

The reigns of Selim and Süleyman were instrumental in the creation of a new Ottoman imperialism as an answer to developments in early modern Eurasia. This new imperialism was supported by the mobilization of large military forces and an expanding administrative apparatus that provided the necessary funds for the military ventures, monitored the members of the ruling elite, and supervised the domain. On the cultural front, it led to the formulation of new ideologies and identities, such as claims to universal monarchy and the caliphate, the promotion of Sunni Islam, and the advocacy of bureaucratic merit. Mustafa helped create the new imperial edifice both through his bureaucratic activity and his contributions to the new ideology. His depictions of the sultan in his works of history, which display a striking dynamism and flexibility, are not mere reproductions of a vocabulary that supposedly existed in the Islamic "tradition," but his answers to specific political and ideological issues and contexts. Beyond the sultan, his imperial imagination dwelled on the distinctive characteristics of a newly created imperial space and on the European Christians, the Mamluks, and the Safavids as the "Others" of the Ottomans. Like other early modern imperialisms, the Ottoman variant produced a powerful language of alterity. This language has usually been ignored, because Ottoman expansion has been seen as a more benign phenomenon than the contemporary European subsets. Early modern Ottomans may not have led to catastrophic events such as the infamous germ genocide or the ruthless enslavement of the peoples of the New World, but they could be very intransigent and violent against millenarian rebels and pro-Safavid military and civilian elements. Mustafa's writings allow us to begin discussing the new languages of empire and the rhetorical violence that emerged as a result of the political, military, and ideological struggles of the era.

Changing Images of Süleyman: From Messianic Conqueror to Pious Lawmaker

There is a striking contrast in the representation of the Ottoman sultans in works of history between the fifteenth and sixteenth centuries. Faced with the absence of a prestigious dynastic lineage, fifteenth-century historians emphasized the martial qualities of the sultans, invented lines of descent from Noah or mythical Turkic ancestors, mentioned divine sanction in the form of a dream, and claimed that the last Anatolian Saljuk sultans had left their mantle to the Ottomans. After the conquest of Constantinople, the level of political confidence grew considerably, and titles referring to Ottoman control over the Black Sea, the Mediterranean, Anatolia, and the Balkans, such as *kayser-i Rūm* or *hākānu'l-bahreyn ve sultānu'l-berreyn*, were utilized. Mehmed II's reign also witnessed the emergence of apocalyptic political themes.[1] Under Süleyman, however, the portrayal of the Ottoman sultan entered a new stage.[2] In tune with the struggles of the period, universalist political theologies portrayed the Ottoman sultan on a world-historical scale, battling the forces of evil and claiming supremacy over both Muslims and Christians. After the messianic fervor of the earlier decades abated, the emphasis changed from apocalyptic warfare to a more docile, culturally and religiously conservative discourse on justice and order.

As shown by Greg Walker in the case of Henry VIII,[3] improvisation played an important role in building the image of early modern monarchs. Frances Yates claims that " ... however different in their modes of expression, in their cult of monarchy both the English and the French traditions belong to the same age, in which the Idea of monarchy was a basic theme, and a theme intimately connected with the religious

---

[1] For early Ottoman portrayals of the sultans, see Imber, "The Ottoman Dynastic Myth"; Leslie P. Peirce, *The Imperial Harem: Women and Sovereignty in the Ottoman Empire* (New York: Oxford University Press, 1993), 156–68; Kafadar, *Between Two Worlds*, 60–117, 151–54; Şahin, "Âşıkpaşa-zâde as Historian," 69–116; Şahin, "Constantinople and the End Time"; Murphey, *Exploring Ottoman Sovereignty*, 77–82.

[2] Woodhead, "Perspectives on Süleyman"; Fleischer, "Lawgiver and Messiah"; Necipoğlu, "Süleymân the Magnificent."

[3] Greg Walker, *Persuasive Fictions: Faction, Faith, and Political Culture in the Reign of Henry VIII* (Aldershot: Ashgate, 1996), 21, 72–98.

problems of the age."[4] The image of the monarch became a central tenet of cultural production, and it reached larger audiences through increased literacy, the circulation of images, architectural patronage, and public ceremonies and rituals. Also in this period, the early modern monarchs and their elites instigated a creative rereading of their respective classical legacies. Whereas Elizabeth I presented herself as Astraea and Henri IV as Hercules, Süleyman's image included references to ancient Iranian kings and Alexander the Great. The early modern monarch became the figure around whom the ancient legacies, the new ideas of universal monarchy, the ideals of religious rectitude and salvation, and the search for justice revolved.[5] In the first half of the sixteenth century, specific images of the Ottoman sultan were created and circulated through diplomatic writings, sultanic decrees, and the letters of victory that followed the campaigns. These writings addressed various constituencies, ranging from Habsburg and Safavid diplomats and elites to Ottoman district judges, members of the ruling elite, and, through the public reading of the letters of victory, the subject population. The production of this sultanic idiom relied as much on tropes from the Arabo-Persian literary heritage as on improvisation within specific contexts. Thanks to its incorporation of materials from the 1520s to the 1550s, Mustafa's *Tabakat* is a repository of the new themes.

Süleyman's early years were characterized by intense tensions among the ruling elite. The contours of a relatively consistent ideological program, claiming the sultan's supremacy over both his realm and his own elite, began to appear only after İbrahim became grand vizier. The first written statement of this program was the preamble to the Egyptian law code (1525).[6] Composed by Mustafa under the guidance of Süleyman

---

[4] Yates, *Astraea*, 126. Also see Robert Zaller, *The Discourse of Legitimacy in Early Modern England* (Stanford: Stanford University Press, 2007), especially chap. 1, "The Discourse of Monarchy," 6–50.

[5] For the rich variety of speculations around the figure of the early modern monarch, also see Anne-Marie Lecoq, *François Ier imaginaire: Symbolique et politique à l'aube de la Renaissance française* (Paris: Macula, 1987); Marie Tanner, *The Last Descendant of Aeneas: The Hapsburgs and the Mythic Image of the Emperor* (New Haven: Yale University Press, 1993); Rainer Wohlfeil, "Grafische Bildnisse Karls V. im Dienste von Darstellung und Propaganda," in *Karl V. 1500–1558: neue Perspektiven seiner Herrschaft in Europa und Übersee*, ed. Alfred Kohler et. al. (Vienna: Verlag der Österreichischen Akademie der Wissenschaften, 2002), 21–56; Sylvène Édouard, *L'empire imaginaire de Philippe II: pouvoir des images et discours du pouvoir sous les Habsbourg d'Espagne au XVIe siècle* (Paris: Honoré Champion, 2005).

[6] Although the preamble is not included in *Tabakat*, it is discussed here as the first major ideological statement from Mustafa's pen.

and İbrahim, it is an expression of Süleyman's hopes and expectations early in his career. First, the document accords Süleyman the title of caliph (ḫalīfe). At this stage, the title of caliph implied a unification of spiritual and temporal authority, or a mixture of divine sanction and personal accomplishment, rather than merely the leadership of Sunni Islam, a meaning the Ottoman elite would prefer later in the century.[7] Next, the preamble calls Süleyman ṣāḥib-ḳırān, the conqueror born under an auspicious astrological conjunction and thus destined to rule over the whole world. Because Süleyman had commanded only two campaigns before 1525, and because the title of ṣāḥib-ḳırān was believed to be both inherited and earned, the preamble foresees a period of conquest for the fulfillment of the sultan's destiny. It then develops a messianic dimension and shows Süleyman as ruling over both the temporal and the spiritual realms. This is not the first instance in which claims of messianic leadership are encountered in Ottoman sultanic ideology, but it is indeed the first time when these are couched within a carefully crafted ideological program. Finally, the preamble defines Süleyman's relationship with his subjects through his guarantee of justice ('adl), peace, and the application of sultanic law (ḳānūn). The Ottoman realm itself is promoted as the perfect abode of peace and justice.[8]

The program outlined in the preamble was subsequently tested on the battlefield, in the Hungarian campaign of 1526. Writing after the Ottoman victory, Mustafa emphasizes Süleyman's messianic and prophetic attributes. The sultan is called mehdī-yi āḫiru'z-zamān (the messiah of the End Time) whose reign will last until the Day of Judgment (ilā yevmi'd-dīn) and the renewer of Islam (müceddid). The messiah/renewer is said to emulate Muhammad's temperament, Joseph's beauty, Moses' austerity, and Jesus' personality. He is God's true caliph who rules over East and West and unifies religious and political authority under the mantle of a messianic conqueror.[9] In the next two campaigns against the Habsburgs, the sultan is presented under a similar light, but his mission is reconfigured according to the ideological needs of the time. After the siege of Vienna, Mustafa explains the campaign as a reaction to Archduke Ferdinand's plans over Hungary and his yearning for titles such as ṣāḥib-ḳırān and Caesar (çesār). The 1529 campaign was meant to remind him

---

[7] See Yılmaz, "The Sultan and the Sultanate," 176–91.

[8] For a more detailed discussion of the preamble, see Buzov, "The Lawgiver and His Lawmakers," 29–38.

[9] Tabakat, 132a–138b passim.

that the Ottoman sultan was the only legitimate holder of these univer-salist titles.[10] The "German" (Alaman) campaign of 1532 is presented as a legitimate reaction to Charles V's coronation as Holy Roman Emperor and his claim to have become *ṣāḥib-ḳırān*.[11] Finally, Mustafa positions the Ottoman sultan as the protector of the "community of Muhammad," without specifying whether this refers to the Sunnis.[12] He thus merges an ideological struggle over universal monarchy (he calls Süleyman the ruler of the inhabited world) with the image of a warrior-caliph who relentlessly fights against his Christian enemies.

The portrayal of the sultan changes around the "Two Iraqs" campaign of 1533–36. In this first campaign against the Safavids, the polemic shifts from the identity of the *ṣāḥib-ḳırān* and universal monarch to intra-Islamic debates. Relinquishing the earlier image of the warrior-caliph, Süleyman's caliphate now relies on the restoration of peace and justice in Muslim territories occupied by heretics.[13] Motivated by Safavid claims of *velāyet ve kerāmet* (sanctity and miracles) and the support of the Twelve Imams, Mustafa offers Süleyman as the only ruler to display signs of sanctity and presents his march from Istanbul to the East with such a large army as his miracle. He laments the fact that the Safavids did not face the Ottoman army in open battle; otherwise, he says, the Ottomans would finally prove that they are the true bearers of sainthood and workers of miracles. The conquest of Baghdad and its vicinity is yet another miracle, according to Mustafa, and one of the signs of the End Time.[14]

Following İbrahim's downfall, in an attempt to compensate the mighty grand vizier's absence, Mustafa's descriptions of Süleyman become even more detailed. In the sections of *Tabakat* on the Karaboğdan campaign of 1538, Mustafa spends entire pages describing the visit of foreign envoys to the sultan, the appointment of new governors-general, the inspection of the army, and the sultan's direction of the military campaign. Following victory at Karaboğdan, the defeat of the Holy League fleet by Hayreddin Barbarossa, and Hadım Süleyman Pasha's rout of the Portuguese and cap-ture of Yemeni coastal cities, Mustafa represents Süleyman on the basis of his achievements, rather than his rivalry with the Habsburgs or the

---

[10] *Ibid.*, 183a–183b.
[11] *Ibid.*, 209b–210a.
[12] *Ibid.*, 224b.
[13] *Ibid.*, 259a.
[14] *Ibid.*, 256b–257a; 272b.

Safavids. This is the first instance of the imperial image's maturation: the more speculative messianic/apocalyptic elements begin to recede into the background, and the sultan is described as an established conqueror, rather than a universal monarch in the making. Mustafa now refers to the sultan as the conqueror of Belgrade, Rhodes, and Baghdad, the ruler of Anatolia and the Balkans, the Arab and Iranian lands, Yemen, Hungary, Egypt, the Frankish lands, and the lands to the north of the Black Sea (Deşt-i Kıpçak).[15] After Stefan Lacusta is crowned king of Moldavia by the Ottomans, Mustafa remarks that Süleyman is a mighty emperor who distributes kingdoms and countries to his subjects.[16] He then lists the names of all the lands and cities from which, he says, messengers are sent to the sultan to inform him of the affairs of his realm.[17] Finally, Mustafa includes justice and munificence (ʿadl ve iḥsān) among Süleyman's attributes.[18] Although he mentions Süleyman's justice in several passages of his work, around the Karaboğdan campaign, he turns it into one of his fundamental qualities.

In the campaigns of 1541 and 1543, organized to prevent Hungary from falling into Habsburg hands after John Szapolyai's death, Mustafa recalibrates the speculative aspects of the title of ṣāḥib-ḳırān by dismissing its apocalyptic overtones and defining it as a secular title based on military success. For instance, he states that Charles V claims to be a ṣāḥib-ḳırān in the "Christian lands" and not in the whole world and adds proudly that the Ottoman control of Hungary prevents him from reaching this stature.[19] In 1543, he again calls Süleyman tāc-bahş, a distributor of crowns.[20] Süleyman's reception of a Polish envoy during the campaign is interpreted as yet another sign of his supremacy over other rulers, and Süleyman is qualified as "the abode of kings, the refuge of sultans, the distinguished ruler whose retinue is formed of kings."[21] In the Safavid campaigns of 1548–49 and 1553–55, the image of a world conqueror is supported with an emphasis on Sunni Muslim identity. Mustafa calls Süleyman the sultan of Islam (padişāh-ı İslām) and caliph, emphasizes that he represents the "true Islam" against the Safavid heresy, and prays

[15] *Ibid.*, 291b.
[16] *Ibid.*, 318b.
[17] *Ibid.*, 319a.
[18] *Ibid.*, 291b.
[19] *Ibid.*, 341a.
[20] *Ibid.*, 347b.
[21] *Ibid.*, 364b.

FIGURE 12. Süleyman receives the ancestral crown of Hungary (detail from Ârifi, *Süleymānnāme*, TSMK, Hazine 1517, 309a). The subsequent gift of the "crown of St. Stephen" to John Szapolyai allowed the Ottomans to portray Süleyman as a king of kings.

to God that the sword of the sultan will always be victorious over the Persians.[22] In 1553, he portrays the sultan as the ruler of all the Muslim countries (*"kişver-i İslām'a ve müslimīne ḥāḳān"*).[23] In the correspondence before the Amasya agreement, which Mustafa either conducted in person or supervised closely, Süleyman is clearly identified as the leader and protector of "true" (i.e., Sunni) Islam.[24]

During these last campaigns, Mustafa begins to establish the foundations for a different sultanic image by developing themes such as Süleyman's piety, his submission to God's will (*tevekkül*), and his kindness toward his subjects.[25] In 1549, when the operations cease due to the sultan's sickness, Mustafa uses this hiatus to ruminate on the factors

[22] *Ibid.*, 399a.
[23] *Ibid.*, 434a.
[24] *Ibid.*, 459a–460a.
[25] *Ibid.*, 385a.

behind Süleyman's success. The sultan's conquest of large territories and his accumulation of great wealth are now explained by Süleyman's submission to God's will. Despite his achievements, the sultan, apparently, never became a slave to vanity, followed the path of modesty and gratitude, and strived to apply the precepts of Sunni Islam.[26] His considerable wealth is not for personal consumption, but for distribution to his servants.[27] The sultan's justice, next to his munificence, also becomes an integral part of his image in this later period. Indeed, as Mustafa states, the greatest duty of a sultan-caliph, his duty vis-à-vis God, is to treat his subjects with munificence and justice and to ensure peace and security in the realm. This duty can only be fulfilled through respect for the Sharia and the abrogation of injustice and heresy from the face of the earth.[28] At this juncture, the image of the sultan as the Lawmaker (Ḳānūnī), his epithet in Ottoman historiography, finds its ideal formulation.

A New Realm for a New Empire

How did the Ottomans define themselves and their realm before the sixteenth century? The ebb and flow of Ottoman expansion and retreat delayed the formation of a "metropole" until the second half of the fifteenth century. A "Rumi" or Roman identity had existed among urban Anatolian Muslims from the thirteenth century onward, mostly based on geography, and the *translatio imperii* in the form of the conquest of Constantinople turned the Ottomans into the true inheritors of the Rumi/Roman/Byzantine legacy. In the sixteenth century, a Rumi identity that denoted an Ottoman sense of distinctness came to the fore.[29] The important cultural capital, represented by recently conquered regions such as Syria, Egypt, and Iraq, was subsumed within this new identity, and these regions were seen as constituent parts of a new *memalik* where, ideally, justice, order, and Sunni Islam reigned, non-Muslims were protected,

---

[26] *Ibid.*, 406b.

[27] *Ibid.*, 435b–436a. Cf. with a poem in 475b, on the sultan's munificence.

[28] *Ibid.*, 437b–438a.

[29] Salih Özbaran, *Bir Osmanlı Kimliği: 14.-17. Yüzyıllarda Rûm/Rûmî Aidiyet ve İmgeleri* (Istanbul: Kitap, 2004), 89–108; Cemal Kafadar, "A Rome of One's Own: Reflections on Cultural Geography and Identity in the Lands of Rum," *Muqarnas* 24 (2007): 7–25; Fleischer, *Mustafa Âli*, 253–61. For the emergence of a distinct Ottoman artistic expression in competition with earlier and contemporary traditions, see Gülru Necipoğlu, "From International Timurid to Ottoman: A change of Taste in Sixteenth-Century Ceramic Tiles," *Muqarnas* 7 (1990): 136–170; "Challenging the Past: Sinan and the Competitive Discourse of Early Modern Islamic Architecture," *Muqarnas* 10 (1993): 169–80.

and commerce and learning flourished.[30] To be sure, this perception was mostly limited to the Ottoman elite, the upper crust of the urban populations, and the literati. The new geographical identity was not rigid and exclusivist, and the Ottoman world remained open to cultural change, integration, and transformation.[31] What happened in the sixteenth century was the creation of what might be called a meta-geography that was supposed to coexist with, and somehow prevail over, local and urban identities.

Expressions of this meta-geography are found in Mustafa's writings, together with references to the supremacy of the new realm over others East and West. New ideas of territoriality are necessarily related to new ideas of political and social control, and in Mustafa's mind, the Ottoman realm is the space where Ottoman justice and Ottoman control are exercised.[32] Hence, *memalik*, in Mustafa's work, denotes a bureaucratic, methodical, and encyclopedic understanding of space as a concatenation of administrative units. This space has to be monitored and managed by the sultan and the ruling elite, and its resources extracted, in return for promises of peace and justice. At the same time, the realm itself is a cultural marker and represents the distinctive aspects of the Ottoman polity.[33] This new understanding of space and geography is a result of Mustafa's ideological position as a defender of Ottoman imperialism,

---

[30] For two recent studies on the rise of a distinct geographical knowledge in the sixteenth century, see Kathryn Ann Ebel, "City Views, Imperial Visions: Cartography and the Visual Culture of Urban Space in the Ottoman Empire, 1453–1603" (PhD diss., University of Texas at Austin, 2002); Mevhibe Pınar Emiralioğlu, "Cognizance of the Ottoman World: Visual and Textual Representations in the Sixteenth-Century Ottoman Empire (1514–1596)" (PhD diss., University of Chicago, 2006).

[31] See Faroqhi, *The Ottoman Empire and the World Around It;* Baki Tezcan, "Ethnicity, Race, Religion and Social Class: Ottoman Markers of Difference," in *The Ottoman World*, ed. Christine Woodhead (London: Routledge, 2012): 159–70.

[32] My discussion of Mustafa's notions of territory, territoriality, and space is based on Jeremy Larkins, "Theorizing Territoriality: Discourse, Culture, History," chap. 3 in *From Hierarchy to Anarchy: Territory and Politics before Westphalia* (New York: Palgrave Macmillan, 2010), 35–52.

[33] For a discussion of the relationship between early modern imperialism and new ideas of space, see Bruce McLeod, "Introduction: Productions of Empire," chap. 1 in *The Geography of Empire in English Literature, 1580–1745* (Cambridge: Cambridge University Press, 1999), 1–31; Lesley B. Cormack, "The Fashioning of an Empire: Geography and the State in Elizabethan England," in *Geography and Empire*, eds. Anne Godlewska and Neil Smith (Oxford: Blackwell, 1994): 15–30. The imagination of a new realm as the target of actual and potential political and cultural agendas is also seen in the memoirs of the first Mughal ruler Babur: *Babur-nama*, trans. Annette S. Beveridge (Lahore: Sang-e-Meel Publications, 2002).

but also of his personal experiences as an Ottoman official who traveled widely. He partook in a veritable "Ottoman age of exploration,"[34] which involved the rediscovery and redefinition of large areas in the Middle East and the Balkans.

Istanbul had been a source of pride as well as anxiety for the Ottomans after 1453. Since the day they conquered the city, they grappled with the daunting logistical tasks of repopulating it, securing its provisioning, and then dealing with the ravage of the 1509 earthquake. Culturally, they tried to overcome the tremendous Byzantine legacy, which dominated the cityscape for a very long time, by building their own structures. The mosques, bathhouses, fountains, madrasas, and markets not only signified royal/imperial patronage and served as contact points for the new Muslim inhabitants, but were also meant to give an Ottoman/Muslim character to the city. By the time of Mustafa's retirement, when he finalized *Tabakat*'s table of contents, the city's demographic, architectural, and cultural panorama had been radically transformed, and Mustafa could clearly see the difference between the present city and the one he relocated to in his early twenties. In his *Selimname*, in a long poem that praises Istanbul, he enumerates its wonders, such as the beautiful neighborhoods and squares, the majestic Hagia Sophia, the tomb of Abu Ayyub al-Ansari, the green gardens of Üsküdar, and the "Frankish/European" neighborhood of Galata and finds the city to be superior to Egypt, which is a wondrous realm in its own right.[35] In *Tabakat*, he promises to devote an entire section to Istanbul, divided into twenty-six subsections. These include the mosque complexes bearing the names of the sultans, the palace, fountains and bathhouses, markets, the port and shipyards, the janissary barracks, the arsenal, and, as the symbol of Ottoman/Muslim conquest, landmarks such as the transformed Hagia Sophia and the tomb and mosque complex of Abu Ayyub. The Byzantine past briefly resurfaces in subsections on the Hippodrome and the ancient monuments and buildings. Finally, the list reflects recent urban transformations through its focus on outlying areas such as Fil Çayırı and Kağıthane, the mansions built alongside the Bosphorus, and Üsküdar.

Mustafa's geographical and cultural interests cover the Balkans and the Middle East as well. The table of contents mentions the natural riches of the governorate-general of Rumeli, the towns and fortresses of Bosnia (where, incidentally, he spent his childhood), the city of Edirne and its new

---

[34] This expression is taken from Giancarlo Casale's *Ottoman Age of Exploration*.
[35] *Selimname*, 48a–48b.

(read "Ottoman") buildings. He promises, when he mentions Buda and the empire's Hungarian possessions, that a description of Russia, Poland, Venice, Dubrovnik, and other Frankish countries will be provided. The outline of the section on the Cezayir governorate-general lists the major Ottoman ports as well as the islands of the Mediterranean; the section on Egypt dwells on Cairo, Alexandria, the irrigation systems around the Nile, and the ancient monuments. The Anadolu governorate-general is organized around the city of Bursa, with its mosques and its royal tombs; the governorate-general of Karaman is represented by the city of Konya and the tomb of the great mystic Mevlana Celaleddin Rumi; Aleppo and Damascus are noted as cities worthy of separate subsections. Baghdad is depicted as an ancient capital of sultans and caliphs recently liberated from the Safavids and a center for both Sunni and Shiite devotion thanks to the presence, in its vicinity, of tombs of important religious figures. The table of contents thus merges newly conquered cities and lands together with the older possessions of the Ottoman dynasty in Western Anatolia, and these cities, lands, fortresses, monuments, tombs, and ports come together to form the new Ottoman realm. Outside the table of contents, throughout *Tabakat*, references to the hills and brooks of Austria, the difficult terrain between Smederevo and Belgrade, the desert-like countryside in Western Iran, the beauty of Amasya and its vicinity, or the vagaries of sea travel in the Mediterranean supply a powerful sense of movement through space and personal observation.

The notion of the land of "Rum" is considerably expanded in Mustafa's other works, as seen in a long list compiled toward the end of his life. The list reflects the realities as well as dreams of Ottoman imperialism, as it states that Western Iran, Andalusia, Abyssinia, and parts of India have submitted to the Ottoman sultan. It mentions Mecca and Medina, Cairo and Damascus, Palestine and Aleppo, Yemen and Oman, the northern African coast, islands and fortresses taken from the "Franks," Circassia, Georgia and Azerbaijan, and Kurdistan and Iraq. This new realm is promoted as "the most select part of the inhabited world" (*zübde-yi ma'mūre-yi rub'-i meskūn*).[36] Mustafa further explains his ideas on the prestige and superiority of the Ottoman realm in a long passage in his *Mevahib*,[37] in which he calls the Ottoman lands "Rum" but also, significantly, "*memālik-i 'Osmāniye*," thus utilizing a dynastic epithet rather than a geographical and/or religious one (such as "the land

---

[36] *Cevahir*, 8a–8b.
[37] *Mevahib*, 87b–89a.

of Islam"). The "Ottoman" land is a star-filled sky on which shine all the virtues and perfections (*feżāil ve kemālāta āsumān ve sipihr-i pürencüm*), it is an ocean brimming with the fruits of learning (*bār-ı ma'ārife deryā-yı ḳulzümdür*). Historically, he says, the civilized parts of the world consisted of Syria, Egypt, Iran, Central Asia, India, China, Morocco and Algeria, Iraq, and Armenia. The traditions and customs (*āyīn ve rüsūm*) of these areas, some of which are located outside Rum, are described in ancient history books and are well known by the intelligent and the educated. He then praises the land of Iran as an exemplary center of learning but, he adds, with the recent emergence of heresy (*rafż*) there, its ancient glory completely disappeared. He thus suggests that the land of Rum is the new center of the Arabo-Persian Islamic learning.

Indeed, says the chancellor, whoever looks with a fair eye will admit that the land of Rum has surpassed all these centers of ancient wisdom in science, talent, eloquence, poetry, prose, court culture and military power, morality, patronage, politics, arts and crafts, individual perfection, piety, and good manners. The Ottoman scholars, especially, are at the forefront of this cultural prestige, by virtue of their knowledge in religious matters, and their talent in solving difficult questions, incorporating wisdom with knowledge and illuminating the darkness of ignorance. Next to the scholars, the inhabitants of Rum are said to constitute a supreme example by virtue of their piety. Rum is an abode for wonderful writers, talented astrologers, skilled craftsmen, knowledgeable merchants and farmers, painters and decorative artists, and victorious soldiers and commanders. Perhaps the most important source of Rum's wealth is its incorporation of so many different groups (*ṭavā'if-i mütenevvi'a, ḳabāil-i müte'addide*), so many individuals with different skills.[38]

This crucial passage points to a very important transformation that occurred in the mind of the Ottoman elite around the middle of the sixteenth century. The overwhelming presence of the Arabo-Persian heritage was always a source of aspiration for the Ottomans previously, and they were acutely aware of being on the margins of the Islamic world. They did not have a dynastic legitimacy that went back to one of the illustrious dynasties of the Arabo-Persian sphere, they did not occupy any territories in this realm, they depended on the skills of Arab and Persian scholars to staff their administration and manage their correspondence. The Balkans and Western Anatolia, the real center of Ottoman power,

---

[38] *Ibid.*, passim.

were rich lands, but they had never been a part of the great Islamic empires such the Abbasids or the Great Saljuks. After the conquests of the sixteenth century, this situation began to change, and the Ottomans finally infiltrated the lands of classical Islam. In this initial stage, however, they were merely conquerors, whose martial skills did not lend immediate access to the cultural capital of these lands. One of the main achievements of Süleyman's reign was to create the idea that the Ottomans were not uncouth soldiers but also writers, scholars, merchants, artisans, and farmers who created a rich culture and a solid economy. They were the rightful heirs of classical Islamic civilization, especially because the land of Iran had fallen into the hands of heretics. It is significant that, when he discusses the issue of cultural prestige, Mustafa does not compare the Ottomans with the Habsburgs, even though he often refers to the political competition between the two sides. It appears from the chancellor's writings that he saw the Safavids as the main cultural competitors of the Ottomans over the legacy of the classical Arabo-Persian civilization. Just as Renaissance humanists, Habsburg propagandists, and French literati laid a claim to the heritage of ancient Greece and Rome, the Ottomans and the Safavids were thus both unified and separated by their respective rediscovery, reimagining, and appropriation of their own classical (Islamic) past, a cultural endeavor that was common to all early modern imperialisms.[39]

The Others of the Empire

The Ottomans always had their Others. The first Ottomans usually subscribed to what may be called nomadic pragmatism and welcomed in their midst individuals and groups who shared similar values. Some of Osman's closest companions have Christian names, and some of them probably never converted to Islam. The soldiers of fortune who gathered around the dynasty's founder looked more like a band of warriors seeking

---

[39] Cf. Barbara Fuchs, "Imperium Studies: Theorizing Early Modern Expansion," in *Postcolonial Moves: Medieval through Modern*, eds. Patricia Clare Ingham and Michelle R. Warren (New York: Palgrave Macmillan, 2003), 73: "Through a wealth of artifacts and representations, the myth of *translatio imperii* undergirds much of European imperialism and nation formation in the sixteenth century, whether or not the practice of early modern imperium bears much resemblance to the Roman original. What makes the cultural legacy so particularly fascinating is the extent to which it is contested by nations attempting to distinguish themselves from each other even as they claim the same imperial legacy."

riches than empire builders with a particular political agenda.[40] In this context, the Others of the first Ottomans were the Christian and Muslim townsmen and agriculturalists who suffered the depredations of Osman's warriors. Later in the fourteenth century, and well into the fifteenth, the major rivals of the Ottomans were the Anatolian Turko-Muslim principalities (and especially the Karamanids), the Serbs, the Byzantines, and the Catholic soldiers of fortune and crusaders who roamed the Balkans and the Eastern Mediterranean.[41] Despite intense struggles, the Ottoman dynasty and its military elite maintained close relations with their peers on the other side. Intermarriage at the dynastic level, frequent alliances, and quickly shifting balances of power made communication and a certain level of collaboration necessary. Further expansion and relative consolidation put the Ottomans in touch with better organized enemies and rivals such as the Hungarians, the Akkoyunlus, and the Mamluks around the middle of the fifteenth century. The defeat of these rivals brought the Ottomans face to face with the Habsburgs in Europe and the Safavids in the East. Very much like the Ottomans, both polities had emerged as a result of tremendous political and military upheavals, and both laid claims to universal politico-religious ideologies. It became of elementary importance to produce a concerted political, religious, and cultural reaction to the respective claims of these formidable rivals, and Mustafa was among those who assumed the task.

Early modern imperialisms produced powerful and widespread discourses of alterity. In the words of Sanjay Subrahmanyam, "... almost any process of early modern empire building was also a process of classification, of identifying difference either in order to preserve it ... or in order to further a civilizing mission of acculturation."[42] Large-scale imperial consolidation necessitated the creation and dissemination of ideas about the empire's identity as well as the identity of its rivals and enemies. The notion of alterity has been used by postcolonial critics to describe the

---

[40] Kafadar, *Between Two Worlds;* Lindner, *Nomads and Ottomans in Medieval Anatolia.*

[41] For the portrayal of these rivalries in a seminal fifteenth-century work of history, see Şahin, "Âşıkpaşa-zâde as Historian," 124–36; for the competition between the Ottomans and the Anatolian principalities, see Emecen, *İlk Osmanlılar ve Anadolu Beylikler Dünyası;* Karadeniz, *Anadolu'da Meşruiyet Mücadelesi;* for the struggles in the Balkans, see Halil İnalcık, "Turkish Settlement and Christian Reaction, 1329–1361," "Ottoman Conquests and the Crusade, 1361–1421," "The Struggle for the Balkans, 1421–1451," in *A History of the Crusades,* ed. Kenneth M. Setton, vol. 6, *The Impact of the Crusades on Europe,* eds. Harry W. Hazard and Norman P. Zacour (Madison: The University of Wisconsin Press, 1989), 222–75.

[42] Subrahmanyam, "Connected Histories," 315.

hegemonic relationship that was established, imagined, and codified by the colonizer vis-à-vis the colonized in the early modern and modern periods. Narrative played an important role in creating and diffusing notions of alterity through travelogues, plays, novels, political treatises, and history writing.[43] In Mustafa's case, the historical narrative fulfills a similar function. His "rhetorical outbursts" about the Mamluks, the European Christians, or the Safavids do not only serve the purpose of propaganda, but also provide clues about the chancellor's ideas on what he saw as his own social and cultural identity and the challenges and dangers that threatened it in the form of war, rebellion, or alternative religious beliefs and political ideals.[44] Mustafa does not talk about the newly conquered territories as colonies in the European sense and assumes that their inhabitants will become Ottoman subjects through the application of law. It is also true, however, that he writes about military conquest and expansion and legitimizes them with reference to various ideological and political arguments, among which notions of alterity/otherness occupy an important place.

The Mamluks of Egypt: The Anti-Ottomans?

When a man named Osman gathered a band of followers and began to organize raids, the Mamluks were the most prestigious and powerful Muslim political entity in the Middle East. Murad I (r. 1359/60–89) and Bayezid I (r. 1389–1402) actively sought Mamluk help against the threat of Timur, and Bayezid, according to Mamluk sources, at least symbolically presented himself as a servant of the Mamluk sultan Barquq (r. 1382–89, 1390–99).[45] Only Bayezid II addressed the Mamluk sultan as his equal, during the last decades of the fifteenth century. The same period also witnessed the first Ottoman–Mamluk war, between 1485 and 1491, and Ottoman reversals in the southeast.[46] Following the end of hostilities, the Ottomans helped the Mamluks defend themselves against

---

[43] Monika Fludernik, "Identity/Alterity," in *The Cambridge Companion to Narrative*, ed. David Herman (Cambridge: Cambridge University Press, 2007), 260–73.

[44] For similar "rhetorical outbursts," in Renaissance France, under the pressure of external and internal threats and the motivation of new ideas on alterity, see Timothy Hampton, *Literature and the Nation in the Sixteenth Century: Inventing Renaissance France* (Ithaca: Cornell University Press, 2001).

[45] Anne F. Broadbridge, *Kingship and Ideology in the Islamic and Mongol Worlds* (Cambridge: Cambridge University Press, 2008), 172–73, 175, 186.

[46] Emire Cihan Muslu, "Ottoman-Mamluk Relations: Diplomacy and Perceptions" (PhD diss., Harvard University, 2007), 87–140; Shai Har-El, *Struggle for Domination in the Middle East: The Ottoman-Mamluk War, 1485–91* (Leiden: Brill, 1995).

Portuguese incursions in the Red Sea by sending experienced mariners and necessary materials. Selim's obliteration of the once-mighty Mamluks, in whose capital the last descendant of the Abbasid caliphs lived, was a cataclysmic event, and Mustafa and his contemporaries strived to explain it. In his *Selimname*, Mustafa provides the classical pro-Ottoman version of the events. Accordingly, after Ismail's defeat by Selim in 1514, the shah sent a letter to Qansuh al-Ghawri, the Mamluk sultan, to ask for help. By agreeing to assist the Safavids, the Mamluks thus partook in their heresy. The Ottomans had to take military measures against the Mamluks, who had already proven, by their attacks during the reign of Bayezid II, that they coveted Ottoman lands.[47] In the spring of 1516, Selim sent letters to the Mamluk sultan to seek his help against the Safavids, but, says Mustafa, the Ottoman envoys were given a cold reception. Selim then asked religious scholars for legal opinions to support his impending attack. Mustafa quotes a legal opinion by Kemalpaşazade Ahmed, which describes the Mamluks as *kuttā'-i tarīk*, "highway robbers," and portrays them as a barrier in front of the Ottoman struggle against heresy.[48]

Through a dialogue between Selim and Piri Mehmed, Mustafa provides another reason for the Ottoman invasion, one that reflects his ideas about justice and the caliphate as the attributes of the Ottoman sultanate. Speaking to the pasha, Selim declares that he is revolted by the servitude of the illustrious Arab lands in the hands of a group of Circassian slaves, referring to the slave backgrounds of the Mamluk ruling class.[49] Selim claims that these individuals are Muslim in appearance only and that to be able to face God and Muhammad without embarrassment on the Day of Judgment, he has to liberate the Arab lands from their injustice and oppression.[50] Mustafa repeats a similar argument when he narrates

---

[47] *Selimname*, 168b–169a.

[48] For the correspondence, see *ibid.*, 174b–178b; for the legal opinion, see 180b–181a. Highway robbery is defined in the Sharia as a crime that requires the direct intervention of the leader of the Muslim community, thus giving the Ottomans an additional reason next to their fight against heresy.

[49] The Mamluks were self-conscious about their slave origins, which were questioned by the Ilkhans and Timur before the Ottomans. As Broadbridge (*Kingship and Ideology*, 16) shows, Mamluk sources focus on the dynasty's military achievements and its services to Muslims to evade the question of their origins.

[50] *Selimname*, 170a. Mustafa calls Selim's army "*'asker-i İslām*" (i.e., the army of Islam). The idea that the Mamluks lost their mandate of rule is mirrored in early Ottoman law codes for the ex-Mamluk areas: Abou-El-Haj, "Aspects of the Legitimization of Ottoman Rule."

Süleyman's stay in Aleppo in the winter of 1553–54. While in Aleppo, the sultan orders a revision of taxes and fees and listens to the grievances of the city dwellers, which gives Mustafa the occasion to compare the Mamluks and the Ottomans. Since the coming of Muhammad, he says, the Arab lands suffered under the rule of a series of tyrants. The Mamluks were especially infamous for their injustices and sins. Indeed, this is the reason why they were punished by God (i.e., were defeated by the Ottomans), whereas Süleyman is careful in preventing the smallest error and sin in his realm.[51] Here too, the Ottomans are promoted as the worthy rulers of an ancient Muslim territory (i.e., the Arab lands), thanks to their justice and good government.

In tune with his gentlemanly ideals, Mustafa portrays the Mamluks as culturally inferior. He often calls them mean (*ḫasīs*) and wicked (*ḫabīs*) and refers to them as the inauspicious/barren Circassians (*Çerākise-yi nāḫise*), the despicable band (*ṭā'ife-yi meẕmūme*), and the vile Circassians (*Çerkes-i nā-kes*).[52] His portrayal of Janbardi al-Ghazali becomes a conduit for the assertion of his own bureaucratic identity within the Ottoman establishment. Because he could not directly criticize Ottoman military administrators, most of whom came from slave backgrounds, Mustafa turns Janbardi into the prototype of an uncultivated military man, a strong-willed but uneducated fighter whose unbridled passions and absence of reason push him into impossible ventures. His speech and appearance prove that he is a base Circassian, his slavish disposition is a servant of envy and jealousy (for political power, that is), but he does not have the necessary knowledge and wisdom.[53] Next, Mustafa attacks the Mamluk system of succession, which was based on an ideal of elective kingship that made all members of the Mamluk military aristocracy eligible. He believes that this practice over-politicized the Mamluk aristocracy, whose members ignored the affairs of the realm and instead engaged in political intrigue. He interprets this as yet another sign of their ignorance (*cehl*). The Mamluks were able to control Cairo and the Holy Cities and establish a mighty kingdom, but, in the absence of a just administration, they incurred the wrath of God and were replaced by the Ottomans.[54] The Mamluks are, in a sense, the anti-Ottomans in the chancellor's idealized scheme of politics. His implication is clear: because

---

[51] *Tabakat*, 440a–b.
[52] Eg. *ibid.*, 22a, 35a, etc.
[53] *Ibid.*, 29a–30b.
[54] *Ibid.*, 104a–b.

it is based on justice, a careful distribution of political and military power, dynastic rule, and a wise and knowledgeable corps of bureaucrats, the Ottoman polity will not suffer the same fate.

The Christians of Europe: Between Prejudice and Pragmatism

The status of the Ottoman non-Muslims was defined by their subjection to a "contract" that guaranteed their well-being. In return, non-Muslim subjects paid a poll tax that symbolized their subjection; other than the poll tax, they faced a variety of barriers in the public sphere.[55] In his works, Mustafa does not necessarily distinguish between Muslim and non-Muslim subjects. In his *Mevahib*, an Ottoman subject is defined according to political and economical principles rather than religious affiliation. On the other hand, the Christians of Europe, the "Franks," as he calls them, play an important role in his historical narrative. Mustafa was a very pious individual, for whom the commandments of God and the principles of Sunni Islam circumscribed every aspect of life. His religiosity, like many of his fellow Ottomans, consisted of a variety of layers, individual as well as political, scholarly as well as popular. On an individual basis, especially late in his life, he was very much concerned with sin and redemption. On the political level, he interpreted *ghaza* both as a religious duty for the sultan and individual Muslims and as a powerful political and military instrument. For instance, after he conquers Belgrade, the sultan is said to have expanded the lands of Islam, defeated the proponents of unbelief/Christianity, and comforted the souls of his ancestors.[56] Moreover, because his sultanate had been given by God, it was his duty to engage in Holy War.[57]

The propagandistic dimension of fights against the European Christians is illustrated by Mustafa's vivid descriptions of battles between the Ottomans and various Christian forces. He utilizes his considerable rhetorical abilities and talks about how the sleeping swords wake up and

---

[55] There is a considerable literature on the place of the non-Muslims in Ottoman society. For a representative compilation, see Benjamin Braude and Bernard Lewis (eds.), *Christians and Jews in the Ottoman Empire*, vol. 1, *The Central Lands*, vol. 2, *The Arabic-Speaking Lands* (New York: Holmes & Meier, 1982); also see Bruce Masters, *Christians and Jews in the Ottoman Arab World: The Roots of Sectarianism* (New York: Cambridge University Press, 2001). For the imperial management of diversity see Karen Barkey, *Empire of Difference: The Ottomans in Comparative Perspective* (Cambridge: Cambridge University Press, 2008).

[56] *Tabakat*, 63a.

[57] Ibid., 65a–b.

put on red garments made of enemy blood, how the weapons are ine-
briated after drinking the wine of the enemy's soul, or how the spears
and lances, once young and straight, fold from the middle like old men
when they enter the bodies of the unbelievers. The soldiers of various
European powers are singled out as debased individuals whose unbelief
manifests itself in their repulsive physique.[58] The battlefield is likened to
a scene from the Day of Judgment where Muslims strive to reach salvation, or to a courthouse where Muslims and Christians adjudicate their
enmity, with the swords assuming the role of judges.[59] Another favorite
trope of Mustafa is the story of the Abyssinian army in the Quran, in
the Surat al-Fil. According to the story, an Abyssinian force planned to
attack Mecca in the days before Islam. However, before reaching Mecca,
the army, fortified with war elephants, was decimated by a flock of swifts
($tuy\bar{u}r$-$\imath$ $eb\bar{a}b\bar{\imath}l$) dropping pebbles from their beaks. In his account of the
naval Battle of Prevesa, Mustafa compares Ottoman cannonballs to the
swifts' pebbles.[60] He often comforts his readers by emphasizing that
the Ottoman dead are martyrs destined to heaven.[61] During their battles,
the Ottomans constantly benefit from the support of God and Muhammad and from the intercession of the angels and the hidden saints.[62] For
instance, Mustafa reports, on the testimony of dervishes who accompanied the army, that Muhammad, his companions, and the hidden saints
fought in the Ottoman ranks at the Battle of Mohacs.[63] The Christians fail
to realize that the Ottoman soldiers will not be stopped by any fortresses
or weapons, as they benefit from the Prophet's intercession.[64]

These enthusiastic passages often hide the fact that Mustafa was a careful observer of European politics and distinguished between European
political actors beyond a generalized anti-Christian paradigm. Although
he uses the trope of Holy War to explain Süleyman's campaign against
the Hospitallers of Rhodes, for instance, he also discusses the strategic
reasons behind the campaign.[65] He carefully monitors Habsburg policies in Europe and often meditates on the ideological dimension of the

---

[58] *Ibid.*, 47b–48a, 146a–149a passim.
[59] *Ibid.*, 233a.
[60] *Ibid.*, 325b.
[61] See for instance, *ibid.*, 92a.
[62] For a typical example of this rhetoric of predestination to victory and divine intercession, see *ibid.*, 282a.
[63] *Ibid.*, 150a.
[64] *Ibid.*, 419a.
[65] *Ibid.*, 66a.

Ottoman-Habsburg rivalry.[66] In a concise analysis of Venice's position in Europe in 1540, he soberly informs his readers about the wealth of the Venetians, the extent of their political power and the expanse of their dominions and cities, their skills in navigation, and, finally, their ambiguous diplomatic position between the Europeans and the Ottomans.[67] When he mentions Ottoman allies such as John Szapolyai and the kings of France, his anti-Christian rhetoric leaves its place to restrained praise. He calls Szapolyai a friend of the holy warriors (*mücāhid*)[68] and praises Francis I for his large dominions, his wealth, and his army, saying that the heroic exploits of his soldiers made Christianity proud.[69] Although he objects to Charles V's use of imperial titles, he nevertheless admits that he is a powerful ruler and the master of many realms.[70] In another passage, he states that he does not have any qualms about becoming friends with Christian powers, as long as these submit to the Ottoman sultan and act in accordance with the sultan's wishes.[71] This more appreciative rhetoric is also seen in the Ottoman diplomatic correspondence of the period, which was to a large extent composed or directed by Mustafa. In his case, the need to entertain a nascent Ottoman public opinion with stories of heroic feats does not preclude the political-bureaucratic necessity of assessing the European political situation with a realistic eye. Despite the bitter tone of the Ottoman–Habsburg ideological competition, European Christians, as the followers of a religion that was supposedly superseded by Islam, do not present a cultural challenge as powerful as the Safavids, whose millenarian ideology and later Twelver Shiism offered powerful intra-Islam critiques of Ottoman Sunnism.

The Safavids: The Power of Intra-Islamic Controversies

Throughout the sixteenth century, the Ottomans and the Safavids profoundly influenced each other's political, religious, and cultural discourse as well as institution building in ways that have not yet been fully acknowledged. The Ottoman and Safavid pasts have played an important role in the self-definition of the Turkish and Iranian nation states in the twentieth century. In both cases, an initial period of emphasis on secularism and on ancient Turkish and Persian history was followed by a focus

---

[66] *Ibid.*, 183b, 209b–210a, 341a–b.
[67] *Ibid.*, 284b.
[68] *Ibid.*, 202a.
[69] *Ibid.*, 215a.
[70] *Ibid.*, 480b.
[71] *Ibid.*, 218a.

FIGURE 13. Süleyman visits the shrine of Husayn. Husayn is revered as the third imam by most Shiites and respected as Muhammad's grandson by Sunnis (*Hünernāme*, vol. 2, TSMK, Hazine 1524, 40a).

on the Ottoman and Safavid Empires as the precursors of the modern nation states. In Turkey, with the decrease of radical Kemalist secularism and the spread of populist and conservative ideologies inspired by Islam, politicians and historians turned to a positive assessment of the Ottoman Empire as a Turkish and Sunni Muslim polity. The adherents of this paradigm portrayed anti-Safavid Ottoman policies as an act of defense against the encroachments of a renegade polity, using a typically Cold War language that stigmatized individuals and groups seen as "rebels," be they Safavids, Armenians, Kurds, or leftists.[72] In Iran, following the Islamic Revolution, the Safavid Empire became the historical founder of the righteous path (i.e., Twelver Shiism) and the heroic fighter against foreign encroachments by the Ottomans, the Portuguese, and the Uzbeks.[73] These respective positions created the fiction of essential, fundamental, and timeless Sunni and Shiite identities and precluded the possibility of any discussion about their historical and constructed natures.

The Ottoman–Safavid conflict, with its complex structure of political, military, religious, and cultural rivalry, is one of the nodal points of early modern Eurasian history because it is a crystallization of the variety of challenges and tensions that characterize this crucial era. Revisiting Mustafa's views about the Safavids shows that an elite Sunni identity, as a combination of religious discourse and political/diplomatic argument, was created in the first half of the sixteenth century to a large extent under the impact of the Safavid challenge. Although the reactions of Ottoman scholars to the Safavid challenge have been studied to a certain extent,[74] Mustafa's writings show that historiography played an important role in the "definition of doctrine" by supporting religious arguments with cultural and political ones.[75] Initially, the ideological competition

---

[72] See, in addition to Kılıç and Kırzıoğlu, Bekir Kütükoğlu, *Osmanlı-İran Siyasi Münasebetleri* (Istanbul: Edebiyat Fakültesi, 1962); Mehmet Saray, *Türk-İran Münasebetlerinde Şiiliğin Rolü* (Ankara: Türk Kültürünü Araştırma Enstitüsü, 1990); Saray, *Türk-İran İlişkileri* (Ankara: Atatürk Araştırma Merkezi, 1999).

[73] See Camron Michael Amin, "*Mujassama-i bud mujassama-i nabud*: The Image of the Safavids in 20th Century Iranian Popular Historiography," in *History and Historiography of Post-Mongol Central Asia and the Middle East: Studies in Honor of John E. Woods*, eds. Judith Pfeiffer and Sholeh A. Quinn (Wiesbaden: Otto Harrassowitz, 2006): 343–59.

[74] See Üstün, "Heresy and Legitimacy;" Elke Eberhard, *Osmanische Polemik gegen die Safawiden im 16. Jahrhundert nach arabischen Handschriften* (Freiburg: Klaus Schwarz, 1970).

[75] I borrow the concept from Daniel Eppley, *Defending Royal Supremacy and Discerning God's Will in Tudor England* (Aldershot: Ashgate, 2007), esp. 5–18.

was profoundly influenced by messianic and apocalyptic ideas that circulated in the Islamic world and the Mediterranean basin in the fifteenth and sixteenth centuries. These eventually revolved into more conservative Sunni and Twelver Shiite positions. In this sense, the Amasya settlement was about ending the state of constant war but also about institutionalizing doctrinal positions while tacitly acknowledging the other side.

Is it possible to claim that the Ottomans and the Safavids contributed to the "confessionalization" of Sunni and Shiite Islam?[76] Using this concept helps bring together a variety of issues that have been discussed separately or ignored altogether, such as the new symbiotic relationship between religion and politics in both empires, the organization of religious establishments in light of the empires' ideological necessities, the growth of external and internal propaganda that reasserted religious principles and moral norms, a new emphasis on ritual and the political supervision of the individual subjects' compliance, and, finally, the territorial demarcation of respective beliefs.[77] Talking about confessionalization opens new vistas for comparative religious history, which is necessary to further specify the particularities of the Catholic/Protestant and Sunni/Shiite experiences.[78] At the same time, the concept presents a variety of challenges for historians of Islamic societies. First of all, it has

---

[76] For discussions of the concept's usefulness in the Ottoman case, see Krstić, *Contested Conversions;* Nikolay Antov, "Imperial Expansion, Colonization, and Conversion to Islam in the Islamic World's 'Wild West:' The Formation of the Muslim Community in Ottoman Deliorman (N.E. Balkans), 15th-16th cc." (PhD diss., University of Chicago, 2011), 171–74. My understanding of the concept is based on Wolfgang Reinhard, "Zwang zur Konfessionalisierung? Prolegomena zu einer Theorie des konfessionellen Zeitalters," *Zeitschrift für historische Forschung* 10 (1983): 257–77; Heinz Schilling, "Confessionalization: Historical and Scholarly Perspectives of a Comparative and Interdisciplinary Paradigm," in *Confessionalization in Europe, 1555–1700. Essays in Honor and Memory of Bodo Nischan*, eds. John M. Headley et. al. (Aldershot: Ashgate, 2004), 21–35; Thomas A. Brady, Jr., "Confessionalization-The Career of a Concept," in *ibid.*, 1–20; R. Po-Chia Hsia, *Social Discipline in the Reformation: Central Europe 1550–1750* (London: Routledge, 1989); Susan R. Boettcher, "Confessionalization : Reformation, Religion, Absolutism, Modernity," *History Compass* 2, no. 1 (2004): 1–10; Alfons Brüning, "Confessionalization in the *Slavia Orthodoxa* (Belorussia, Ukraine, Russia)? – Potential and Limits of a Western Historiographical Concept," in *Religion and the Conceptual Boundary in Central and Eastern Europe: Encounters of Faiths*, ed. Thomas Bremer (Basingstoke, Hampshire: Palgrave Macmillan, 2008), 66–97.

[77] Antov, "Imperial Expansion," 174–83. It is worth noting that the change in the notions of Muslim religious identity also led to a reassertion of the Muslim/non-Muslim difference within the empire (*ibid.*, 173; Kafadar, "A Rome of One's Own").

[78] Schilling, "Confessionalization," 27.

been used so exclusively to discuss the Protestant Reformation and the Catholic Counter-Reformation that, like the Renaissance and the Enlightenment, it automatically refers to a Eurocentric approach. Moreover, an institution such as the Catholic Church, a major political and religious actor, did not exist in the Ottoman case, even though the new symbiosis between the political authorities and the religious scholars, the development of the madrasa system, and new technologies of governance and control allowed the Ottoman political center unprecedented advantages in the production, dissemination, and supervision of religio-political doctrines. The Shiite Safavid clergy was somehow similar to the Catholic clergy in terms of hierarchical organization and the claim to hold the ultimate truth, but, at least in the sixteenth century, it did not have the power and resources of the Catholic Church. Finally, the discussion on confessionalization emphasizes education and social disciplining through education (especially elementary education), whereas the Ottoman and Safavid Empires did not have the vision, or the resources, or both, to create a widespread system of elementary education that is seen, for instance, in the early modern German principalities.

Thomas Kaufmann's warning against the risk of overstressing the uniformity of rival confessions and his emphasis on mutual exchange and plurality are particularly important in the Ottoman–Safavid case.[79] The elites, on both sides, continued to refer to the legacy of the Perso-Islamic tradition, despite the more frequent use of Ottoman Turkish in the sixteenth century.[80] Bi- or trilingualism (knowledge of Ottoman Turkish, Arabic, and Persian) was frequent, and the conflict itself contributed to intellectual curiosity on both sides. The sheer geographical scope of the empires made the imposition of a single confession logistically difficult. Moreover, although the number of Sunnis in Safavid territories continued to diminish under forced conversion or simple cultural accommodation, sizeable communities belonging to various proto-Shiite and Shiite denominations lived in Ottoman territories. This necessitated a level of "administrative pragmatism" that often ran counter to the diatribes produced in

---

[79] Thomas Kaufmann, "La culture confessionnelle luthérienne de la première modernité. Remarques de méthode," *Études Germaniques* 57, no. 3 (2002): 421–39.

[80] For the circulation of manuscripts between the two sides, see Filiz Çağman and Zeren Tanındı, "Remarks on Some Manuscripts from the Topkapı Palace Treasury in the Context of Ottoman-Safavid Relations," *Muqarnas* 13 (1996): 132–148. A plethora of beliefs, superstitions, myths, and tropes were shared on a more popular level, as discussed by John Perry, "Cultural Currents in the Turco-Persian World of Safavid and Post-Safavid Times," in *New Perspectives on Safavid Iran*, 84–96.

Istanbul by the likes of Mustafa.[81] At the same time, however, Mustafa, together with other historians, scholars, and literati, engaged in a conscious and relatively organized attempt to define and promote the correct version of Islam (Sunni Islam, in this particular case) and denounce deviations from it. The persecution of non-Sunnis was not systematic, but the association of the empire and its ruling class with Sunni Islam was to be a long-lasting legacy of the sixteenth century. This politico-religious doctrine and elite culture eventually trickled down to create less official and more devotional forms of Ottoman Sunnism.[82] Mustafa and his generation thus played an important role in the introductory stages of a wave of confessionalization or a politicized Sunnism which, born from the struggles of a particular age, would become essentialized and de-historicized in the next centuries.

An anti-Safavid idiom had been developing since the early sixteenth century, but it found its most elaborate expression in Mustafa.[83] Throughout *Tabakat*, he treats the Safavids as a perverted group, a band of rebels and mischief makers.[84] The battles between the Ottomans and the Safavids are characterized as struggles between the defenders and detractors of Sunni Islam, between a divinely supported group and a community of sinners. Whereas he usually refers to Christians as infidels, Mustafa's anti-Safavid epithets are more specific. Safavids create divisions within the Muslim community (*fitne*), preach what may be translated as heresy or deviance (*ilḥād*),[85] obliterate the legal schools of thought and indeed religion itself, and propagate the refusal of the true faith (*mezāhib-ḥırāş . . . dīn-tırāş ve rafż-fāş*). Mustafa goes so far as to call them a community without a religion (*bī-dīn*).[86] He states, for instance, that they do not pray in mosques and do not pay the customary Muslim alms.[87] He thus deploys a custom-built Sunni rhetoric, also witnessed in the trial of Molla Kabız, but conspicuously absent in the previous centuries.

---

[81] See Stefan Winter, "Shiism in the Ottoman Empire: Between Confessional Ambiguity and Administrative Pragmatism," chap. 1 in *The Shiites of Lebanon under Ottoman Rule, 1516–1788* (Cambridge: Cambridge University Press, 2010), 7–30.

[82] Derin Terzioğlu, "How to Conceptualize Ottoman Sunnitization: A Historiographical Discussion" (conference presentation, Boğaziçi University, 14 December 2011).

[83] For earlier forms of an anti-Safavid Ottoman rhetoric found in histories, see Emecen, "'Şark Meselesi'nin Ortaya Çıkışı."

[84] *Tabakat*, 21b.

[85] For the historical development and Ottoman usage of this critical term, see Ocak, *Zındıklar ve Mülhidler*, 1–15 passim.

[86] Eg. *Tabakat*, 273a, 295b, 381a.

[87] *Ibid.*, 250b.

These ideas are then applied to the battlefield. Mustafa presents
Ottoman attacks against the Safavids as *ghaza*. He insists that it is not
a sin to kill those who wear the red headgear (*kızılbāş*), that it is the
duty of the Ottoman sultan, as the protector of Sharia and the representative of true religion, to punish heretics. He portrays the Ottoman
conquest of lands from the Safavids as liberation and restitution to their
rightful owners. Just as he argues, in the case of the Mamluks, that
their injustices voided their sovereignty over the Arab lands, the Safavid
heresy supposedly destroys any claims of the shah to rule over the old
cities of Islamic civilization. This is apparent in the chancellor's narrative of İbrahim Pasha's capture of Tabriz in 1534. This beautiful city,
famous for its gardens, the civility of its population, and the learning
of its scholars, had become a center of heresy and a source of evil and
sedition. The occupiers of the city had instituted a new religion and abandoned the commandments of Islam, whereas the Ottomans restored the
"ancient Muhammadan/Sunni tradition" ('*ādet-i maḥmūde-yi kadīme*).[88]
Baghdad, says the chancellor, had been a center of Muslim kings and
caliphs, but had fallen into the hands of the religion-abrogating, heresy-
preaching *kızılbāş*, who turned it into a center of injustice and evil. The
Ottoman sultan, the protector of Sharia (*şeri'at-penāh*) and the defender
of justice, liberated the city with his victorious sword.[89] On a more secular level, Mustafa constantly interprets the Safavid hit-and-run tactics as
a sign of cowardice. During the campaign of 1547–48, for instance, after
noting that Safavid raiders killed the livestock they were not able to carry
away, he wryly remarks that slaughtering sheep and cattle is their true
military skill.[90]

Ottoman–Safavid polemics reached a turning point in 1555. The correspondence of 1554–55, in which Mustafa played a crucial role, illustrates the respective Ottoman and Safavid positions on doctrinal issues.
In a letter from July 1554, after the customary invitation to battle, the
Ottomans reiterate the famous fatwa issued by Kemalpaşazade Ahmed
around 1513.[91] In another letter to Tahmasb, signed by the Ottoman
viziers, the Safavids are accused of ignoring daily prayers, eschewing
the Friday prayer, and abandoning the Sharia. The "Safavid creed" is

---

[88] *Ibid.*, 250a, 274b.
[89] *Ibid.*, 19b.
[90] *Ibid.*, 393b.
[91] *Ibid.*, 459a–460b. For the legal opinion, see Üstün, "Heresy and Legitimacy," 49–59. It
states, most notably, that because the Safavids abandoned Islam and entered the path of
unbelief, killing and expropriating them is permissible.

described as a fifty-year old invention, whereas true (i.e., Sunni) Islam has existed for 961 years.[92] In yet another missive to the shah, signed by the governor-general of Erzurum, the Safavid practice of cursing the first three Sunni caliphs is denounced.[93] The Safavid answer on the eve of Amasya denies the Ottoman accusations of infidelity (küfr), because Safavids worship Allah and praise Muhammad. Quoting verses from the Quran, they argue that the killers of fellow Muslims are doomed to hell. In an important missive called the "belt letter" by Colin Mitchell (because Tahmasb talks about his faith as girding the belt of love for Ali), the Safavids compare their struggles with the Ottomans with the fights between the Umayyad oppressors and the supporters of Ali and present their realm as the protected abode of Shiism. Mirroring the aggressive language of the Ottomans, the Safavids accuse the first three Sunni caliphs of usurping Ali's legitimate right to leadership and call Istanbul the abode of infidelity.[94]

This aggressive tone eventually changed into a more conciliatory one, and a peace settlement was reached between the two sides. Mustafa's reactions to the settlement reveal his ambiguity about the Safavid problem. On the one hand, he laments the destructions of war and welcomes the cessation of the hostilities. He accepts Tahmasb as the ruler of the East (Şāh-ı Şarḳ), rather than the leader of a band of cowardly heretics. As a sign of his individual dissatisfaction, however, he interrupts the historical account and begins narrating anti-Shiite anecdotes. In the first anecdote, a man who converts to Shia from Sunna is punished by none other than Ali himself for his disrespect against the first three caliphs. In the second anecdote, the corpses of Shiites killed by a Sunni, as punishment for their disrespect of the first three caliphs, are transformed into pig carcasses. The third anecdote narrates an encounter between French and Safavid diplomats in the imperial council. The French envoy expresses his surprise at the inconsistency between the Shiites' reverence for Muhammad and their reviling of some of his companions and further illustrates his point by claiming that Christians respect all of Jesus' apostles. When İbrahim Pasha has this exchange translated for the Safavid envoy, the latter, says Mustafa, is embarrassed and reluctantly states that only ignoramuses among the Safavids make such claims.[95] Thus,

[92] Tabakat, 467a–468b.
[93] Ibid., 469a–470a.
[94] Mitchell, The Practice of Politics, 81–87.
[95] Tabakat, 488a–491a.

although a settlement is finally reached with the Safavids, the chancellor feels the need to assert the irreconcilable differences between the two sides. Even though the Ottoman–Safavid frontier is finally peaceful, the frontier in the chancellor's mind is still a scene of confrontation and conflict.

7

Managing the Empire

Institutionalization and Bureaucratic Consciousness

During Mustafa's lifetime, early modern Eurasia witnessed the development of new overland and overseas channels of commercial and intellectual exchange that connected various parts of this geographical, economic, and cultural zone. The complex imperialist rivalries among the Ottomans, the Habsburgs, the Safavids, the Portuguese, the Mughals, the French, the Venetians, and various other actors led, among other things, to the emergence of more centralized administrations, better organized armies, more efficient fiscal institutions, and new ideologies focusing on monarchic and dynastic ideals, confessional problems, and the role of law and legality. Newly conquered territories needed to be controlled, elites needed to be co-opted and managed, records needed to be kept, and instruments of legitimacy (diplomatic correspondence, histories, political treatises) needed to be created. Secretaries were promoted, mostly from the lower ranks of elites and nobilities, to assist the monarchs in these complex tasks.

This was the time when the fiction of an absolute monarch being served by selfless secretaries was created and displayed to the benefit of centralizing tendencies.[1] The administrative centralization was never complete, and secretaries never overcame members of the better entrenched and more numerous groups such as the aristocracy and the clergy or, in the Ottoman case, the military administrators, the janissaries, and the scholars. However, they were able to create a bureaucratic esprit de

---

[1] By fiction I mean both a "conceptual abstraction" and a "narrative." See Dorrit Cohn, *The Distinction of Fiction* (Baltimore: The Johns Hopkins University Press, 1999), 2.

corps and formulate an ideology based on raison d'état, which would be successfully manipulated in the following centuries to defend nascent nation states. In terms of state/empire formation, the creation of new loci for political power, and the forging of ideas of governance based on reason, efficiency, merit, and law, the sixteenth century represents a crucial period of transition in world history. Mustafa's life and career may help us better explain the Ottoman case and, by extension, the modalities of state/empire formation in early modern Eurasia.

New Men in Ottoman Service: The Rise of the Secretaries

Although many scholars have argued that an orderly administrative apparatus reflecting a Near Eastern or Turkish political culture existed since the first days of the Ottoman polity, early Ottoman administrative practices mostly consisted of temporary pragmatic arrangements.[2] The sultans' secretaries, in the fourteenth and fifteenth centuries, came from a variety of ethnic, linguistic, religious, and cultural backgrounds. Men with a madrasa education served various Anatolian principalities, and some of them offered their services to Ottoman rulers. They were joined by educated individuals from other parts of the Islamic world. Ottoman rulers eagerly sought the services of learned men who could provide a crucial know-how in managing the affairs of the swiftly expanding Ottoman enterprise.[3] These migrant scholars were sometimes met with suspicion by the representatives of the so-called ghazi-dervish milieus, because they were seen as the instigators of oppressive practices such as over-taxation and the increase of sultanic power. Acrimonious references to the "Persian scholars" (i.e., learned man from the East) are often encountered in fifteenth-century Ottoman histories.[4]

Secretaries came from other backgrounds as well. In the words of Joel Shinder, the Ottomans "pursued an articulated policy which employed

[2] See Joel Shinder, "Early Ottoman Administration in the Wilderness: Some Limits on Comparison," *IJMES* 9, no. 4 (November 1978): 497–517.

[3] Cornell H. Fleischer, "Scribal Training and Medrese Education in the Sixteenth-Century Ottoman Empire," *TSAB* 8, no. 1 (1984): 27–29; Bilgin Aydın, "Osmanlı Bürokrasisinde Divan-ı Hümâyun Defter Formlarının Ortaya Çıkışı ve Gelişimi (XV-XVI. Yüzyıl)" (PhD diss., Marmara Üniversitesi, 2003), 1–4; Resul Ay, "Ortaçağ Anadolu'sunda Bilginin Seyahati: Talebeler, Âlimler, Dervişler," *TTYY* 3 (Spring 2006): 17–53; Abdurrahman Atçıl, "The Formation of the Ottoman Learned Class and Legal Scholarship" (PhD diss., University of Chicago, 2010), 34–66.

[4] Şahin, "Âşıkpaşa-zâde as Historian," 127–33.

all human resources at hand without any kind of ideological orientation reflected in such terms as ghazi, hinterlander, ethical fraternity, or mystical order." Men with knowledge of local custom and law were critical in incorporating newly conquered territories, and Byzantine and Serbian secretaries could thus find themselves a place within the early Ottoman administration. These practices made the early Ottoman administration a multilingual, multiethnic environment, where pragmatism prevailed over adherence to an imagined Near Eastern/Turkish inheritance.[5] As late as 1430, as reported by the Byzantine historian Doukas, a secretary of Serbian origin named George managed the sultan's correspondence in Turkish, Slavic, and Greek.[6] Mehmed II employed Grecophone secretaries, both Byzantine Greeks and converts to Islam, whose activities included translation from, and composition of, works in classical Greek.[7] Some secretaries were originally taken into the sultan's household through the levy of Christian children; others were war captives. In 1473, for instance, Mehmed II brought captured Akkoyunlu secretaries to Istanbul after he defeated the Akkoyunlu sultan at Otlukbeli.[8]

What distinguishes the sixteenth century from the fifteenth in terms of personnel is, first, the near-exclusive recruitment of secretaries from among the graduates of Ottoman madrasas and/or the sons of the 'askeri class.[9] In earlier periods, scholar-secretaries were mobile because they could offer their services to other Muslim rulers, whereas slave-secretaries remained members of the sultan's household. The new secretaries working for the Ottoman administration during Mustafa's professional career were, in this sense, more Ottoman and local. This allowed for further cohesion, as some secretaries studied together, belonged to the same local networks, the same religious orders, and so forth. It also facilitated their identification with the political and cultural agendas of Ottoman imperialism. Unlike the slave-secretaries of the previous century, on the other hand, the new secretaries did not belong to the sultan's household and constituted a separate entity. Although they were madrasa graduates, they were differentiated, through the nature of their work, from the religious scholars as well as the administrators and military commanders, most of

---

[5] Shinder, "Early Ottoman Administration," 514–15.

[6] Uzunçarşılı, *Merkez ve Bahriye Teşkilâtı,* 226.

[7] See Julian Raby, "Mehmed II's Greek Scriptorium," *Dumbarton Oaks Papers* 37 (1983): 15–34.

[8] Aydın, "Divan-ı Hümâyun," 16.

[9] Fleischer, "Scribal Training," 27–29; Linda Darling, "Ottoman Salary Registers as a Source for Economic and Social History," *TSAB* 14, no. 1 (1990): 25–27.

whom were of *devşirme* origin. It is true that patronage played an important role in recruitment; moreover, some secretaries continued to engage
in *extra muros* economic activities.[10] Despite these dynamics, which may
be seen by a strict Weberian approach as hampering the formation of a
distinct bureaucratic apparatus, the secretarial career continued to evolve
into a distinct professional, cultural, and political trajectory in Süleyman's
reign.

The promotion of the secretarial career as a road to upward mobility
is not limited to the Ottoman polity of the sixteenth century. Medieval
English chroniclers and moralists bitterly complained about the arrival
of "new men" at the expense of the deserving nobles, and members of
the military caste viewed these secretaries, who earned "reward through
dull work of administration or worse, through flattery and influence-
peddling," as a threat to their special status. However, the increased use
of the written word in the administration and the need to introduce relatively routine procedures managed by "reason" required a certain type
of individual. "Ambitious knights or sons of humbler freemen" went to
schools to qualify for the newly available posts, which gave them a place
in the center of power.[11] These trends were further accentuated in the
sixteenth century because the need to create institutions of management
and control was particularly pressing under the impact of international
military, political, and ideological competition. As Perez Zagorin notes,
even the aristocratic order itself "gradually tended to exhibit in certain
respects the characteristic of a nobility of service whose main political orientation lay increasingly toward the governments and courts of
royal masters and the political careers of whose more ambitious members were likely to be closely tied to royal interests." The central administrations in the English, Spanish, and French monarchies were "mainly
managed by men whose social origins lay in the lesser nobility or gentry,
the bourgeoisie, and sometimes even humbler strata." These new groups,
which included "secretaries of state, ministers, councilors, legal and financial administrators exemplifying traditions of professional expertise and
fidelity to royal interests," became the main supporters of monarchical
prerogatives in the early modern period and represented their respective

---

[10] For a few cases from the 1520s and 1530s, see Cornell H. Fleischer, "Between the Lines:
Realities of Scribal Life in the Sixteenth Century," in *Studies in Ottoman History in
Honour of Professor V. L. Ménage*, 45–61.

[11] Ralph V. Turner, *Men Raised from the Dust: Administrative Service and Upward Mobility in Angevin England* (Philadelphia: University of Pennsylvania Press, 1988), 1–2, 3,
11–12.

monarchies and empires against what they saw as factional, local, and regional interests.[12]

A more effective and centralized control of Ottoman revenue sources began to be developed under Mehmed II and Bayezid II. A legal/ administrative framework for the regular extraction of resources was created, and the number of treasury secretaries and financial posts increased. Selim's conquests in the Middle East necessitated yet another level of financial supervision and expansion.[13] The combination of conquest and administrative control continued during the first half of Süleyman's reign and allowed the Ottoman political center access to larger financial means, which were utilized both for war and elite management.[14] In the words of Sam White, the coincidence of favorable ecological conditions with a better organized administrative center created an "imperial ecology:"

> Goods had to keep pouring from the peripheries into the core; and settlement had to reach as far as possible for agriculture, extraction, and transportation. Resources had to be harvested, requisitioned, and managed to secure supply. The peasantry had to be taxed, cajoled, coerced, and sometimes moved about for imperial ends, and yet at the same time protected, secured, and held loyal to the imperial dynasty.[15]

During his career, next to the increase in the number of secretaries, Mustafa witnessed other developments such as the intensification of the imperial council's activities, the rise of the office of the chancellor, and the differentiation of the chancery and financial branches. Budgets and gift, expense, and salary registers from the period display both the increase in

---

[12] Perez Zagorin, *Rebels and Rulers, 1500–1660, vol. 1, Society, States, and Early Modern Revolution: Agrarian and Urban Rebellions* (Cambridge: Cambridge University Press, 1982), 95–96, 97–98.

[13] Linda T. Darling, *Revenue-Raising and Legitimacy: Tax Collection and Finance Administration in the Ottoman Empire, 1560–1660* (Leiden: Brill, 1996), 52–54; Bilgin Aydın and Rıfat Günalan, *XV.–XVI. Yüzyıllarda Osmanlı Maliyesi ve Defter Sistemi* (Istanbul: Yeditepe, 2008), 19–26.

[14] Darling, *Revenue-Raising*, 55–67.

[15] White, *The Climate of Rebellion*, 17. Also see *ibid.*, 20–51, for a detailed analysis of the ecological environment that underwrote the empire's success. For the expansion of the central treasury's revenues, and the new relationship between the administrative center and the peasantry, see Erol Özvar, "Osmanlı Devletinin Bütçe Harcamaları," in *Osmanlı Maliyesi: Kurumlar ve Bütçeler*, vol. 1, eds. Mehmet Genç and Erol Özvar (Istanbul: Osmanlı Bankası Arşiv ve Araştırma Merkezi, 2006), 197–218; Huri İslamoğlu-İnan, *State and Peasant in the Ottoman Empire. Agrarian Power Relations and Regional Economic Development in Ottoman Anatolia during the Sixteenth Century* (Leiden: Brill, 1994).

numbers and the process of professional specialization. (The exact number of secretaries is difficult to ascertain. Some were paid through the assignment of land grants and worked outside the capital, and are not listed in these registers.) A register from 1478–80 mentions secretaries without referring to any independent administrative units; secretaries are listed under the palace units for which they work. A budget from 1494–95, showing disbursements made from the treasury, lists only twenty-five secretaries and apprentice-secretaries; five of them are said to work for the imperial council, and twenty for the treasury. This number increases to thirty-six in 1514–15, a few years before Mustafa entered the service as a secretary of the imperial council. A register of gifts, covering 1527–35, displays crucial changes. First, in 1527, the imperial council secretaries are divided into two groups, as those serving the treasurer (seven in total) and the chancellor (eleven in total). The same entry lists thirty-six treasury secretaries and their twenty-four apprentices. This means that the activities of the imperial council now required three times as many secretaries as they did a few decades before. The building of new offices for the imperial council after İbrahim's grand vizierate, and the regularization of the council's meeting days and times, is another testimony of this growth.[16] Four years later, in 1531, the chancellor's secretaries are fifteen in number. In yet another move toward more specialization, the chief of the land registry (*defter emini*) is listed separately, together with six secretaries working in this particular office, also supervised by the chancellor. The land registry had presumably existed since the second half of the fifteenth century, but, like so many other offices, it became a recognizable and distinct bureau in Süleyman's reign.[17] In January 1536, two apprentice secretaries for the imperial council are mentioned, and this number increases to ten in May 1537. A payment register from 1548–49 includes nineteen secretaries of the imperial council and five imperial council apprentice-secretaries. The presence of apprentices for both the financial and the council/chancery branches shows that on-the-job training emerged in this period as an alternative to madrasa education, because increased specialization required individuals with a specific knowledge rather than the more generalized formation provided by the

[16] Uzunçarşılı, *Merkez ve Bahriye Teşkilatı*, 3–4, 8; Abdurrahman Sağırlı, "Şâhnâme-i Âl-i Osman'a Göre Kanuni Döneminde Divân-ı Hümâyûn," in *Eski Çağ'dan Günümüze Yönetim Anlayışı ve Kurumlar*, ed. Feridun Emecen (Istanbul: Kitabevi, 2009), 59–65.

[17] See Douglas Howard, "The Historical Development of the Ottoman Imperial Registry (Defter-i Hakanî): mid-Fifteenth to mid-Seventeenth Centuries," *Archivum Ottomanicum* 11 (1986): 214–217; Erhan Afyoncu, "Defter Emini," *TDVİA* 9: 91–93.

FIGURE 14. A sixteenth-century imperial council meeting. The chancellor is on the lower left corner (detail from Ârifi, *Süleymânnâme*, TSMK, Hazine 1517, 38a).

madrasas.[18] The increase in personnel and specialization meant that the secretary became a ubiquitous figure within the Ottoman elite and provided a counterpoint to powerful factions headed by military men or religious scholars. The secretaries closely associated themselves with the sultan because their political and social power was weaker than the other groups. In return, through their supervision of the distribution of land grants, they offered the sultan better control over his own ruling elite.

An Office to Manage the Empire: The Rise of the Chancellor

Mustafa's rise in Ottoman service coincided with, and was helped by, these structural changes. His personal skills were recognized relatively early, and this recognition was reflected in large annual bonuses.[19] He

---

[18] This summary is based on Fleischer, "Preliminaries," 137–140; Yılmaz, "Koca Nişancı," 10–13; BOA, KK 1764; BOA, Maliyeden Müdevver 7118. For the separation of the chancery and financial branches and the rise of the secretary as a new figure see Fleischer, *Mustafa Âli*, 216–224.

[19] For the monetary benefits of his promotion to chief secretary, see various entries in BOA, KK 1764. Between his appointment to chief secretary and his becoming chancellor,

established a close working relationship with Piri Mehmed, in an environment with relatively few secretaries working for the imperial council and the grand vizier. His collaboration with İbrahim catapulted him to new heights. His appointment as chief secretary in 1525 was obviously a reward for his services in Egypt. It was also an attempt at creating an intermediary figure between the larger number of imperial council secretaries and the office of the chancellor. As chief secretary, one of his main tasks was to write the sultan and the grand vizier's official correspondence and, in general, act as a trusted man in difficult circumstances, such as the interrogation of defeated Ottoman military commanders in Anatolia in 1527 or the composition of the official decree appointing İbrahim commander-in-chief. The placement of the imperial registry under the chancery allowed Mustafa to familiarize himself with the preparation of the detailed land surveys, the basis of the empire's military-financial system. His appointment as chancellor further magnified his position within the Ottoman elite and also gave him new responsibilities, especially in the matter of legislation.

After the passing of Seydi Bey, his old mentor, Mustafa was the obvious successor thanks to his service and skills. The title *nişancı* implies an official who places the *nişan*, the sultan's stamp, on official documents. Although earlier Ottoman sultans are said to have employed chancellors, the position was probably created under Mehmed II. In Mehmed II's administrative law code, those eligible for becoming *nişancı* are described as either an official or scholar with knowledge of religious law, or a secretary with experience in the Ottoman administration, financial or otherwise. Karamani Mehmed (d. 1481), who served as chancellor in 1464–77, was a madrasa teacher before he became a secretary, but his professional activity involved a considerable amount of financial supervision. Tacizade Cafer, who served under both Bayezid II and Selim I, in 1497–1511 and 1512–14, also came from a teaching background and was the first individual to create an aura of intellectual aspiration and literary prowess around the office.[20] The expansive activities of the chancellor's office, such as managing the sultan's correspondence (including texts of negotiations and settlements with other polities),

---

Mustafa consistently received yearly bonuses that were considerably higher than those of other secretaries.

[20] Franz Babinger, "Nishandji," *EI 2*; M. Tayyib Gökbilgin, "Nişāncı," *İA*, vol. 3, 299–302; Aydın, "Divan-ı Hümâyun," 11–12; Woodhead, "After Celalzade". About Tacizade's recognition as a master stylist, see Yılmaz, "Koca Nişancı," 176–78.

preparing official copies of the imperial council decisions when needed, revising and correcting land survey registers, and issuing *kanun* in the name of the sultan, were probably crystallized under Süleyman.[21] Similar institutions sprouted all over early modern Eurasia. As representatives of royal, imperial, monarchic, and dynastic powers, the Safavid and Mughal *dar al-insha* or the French *chancellerie* responded to the twin requirements of controlling the realm in the name of their rulers and producing answers to the large-scale political and religious shifts of early modern Eurasia, while Mercurino Gattinara's chancery fought to impose an often unrealizable unity to the vast Habsburg domains.[22]

Mustafa was aware of the chancellor's new political and ideological functions, and he summarizes them when he informs his readers of his new appointment. He prefaces his reflections with a comparison between the pen and the sword and concludes that the pen is more constructive and productive. Next, he introduces the figure of the virtuous secretary (*debīr-i kāmil*) and argues that, unlike the members of other groups, he is rare and irreplaceable. By himself, the secretary is able to secure the control of the realm (*żabṭ-ı memālik*). In his absence, the harmony of the realm and the subject population (*ḳıvām-ı mülk ve millet*) is upset, and the matters pertaining to the realm's order (*umūr-ı niẓām*) become destitute. Thus, the chancellor's first task is to help the sultan control and manage the realm. Second, the chancellor is the conduit between the sultan and the subject population, because he is the one who issues official documents with the sultan's name and stamp. Third, the chancellor is distinguished from the members of the sultan's household because, unlike them, his stipend comes from a land grant and not from the imperial treasury. This, in Mustafa's mind, is a sign of financial and professional independence. Fourth, there is a link between the office and the realization of justice. The oppressors of the subjects often use the rules

---

[21] The most comprehensive account of the Ottoman chancery is Josef Matuz, *Das Kanzleiwesen Sultan Süleymāns des Prächtigen* (Wiesbaden: F. Steiner, 1974).

[22] See Willem Floor, *Safavid Government Institutions* (Costa Mesa: Mazda Publishers, 2001), 40–55; Momin Mohiuddin, *The Chancellery and Imperial Epistolography under the Mughals* (Calcutta: Iran Society, 1971); Sylvie Charton-Le Clech, *Chancellerie et culture au XVIe siècle (les notaires et secretaires du roi de 1515 à 1547)* (Toulouse: Presses universitaires du Mirail, 1993); Headley, *The Emperor and His Chancellor*. While he discusses the last decades of the sixteenth century, another study that is crucial in understanding the specific role played by the chanceries is Colin P. Mitchell, "Out of Sight, Out of Mind: Shah Mohammad Khodābanda and the Safavid *Dār al-enshā*," *Studies on Persianate Societies* 3 (2005): 65–98.

issued by the sultans in their fraud (*tezvīr*), and the chancellors have to ensure that the rules and regulations won't be conducive to oppression and error (*żulm ve ḍalāl-āmīz*). By doing so, they ensure that sultans will enjoy a long reign, a good reputation, and divine grace after death. Finally, Mustafa claims that the chancellor has to be aware of the stature of other rulers, to better represent Süleyman in his shining glory. This is a reference to the diplomatic duties of the chancellor, who was given the task to depict the sultan's stature and achievements in his dispatches.[23]

Mustafa was expected to lend his considerable skills to the office, and he was willing to oblige. As Halil İnalcık noted, under his tenure, land survey registers became more detailed, and separate registers were prepared for land grants and endowments. The organization of the information in the registers was improved, and the introduction of what might be called indexes facilitated the location of specific entries.[24] This was the result of a need, on the part of the political center, to better control the land grant appointments as a means to exercise authority over the members of the military class, ensure the participation of the land grant holders in campaigns, and limit the powers of provincial governors and governors-general whose right to assign land grants was made conditional on sultanic approval in 1531.[25] Land surveys, which were usually conducted when the need arose in the fifteenth century, became a more regular practice in the sixteenth century, not only as a means to incorporate newly acquired territories, but also as a method of governance.

The regularization of documentary practices and the increase in the volume of documents is also observed in the language, style, and number of letters sent to foreign rulers from Süleyman's chancery. As mentioned previously, the Ottoman sultans' correspondence before the sixteenth century was multilingual. Mehmed II's letters of victory to the Mamluks and the hereditary guardians of Mecca (*sharif*) were composed in Arabic, and his letters to various Turko-Persian rulers were in Persian.[26]

[23] *Tabakat*, 259b–260b.

[24] İnalcık, "State, Sovereignty and Law," 81–82.

[25] Klaus Michael Röhrborn, *Untersuchungen zur osmanischen Verwaltungsgeschichte* (Berlin: W. de Gruyter, 1973), 39–40. Cf. M. Tayyib Gökbilgin, "Kanûnî Sultan Süleyman'ın Timar ve Zeamet Tevcihi ile İlgili Fermanları," *Tarih Dergisi* 22 (1967): 37–43.

[26] Ahmet Ateş, "İstanbul'un Fethine Dair Fatih Sultan Mehmed Tarafından Gönderilen Mektuplar ve Bunlara Gelen Cevablar," *Tarih Dergisi* 4, no. 7 (1953): 11–50; Necati

Multilingualism did not completely disappear under Süleyman. His letter of accession, sent to Mecca, was in Arabic, the inquiry sent to Gilan to ascertain Shah Ismail's death in Persian, and a diploma sent to the lord of Bahrayn in Arabic.[27] Ottoman officials in the Balkans continued to use local languages in their correspondence and everyday activity. On the other hand, the overwhelming majority of the sultan's letters were composed in Ottoman, in a flowery style that was meant to reflect Süleyman's political and cultural prestige. Hans Theunissen's survey of Ottoman–Venetian documents supports these observations. Before 1482, treaties regulating political and commercial affairs were either in Greek or in Italian. Under Bayezid II, they were in both Ottoman and Greek, whereas under Selim, one document is in Ottoman Turkish and another is in Ottoman and Italian. The two treaties under Süleyman and after are exclusively in Ottoman. Around the middle of the sixteenth century, as Hans Theunissen remarks, differences between documents sent to Poland, Venice, and Dubrovnik/Ragusa began to disappear, and a standardized Ottoman diplomatic form of writing emerged.[28] Süleyman's chancery addressed new interlocutors in this period and did so more often. The entire correspondence with Safavid Iran, the Habsburgs, and France was conducted in Ottoman. Süleyman's famous letter to Francis I, after the Battle of Pavia, was composed in Ottoman, and the Ottoman–French correspondence continued in the same vein. In a telling example of the intensification of diplomatic correspondence, the Ottomans informed Venice, France, and the Habsburgs about the developments of the Two Iraqs campaign, and İbrahim continued his diplomatic negotiations with the Venetians and the Habsburgs while he was in the East.[29] Under Mustafa's personal supervision, new features such as an *invocatio* in Arabic; an

Lugal and Adnan Erzi, "Fâtih Sultan Mehmed'in Muhtelif Seferlerine Ait Fetih-Nâmeleri," *İstanbul Enstitüsü Dergisi* 1 (1955): 169–84.

[27] Feridun Bey, *Mecmū'a-yı Münşe'āt*, 1:500–501 (to Mecca), 540–41 (to Gilan), 610–12 (to Bahrayn).

[28] Theunissen, "Ottoman-Venetian Diplomatics," 191, 308. Cf. Gökbilgin, "Timar ve Zeamet Tevcihi," 39–54, for a change in style and content from Bayezid II to Süleyman. Also see Yılmaz, "Koca Nişancı," 173–74.

[29] See Gökbilgin, "Venedik Devlet Arşivindeki...," for two letters to France (111–14) and another to Venice (54–56); Gisele Procházka-Eisl and Claudia Römer, *Osmanische Beamtenschreiben und Privatbriefe der Zeit Süleymāns des Prächtigen aus dem Haus-, Hof-, un Staatsarchiv zu Wien* (Vienna: Verlag der Österreichischen Akademie der Wissenschaften, 2007) for a letter from İbrahim to Ferdinand renewing the Ottoman-Habsburg ceasefire (41–42) and another, sent from Diyarbekir and announcing the campaign's success (42–44).

Ottoman section on God, Muhammad, and the four Sunni caliphs; and a detailed *intitulatio* enumerating the titles of the sultan were added to the official letters sent to foreign rulers.[30] Dispatches from Süleyman and the Ottoman grand viziers to Ferdinand I, Charles V, and Maximilian II and letters to the kings of Poland and to Muslim local rulers in India were composed in the new idiom of the empire, and subsequent letters to Mecca and Bahrayn were written in Ottoman rather than Arabic.[31]

The increased volume of these documents shows that, within an interconnected early modern Eurasia, communication, information gathering, correspondence, and diplomacy became a crucial component of governance. The Venetians, the Genoese, and the Catalans had maintained relations with various powers in the Eastern Mediterranean and the Middle East throughout the late Middle Ages, and the Ottomans, very early on, became a part of these networks of communication. Before they became part of the so-called Renaissance diplomacy in the late fifteenth century through the Prince Cem affair, through their relations with the Byzantines, the Serbs, the Hungarians, and the Wallachians, they were able to gather information from the Balkans. The traveling scholars, secretaries, and military men from the East carried information next to knowhow. The sixteenth-century diplomatic transformation, on the other hand, was a result of increased imperialist competition.[32] On the European front, struggles over the control of Italy after the end of the fifteenth century made Venice a major international actor, and the Ottomans were connected to this scene through them and then through their own relations

---

[30] Victor L. Ménage, "On the Constituent Elements of Certain Sixteenth-Century Ottoman Documents," *BSOAS* 48, no. 2 (1985), 285–87, passim.

[31] For the letters to the Habsburgs, see previously mentioned works by Procházka-Eisl and Römer, and Schaendlinger and Ro¨mer. For the Ottoman-Polish correspondence, see Dariusz Kołodziejczyk, *Ottoman-Polish Diplomatic Relations (15th-18th Century): An Annotated Edition of 'Ahdnames and Other Documents* (Leiden: Brill, 2000). Also see Feridun Bey, *Mecmū'a-yı Münşe'āt*, 1: 613–14 (to Mecca), 617–18 (to Receb Han on the coast of Gujarat), 618–19 (to Bahrayn).

[32] This diplomatic expansion has been interpreted as another specifically European phenomenon, even though it clearly encompassed all the actors in early modern Eurasia. The Eurocentric approach is exemplified by Garrett Mattingly, *Renaissance Diplomacy* (Baltimore: Penguin, 1964). For Ottoman diplomacy, see Bülent Arı, "Early Ottoman Diplomacy: Ad Hoc Period," in *Ottoman Diplomacy: Conventional or Unconventional?*, ed. Nuri Yurdusev (Basingstoke, Hampshire: Palgrave Macmillan, 2004), 36–65. Despite its merits, the article labels all Ottoman diplomatic activity before the late eighteenth century as "ad hoc." For a list of works on the rise of a very active Safavid diplomacy see Colin P. Mitchell, "Safavid Imperial *Tarassul* and the Persian *Inshā'* Tradition," *Studia Iranica* 26 (1997): 174–176nn1–2.

with the Habsburgs and the French.[33] Mustafa, unlike his predecessors, thus found himself in negotiations with the Habsburgs and the Safavids, composed documents in which he defended Ottoman claims to universal monarchy or the leadership of Sunni Islam, and wrote letters that traveled from Istanbul and the sultan's army camp to Vienna, North Africa, the Persian Gulf, Paris, Brussels, and Gujarat. The Safavid chancery, under Tahmasb, was invested with the same task and played an important role in the creation of an official Shiite discourse through dispatches to the Uzbeks and the Ottomans.[34] In Mustafa's case, already in the mid-1520s, his letters to the Habsburgs included the names of the four Sunni caliphs and the Ottoman claims to the leadership of Sunni Islam, which shows that a seemingly intra-Muslim conflict was presented to a European Christian audience.[35] Ottoman military supremacy led to the disappearance of the reciprocal clauses found in earlier Venetian–Ottoman treaties and to the emergence of a "diplomatic fiction" whereby the Ottoman side granted privileges and received submission.[36] Like Mercurino Gattinara or Charles V's Latin secretary, Alfonso de Valdès, Mustafa defended the Ottoman version of empire on the written page, in an international environment.[37]

The use of a standardized language was another widespread development. The royal ordinance of Villers-Cotterêts in 1539 made French the language of administration, and a similar measure was taken in Poland, also in 1539. The Act of Union of 1536 subsumed Welsh jurisdiction under English and ordered court records to be kept and oaths to be taken in English.[38] Around the same time, Persian became the language of the Mughal and Safavid administrations.[39] The monarchies continued

---

[33] Daniel Goffman, "Negotiating with the Renaissance State: The Ottoman Empire and the New Diplomacy," in *Early Modern Ottomans*, 61–74; Marie F. Viallon, *Venise et la porte Ottomane (1453–1566): un siècle de relations vénéto-ottomanes, de la prise de Constantinople à la mort de Soliman* (Paris: Economica, 1995); Turan, "The Sultan's Favorite;" *The Papacy and the Levant 3*.

[34] See Mitchell, *The Practice of Politics*, passim; Mitchell, "Out of Sight, Out of Mind."

[35] Ménage, "Constituent Elements," 301–02.

[36] Theunissen, "Ottoman-Venetian Diplomatics," 239–40.

[37] Headley, *The Emperor and His Chancellor*; Headley, "Germany, the Empire and *Monarchia* in the Thought and Policy of Gattinara," in *Das Römisch-Deutsche Reich im politischen System Karls V.*, ed. Heinrich Lutz (Munich: R. Oldenbourg, 1982): 15–33; J. A. Fernández-Santamaria, *The State, War and Peace: Spanish Political Thought in the Renaissance 1516–1559* (Cambridge: Cambridge University Press, 1977), 38–49.

[38] Peter Burke, *Languages and Communities in Early Modern Europe* (Cambridge: Cambridge University Press, 2004), 72–76.

[39] Muzaffar Alam, *The Languages of Political Islam: India, 1200–1800* (Chicago: University of Chicago Press, 2004), 122–33; Alam and Sanjay Subrahmanyam, "The Making

to rule over multilingual societies, but a unified administrative language was expected to help better manage the realm and create a cultural and professional cohesion within the ruling elite. The elitist cultural implications of the new administrative idioms are best illustrated by the use of a specific idiom, *insha*, in Ottoman, Mughal, and Safavid chanceries. This synthesis of honorific formulae and rhyming prose (*saj'*) had been utilized by Muslim chanceries for many centuries, in its Arabic and Persian variants, and its mastery was seen as a necessary qualification for any scholar or secretary.[40] The Ottomans were exposed to this bureaucratic and belles-lettres tradition through mostly Persian, and some Arabic, compilations. Ottoman *insha* compilations emerged in the fifteenth century but, compared with sixteenth-century compendia, these display a more rudimentary idiom based on repetitive formulas gleaned from Arabo-Persian collections.[41] In the sixteenth century, the Ottomans began to create their own brand of *insha*, in tune with the emergence of a new cultural self-consciousness.[42] The result was, in the words of Christine Woodhead, "[a]n amalgam of lexical and syntactical elements from the Arabic, Persian and Turkish languages, embellished with a daunting range of allusions and word-play, and with the distinctive cadences of rhymed phrasing."[43] Mustafa's particular contribution, recognized by his contemporaries as well as by posterity, was to politicize this idiom and adapt it to the political and ideological realities of the day without sacrificing the literary dimension.[44] By uniting belles-lettres, secretarial functions, and the defense of Ottoman imperialism, Mustafa established a new

of a Munshi," *Comparative Studies of South Asia, Africa and the Middle East* 24, no. 2 (2004): 61–62; Mitchell, *The Practice of Politics;* Mitchell, "Safavid Imperial *Tarassul*."

[40] For the historical development of *insha*, see Mitchell, "Safavid Imperial *Tarassul*," 179–190; Ishtiyaq Ahmad Zilli, "Development of *Inshā* Literature to the End of Akbar's Reign," in *The Making of Indo-Persian Culture: Indian and French Studies* ed. Muzaffar Alam et. al. (New Delhi: Manohar Publishers & Distributors, 2000), 309–21; Rajeev Kinra, "Secretary-Poets in Mughal India and the Ethos of Persian: the Case of Chandar Bhān Brahman" (PhD diss., University of Chicago, August 2008), 55–92; Yılmaz, "Koca Nişancı," 165–72. For its function in Safavid and Mughal administrative/secretarial circles see, respectively, Mitchell, "Safavid Imperial *Tarassul*," 190–205; Zilli, "Development of *Inshā* Literature," 327–44.

[41] For the circulation of Mamluk, Ilhanid and other *insha* collections in the Ottoman lands, see Aydın, "Divan-ı Hümâyun," 4. For an early Ottoman *insha* collection, see Şinasi Tekin, "Fatih Devrine Ait Bir İnşa Mecmuası," *JTS* 20 (1996): 267–311.

[42] Yılmaz, "Koca Nişancı," 174–82.

[43] "Ottoman İnşa and the Art of Letter-Writing. Influences upon the Career of the Nişancı and Prose Stylist Okçuzade (d. 1630)," *Osmanlı Araştırmaları* 7–8 (1988): 144–45. For a description of the application of *inşa*, see Andreas Tietze, "Muṣṭafā 'Ālī of Gallipoli's Prose Style," *Archivum Ottomanicum* 5 (1973): 297–319.

[44] Yılmaz, "Koca Nişancı," 182–88.

set of credentials for the current and aspiring literati-secretaries of the empire.[45]

Mustafa's purview also extended into the supervision of land grants and surveys and the preparation of sultanic law (*kanun*).[46] The legal rights and prerogatives of secular rulers, which had always existed in practice, were further formalized in the Islamic world in the post-Mongol period. The waning of the caliphate as a representative of legal universalism was compensated by the idea that a Muslim ruler, respectful of the Sharia, could guarantee a lawful society and that individual Muslims should recognize his legislative authority.[47] In a majority of cases, this legal authority consisted of recognizing local traditions and customary law, and the Ottomans, like other societies in early modern Eurasia, lived in an environment of legal pluralism. Early Ottoman sultans exercised their discretion on various affairs and understood *kanun* as the right to exercise that discretion, rather than a collection of relatively standardized and detailed body of *written* law. This earlier notion began to change in the second half of the fifteenth century, when Mehmed II's expanding dynastic kingdom needed, first of all, to create a hierarchy within the ruling elite and better regulate the process of extracting resources from the subject population. Various law codes from the era show that the sultan first and foremost tried to overcome his competitors inside the ruling elite. For instance, in a text regulating silver mining in the Balkans, Mehmed felt the need to warn his own men about not interfering in the mines, because the wealth they generated belonged to the sultan.[48] More importantly, Mehmed II understood *kanun* as a mutable, flexible form of legislation that needed to be modified and improved by posterity.[49]

Ottoman law codes, *kanunnames*, were issued in different forms after the mid-fifteenth century, such as sultanic decrees addressing a specific issue or correcting a specific application, regulations for specific localities (listed at the beginning of the land survey registers), regulations for

---

[45] For the conflation of secretarial and cultural ideals, although in a slightly later period, see Christine Woodhead, "From Scribe to Litterateur: The Career of a Sixteenth Century Ottoman *Kātib*," *Bulletin of the British Society for Middle Eastern Studies* 9, no. 1 (1982): 55–74; Fleischer, *Mustafa Âli*, passim. For a similar mindset among European diplomats, see Timothy Hampton, *Fictions of Embassy: Literature and Diplomacy in Early Modern Europe* (Ithaca: Cornell University Press, 2009).

[46] For two definitions of *kanun*, both very influential among Ottomanists, see Halil İnalcık, "*Kānūn*," *EI 2*; Imber, *Ebu's-su'ud*, 40–51.

[47] See Buzov, "The Lawgiver and His Lawmakers," 114–16.

[48] Ahmed Akgündüz, *Osmanlı Kanunnâmeleri ve Hukukî Tahlilleri*, vol. 1, *Osmanlı Hukukuna Giriş ve Fatih Devri Kanunnâmeleri* (Istanbul: Fey Vakfı, 1990–), 498.

[49] Fleischer, *Mustafa Âli*, 197–200.

specific ethnic/demographic/professional groups, and regulations apply-
ing to all the subjects.[50] Bayezid II's reign witnessed a proliferation in
legal production, increasingly seen as a useful instrument of resource
extraction and conflict resolution. However, written law continued to be
issued when needed, rather than regularly. Moreover, before Süleyman,
*kanunname*s usually addressed specific groups and not specific territories. The land survey registers might include legal clauses, but these were
spread throughout the registers rather than being presented as a formal
introduction. Finally, laws issued in the form of sultanic decree (*hükm*)
were not included in registers.[51] These features changed under Süleyman
and, in the words of Snjezana Buzov, a level of "compilation, consolidation, and systematization" was reached. This was a task that Mustafa
assumed, together with the legal scholar and administrator, Ebussu'ud.
Thanks to their efforts, the preparation and application of the law became
an important tenet of Ottoman ideas of sovereignty.[52]

Mustafa's role in the codification of *kanun* has been duly recognized by
Halil İnalcık.[53] Even though previous chancellors engaged in related activ-
ities, the office's legal function was re-asserted during Mustafa's tenure.
Mustafa, as a madrasa graduate, was obviously knowledgeable about the
Sharia, having studied some of the classical texts of the Islamic tradition.
Mustafa and his contemporaries did not see a necessary contradiction
between Sharia and *kanun* but, rather, a complementary relationship.
Mustafa envisioned *kanun* as the practical arm of the Ottoman sultan,
and an extension of Süleyman's identity as the caliph of Muslims and
the guarantor of justice to all his subjects. *Kanun* was the basis for good
and just governance and social harmony.[54] By placing law codes at the
beginning of land surveys, *kanun* was given a practical basis, and the land
survey was endowed with a more abstract level of legitimacy. Mustafa
also prepared rules and regulations for the hierarchy within the Ottoman
ruling elite, and drafted a general law code that includes various provisions about what would today be called criminal and civil law.[55] As an
answer to the enlargement of the ruling elite and new ideas of hierarchy,
he designed a standing order regulating where officials would stand with

[50] Halil İnalcık, "*Ḳānūnnāme*," EI 2.
[51] Buzov, "The Lawgiver and His Lawmakers," 116–23.
[52] For a survey of Ottoman law to the end of Süleyman's reign, see *ibid.*, 116–30. For
Ebussu'ud's legal activity, see *ibid.*, 77–111, 161–71; Imber, *Ebu's-su'ud*, passim.
[53] İnalcık, "State, Sovereignty and Law," 78–79.
[54] Buzov, "The Lawgiver and His Lawmakers," 172–189.
[55] For Mustafa's regulations about hierarchy, see Akgündüz, *Osmanlı Kanunnameleri 4:*
449–50; his general law code is in *ibid.*, 365–431.

regard to the sultan and to each other in official gatherings and ceremonial occasions. His general law code, prepared in the late 1530s–early 1540s on the request of the grand vizier Lütfi Pasha, reflects the preoccupations of an imperial elite whose legitimacy is based on creating and preserving order. Uriel Heyd's comparison of the law code with earlier texts shows that Mustafa's definition of crimes is more detailed, with a more pronounced moral dimension. More consideration is given to crimes such as sodomy, wine drinking, forgery, the neglect of prayer, breaking the Ramadan fast before sunset, and disturbing the public order.[56] This is the product of a period in which the central administration wanted to infiltrate the lives of the subjects and preach an official religious doctrine while promising justice, peace, order, and prosperity.

Mustafa as a Political Writer and Moralist

Political/moral treatises, alternately called ādāb (in Arabic) and siyāsat-nāmah (in Persian), attracted a considerable number of authors and readers throughout Islamic history. Military administrators, philosophers, secretaries, and literati used this form to expound their views on various subjects. Works that found the right patron could bring remuneration and promotion, and a few became veritable classics studied by every generation. In these works, anecdotes about the ancient Persian kings exist side by side with stories on Muslim caliphs and Indian animal fables. Although some authors prefer to indulge in longwinded monologues on morality and piety, others deal with specific issues, such as the importance of irrigation for agriculture or the necessity of a postal system for efficient administration. However, they all share a few common points. First, they emphasize the importance of piety and morality in the conduct of public affairs and address the tension between religious/moral ideals and the conduct of everyday policy. Second, many of them are written with a particular emphasis on style and are meant to be examples of the Arabic or Persian belles lettres. Third, despite the overgeneralizations and anachronisms they may manifest, they often address pressing contemporary issues, sometimes through allusions and sometimes directly.[57]

---

[56] Uriel Heyd, Studies in Old Ottoman Criminal Law, ed. Victor L. Ménage (Oxford: Clarendon Press, 1973), 24–31. For a text of the law code utilized by Heyd, see 56–93 (the Ottoman original), 95–131 (English translation).

[57] For a concise overview of the genre, see C.E. Bosworth, "Naṣīḥat al-Mulūk," EI 2, and Louise Marlow, "Advice and advice literature," EI 3. The genre has been the subject

The political and cultural developments of the sixteenth century in the Ottoman lands motivated officials, scholars, and authors outside the ruling elite to write works in the *siyāsat-nāmah* tradition. These works, composed in Arabic, Persian, or Ottoman Turkish, discuss different aspects of the Ottoman sultanate and administration.[58] Until relatively recently, the Ottoman literature of political advice was discussed within the so-called "decline paradigm," according to which the empire entered a period of irrecoverable political and economic decline after the end of the sixteenth century. The composition of treatises on politics and morals supposedly reflected a reaction to decline.[59] More recently, the emphasis has been shifted from the "decline paradigm" to the striking variety displayed by the Ottoman political literature and a more nuanced analysis of political criticism. Arguing that a critical dimension existed in political treatises well before the end of the sixteenth century, and pointing to the tension between morals and politics, Cornell Fleischer emphasized the dimension of adjustment and adaptation:

> ...this style of critical analysis became important to the intellectuals of a frontier conquest state in the process of becoming a centralized Islamic empire. This evolution required that the administrative goals of the state be integrated with its religious and cultural ideals, and the fact that dynastic legitimacy rested primarily on an active concern for universal justice lent special significance to the dialectical process.[60]

Rifa'at Abou-El-Haj and Douglas Howard brought to the fore the creative attempts of the authors at coping with political and social change

---

of multiple studies. A representative sample that has been used for the purposes of the present discussion is Ann K. S. Lambton, "*Quis custodiet custodes*: Some Reflections on the Persian Theory of Government I," *StIsl* 5 (1956): 125–48; Lambton, "*Quis custodiet custodes*: Some Reflections on the Persian Theory of Government (Conclusion)," *StIsl* 6 (1956): 125–46; Lambton, "Islamic Mirrors for Princes," in *Atti del Convegno internazionale sul tema: La Persia nel Medieovo* (Rome: Accademia nazionale dei Lincei, 1971), 419–42; Louise Marlow, *Hierarchy and Egalitarianism in Islamic Thought* (Cambridge: Cambridge University Press, 1997), 117–42; Aziz al-Azmeh, *Muslim Kingship: Power and the Sacred in Muslim, Christian, and Pagan Polities* (London: I. B. Tauris, 1997).

[58] For these authors, their works, and their political and cultural motivations, see Yılmaz, "The Sultan and the Sultanate," 65–134.

[59] This approach was first formulated by Bernard Lewis, "Ottoman Observers of Ottoman Decline," *Islamic Studies* 1 (1962): 71–87.

[60] Cornell H. Fleischer, "From Şeyhzade Korkud to Mustafa Âli: Cultural Origins of the Ottoman *Nasihatname*," in *Proceedings of the Third Congress on the Social and Economic History of Turkey*, eds. Heath W. Lowry and Ralph S. Hattox (Istanbul: Isis, 1990), 77.

and emphasized the impact of the authors' personal and professional identities and concerns on their works.[61] In his discussion of a seminal sixteenth-century text by Kınalızade Ali (d. 1571), *Aḫlāḳ-ı ʿAlāī*, Baki Tezcan illustrated how piety and morality were utilized to portray the strife-ridden sphere of politics as a legitimate locus of action.[62] Like history writing, the political advice literature discussed the nature of the system through a personal lens. Unlike history writing, it legitimized individual/collective concerns and the system not through its depiction of imperial rivalry, but through moralistic discussions of duty and piety that aimed to bridge the gap between Sunni Muslim ideals of perfect order and the inescapable entanglements of everyday politics.

Mustafa's political treatise, *Mevahib*, is a repository of multiple tensions and concerns. It is a translation/re-writing of Husayn Vaiz Kashifi's Persian *Akhlāq-i Muḥsinī*. The choice of this particular work is not a coincidence, because Kashifi represented and extolled the men of the pen in his life and works in post-Timurid Central Asia, an era and location idealized by the Ottoman literati.[63] Kashifi's *insha* collection reached the Ottoman palace during the last years of Bayezid II's reign, and Mustafa most likely used it in developing his own style.[64] Next to his addition of a lengthy section on the ninety-nine names of Allah at the beginning of his Ottoman version, Mustafa approached Kashifi's original creatively. He rendered Kashifi's list of positive virtues more nuanced through his addition of chapters on envy and calumny; unsurprisingly, he also added a chapter on reason (*ʿaḳl*), one of his cardinal concepts. He divided Kashifi's last chapter (entitled "On the Servants of a Ruler") into two ("On the Vizierate" and "On the Sultanate") and developed and rewrote the original passages. This division signifies Mustafa's desire to separate

---

[61] Rifaat Abou-El-Haj, "The Ottoman Nasihatname as a Discourse over 'Morality,'" in *Mélanges Professeur Robert Mantran*, ed. Abdeljelil Temimi (Zaghouan: CEROMDE, 1988), 17–30; Abou-El-Haj "The Expression of Ottoman Political Culture in the Literature of Advice to Princes (Nasihatnameler), Sixteenth to Twentieth Centuries," in *Sociology in the Rubric of Social Science: Professor Ramkrishna Mukherjee Felicitation Volume*, ed. R. K. Bhattacharya and Asok K. Ghosh (Calcutta: Ministry of Human Resource Development, 1995), 282–92; Howard, "Genre and Myth."

[62] Baki Tezcan, "Ethics as a Domain to Discuss the Political: Kınalızâde Ali Efendi's *Ahlâk-ı Alâî*," in *Proceedings of the International Congress on Learning and Education in the Ottoman World: Istanbul, 12–15 April 1999*, ed. Ali Çaksu (Istanbul: IRCICA, 2001), 109–20.

[63] Colin P. Mitchell, "To Preserve and Protect: Husayn Vaʿiz-i Kashifi and Perso-Islamic Chancellery Culture," *IrSt* 36, no. 4 (December 2003): 500–05.

[64] *Makhzan al-inshāʾ*, ms. TSMK, Revan Köşkü, 1049.

the secretaries from the sultan's servants and portray them as semi-independent actors serving the realm by their own volition.

As a whole, *Mevahib* represents Mustafa's attempt to harmonize the moral restraints placed upon a pious Muslim with the professional demands expected of a meritocratic bureaucrat. As seen in the introduction of his *Selimname*, Mustafa was in a repentant mood in the last years of his life and admitted that he may have engaged in acts that caused injustice and oppression. In *Mevahib*, political action is redeemed, or at the very least excused, through the imposition of moral and religious values and ideals. In professional terms, the work aims at elevating the secretaries above the other groups within the Ottoman elite. Although Mustafa's historical writings already show secretaries and bureaucratic values under a positive light, *Mevahib* provides a more general and timeless theory of bureaucratic merit and efficiency. Finally, the political genre allows Mustafa to discuss the thorny issue of the sultan's duties and responsibilities within the imperial struggles of the sixteenth century. The work's critical dimension is not very visible at first, as Mustafa does not directly discuss issues such as favoritism, which had become especially prevalent during Rüstem Pasha's tenure as grand vizier. At the same time, his constant references to a perfect system suggest that there is room, indeed need, for improvement, and that this can only be realized through the prominence of secretaries and secretarial virtues.

Reason (*'akl*) as a Key to Success and a Tool for Criticism

Reason plays a dramatic role in Mustafa's works and is presented as the chief instrument of governance and the main condition for a virtuous life. By its presence or absence, by its use or its abandonment, reason affects individual destinies as well as the entire realm's fate. Mustafa does not promote a secular, self-referential rationalism but, rather, a neo-Platonic approach that brings together the use of mental faculties with the obeisance of moral and religious prerogatives. Muzaffar Alam has shown that early modern Muslim authors of moralistic and political works evaluate the Sharia in a practical way, as a set of values that defines and guides moral precepts and builds a political and public character.[65] Mustafa's approach to reason, morality, piety, and law is very similar. His thoughts do not belong to a pre-Cartesian universe where reason is supposedly

---

[65] Alam, "*Akhlāqī* Norms and Mughal Governance," in *The Making of Indo-Persian Culture*, 67–95; Alam, *Languages of Political Islam*, 54–61.

overshadowed by faith and superstition, but, at the same time, he does not see a necessary contradiction between reason and faith. Daniel Engster argues, in the case of sixteenth-century European political thinkers, that they conceived of the state not as a secular body, but "as a metaphysically ordained instrument that would bring harmony to the disorderly forces of the temporal/secular world."[66] Similarly, Mustafa's notion of reason, which is neither completely secular nor entirely religious, is of a God-given instrument to be utilized in bringing order and justice to the world. Thus, says Mustafa, the best vizier a sultan can employ is reason itself.[67]

Mustafa's understanding of reason is both elitist and pragmatic. In the first page of his *Mevahib*, he states that reason is the prerogative of the worthy members of mankind (*aṣḥāb-ı fażl*).[68] Muhammad, for instance, was also the most intelligent man who ever lived.[69] According to this elitist worldview, mankind consists of three groups: the intelligent/wise (*ʿāḳil*), the fool (*aḥmaḳ*), and the sinner (*fācir*).[70] This worldview, developed by classical Muslim philosophers, envisages "an abstract hierarchy of intellects affiliated to a scale of spiritual and political authority." "[S]ince the proper qualifications for the exercise of political power are knowledge and wisdom, those possessed of a lower degree of intellectual aptitude have commensurately less authority."[71] Furthermore, Mustafa asserts that every individual quality is a reflection of reason: one's speech and writing, the gifts he gives, his ability to cultivate good relations, dress style, cleanliness, and so forth.[72] Reason is a key to salvation, because it allows individuals to recognize the greatness of God. A person endowed with reason realizes that life in this world is transitory and engages in good deeds and prayer, rather than worldly pleasures.[73] In a more practical sense, although reason is superior to experience and trial (*tecrübe ve imtiḥān*),[74] it requires them to appropriately respond to

---

[66] Daniel Engster, *Divine Sovereignty: The Origins of Modern State Power* (DeKalb: Northern Illinois University Press, 2001), 10.

[67] *Mevahib*, 239a. Cf. Hayrettin Yücesoy, "Justification of Political Authority in Medieval Sunni Thought," in *Islam, the State, and Political Authority: Medieval Issues and Modern Concerns*, ed. Asma Afsaruddin (New York: Palgrave Macmillan, 2011), 9–33.

[68] *Mevahib*, 2a.

[69] *Ibid.*, 201a.

[70] *Ibid.*, 276b–277a.

[71] Marlow, *Hierarchy and Egalitarianism*, 49–50.

[72] *Mevahib*, 120b.

[73] *Ibid.*, 82b, 329b.

[74] *Ibid.*, 119b.

specific situations.[75] Similarly, it benefits from the exercise of patience, prudence, reflection, and composure. The synthesis of knowledge (ʿilm), reason, and prudence (ḥilm) creates a perfect individual.[76]

Mustafa's historical writings offer vivid tableaus in which he illustrates these more abstract notions and ideas to promote a secretary-centered view of political and administrative action. Reason becomes a litmus test used to laud or criticize individuals. In his *Selimname*, after haranguing Bayezid II's viziers, Mustafa claims that the good fortune and felicity of rulers depend on their viziers' and advisors' intelligence, piety, trustworthiness, and loyalty (kemāl-i ʿaḳl ve diyānetleri ve ḥüsn-i emānet ve ṣadāḳatleri). For the sultan's good fortune to increase, the viziers must be righteous Muslims of unblemished faith. They have to be wise and knowledgeable about the affairs of the world as well.[77] Piri Mehmed, Mustafa's first mentor, emerges in the early pages of *Tabakat* as a scholar/administrator whose clear mind (ẕihn-i pāk) is a sea of learning and whose perceptive intellect (ʿaḳl-ı derrāk) is a mirror that reflects felicity.[78] He is distinguished by his virtues and his knowledge of various sciences (envāʿ-ı kemālāt ve ʿulūm).[79] İbrahim Pasha displays the best personal attributes and moral virtues (ecmel-i aḫlāḳ ve evṣāf) and refrains from unlawful/illegitimate and *unreasonable* affairs (nā-meşrūʿ ve nā-maʿḳūl umūra irtikābdan iḥtirāz ve perhīz iderdi).[80] Mustafa praises the pasha's comprehension of counsel and his readiness to accept and follow it (söz fehminde pehlivān, iẕʿān ve ḳabūlde ʿālī-şān). Before he succumbs to vanity at the end of his life, he follows Ottoman laws and practices in their entirety (Ḳānūn-ı ḳadīmden cüzʾī ve küllī inḥirāfa ḳāil değiller idi).[81]

Grand viziers from a military background are similarly presented to the readers through their mental and administrative capabilities, rather than their military credentials and achievements. Ayas Pasha, who succeeded İbrahim, is a man of precaution who manages well the affairs of the realm and who cures the ills of the land with the medicine of his administration.[82] His successor, Lütfi, is praised for his clear mind,

---

[75] *Ibid.*, 331a.
[76] *Ibid.*, 273a–b.
[77] *Selimname*, 148b.
[78] *Tabakat*, 21b.
[79] *Ibid.*, 86a.
[80] *Ibid.*, 168b.
[81] *Ibid.*, 178b.
[82] *Ibid.*, 300b.

his understanding of the realm's affairs, his mercy, and his fondness for religious sciences (*'ulūm-ı dīniyye*).[83] Even the famous naval commander Hayreddin Barbarossa is qualified as a man on whose face shines the light of wisdom.[84] While he is still the governor-general of Anadolu, Rüstem Pasha is called the most intelligent and virtuous administrator of the time (*ā'ḳal-ı ümerā-yı devrān, ekmel-i kūberā-yı 'asr ve āvān*).[85] After he becomes grand vizier, his clear mind (*ẕihn-i pāk*) and his perception and comprehension (*idrāk-ı derrāk*) are emphasized. His piercing thoughts, which never miss their target (*efkār-ı sāḳıbe-yi iṣābet-āsār*), act as a doctor who cures the ills of the realm.[86]

The counterpoint to these praises is provided by those who stray from the precepts of reason, be they rebels or inept Ottoman administrators. Their covetous nature pushes them to seek political and economic gain, their ignorance ensures their defeat, and their disrespect of law and religion dooms them to the fires of hell. Their activities result in oppression (*ẕulm*); they abrogate the just order established by the sultan and substitute it with injustice and tyranny.[87] For instance, although Janbardi al-Ghazali's intelligence was worth naught in the bazaar of learned men, says Mustafa, he dared enter the path of rebellion. In fact, his ignorance (*cehl*) is *the* reason behind his rebellion. In a poem about the Janbardi affair, Mustafa claims that only men of reason know how to conquer a territory, whereas ignorant men cannot distinguish between what is beneficial and what is harmful.[88] Şehsuvaroğlu Ali Bey is another example of the cycle of ignorance, rebellion, oppression, and personal demise. In his account of the affair, significantly enough, Mustafa first divides humanity into two categories. The first category is bestowed reason and piety by God, whereas the second category is akin to animals in the sense that it has only a patina of reason and intelligence. Those who belong to the latter category, such as Şehsuvaroğlu Ali Bey, venture into risky situations and expose themselves to an eventual punishment. Ali Bey surrenders to his pride, the task of administration constitutes a heavy burden for his weak

---

[83] *Ibid.*, 285b.

[84] *Ibid.*, 245b.

[85] *Ibid.*, 298a.

[86] *Ibid.*, 380b.

[87] In Ottoman usage, *ẕulm* denoted a legal/administrative as well as ethical/religious infraction. See Gottfried Hagen, "Legitimacy and World Order," in *Legitimizing the Order*, 71–73.

[88] *Tabakat*, 30b.

character, and he thus extinguishes the flame of justice that illuminates the subjects' hearts.[89]

Piri Mehmed's nemesis, Ahmed Pasha, is presented as the stereotype of the headstrong military administrator. When Selim I dies, Piri Mehmed does not inform Ahmed of the sultan's passing, because the latter is of lowly character, impetuous and uncivil (*erāzil-ḥaseb, mütehevvir ve bī-edeb*). He is unable to comprehend the secrets of the sultanate (*Havṣalası esrār-ı salṭanat ḥażmına mütehammil değil idi*).[90] While Mustafa talks about the tensions between Piri Mehmed and Ahmed during the Belgrade campaign, he accuses Ahmed of being proud and vain (*maġrūr*), ignorant (*cāhil*), seditious, and malicious (*müfsid ve şerīr*). He also mentions the pasha's Georgian origin as a negative trait, pointing to his non-Muslim and slave background.[91] The negative portrait is completed with the addition of two final traits: Ahmed's impiety and his inability to grasp the significance of the grand vizierate. The pasha's rebellion is closely associated with the absence of faith in his heart.[92] Furthermore, he is utterly unaware that the grand vizierate is the main support of the administration, the instance where the ruler's sultanate and caliphate are exercised, and the locus for the application of the commandments of God and the stipulations of Muhammad.[93]

Mustafa passes similar judgments for other administrators, all of whom had conveniently fallen from favor at the time of his writing. Hürrem Pasha, the governor-general of Karaman who was defeated by rebels in 1527, has an empty mind (*ḥālī-yi zihn*) and displays signs of stupidity (*ḥamākat-şi'ār*).[94] Kara Ahmed Pasha, who served as grand vizier between October 1553 and his execution in September 1555, is similarly found guilty of not listening to advice useful for both religious and administrative purposes (*dīn ve devlete lāyıḳ olan kelimāt-ı ḥikmet-āyāt ve nuṣḥ-ġāyāt*) and associating with lowly characters (*aḥass-ı erāzil, erbāb-ı rezāil*). When he was appointed to the grand vizierate, he had given the impression of being a virtuous individual; however, once in office, he did not have enough endurance to assume the heavy burden of the grand vizierate and floundered under the weight of the affairs of the

---

[89] *Ibid.*, 68a–b.
[90] *Ibid.*, 24b.
[91] *Ibid.*, 46a.
[92] *Ibid.*, 109b.
[93] *Ibid.*, 110b.
[94] *Ibid.*, 159b.

realm. The pasha's character (*cibilliyet*) prevented him from following the commandments of God, implementing the just laws of the sultan, or understanding the truth behind the affairs of the sultanate.[95]

Mustafa, in Daniel Engster's words, believed in the "constructive powers of human virtue."[96] Reason, morality, piety, and service to the dynasty occupied an important place in his public and private ideals and constituted the foundations of what might be called his political and moral philosophy. He viewed these ideals through a practical lens and believed that they succeeded or failed through individual action. Mustafa was a true Renaissance man in this regard, because he brought together moral virtue and political action as conditions for character building as well as good government. A successful realization of these ideals, he claimed, would serve the interests of both the dynasty and the subject population. Unfortunately, government matters were entrusted to men, who were by nature open to error. Human frailty gave a tragic tenor to human history, as those with reason and intelligence had to struggle with the ignorant, and the virtuous were constantly in conflict with the wicked. A good bureaucrat, unlike military administrators, represented by default the side of intelligence and virtue in this struggle.

The Pen, the Secretary, and the Sultan: Toward an Ideology of Service

The theme of the pen and the sword emerged in Islamic literature as early as the ninth century, mostly in poetry. From the thirteenth century onward, comparisons between the pen and the sword became a standard feature of the political advice literature. These works usually emphasized the complementary aspects of the pen and the sword. Moreover, the concept of "men of the pen" was used to define both secretaries and religious scholars.[97] Mustafa did not necessarily see a tension between the secretaries and the religious scholars, and he came from a madrasa background himself. On the other hand, he believed that, in the realm's management, his own professional group, the secretaries, offered genuine benefits. He was not alone in this endeavor; the idea of the pen's supremacy over the sword was developed and defended by a number of Ottoman authors. These authors shared Mustafa's madrasa background, as well as his desire

---

[95] *Ibid.*, 500a–501b.
[96] Engster, *Divine Sovereignty*, 7.
[97] Marlow, *Hierarchy and Egalitarianism*, 168–73.

FIGURE 15. Süleyman listens to the grievances of an old lady (*Hünernāme*, vol. 2, TSMK, Hazine 1524, 153a).

to redefine the vizierate as the seat of knowledgeable bureaucrats rather than military men.[98]

In his translation of Prophet Joseph's vita, his *Cevahir*, while discussing the select groups among mankind, Mustafa describes the secretaries as the circumambulators of the Kaaba of the Pen, the devotees of the holy realm of purity, and the custodians of numbers. They carry the diamonds of speech and transmit the gems of reports; the tongue of their pens showers the readers with fruits and sweets, and the language of their reeds provides comfort and joy. A clear mind, devoid of the calamities of jealousy, says Mustafa, will easily admit this truth. The pen is a joyful storyteller, an unambiguous translator, a wise raconteur. The virtuous secretary, using such a mighty instrument, holds the keys to universal order (*niẓām-ı 'ālem*).[99] In *Mevahib*, Mustafa likens the secretary to the eyes, ears, and hands of a ruler. In dark times, such as enemy invasion, the secretary's presence is a beacon that shows the road to salvation. The holders of the pen, who are the commanders of the army of knowledge, secure the order of the realm, attend to the problems of the subjects, and gather riches for the sultan, so much so that fighting with and defeating the enemies depend on the activities of the wise and knowledgeable secretary (*kātib-i 'ārifü'l-merātib*). In his hands, the pen becomes an instrument of peace as well as war. Like a victorious standard paraded in battlefields, the pen saves the world from injustice and oppression.[100] Another weapon is *inşā'*, the secretaries' flowery prose. Just as sorrow needs joy, turmoil needs comfort, and illness needs cure, a sultan needs a secretary armed with *inşā'*. The sword of *inşā'* defeated the soldiers of rebellion many times; well-prepared armies were routed by *inşā'*; countless fortresses, whose fortifications rose to the skies, were conquered by the help of *inşā'*.[101] Through these military metaphors, Mustafa conveys the idea that military success itself is a result of bureaucratic efficiency.

Mustafa goes so far as to claim that, because *kātib* (secretary) also means "vizier" in Persian, these two titles are interchangeable.[102] As a secretary who closely worked with viziers from a military background, Mustafa is surprisingly adamant in his conflation of bureaucratic and

---

[98] Yılmaz, "The Sultan and the Sultanate," 332–45. For a similar tension in Habsburg Spain, see James M. Boyden, *The Courtier and the King: Ruy Gómez de Silva, Philip II, and the Court of Spain* (Berkeley: University of California Press, 1995), 94–115.

[99] *Cevahir*, 6a–6b.

[100] *Mevahib*, 197b–198b.

[101] *Ibid.*, 210b.

[102] *Ibid.*, 229b.

vizirial attributes. A good vizier, very much like a good secretary, has to be a man of learning; more importantly, he has to stay away from pride and arrogance. He has to be foresighted and has to take precautions to protect the realm from danger.[103] Mustafa further supports the necessity of advisors and counselors by emphasizing the concept of *meşveret* (consultation). According to him, *meşveret* is related to reason; Prophet Muhammad, the most intelligent man who ever lived, was aware of the importance of counsel and often had recourse to it. In fact, receiving counsel is so important that even the advice of intelligent non-Muslims can be followed.[104] Because counsel is a prerogative of reason, and because it is of utmost political and practical value, rulers need to be surrounded by intelligent men, as seen in the example of the ancient Persian rulers who were famous for having scholars and wise men in their courts.[105]

The sultanate is defined by Mustafa as a dynamic position that requires vigilance and incessant activity. In his chapter on the sultanate,[106] after defining the sultan as the best of humans and the refuge of peace and order, he states that a sultan has to divide his time among a series of tasks: the scrutiny of the affairs of the realm (*"meṣāliḥ-i mülke naẓar"*), the investigation of the subject population's condition (*"reʿāyā-yı raʿiyyetin keşfī"*), the gathering of armies and the execution of military duties (*"duḫūl-i cünd ve edā-yı vaẓīfe-yi ʿasker"*), and the fulfillment of divine commandments and prayer. While doing this, he must exercise caution for fear of confiding any tasks to the ignorant, the unwary, and the unworthy.[107] Besides these four duties, says Mustafa, the sultan has to manage ten interrelated matters: the defense of the realm of Islam; the inspection and repair of castles and fortresses; the pursuit of mischief makers and oppressors (*müfsid ve ẓālim*) and the maintenance of the security of the roads; the application of the punishments proscribed by the Sharia (*ḥudūd-ı ilāhī*); the application of the Sharia through the appointment of judges and administrators; the distribution of land grants to the ruling elite; the protection of the subject population (*reʿāyā*) to secure the prosperity of the land; the recognition and acceptance of the advice of worthy people; the granting of audiences to the population to discover cases of injustice; the engagement of informers who will tell the sultan of

---

[103] *Ibid.*, 199a–b.
[104] *Ibid.*, 246b–247a.
[105] *Ibid.*, 330b.
[106] *Ibid.*, 162b–197b.
[107] *Ibid.*, 162b, 164b, 165a.

the new developments in the realm.[108] In all these tasks, the sultan will benefit from the help of his advisors who will direct him to the true path, because a single individual, however talented, cannot assume all these tasks singlehandedly. Mustafa's discussion of the relationship between the viziers and the sultans, and his views on the sultans' duties, run counter to arguments according to which Ottoman rulers were Oriental despots with unbridled power or patrimonial monarchs whose arbitrary actions were tantamount to law. While debates on universal sovereignty and the caliphate occupied the forefront of Ottoman political thought, new understandings of law and legality (which required the sultan to behave justly and equitably), a renewed emphasis on counsel, and the idea that the sultan as an individual believer had to follow divine commandments suggested limits on the sultan's authority.

[108] *Ibid.*, 165a–165b.

Conclusion

Beyond Ottoman and European Exceptionalism: Empire and Power in Sixteenth-Century Eurasia

The study of the first three Ottoman centuries, especially when it comes to defining the nature of the administrative apparatus and the origins and development of Ottoman political culture, is hampered by a variety of problems. The main challenges, of a historiographical nature, are related to the political and cultural tensions of the late Ottoman Empire and the Turkish republic. The empire's catastrophic last decade (1912–22) and the republic's establishment in 1923 as an authoritarian nation-state required a thorough reassessment of Ottoman history. The major fault lines in Ottoman historiography emerged during the first decades of the republic. Some saw the empire as a decrepit, corrupt, and cosmopolitan enterprise doomed to collapse, an Islamic/Oriental version of the Dark Ages. Others, however, were ready to hail it as a relatively institutionalized conquest "state" that had seen its heyday in 1450–1600. Ömer Lütfi Barkan's influential works were especially instrumental in locating the origins of a "secular," bureaucratic, law-based Turkish state in Ottoman history.[1]

---

[1] For different approaches to Ottoman history during the first decades of the republic, see Büşra Ersanlı, "The Ottoman Empire in the Historiography of the Kemalist Era: A Theory of Fatal Decline," in *The Ottomans and the Balkans: A Discussion of Historiography*, eds. Fikret Adanır and Suraiya Faroqhi (Leiden: Brill, 2002), 115–54. A collection that reflects Barkan's statist approach is *Osmanlı Devleti'nin Sosyal ve Ekonomik Tarihi: Osmanlı Devlet Arşivleri Üzerinde Tetkikler-Makaleler*, ed. Hüseyin Özdeğer, 2 vols. (Istanbul: Istanbul Üniversitesi Rektörlüğü, 2000). For a concise critique of Barkan, see

Was the Ottoman state a "Leviathan or paper tiger? Inexorable instrument of political and fiscal centralization, or mere carapace?"[2] This question continued to occupy scholars in the 1960s and 1970s. Marxian works asked whether the Ottoman Empire was feudal or was characterized by the so-called Asiatic mode of production. These studies sought to identify the role of the state in Ottoman history and the mechanisms of exploitation and resource distribution. The Asiatic mode of production argument posited a rapacious central state exploiting a vast peasantry, whereas the feudalism argument offered a more fragmented, weaker structure that allowed local magnates to exploit mercilessly the same vast, immobile peasantry.[3] (Similar debates, which agreed on the fundamental backwardness of any polity that did not partake in capitalist modernity, were popular among scholars investigating the history of India, Iran, Russia, and China.[4]) Balkan historians, nationalist and Marxist alike, mostly saw the Ottoman Empire as a machine of conquest, exploitation, and Islamization; the newly resurgent Baath and its ideology of Arab socialism harbored similar suspicions vis-à-vis Ottoman rule. On the other side of the political spectrum, the emergence and consolidation of the so-called Turco-Islamic synthesis from the 1950s onward promoted the idea of a bureaucratic, state-like imperial administration by ascribing a Turkish and Sunni Muslim character to it.[5] The autocratic atmosphere following the coup d'état of September 12, 1980,[6] and the recent successes of political Islam, supported and popularized the image of a Turkish and Sunni empire-state that was tolerant

Halil Berktay, "Dört Tarihçinin Sosyal Portresi," *Toplum ve Bilim* 54 (Summer-Fall 1991): 34–41.

[2] Alam and Subrahmanyam, "Introduction," in *The Mughal State*, 2. It is meaningful that Mughal historians have had to grapple with similar historiographical problems.

[3] Two representatives of these arguments are, respectively, Sencer Divitçioğlu, *Asya Üretim Tarzı ve Osmanlı Toplumu* (Istanbul: Köz, 1971), and Mehmet Ali Kılıçbay, *Feodalite ve Klasik Dönem Osmanlı Üretim Tarzı* (Ankara: Gazi Üniversitesi İktisadi ve İdari Bilimler Fakültesi, 1982).

[4] Timothy Brook (ed.), *The Asiatic Mode of Production in China* (Armonk, N.Y.: M.E. Sharpe, 1989); Brendan O'Leary, *The Asiatic Mode of Production: Oriental Despotism, Historical Materialism, and Indian History* (Oxford: Blackwell, 1989); Abbas Vali, *Pre-Capitalist Iran: A Theoretical History* (New York: NYU Press, 1993).

[5] For an elucidation of this thesis by one of its founders, see İbrahim Kafesoğlu, *Türk-İslâm Sentezi* (Istanbul: Aydınlar Ocağı, 1985). For a critical assessment, see Gökhan Çetinsaya, "Rethinking Nationalism and Islam: Some Preliminary Notes on the Roots of 'Turkish-Islamic Synthesis' in Modern Turkish Political Thought," *The Muslim World* 89, nos. 3–4 (July–October 1999): 368–76.

[6] Özel and Çetinsaya, "Türkiye'de Osmanlı Tarihçiliğinin Son Çeyrek Yüzyılı," 11–19.

toward its subjects, but adamant in its defense of national and religious values.[7]

A related problem, also teleological in nature, is observed in the issue of administrative development and change in the Ottoman polity from the early-fourteenth to the mid-sixteenth centuries. Various works by the founding fathers of Ottoman studies, such as Tayyib Gökbilgin, Halil İnalcık, and İsmail Hakkı Uzunçarşılı, have contributed to the idea that the Ottomans always had a relatively organized administrative structure, which became more developed and sophisticated with every new ruler. Uzunçarşılı's detailed studies on the Ottoman administration assumed that administrative personnel and offices that existed in the late sixteenth and seventeenth centuries must have been present before. For instance, the imperial council (*divan*), Uzunçarşılı claimed, was established under Orhan (r. 1324–61) or even Osman.[8] It is quite likely that Orhan, like any dynastic ruler, sought counsel and granted audiences to his followers. However, these activities occurred in a setting that was different from the sixteenth-century *divan*, with its fairly regular meeting schedule, its workload, its system of record-keeping, and a new group of secretaries serving the council's needs. The argument of administrative and institutional continuity was supported with reference to Near Eastern and Islamic practices, which the Ottomans purportedly inherited from the Ilkhans, the Anatolian Seljuks and various Anatolian Muslim principalities. Uzunçarşılı admitted that he developed this argument against scholars who proposed a heavy Byzantine administrative influence in the early Ottoman polity.[9] Another enthusiastic critique of the Byzantine influence argument, Mehmet Fuat Köprülü, argued that Ottoman institutions had a *sui generis* nature, in tune with his Turkish nationalist reading of Anatolian and early Ottoman history.[10]

---

[7] For a more detailed analysis on how the Ottoman Empire became a prominent subject of discussion in Turkish political Islam, see Baki Tezcan, "Lost in Historiography: An Essay on the Reasons for the Absence of a History of Limited Government in the Early Modern Ottoman Empire," *Middle Eastern Studies* 45, no. 3 (May 2009): 488–95.

[8] Uzunçarşılı, *Merkez ve Bahriye Teşkilâtı*, 1–2. This foundational myth continued to be reproduced in later works. See, for instance, M. Tayyib Gökbilgin, *Osmanlı Müesseseleri Teşkilâtı ve Medeniyeti Tarihine Genel Bakış* (Istanbul: Edebiyat Fakültesi Matbaası, 1977); Yusuf Halaçoğlu, *XIV–XVII. Yüzyıllarda Osmanlılarda Devlet Teşkilâtı ve Sosyal Yapı* (Ankara: Türk Tarih Kurumu, 1991).

[9] *Osmanlı Devleti Teşkilâtına Medhal. Büyük Selçukîler, Anadolu Selçukîleri, Anadolu Beylikleri, İlhanîler, Karakoyunlu ve Akkoyunlularla Memlûklerdeki Devlet Teşkilâtına Bir Bakış* (Istanbul: Maarif Matbaası, 1941).

[10] See Köprülü, "Bizans Müesseselerinin Osmanlı Müesselerine Tesiri Hakkında Bâzı Mülâhazalar," *Türk Hukuk ve İktisat Tarihi Mecmuası* 1 (1931): 165–313; for an

Far away from Turkey, Norman Itzkowitz produced the first elaborate English version of the Islamic continuity argument, presenting it together with yet another famous paradigm, the "decline theory."[11] With the publication of Halil İnalcık's influential study of the Ottoman "Classical Age," the idea of Near Eastern and Islamic administrative continuity came to represent the scholarly consensus in Ottoman studies.[12] In their comparative studies on the Ottomans, the Safavids, and the Mughals, Marshall Hodgson and, more recently, Stephen Dale have shown that these three polities were inspired not by an essentialist Near Eastern legacy that represented the continuation of a conservative bureaucratic tradition, but by a complex set of Eurasian, Islamic, Persian, and Timurid legacies, which they in turn refashioned according to their own political and cultural needs.[13] Although these studies are useful (and Marshall Hodgson's hasty characterization of these polities as "absolutist" and doomed to decline has to be revised), the Ottoman experience in the sixteenth century is better understood within an even larger context that involves a European dimension.

While looking for alternatives beyond these historiographical legacies, the literature on state/empire formation in Europe presents various opportunities and challenges. The challenges range from the persistence of Eurocentrism to the evaluation of early modern political entities solely as precursors to modern European nation states; from the popularity of Weberian approaches that have traditionally fuelled patronizing and exclusionary analyses of non-Western polities to the definition and widespread use of absolutism as a universal marker of early modern polities. Immanuel Wallerstein and Perry Anderson, proponents of global approaches to state/empire formation, nevertheless identify the Ottomans as non-Europeans. Wallerstein's judgment is based on his schematic division of the globe into economic cores and peripheries, while Anderson reproduces some of the most essentialist clichés of the Asiatic mode of production approach and sees the Ottomans as a cultural and political oddity that somehow found its way to the immediate vicinity of

---

annotated English edition see *Some Observations on the Influence of Byzantine Institutions on Ottoman Institutions*, ed. and trans. Gary Leiser (Ankara: Türk Tarih Kurumu, 1999). On Köprülü, in addition to his article cited above, see Halil Berktay, *Cumhuriyet İdeolojisi ve Fuat Köprülü* (Istanbul: Kaynak, 1983).

[11] *Ottoman Empire and Islamic Tradition* (New York: Alfred A. Knopf, 1972).

[12] İnalcık, *The Classical Age*. For an illustration of how this argument became the credo of any Ottomanist trying to explain sixteenth-century administrative developments see Yılmaz, "Koca Nişancı," 3–6, 165–73.

[13] Hodgson, *The Venture of Islam 3*; Dale, *The Ottomans, Safavids, and Mughals.*

Europe.[14] Even when it is not seen as the sempiternal non- or anti-
European, the Ottoman polity is classified together with other outliers, as
when it is lumped together with Denmark, Sweden, Poland-Lithuania,
and Muscovy/Russia under the rubric "The Outsiders of Europe."[15]
Many scholars, in otherwise excellent works, define the state as a purely
European phenomenon and describe its emergence and development with
reference to the internal dynamics of European societies.[16] A recent work
on conflict and international change in sixteenth-century Europe, for
instance, focuses on the Habsburgs and the Protestants without recognizing that the Ottomans were one of the most prominent participants in
the same international scene.[17]

The persistence of Weberian notions, tailored in the first place to
explain European particularities, renders the task of comparison even
more difficult. Weber's emphasis on cultural, religious, and symbolic
factors in the lives of individuals, groups, and institutions is a panacea
against economic reductionism; however, his views of rationality and
modernity as exclusively Western European processes, and his thoughts
on "sultanism" as a particularly resilient form of patrimonialism, serve
to depict non-Western societies as lagging behind Europe, mired in a pre-
rational political state.[18] The ruler's personal authority runs supreme,

---

[14] Immanuel Wallerstein, *The Modern World-System*, vol. 1, *Capitalist Agriculture and
the Origins of the European World-Economy in the Sixteenth Century* (New York: Academic Press, 1974), 133–62; Perry Anderson, *Lineages of the Absolutist State* (London:
NLB, 1974), 361–94. Also see Abou-El-Haj's criticism of Anderson in his *Formation of
the Modern State*, 3–5.

[15] Bonney, *European Dynastic* States, 242–301.

[16] Kenneth Dyson, *The State Tradition in Western Europe: A Study of an Idea and Institution* (Oxford: Martin Robertson, 1980); Thomas Ertman, *Birth of the Leviathan:
Building States and Regimes in Medieval and Early Modern Europe* (Cambridge: Cambridge University Press, 1997); Wolfgang Reinhard, *Geschichte der Staatsgewalt: eine
vergleichende Verfassungsgeschichte Europas von den Anfängen bis zur Gegenwart*
(Munich: C. H. Beck, 1999), etc.

[17] Daniel H. Nexon, *Struggle for Power in Early Modern Europe: Religious Conflict,
Dynastic Empires, and International Change* (Princeton: Princeton University Press,
2009).

[18] For Weber's ideas on rationality and modernity, see Sam Whimster and Scott Lash,
eds., *Max Weber, Rationality, and Modernity* (London: Allen and Unwin, 1987). For
sultanism and patrimonialism, see Susan K. Croutwater, "Weber and Sultanism in the
Light of Historical Data," in *Theory of Liberty, Legitimacy and Power: New Directions in the Intellectual and Scientific Legacy of Max Weber*, ed. Vatro Murvar (London:
Routledge and Kegan Paul, 1985), 168–84; Vatro Murvar, "Patrimonialism, Modern
and Traditionalist: A Paradigm for Interdisciplinary Research on Rulership and Legitimacy," in *ibid.*, 40–85. For an attempt at a critical reading of Weber, see Bryan S.
Turner, *Weber and Islam: A Critical Study* (Boston and London: Routledge and Kegan
Paul, 1974). However, lacking sufficient historical data and specific contextual analyses,

and an amorphous group of servants, whose everyday activities are characterized by favoritism and corruption, inefficiently fulfill various tasks. Embryonic bureaucracies may emerge, but can never evolve into independent institutions serving an abstract idea of rule and statehood. Another typical Weberian approach is to bring together "Oriental" societies with reference to their non-Western attributes and place the Mughals, the Safavids, the Tokugawa, and the Ming on the same level of analysis.[19] "Oriental" societies, the Ottomans among them, are thus defined in a self-referential fashion, in contradistinction to European societies.[20]

Beyond Eurocentric approaches and Weberian ideal types, the literature on early modern European state/empire formation presents rich opportunities for incorporating the Ottomans, Safavids, and Mughals within larger debates. If we were to look for general trends, we could easily expand Perry Anderson and Perez Zagorin's descriptions of European societies to the rest of Eurasia. The sixteenth century, in this sense, symbolizes the beginning of trends toward the creation of standing armies, new offices and office holders, relatively unified markets and legal regimes, and powerful dynastic ideologies, despite the persistence of local particularisms. These polities were not yet modern, as Anderson suggests, and ideas of bourgeois efficiency did not prevail in imperialist political agendas and military ventures. As Zagorin argues, on the other hand, absolutism often remained a political ideal that was not fully realized.[21] Moreover, warfare, violence, and coercion contributed to the rise of better managed political and fiscal structures not only in Europe, but throughout the whole Eurasia, as seen in the relatively rapid adoption of gunpowder weapons by the Safavids and the Mughals and the close relationship between fiscal systems and military organization.[22] Although it still

---

Turner tends to succumb to various suggestions made by Weber about the seemingly irreducible differences of Islamic societies.

[19] Stephen P. Blake, "The Patrimonial-Bureaucratic Empire of the Mughals," *Journal of Asian Studies* 39, no. 1 (November 1979): 77–94.

[20] Halil İnalcık, "Comments on 'Sultanism': Max Weber's Typification of the Ottoman Polity," *Princeton Papers in Near Eastern Studies* 1 (1992): 49–72; İnalcık, "Decision Making in the Ottoman State," in *Essays in Ottoman History* (Istanbul: Eren, 1998), 113–21.

[21] Anderson, *Lineages of the Absolutist State*, 15–42; Zagorin, "Monarchy, Absolutism, Political System," chap. 4 in *Rebels and Rulers, 1500–1660*, 1: 87–121.

[22] The classical works about this correlation are Charles Tilly, *Coercion, Capital, and European States, AD 990–1992*, second printing (Cambridge, MA: Blackwell, 1992); Geoffrey Parker, *The Military Revolution: Military Innovation and the Rise of the West, 1500–1800*, second edition (Cambridge: Cambridge University Press, 1996); also see

awaits a thorough study, the new relationship between dynasties and religion, and especially the Sunni–Shiite conflict, also exerted a considerable impact on ideas and institutions of governance.[23] At the very least, new forms of morality permeated Ottoman society, and courts and communities produced, controlled, and enforced new social norms in the sixteenth century.[24] New political ideas, usually thought of as products of the Renaissance and the Reformation, circulated within the rest of Eurasia and created debates about the nature of government, the necessity of justice, and the problems of social mobility.[25] "A more dynamic vision of social order emphasizing fortune and contingency and the constructive powers of human virtue" became a global phenomenon, and men from Delhi to Tabriz, from Istanbul to Venice, from Paris to London "portrayed the state as a metaphysically privileged institution responsible for instituting a static and universal political order within the contingent and disorderly temporal world."[26]

What might be called an Ottoman "state," as the managing component of the empire, thus began to be formed under the impact of early modern Eurasian tensions, as a result of military and religious pressures,

Philippe Contamine, ed., *War and Competition between States*, Theme A of *The Origins of the Modern State in Europe, 13th to 18th Centuries*, eds. Wim Blockmans and Jean-Philippe Genet (Oxford: Clarendon Press; New York: Oxford University Press, 2000). For the Ottomans see Gábor Ágoston, "Empires and Warfare in East-Central Europe, 1550–1750: The Ottoman Habsburg Rivalry and Military Transformation," in *European Warfare, 1350–1750*, eds. Frank Tallett and D. J. B. Trim (Cambridge: Cambridge University Press, 2010), 110–34; Rhoads Murphey, "Ottoman Military Organisation in South-Eastern Europe, c. 1420–1720," in *ibid.*, 135–58. For the Mughals, see Jos Gommans, *Mughal Warfare: Indian Frontiers and High Roads to Empire, 1500–1700* (London: Routledge, 2002).

[23] For the European case, see Philip S. Gorski, "Calvinism and State Formation in Early Modern Europe," in *State/Culture. State-Formation after the Cultural Turn*, ed. George Steinmetz (Ithaca: Cornell University Press, 1999), 147–81; Gorski, *The Disciplinary Revolution: Calvinism and the Rise of the State in Early Modern Europe* (Chicago: University of Chicago Press, 2003); Gorski, "The Protestant Ethic and the Bureaucratic Revolution: Ascetic Protestantism and Administrative Rationalization in Early Modern Europe," in *Max Weber's Economy and Society: A Critical Companion*, eds. Charles Camic et. al. (Stanford: Stanford University Press, 2005), 267–96; Heinz Schilling, *Konfessionskonflikt und Staatsbildung: eine Fallstudie über das Verhältnis von religiösem und sozialem Wandel in der Frühneuzeit am Beispiel der Grafschaft Lippe* (Gütersloh: Gütersloher Verlagshaus Gerd Mohn, 1981). Even though she focuses on non-Muslims and does not discuss non-Sunnis in detail, Karen Barkey shows that state management of religion became an important concern in the early modern Ottoman case. See *Empire of Difference*.

[24] See Leslie Peirce, *Morality Tales: Law and Gender in the Ottoman Court of Aintab* (Berkeley: University of California Press, 2003).

[25] Darling, "Early Modern Mediterranean World."

[26] Engster, *Divine Sovereignty*, 7, 9.

incorporation within a larger political and economic global system, and, more importantly, imperial rivalry. As Mustafa's career shows, military and administrative organization was achieved through the agency of record keeping, sustained through intense legislative activity, and legitimized by the sultan's promise to provide security, order, peace, and prosperity. The essentialist Weberian approaches to the Ottoman case fail to see the processes of institution building, the emphasis on rationality and efficiency, and the move toward the idea of bureaucratic autonomy. Moreover, the fiction of an all-powerful sultan as the paragon of what would later be called sultanism was manufactured by the likes of Mustafa in the sixteenth century, as an answer to an uncertain internal and international environment rife with military, political, and cultural crises and challenges. Even in this case, the litterateur-secretary preferred to set limits to the ruler's discretionary powers by referring to religion and morality, or laws and regulations.

Focusing on the development and building of new institutions and ideologies should not overshadow the fact that, in the words of John Elliott, the early modern state remained a "Leviathan *manqué*." "If a state can be defined as an organization that wields sovereign control over territories and populations, in the last instance by force," says Julia Adams, "then early modern European states were emphatically states in the making."[27] In the absence of the dubious comforts that might be provided by sultanism or absolutism, the Ottoman administration had to cope with a dynamic social panorama within which nomads, peasants, merchants, and members of the elite pursued their own individual, local, and communal interests, and where the Ottoman ruling elite was a class among others, a *primus inter pares* trying to create and then supervise spaces of negotiation for various interests.[28] Indeed, the tensions within the Ottoman ruling elite made it a coalition of what Nicos Poulantzas, in his work on state formation, called "class fractions" with distinct interests and agendas.[29] Michael Braddick's study on the early modern English

---

[27] John H. Elliott, "Power and Propaganda in the Spain of Philip IV," in *Rites of Power*, 145; Julia Adams, *The Familial State: Ruling Families and Merchant Capitalism in Early Modern Europe* (Ithaca: Cornell University Press, 2005), 13.

[28] See Suraiya Faroqhi, "Politics and Socioeconomic Change in the Ottoman Empire in the Later Sixteenth Century," in *Süleyman the Magnificent and His Age*, 91–113.

[29] Nicos Poulantzas, *Political Power and Social Classes*, trans. Timothy O'Hagan (London: NLB, 1973). Poulantzas focuses on the modern capitalist states, but his analysis of intra- and inter-class relations is relevant, in an anthropological sense, for the study of the construction of power in human societies.

state shows that the growth of the state, as a "coordinated and territorially bounded network of agents exercising political power," was an incremental and multifaceted process. The English monarchy consisted of "a network of offices." The bureaucratic apparatus was small but, at the same time, included relatively well-defined institutions with relatively well-defined purviews. Monarchs had to take counsel and accept the placement of various constraints on their discretionary powers. In this context, beyond the individual monarchs, legislation and the administration of justice became important provinces of the central institutions.[30] Another historian of early modern England, Steve Hindle, finds this period remarkable with regard to the "increase of governance": relative administrative centralization was accompanied by the participation of individuals and groups at various levels, and the increase of governance led to the institutionalization of power relations via "a series of multilateral initiatives to be negotiated across space and through the social order."[31]

In the Ottoman case too, new power relations came to the fore in the sixteenth century. The legitimacy of political power stemmed, in the words of Michael Mann, from the "usefulness of centralized, institutionalized, territorialized regulation of many aspects of social relations."[32] The power wielded by the sultan and his administrators was "not just the ability of one (individual, class, regime, polity) to realize its (political, economic, social) interests at the expense of another (individual, class, regime, polity) but . . . the capacity to constitute interests and determine their significance within the management of existing conditions."[33] The symbolic and imagined aspect of this power was as important as its institutional aspect, if not more. Mustafa, in his bureaucratic activity and in his historical works, introduced and defended practices that were meant to "perpetuate the existing political order within a discursive framework that generates the allegiance of subjects," or, at least, the allegiance of the elite.[34] The political center accumulated a significant amount of political and symbolic capital in this period and displayed

---

[30] Michael J. Braddick, *State Formation in Early Modern England, c. 1550–1700* (Cambridge: Cambridge University Press, 2000), 6, 20–27, 45–46.

[31] Steve Hindle, *The State and Social Change in Early Modern England, c. 1550–1640* (Basingstoke: Macmillan; New York: St. Martin's Press, 2000), 2–34 passim., 23.

[32] Michael Mann, *The Sources of Social Power*, vol. 1, *A History of Power from the Beginning to A.D. 1760* (Cambridge: Cambridge University Press, 1986), 26, 22–27.

[33] Adam T. Smith, *The Political Landscape: Constellations of Authority in Early Complex Polities* (Berkeley: University of California Press, 2003), 108.

[34] *Ibid.*

it successfully to create a "state effect."[35] The story of Mustafa's life within the sixteenth-century Ottoman administration, and an analysis of his ideas about empire, sovereignty, and bureaucratic merit, are a suitable starting point for the reconsideration of the formation of new institutions and ideas about power, legality, and governance in early modern Eurasia.

---

[35] For a discussion of various forms of capital utilized in building and reproducing governing structures, see Pierre Bourdieu, "Rethinking the State: Genesis and Structure of the Bureaucratic Field," in *State/Culture*, 53–75. I am borrowing the concept from Timothy Mitchell, "Society, Economy, and the State Effect," in *ibid.*, 76–97.

Bibliography

Archival and Manuscript Sources

Başbakanlık Osmanlı Arşivleri

Kamil Kepeci 1764, 1766
Maliyeden Müdevver 664m, 7118, 22082

Topkapı Sarayı Arşivi

D. 9555, 10151
E. 5013, 6142, 6146/2, 6551, 11969, 11997

Manuscripts and Published Literary and Archival Sources

Abu al-Fazl ibn Mubarak. *The Āʾīn-i Akbarī*. Vol. 1, translated by H. Blochmann, edited by D. C. Phillott. New Delhi: Oriental Books Reprint Corporation, 1977. *Vol.* 2, translated by H. S. Jarrett, edited by Jadunath Sarkar. Calcutta: Royal Asiatic Society of Bengal, 1949. *Vol.* 3, translated by Jarrett, edited by Sarkar. New Delhi: Oriental Books Reprint Corporation, 1978.

Ahmed Resmi Efendi. *Ḥalīfetü'r-rüʾesā*. Istanbul: n.p., 1853.

Akgündüz, Ahmed. *Osmanlı Kanunnameleri ve Hukuki Tahlilleri*. Vols. 1–7. Istanbul: Fey Vakfı, 1990.

Âşık Çelebi. *Meşāʿirüʾş-şuʿarā*. Edited by G. M. Meredith-Owens. London: Luzac, 1971.

Ateş, Ahmet. "İstanbul'un Fethine Dair Fatih Sultan Mehmed Tarafından Gönderilen Mektuplar ve Bunlara Gelen Cevablar." *Tarih Dergisi* 4, no. 7 (1953): 11–50.

Atıl, Esin, ed. *Süleymanname: The Illustrated History of Süleyman the Magnificent*. Washington: National Gallery of Art; New York: H.N. Abrams, 1986.

Babur, Zahiru'd-dīn Muḥammad. *Babur-nama*. Translated by Annette S. Beveridge. Lahore: Sang-e-Meel Publications, 2002.

Beyani. *Tezkire-yi şu'arā-yı Beyānī*. Ms. İstanbul Üniversitesi T.Y. 2568, Halis Efendi.

de Busbecq, Ogier Ghiselin. *Les lettres turques*. Translated and annotated by Dominique Arrighi. Paris: Honoré Champion, 2010.

Blackburn, Richard, ed. and trans. *Journey to the Sublime Porte: The Arabic Memoir of a Sharifian Agent's Diplomatic Mission to the Imperial Court in the Era of Suleyman the Magnificent*. Beirut-Würzburg: Orient-Institut Berlin, Ergon Verlag, 2005.

Bostan Çelebi. *Süleymānnāme*. Ms. SK, Ayasofya 3317.

Celalzade Mustafa. *Cevāhiru'l-aḫbār fī ḥaṣā'ili'l-aḫyār*. Ms. SK, Nuruosmaniye 2356.

———. *Delā'il-i Nübüvvet-i Muḥammedī (Ma'āricü'n-nübüvve)*. Ms. SK, Fatih 4289.

———. *Geschichte Sultan Süleymān Ḳānūnīs von 1520 bis 1557, oder, Ṭabaḳāt ül-Memālik ve Derecāt ül-Mesālik/von Celālzāde Muṣṭafā genannt Ḳoca Nişāncı*. Edited by Petra Kappert. Wiesbaden: Steiner, 1981.

———. *Ḳānūnnāme*. Ms. SK, Hacı Mahmud Efendi, 913/2.

———. *Ḳānūnnāme*. Ms. SK, Ayasofya 2894, 63a–101a.

———. *Ḳānūnnāme*. Ms. SK, Fatih 3507, 1a–78b.

———. *Mevāhibu'l-ḫallāḳ fī merātibi'l-aḫlāḳ*. Ms. SK, Fatih 3521.

———. Poems. Ms. SK, Hacı Mahmud Efendi 3563, 25b–26a.

———. *Tārīḫ-i Sulṭān Selīm*. Ms. *British Museum Add.* 7848.

Celalzade Salih. *Münşe'āt*. Ms. SK, Kadızade Mehmed, 557.

Charrière, Ernest, ed. *Négociations de la France dans le Levant . . .* Vol. 1, *1515–1547*. Vol. 2, *1547–1566*. Paris: Imprimerie nationale, 1848–60.

Erünsal, İsmail E. "Türk Edebiyatı Tarihinin Arşiv Kaynakları II: Kanunî Sultan Süleyman Devrine Ait Bir İn'âmât Defteri." *Osmanlı Araştırmaları* 4 (1984): 1–17.

Erzi, Adnan and Necati Lugal. "Fatih Sultan Mehmed'in Muhtelif Seferlerine Ait Feth-nâmeleri." *İstanbul Enstitüsü Dergisi* 1 (1955): 169–84.

Eskandar Beg Monshi. *The History of Shah 'Abbas the Great (Tārīḵ-e 'ālamārā-ye 'Abbāsī)*. 2 volumes. Translated by Roger M. Savory. Boulder, CO: Westview Press, 1978.

Feridun Ahmed Bey. *Mecmū'a-yı Münşe'āt-ı Ferīdūn Bey*. 2 volumes. Istanbul: Daru't-tıbaati'l Âmire, 1848–57.

Gökbilgin, M. Tayyib. "Arz ve Raporlarına Göre İbrahim Paşa'nın Irakeyn Seferindeki İlk Tedbirleri ve Fütuhatı." *Belleten* 21, nos. 81–84 (1957): 450–82.

———. "Kanûnî Sultan Süleyman'ın Timar ve Zeamet Tevcihi ile İlgili Fermanları." *Tarih Dergisi* 22 (1967): 35–48.

———. "Venedik Devlet Arşivindeki Türkçe Belgeler Kolleksiyonu ve Bizimle İlgili Diğer Belgeler." *Belgeler* 5–8, nos. 9–12 (1968–71): 1–151.

Gülsoy, Ersin. *Malatya Divriği ve Darende Sancaklarının İlk Tahriri (1519)*. Erzurum: Fenomen, 2009.

von Hammer-Purgstall, Joseph. *Geschichte des Osmanischen Reiches*. Volume 3, *Vom Regierungsantritte Suleiman des Ersten bis zum Tode Selim's II*. Pest: C.A. Hartleben, 1828.

Husayn Vaiz Kashifi. *Makhzan al-inshā'*. Ms. TSK, Revan Köşkü, 1049.

———. *Aḫlāḳ-ı Aḥmedī*. Translated by Osmanzade Taib. Istanbul: Matbaa-yı Daru'l-hilafe, 1840–41.

———. *Akhlak-ı Muhsini, or, the Morals of the Beneficient*. Translated by Henry George Keene. Hertford: Stephen Austin, 1850.

———. *Akhlāq-i Muḥṣinī*. Lucknow: Tij Kumar, 1972.

Hüseyin Hüsameddin. *Nişāncılar Durağı*. Ms. İslam Araştırmaları Merkezi.

İlhan, M. Mehdi. *Amid (Diyarbakır). 1518 Tarihli Defter-i Mufassal*. Ankara: Türk Tarih Kurumu, 2000).

Kemalpaşazade Ahmed. *Tevārīḫ-i Āl-i 'Os̱mān. X. Defter*. Edited and transliterated by Şerafettin Severcan. Ankara: Türk Tarih Kurumu, 1996.

Kınalızade Hasan. *Teẕkiretü'ş-şu'arā*. 2 volumes. Edited by İbrahim Kutluk. Ankara: Türk Tarih Kurumu, 1978.

Kołodziejczyk, Dariusz. *Ottoman-Polish Diplomatic Relations (15th–18th Century): An Annotated Edition of 'Ahdnames and Other Documents*. Leiden: Brill, 2000.

Latifi. *Teẕkiretü'ş- şu'arā*. Istanbul: İkdam Matbaası, 1896–97.

Lütfi Paşa. *Tevārīḫ-i Āl-i 'Os̱mān*. Edited by Âlî Bey. Istanbul: Matbaa-yı Âmire, 1922–23.

Mahmud bin Mustafa. *Münşe'āt*. Ms. SK, Hüsrev Paşa 564.

Matrakçı Nasuh. *Beyān-ı Menāzil-i Sefer-i Irāḳeyn-i Sulṭān Süleymān Ḫān*. Edited by Hüseyin G. Yurdaydın. Ankara: Türk Tarih Kurumu, 1976.

Mecdi Efendi. *Terceme-yi Şaḳā'ıḳ-ı nu'māniyye*. Istanbul: Tabhane-yi Amire, 1853.

Meredith-Owens, G. M. "Traces of a Lost Autobiographical Work by a Courtier of Selim II." *BSOAS* 23, no. 3 (1960): 456–73.

Mevlana Neşri. *Kitāb-ı Cihān-nümā*. 2 volumes. Edited by F. R. Unat and M. A. Köymen. Ankara: Türk Tarih Kurumu, 1949–57.

Mustafa Âli. *Künhü'l-Ahbâr'ın Tezkire Kısmı*. Edited by Mustafa İsen. Ankara: Atatürk Kültür, Dil ve Tarih Yüksek Kurumu, 1994.

Müstakimzade Süleyman Sa'deddin Efendi. *Tuḥfetü'l-ḫaṭṭāṭīn*. Istanbul: Devlet Matbaası, 1928.

Parmaksızoğlu, İsmet. "Kuzey Irak'ta Osmanlı Hâkimiyetinin Kuruluşu ve Memun Bey'in Hatıraları." *Belleten* 37, no. 146 (1973): 191–230.

Peçevi İbrahim Efendi. *Tārīḫ-i Peçevī*. Edited by Fahri Ç. Derin and Vahit Çabuk. Istanbul: Enderun Kitabevi, 1980.

Procházka-Eisl, Gisele, and Claudia Römer, eds. *Osmanische Beamtenschreiben und Privatbriefe der Zeit Süleymāns des Prächtigen aus dem Haus-, Hof-, un Staatsarchiv zu Wien*. Vienna: Verlag der Österreichischen Akademie der Wissenschaften, 2007.

Riyazi. *Teẕkire-yi Riyāżī*. Ms. Millet Genel Kütüphanesi 765.

Schaendlinger, Anton C. and Claudia Römer. *Die Schreiben Süleymāns des Prächtigen an Karl V., Ferdinand I. und Maximilian II*. 2 volumes. Vienna: Verlag der Österreichischen Akademie der Wissenschaften, 1983.

Sehi. *Teẕkire-yi Sehī*. Istanbul: Matbaa-yı Âmidî, 1907.

Siraj al-Din Abi Khafs Umar. *Zahr al-Qimam fī Qiṣṣa Yūsuf 'alayhi as-Salām*. Edited by Kamal al-Din Allam. Beirut: Dar al-kutub al-ilmiyya, 2003.

Şakiroğlu, Mahmut. "1521 Tarihli Osmanlı-Venedik Andlaşmasının Aslî Metni." *İÜEF Tarih Enstitüsü Dergisi* 12 (1982): 387–404.

Şeref Han. *Şerefname*. Translated by Mehmet Emin Bozarslan. 2 volumes. Istanbul: Ant, 1971.

Şah Tahmasb-ı Safevî. *Tezkire*. Translated by Hicabi Kırlangıç. Istanbul: Anka, 2001.

Tekin, Şinasi. "Fatih Devrine Ait Bir İnşa Mecmuası." *JTS* 20 (1996): 267–311.

Theunissen, Hans. "Ottoman-Venetian Diplomatics: the ʿAhd-names. The Historical Background and the Development of a Category of Political-Commercial Instruments together with an Annotated Edition of a Corpus of Relevant Documents." *Electronic Journal of Oriental Studies* 1, no. 2 (1998): 1–698.

Tursun Beg. *Tārīḫ-i Ebū'l-fetḥ*. Edited by Mertol Tulum. Istanbul: Baha Matbaası, 1977.

Studies

Abisaab, Rula Jurdi. *Converting Persia: Religion and Power in the Safavid Empire*. London: I.B. Tauris, 2004.

Abou-El-Haj, Rifaat Ali. "Aspects of the Legitimization of Ottoman Rule as Reflected in the Preambles of Two Early Liva Kanunnameler." *Turcica* 21–23 (1991): 371–83.

––––––. "The Expression of Ottoman Political Culture in the Literature of Advice to Princes (Nasihatnameler), Sixteenth to Twentieth Centuries." In *Sociology in the Rubric of Social Science: Professor Ramkrishna Mukherjee Felicitation Volume*, edited by R. K. Bhattacharya and Asok K. Ghosh, 282–92. Calcutta: Ministry of Human Resource Development, 1995.

––––––. *Formation of the Modern State: The Ottoman Empire, Sixteenth to Eighteenth Centuries*. 2nd edition. Syracuse: Syracuse University Press, 2005.

––––––. "The Ottoman Nasihatname as a Discourse over 'Morality.'" In *Mélanges Professeur Robert Mantran*, edited by Abdeljelil Temimi, 17–30. Zaghouan: CEROMDE, 1988.

Adams, Julia. *The Familial State: Ruling Families and Merchant Capitalism in Early Modern Europe*. Ithaca: Cornell University Press, 2005.

Afyoncu, Erhan. "Defter Emini." *TDVİA*, vol. 9.

––––––. "Osmanlı Siyasî Tarihinin Ana Kaynakları: Kronikler." *Türkiye Araştırmaları Literatür Dergisi* 1, no. 2 (2003): 101–72.

Ágoston, Gábor. "Empires and Warfare in East-Central Europe, 1550–1750: The Ottoman Habsburg Rivalry and Military Transformation." In *European Warfare, 1350–1750*, edited by Frank Tallett and D. J. B. Trim, 110–34. Cambridge: Cambridge University Press, 2010.

––––––. "A Flexible Empire: Authority and Its Limits on the Ottoman Frontiers." *IJTS* 9, nos. 1–2 (2003): 15–31.

––––––. "Ideologie, Propaganda und politischer Pragmatismus: Die Auseinandersetzung der osmanischen und habsburgischen Grossmächte und die mitteleuropäische Konfrontation." In *Kaiser Ferdinand I. – Ein mitteleuropäischer Herrscher*, edited by Martina Fuchs, Teréz Oborni and Gábor Újvári. 207–33. Münster: Aschendorff, 2005.

––––––. "Information, Ideology, and Limits of Imperial Policy: Ottoman Grand Strategy in the Context of Ottoman-Habsburg Rivalry." In *The Early Modern Ottomans: Remapping the Empire*, edited by Virginia H. Aksan and Daniel Goffman, 75–103. Cambridge: Cambridge University Press, 2007.

Akgündüz, Hasan. *Klasik Dönem Osmanlı Medrese Sistemi: Amaç-Yapı-İşleyiş.* Istanbul: Ulusal, 1997.

Aköz, Alaaddin and İbrahim Solak. "Dulkadirli Beyliğinin Osmanlı Devletine İlhakı ve Sonrasında Çıkan İsyanlar." *Türk Dünyası Araştırmaları* 153 (November–December 2004): 41–50.

––––––. "Dulkadirli Eyâletine Ait Bir Kânûnnâme (1533–1546)." *Kırgızistan "Manas" Üniversitesi Sosyal Bilimler Dergisi* 9 (2004): 9–29.

Aksan, Virginia H. *An Ottoman Statesman in War and Peace: Ahmed Resmi Efendi, 1700–1783* (Leiden: Brill, 1995).

Alam, Muzaffar. "*Akhlāqī* Norms and Mughal Governance." In *The Making of Indo-Persian Culture: Indian and French Studies*, edited by Muzaffar Alam, Françoise 'Nalini' Delvoye, Marc Gaborieau, 67–95. New Delhi: Manohar Publishers & Distributors, 2000.

––––––. *The Languages of Political Islam: India, 1200–1800.* Chicago: University of Chicago Press, 2004.

––––––. "The Making of a Munshi." *Comparative Studies of South Asia, Africa and the Middle East* 24, no. 2 (2004): 61–72.

Alam, Muzaffar and Sanjay Subrahmanyam. "Introduction." In *The Mughal State 1526–1750, 1–71.* Delhi: Oxford University Press, 1998.

Alford, Stephen. *Burghley: William Cecil at the Court of Elizabeth I.* New Haven: Yale University Press, 2008.

Ali, M. Athar. "Political Structures of the Islamic Orient in the Sixteenth and Seventeenth Centuries." In *Medieval India 1: Researches in the History of India, 1250–1750*, edited by Irfan Habib, 129–40. Delhi: Oxford University Press, 1992.

Allouche, Adel. *The Origins and Development of the Ottoman-Ṣafavid Conflict (906–962/1500–1555).* Berlin: Klaus Schwarz, 1983.

d'Amico, Juan Carlos. *Charles Quint, maître du monde: entre mythe et réalité.* Caen: Presses Universitaires de Caen, 2004.

Amin, Camron Michael. "*Mujassama-i bud mujassama-i nabud*: The Image of the Safavids in 20th Century Iranian Popular Historiography." In *History and Historiography of Post-Mongol Central Asia and the Middle East: Studies in Honor of John E. Woods*, edited by Judith Pfeiffer and Sholeh A. Quinn, 343–59. Wiesbaden: Otto Harrassowitz, 2006.

Anderson, Perry. *Lineages of the Absolutist State.* London: NLB, 1974.

Andrews, Walter G. "Literary Art of the Golden Age: The Age of Süleymân." In *Süleymân the Second and His Time*, edited by Halil İnalcık and Cemal Kafadar, 353–68. Istanbul: The Isis Press, 1993.

––––––. *Poetry's Voice, Society's Song: Ottoman Lyric Poetry.* Seattle: University of Washington Press, 1985.

Andrews, Walter G. and Mehmet Kalpaklı. *Age of Beloveds: Love and the Beloved in Early Modern Ottoman and European Culture and Society.* Durham: Duke University Press, 2005.

Anglo, Sydney. *Spectacle, Pageantry, and Early Tudor Policy*. Second edition. Oxford: Clarendon Press; New York: Oxford University Press, 1987.

Ankersmit, Frank N. *Historical Representation*. Stanford: Stanford University Press, 2001.

Antov, Nikolay. "Imperial Expansion, Colonization, and Conversion to Islam in the Islamic World's 'Wild West:' The Formation of the Muslim Community in Ottoman Deliorman (N.E. Balkans), 15th-16th cc." Ph. D. diss., University of Chicago, 2011.

Arı, Bülent. "Early Ottoman Diplomacy: Ad Hoc Period." In *Ottoman Diplomacy: Conventional or Unconventional?*, edited by Nuri Yurdusev, 36–65. Basingstoke, Hampshire: Palgrave Macmillan, 2004.

Atçıl, Abdurrahman. "The Formation of the Ottoman Learned Class and Legal Scholarship." PhD diss., University of Chicago, 2010.

Ay, Resul. "Ortaçağ Anadolu'sunda Bilginin Seyahati: Talebeler, Âlimler, Dervişler." *TTYY* 3 (Spring 2006): 17–53.

Aydın, Bilgin. "Osmanlı Bürokrasisinde Divan-ı Hümâyun Defter Formlarının Ortaya Çıkışı ve Gelişimi (XV–XVI. Yüzyıl)." PhD diss., Marmara Üniversitesi, 2003.

Aydın, Bilgin and Rıfat Günalan. *XV.–XVI. Yüzyıllarda Osmanlı Maliyesi ve Defter Sistemi*. Istanbul: Yeditepe, 2008.

al-Azmeh, Aziz. *Muslim Kingship: Power and the Sacred in Muslim, Christian, and Pagan Polities*. London: I.B. Tauris, 1997.

Babayan, Kathryn. *Mystics, Monarchs, and Messiahs: Cultural Landscapes of Early Modern Iran*. Cambridge, MA: Center for Middle Eastern Studies of Harvard University, Harvard University Press, 2002.

Babinger, Franz. *Die Geschichtsschreiber der Osmanen und ihre Werke*. Leipzig: Otto Harrassowitz, 1927.

———. "Nishandji." *EI 2*.

Bacqué-Grammont, Jean-Louis. "Autour d'une correspondance entre Charles-quint et İbrâhîm Paşa." *Turcica* 15 (1983): 231–46.

———. "Sur deux lettres de Ferdinand Ier à İbrâhîm Paşa." *Turcica* 19 (1987): 175–93.

———. "The Eastern Policy of Süleymân the Magnificent, 1520–1533." In İnalcık and Kafadar, *Süleymân the Second and His Time*, 219–28.

———. "Une lettre d'İbrâhîm Paşa à Charles Quint," in *Comité international d'études pré-ottomanes et ottomanes, 6th Symposium, Cambridge, 1st-4th July 1984*, edited by idem and E.J. van Donzel (Istanbul: Divit, 1987): 65–88.

———. *Les Ottomans, les Safavides et leurs voisins: contribution à l'histoire des relations internationales dans l'Orient islamique de 1514 à 1524*. Istanbul: Nederlands Historisch-Archaeologisch Instituut te Istanbul, 1987.

———. "Un rapport inédit sur la révolte anatolienne de 1527. *StIsl* 62 (1985): 155–71.

Bakhit, Adnan. *The Ottoman Province of Damascus in the Sixteenth Century*. Beirut: Librairie du Liban, 1982.

Balabanlılar, Lisa. *Imperial Identity in the Mughal Empire: Memory and Dynastic Politics in Early Modern South and Central Asia*. London: I.B. Tauris, 2011.

Baltacı, Câhid. *XV-XVI. Asırlar Osmanlı Medreseleri: Teşkilât, Tarih.* Istanbul: İrfan Matbaası, 1976.

Barkan, Ömer Lütfi. *Osmanlı Devleti'nin Sosyal ve Ekonomik Tarihi: Osmanlı Devlet Arşivleri Üzerinde Tetkikler-Makaleler.* Edited by Hüseyin Özdeğer. 2 volumes. Istanbul: Istanbul Üniversitesi Rektörlüğü, 2000.

Barkey, Karen. *Bandits and Bureaucrats: The Ottoman Route to State Centralization.* Ithaca: Cornell University Press, 1994.

————. *Empire of Difference: The Ottomans in Comparative Perspective.* Cambridge: Cambridge University Press, 2008.

Bashir, Shahzad. "Deciphering the Cosmos from Creation to Apocalypse: The Hurufiyya Movement and Medieval Islamic Esotericism." In *Imagining the End: Visions of Apocalypse from the Ancient Middle East to Modern America,* edited by Abbas Amanat, 168–84. London: I.B. Tauris, 2002.

————. *Messianic Hopes and Mystical Visions: The Nurbakhshiya between Medieval and Modern Islam.* Columbia, SC: South Carolina University Press, 2003.

Bayly, C.A. *The Birth of the Modern World, 1780–1914: Global Connections and Comparisons.* Malden, MA: Blackwell, 2004.

Bayrak, M. Orhan *"Osmanlı Tarihi" Yazarları.* Expanded second edition. Istanbul: Milenyum, 2002.

Beckjord, Sarah H. *Territories of History: Humanism, Rhetoric, and the Historical Imagination in the Early Chronicles of Spanish America.* University Park, Penn.: Pennsylvania State University Press, 2007.

Bentley, Jerry H. "Early Modern Europe and the Early Modern World." In *Between the Middle Ages and Modernity: Individual and Community in the Early Modern World,* edited by Charles H. Parker and Jerry H. Bentley, 13–31. Lanham: Rowman & Littlefield, 2007.

Berkey, Jonathan. *The Transmission of Knowledge in Medieval Cairo: A Social History of Islamic Education.* Princeton, NJ: Princeton University Press, 1992.

Berktay, Halil. *Cumhuriyet İdeolojisi ve Fuat Köprülü.* Istanbul: Kaynak, 1983.

————. "Dört Tarihçinin Sosyal Portresi." *Toplum ve Bilim,* 54 (Summer–Fall 1991): 34–41.

————. "Three Empires and the Societies They Governed: Iran, India and the Ottoman Empire." In *New Approaches to State and Peasant in Ottoman History,* edited by Halil Berktay and Suraiya Faroqhi, 242–63. London: Frank Cass, 1992.

Bilge, Mustafa. *İlk Osmanlı Medreseleri.* Istanbul: Edebiyat Fakültesi, 1984.

Binbaş, İlker Evrim. "Sharaf-al-Dīn ʿAlī Yazdī (*ca.* 770s-858/*ca.* 1370s–1454): Prophecy, Politics, and Historiography in Late Medieval Islamic History." PhD diss., University of Chicago, 2009.

Blake, Stephen P. "The Patrimonial-Bureaucratic Empire of the Mughals." *Journal of Asian Studies* 39, no. 1 (November 1979): 77–94.

Boettcher, Susan R. "Confessionalization: Reformation, Religion, Absolutism, Modernity." *History Compass* 2, no. 1 (2004): 1–10.

Bonney, Richard. *The European Dynastic States, 1494–1660.* Oxford: Oxford University Press, 1991.

Bosbach, Franz. "The European Debate on Universal Monarchy." In *Theories of Empire, 1450–180*, ed. David Armitage, 81–98. Aldershot: Ashgate, 1998.

———. "*Imperium Turcorum* oder *Christianorum Monarchia* – Die Osmanen in der heilsgeschichtlichen Deutung Mercurino Gattinaras." In *Das Osmanische Reich und die Habsburgermonarchie*, edited by Marlene Kurz et. al., 167–180. Vienna: R. Oldenbourg, 2005.

Bostan, İdris. "Cezâyir-i Bahr-i Sefîd Eyaletinin Kuruluşu." *Tarih Dergisi* 38 (2003): 61–78.

Bosworth, C.E. "Naṣīḥat al-Mulūk." *EI 2*.

Bourdieu, Pierre. "Rethinking the State: Genesis and Structure of the Bureaucratic Field." In *State/Culture: State-Formation after the Cultural Turn*, edited by George Steinmetz, 53–75. Ithaca: Cornell University Press, 1999.

Boyden, James M. *The Courtier and the King: Ruy Gómez de Silva, Philip II, and the Court of Spain*. Berkeley: University of California Press, 1995.

Braddick, Michael J. *State Formation in Early Modern England, c. 1550–1700*. Cambridge: Cambridge University Press, 2000.

Brady, Jr., Thomas A. "Confessionalization-The Career of a Concept." In *Confessionalization in Europe, 1555–1700: Essays in Honor and Memory of Bodo Nischan*, edited by John M. Headley, Hans J. Hillerbrand and Anthony J. Papalas, 1–20. Aldershot: Ashgate, 2004.

Brannigan, John. *New Historicism and Cultural Materialism*. New York: St. Martin's Press, 1998.

Braude, Benjamin and Bernard Lewis, eds. *Christians and Jews in the Ottoman Empire*, vol. 1, *The Central Lands*, vol. 2, *The Arabic-Speaking Lands*. New York: Holmes & Meier, 1982.

Braudel, Ferdinand. *The Mediterranean and the Mediterranean World in the Age of Philip II*. Translated by Siân Reynolds. 3 volumes. London: The Folio Society, 2000.

Brook, Timothy, ed. *The Asiatic Mode of Production in China*. Armonk, N.Y.: M.E. Sharpe, 1989.

Brummett, Palmira. "The Overrated Adversary: Rhodes and Ottoman Naval Power." *The Historical Journal* 36, no. 3 (1993): 517–41.

Brüning, Alfons. "Confessionalization in the *Slavia Orthodoxa* (Belorussia, Ukraine, Russia)? – Potential and Limits of a Western Historiographical Concept." In *Religion and the Conceptual Boundary in Central and Eastern Europe: Encounters of Faiths*, edited by Thomas Bremer, 66–97. Basingstoke, Hampshire: Palgrave Macmillan, 2008.

Burke, Peter. *Languages and Communities in Early Modern Europe*. Cambridge: Cambridge University Press, 2004.

Bursalı Mehmet Tahir Efendi. *Osmanlı Müellifleri 1299–1915*. Edited by İsmail Özen. Istanbul: Meral, 1975.

Buzov, Snjezana. "The Lawgiver and His Lawmakers: The Role of Legal Discourse in the Change of the Ottoman Imperial Culture." Ph. D. *diss*., University of Chicago, 2005.

———. "History." In *Key Themes for the Study of Islam*, edited by Jamal J. Elias, 182–99. Oxford: Oneworld, 2010.

Casale, Giancarlo. *The Ottoman Age of Exploration.* Oxford: Oxford University Press, 2010.

Charton-Le Clech, Sylvie. *Chancellerie et culture au XVIe siècle (les notaires et secretaires du roi de 1515 à 1547).* Toulouse: Presses universitaires du Mirail, 1993.

Clark, Elizabeth A. *History, Theory, Text: Historians and the Linguistic Turn.* Cambridge, MA: Harvard University Press, 2004.

Cohn, Dorrit. *The Distinction of Fiction.* Baltimore: The Johns Hopkins University Press, 1999.

Colebrook, Claire. *New Literary Histories: New Historicism and Contemporary Criticism.* Manchester: Manchester University Press, 1997.

Cole, Alison. *Virtue and Magnificence: Art of the Italian Renaissance Courts.* New York: H.N. Abrams, 1995.

Contamine, Philippe, ed. *War and Competition between States,* Theme A of *The Origins of the Modern State in Europe, 13th to 18th Centuries,* edited by Wim Blockmans and Jean-Philippe Genet. Oxford: Clarendon Press; New York: Oxford University Press, 2000.

Cormack, Lesley B. "The Fashioning of an Empire: Geography and the State in Elizabethan England." *In Geography and Empire,* edited by Anne Godlewska and Neil Smith, 15–30. Oxford: Blackwell, 1994.

Croutwater, Susan K. "Weber and Sultanism in the Light of Historical Data." In *Theory of Liberty, Legitimacy and Power: New Directions in the Intellectual and Scientific Legacy of Max Weber,* edited by Vatro Murvar, 168–84. London: Routledge and Kegan Paul, 1985.

Crouzet, Denis. *La sagesse et le malheur: Michel de l'Hospital, Chancelier de France.* Seyssel: Champ Vallon, 1998.

Çağman, Filiz and Zeren Tanındı. "Remarks on Some Manuscripts from the Top-kapı Palace Treasury in the Context of Ottoman-Safavid Relations." *Muqarnas* 13 (1996): 132–48.

Çetinsaya, Gökhan. "Rethinking Nationalism and Islam: Some Preliminary Notes on the Roots of 'Turkish-Islamic Synthesis' in Modern Turkish Political Thought," *The Muslim World* 89, nos. 3–4 (July–October 1999): 350–76.

Çıpa, Erdem Hakkı. "The Centrality of the Periphery: The Rise to Power of Selim I, 1481–1512." PhD diss., Harvard University, 2007.

Çulpan, Cevdet. "İstanbul Süleymaniye Camii Kitabesi." In *Kanunî Armağanı,* edited by Uluğ İğdemir, 291–99. Ankara: Türk Tarih Kurumu, 1970.

Dale, Stephen F. *The Muslim Empires of the Ottomans, Safavids, and Mughals.* Cambridge: Cambridge University Press, 2010.

———. "Steppe Humanism: The Autobiographical Writings of Zahir al-Din Muhammad Babur, 1483–1530," *IJMES* 22, no. 1 (February 1990): 37–58.

Danişmend, İsmail Hami. *İzahlı Osmanlı Tarihi Kronolojisi. Vol. 2, M. 1513–1573/H. 919–981.* Istanbul: Türkiye Basımevi, 1948.

Darling, Linda. "Ottoman Salary Registers as a Source for Economic and Social History." *TSAB* 14, no. 1 (1990): 13–33.

———. "Political Change and Political Discourse in the Early Modern Mediterranean World." *Journal of Interdisciplinary History* 38, no. 4 (Spring 2008): 505–31.

———. *Revenue-Raising and Legitimacy: Tax Collection and Finance Administration in the Ottoman Empire, 1560–1660.* Leiden and New York: Brill, 1996.

Darwin, John. *After Tamerlane: The Global History of Empire since 1405.* London: Allen Lane, 2007.

Decei, Aurel. "Un "Fetih-nâme-i Karaboğdan" (1538) de Nasuh Matrakçı." In *60. Doğum Yılı Münasebetiyle Fuad Köprülü Armağanı.* Istanbul: Osman Yalçın Matbaası, 1953.

Deny, Jean. "Re'īs ül Küttāb." *EI 2.*

Dilger, Konrad. *Untersuchungen zur Geschichte des osmanischen Hofzeremoniells im 15. und 16. Jahrhundert.* Munich: Rudolf Trofenik, 1967.

Dirimtekin, Feridun. "Belgrad'ın İki Muhasarası." *İstanbul Enstitüsü Dergisi 2* (1956): 51–76.

Divitçioğlu, Sencer. *Asya Üretim Tarzı ve Osmanlı Toplumu.* Istanbul: Köz, 1971.

Diyanet, A. Ekber. *İlk Osmanlı-İran Anlaşması (1555 Amasya Musalahası).* Istanbul: Edebiyat Fakültesi, 1971.

Dyson, Kenneth. *The State Tradition in Western Europe: A Study of an Idea and Institution.* Oxford: Martin Robertson, 1980.

Ebel, Kathryn Ann. "City Views, Imperial Visions: Cartography and the Visual Culture of Urban Space in the Ottoman Empire, 1453–1603." PhD diss., University of Texas at Austin, 2002.

Eberhard, Elke. *Osmanische Polemik gegen die Safawiden im 16. Jahrhundert nach arabischen Handschriften.* Freiburg: Klaus Schwarz, 1970.

Édouard, Sylvène. *L'empire imaginaire de Philippe II: pouvoir des images et discours du pouvoir sous les Habsbourg d'Espagne au XVIe sie'cle.* Paris: Honoré Champion, 2005.

Ellenius, Allan, ed. *Iconography, Propaganda, and Legitimation.* Oxford: Clarendon Press, 1998.

Elliott, John H. "Ottoman-Habsburg Rivalry: The European Perspective." In İnalcık and Kafadar, *Süleymân the Second and His Time,* 153–62.

———. "Power and Propaganda in the Spain of Philip IV." In *Rites of Power: Symbolism, Ritual, and Politics since the Middle Ages,* edited by Sean Wilentz, 145–74. Philadelphia: University of Pennsylvania Press, 1985.

Emecen, Feridun M. 'Büyük Türk'e Pannonia Düzlüklerini Açan Savaş Mohaç 1526." In *Muhteşem Süleyman,* edited by Özlem Kumrular, 45–92. Istanbul: Kitap, 2007.

———. *İlk Osmanlılar ve Batı Anadolu Beylikler Dünyası.* Istanbul: Kitabevi, 2001.

———. "Osmanlı Devleti'nin 'Şark Meselesi'nin Ortaya Çıkışı: İlk Münasebetler ve İç Yansımaları." In *Tarihten Günümüze Türk-İran İlişkileri Sempozyumu,* 33–48. Ankara: Türk Tarih Kurumu, 2003.

Emiralioğlu, Mevhibe Pınar. "Cognizance of the Ottoman World: Visual and Textual Representations in the Sixteenth-Century Ottoman Empire (1514–1596)." PhD diss., University of Chicago, 2006.

Emre, Side. "İbrahim-i Gülşeni (ca. 1442–1534): Itinerant Saint and Cairene Ruler." PhD diss., University of Chicago, 2009.

Engel, Pál. *The Realm of St. Stephen: A History of Medieval Hungary, 895–1526.* Translated by Tamás Pálosfalvi. London: I.B. Tauris, 2001.

Engster, Daniel. *Divine Sovereignty: The Origins of Modern State Power*. DeKalb: Northern Illinois University Press, 2001.

Ersanlı, Büşra. "The Ottoman Empire in the Historiography of the Kemalist Era: A Theory of Fatal Decline." In *The Ottomans and the Balkans: A Discussion of Historiography*, edited by Fikret Adanır and Suraiya Faroqhi, 115–54. Leiden: Brill, 2002.

Ertman, Thomas. *Birth of the Leviathan: Building States and Regimes in Medieval and Early Modern Europe*. Cambridge: Cambridge University Press, 1997.

Erünsal, İsmail E. *The Life and Works of Tâcî-zâde Ca'fer Çelebi*. Istanbul: İstanbul Üniversitesi Edebiyat Fakültesi, 1983.

Eryılmaz, Fatma Sinem. "The *Shehnameci*s of Sultan Süleyman: 'Arif and Eflatun and Their Dynastic Project." PhD diss., University of Chicago, 2010.

Faroqhi, Suraiya. *The Ottoman Empire and the World around It*. London: I.B. Tauris, 2004.

———. "Politics and Socioeconomic Change in the Ottoman Empire in the Later Sixteenth Century." In *Süleyman the Magnificent and His Age*, edited by Metin I. Kunt and Christine Woodhead, 91–113. London: Longman, 1995.

Fernández-Santamaria, J. A. *The State, War and Peace: Spanish Political Thought in the Renaissance 1516–1559*. Cambridge: Cambridge University Press, 1977.

Fetvacı, Emine. "The Office of the Ottoman Court Historian." In *Studies on Istanbul and Beyond. The Freely Papers, Volume I*, edited by Robert G. Ousterhout, 7–21. Philadelphia: University of Pennsylvania Museum of Archaeology and Anthropology, 2007.

———. "Viziers to Eunuchs: Transitions in Ottoman Manuscript Patronage, 1566–1617." PhD diss., Harvard University, 2005.

Findley, Carter V. *Bureaucratic Reform in the Ottoman Empire: The Sublime Porte, 1789–1922*. Princeton, NJ: Princeton University Press, 1980.

———. *Ottoman Civil Officialdom: A Social History*. Princeton, NJ: Princeton University Press, 1988.

Finkel, Caroline. *Osman's Dream: The Story of the Ottoman Empire, 1300–1923*. New York: Basic Books, 2006.

Finlay, Robert. "'I am the Servant of the Turkish Sultan:' Venice, the Ottoman Empire, and Christendom, 1523–1534." In *Venice Besieged: Politics and Diplomacy during the Italian Wars, 1494–1534*, Chapter X. Aldershot: Ashgate Variorum, 2008.

———. "Prophecy and Politics in Istanbul: Charles V, Sultan Süleyman, and the Habsburg Embassy of 1533–1534." *JEMH* 2, no. 1 (1998): 1–31.

Fischer-Galati, Stephen A. *Ottoman Imperialism and German Protestantism 1521–1555*. Cambridge: Harvard University Press, 1959.

Fisher, Alan. "The Life and Family of Süleymân I." In İnalcık and Kafadar, *Süleyman the Second and His Time*, 9–27.

Fleischer, Cornell H. "Alqās Mīrzā Safawī." *Encyclopædia Iranica*, vol. 1.

———. "Between the Lines: Realities of Scribal Life in the Sixteenth Century. In *Studies in Ottoman History in Honour of Professor V. L. Ménage*, edited by Colin Heywood and Colin Imber, 45–61. Istanbul: The Isis Press, 1994.

———. *Bureaucrat and Intellectual in the Ottoman Empire: The Historian Mustafa Âli (1541–1600)*. Princeton, NJ: Princeton University Press, 1986.

———. "From Şeyhzade Korkud to Mustafa Âli: Cultural Origins of the Ottoman Nasihatname." In *Proceedings of the Third Congress on the Social and Economic History of Turkey*, edited by Heath W. Lowry and Ralph S. Hattox, 67–77 Istanbul: Isis, 1990.

———. "The Lawgiver as Messiah: The Making of the Imperial Image in the Reign of Süleymân." In *Soliman le magnifique et son temps, Actes du Colloque de Paris. Galeries Nationales du Grand Palais, 7–10 Mars 1990*, edited by Gilles Veinstein, 159–77. Paris: La Documentation Française, 1992.

———. "Mahdi and Millenium: Messianic Dimensions in the Development of Ottoman Imperial Ideology." In *The Great Ottoman-Turkish Civilization. Vol. 3, Philosophy, Science and Institutions*, edited by Kemal Çiçek, 42–54. Ankara: Yeni Türkiye, 2000.

———. "Preliminaries to the Study of Ottoman Bureaucracy." *JTS* 10 (1986): 135–41.

———. "Scribal Training and Medrese Education in the Sixteenth-Century Ottoman Empire." *TSAB* 8, no. 1 (1984): 27–29.

———. "Secretaries' Dreams: Augury and Angst in the Ottoman Scribal Service." In *Armagan: Festschrift für Andreas Tietze*, edited by Ingeborg Baldauf, 77–88. Prague: Enigma, 1994.

———. "Shadows of Shadows: Prophecy and Politics in 1530s Istanbul." *IJTS* 13, no. 1–2 (2007): 51–62.

Flemming, Barbara. "Public Opinion under Sultan Süleymân." In İnalcık and Kafadar, *Süleymân the Second and His Time*, 59–67.

———. "Ṣāḥib-ḳirān und Mahdī: Türkische Endzeiterwartungen im ersten Jahrzehnt der Regierung Süleymāns." In *Between the Danube and the Caucasus*, edited by György Kara, 43–62. Budapest: Akadémiai Kiadó, 1987.

Fletcher, Joseph. "Integrative History: Parallels and Interconnections in the Early Modern Period." In *Studies on Chinese and Islamic Inner Asia*, article no. X. Edited by Beatrice Forbes Manz. Aldershot: Ashgate Variorum, 1995.

———. "Turco-Mongolian Monarchic Tradition in the Ottoman Empire." *Harvard Ukrainian Studies* 3–4 (1979–80): 236–51.

Floor, Willem. *Safavid Government Institutions*. Costa Mesa: Mazda Publishers, 2001.

Fludernik, Monika "Identity/Alterity." In *The Cambridge Companion to Narrative*, edited by David Herman, 260–73. Cambridge: Cambridge University Press, 2007.

Fodor, Pál. "Ottoman Policy Towards Hungary, 1520–1541." *Acta Orientalia Academiae Scientiarum Hungaricae* 45, nos. 2–3 (1991): 271–345.

———. "The View of the Turk in Hungary: The Apocalyptic Tradition and the Legend of the Red Apple in Ottoman-Hungarian Context." In *Les traditions apocalyptiques au tournant de la chute de Constantinople*, edited by Benjamin Lellouch and Stéphane Yérasimos, 99–131. Paris: Harmattan; Istanbul: Institut français d'études anatoliennes Georges-Dumézil, 2000.

Fortna, Benjamin C. *Imperial Classroom: Islam, the State, and Education in the Late Ottoman Empire*. Oxford: Oxford University Press, 2002.

Galotta, Aldo. "Khayral-Dīn (Khiḍîr) Pasha, Barbarossa." *EI 2*.

Geary, Patrick J. *Phantoms of Remembrance: Memory and Oblivion at the End of the First Millennium.* Princeton, NJ: Princeton University Press, 1994.

Giesey, Ralph E. "Models of Rulership in French Royal Ceremonial." In Wilentz, *Rites of Power*, 41–64.

Goffman, Daniel. "Negotiating with the Renaissance State: The Ottoman Empire and the New Diplomacy." In Aksan and Goffman, *The Early Modern Ottomans*, 61–74.

———. *The Ottoman Empire and Early Modern Europe.* Cambridge: Cambridge University Press, 2002.

Goldstone, Jack A. "Neither Late Imperial nor Early Modern: Efflorescences and the Qing Formation in World History." In *The Qing Formation in World-Historical Time*, edited by Lynn A. Struve, 242–302. Cambridge, MA: Harvard University Asia Center, Harvard University Press, 2004.

———. "The Problem of the 'Early Modern' World." *Journal of the Economic and Social History of the Orient* 41, no. 3 (1998): 249–84.

Gommans, Jos. *Mughal Warfare: Indian Frontiers and High Roads to Empire, 1500–1700.* London: Routledge, 2002.

Goody, Jack. *The Eurasian Miracle* (Cambridge: Polity, 2011).

Gorski, Philip S. "Calvinism and State Formation in Early Modern Europe." In Steinmetz, *State/Culture*, 147–81.

———. *The Disciplinary Revolution: Calvinism and the Rise of the State in Early Modern Europe.* Chicago: University of Chicago Press, 2003.

———. "The Protestant Ethic and the Bureaucratic Revolution: Ascetic Protestantism and Administrative Rationalization in Early Modern Europe," In *Max Weber's Economy and Society: A Critical Companion*, edited by Charles Camic, Philip S. Gorski, and David M. Trubek, 267–96. Stanford: Stanford University Press, 2005.

Gökbilgin, M. Tayyib. "Kanunî Sultan Süleyman'ın Macaristan ve Avrupa Siyasetinin Sebep ve Âmilleri, Geçirdiği Safhalar." In İğdemir, *Kanunî Armağanı*, 5–40.

———. "Nişâncı." *İA*, vol. 3, 299–302.

———. *Osmanlı Müesseseleri Teşkilâtı ve Medeniyeti Tarihine Genel Bakış.* Istanbul: Edebiyat Fakültesi, 1977.

———. "Rüstem Paşa ve Hakkındaki İthamlar." *Tarih Dergisi* 8, no. 11 (1955): 11–50.

Hagen, Gottfried. "Legitimacy and World Order." In *Legitimizing the Order. The Ottoman Rhetoric of State Power*, edited by Hakan T. Karateke and Maurus Reinkowski, 55–83. Leiden: Brill, 2005.

———. "Translations and Translators in a Multilingual Society: A Case Study of Persian-Ottoman Translations, Late Fifteenth to Early Seventeenth Century." *Eurasian Studies* 2, no. 1 (2003): 95–134.

Halaçoğlu, Yusuf. *XIV–XVII. Yüzyıllarda Osmanlılarda Devlet Teşkilâtı ve Sosyal Yapı.* Ankara: Türk Tarih Kurumu, 1991.

Hampton, Timothy. *Fictions of Embassy: Literature and Diplomacy in Early Modern Europe.* Ithaca: Cornell University Press, 2009.

———. *Literature and the Nation in the Sixteenth Century: Inventing Renaissance France.* Ithaca: Cornell University Press, 2001.

Hanna, Nelly. *In Praise of Books: A Cultural History of Cairo's Middle Class, Sixteenth to the Eighteenth Century.* Syracuse, NY: Syracuse University Press, 2003.

———. "Literacy and the 'Great Divide' in the Islamic World, 1300–1800." *Journal of Global History* 2 (2007): 175–93.

Har-El, Shai. *Struggle for Domination in the Middle East: The Ottoman-Mamluk War, 1485–91.* Leiden: Brill, 1995.

Hathaway, Jane. "Problems of Periodization in Ottoman History: The Fifteenth through the Eighteenth Centuries." *TSAB* 20, no. 2 (Fall 1996): 25–31.

Hattox, Ralph. *Coffee and Coffeehouses: The Origins of a Social Beverage in the Medieval Near East.* Seattle: University of Washington Press, 1985.

Headley, John M. *The Emperor and His Chancellor: A Study of the Imperial Chancellery under Gattinara.* Cambridge: Cambridge University Press, 1983.

———. "Germany, the Empire and *Monarchia* in the Thought and Policy of Gattinara." in *Das Römisch-Deutsche Reich im politischen System Karls V.,* edited by Heinrich Lutz, 15–33. Munich: R. Oldenbourg, 1982.

———. "The Habsburg World Empire and the Revival of Ghibellinism." *Medieval and Renaissance Studies* 7 (1975): 93–127.

———. "Rhetoric and Reality: Messianic, Humanist, and Civilian Themes in the Imperialist Ethos of Gattinara." In *Prophetic Rome in the Renaissance Period,* edited by Marjorie Reeves, 241–69. Oxford: Clarendon Press, 1992.

Hess, Andrew. *The Forgotten Frontier: A History of the Sixteenth-Century Ibero-African Frontier.* Chicago: University of Chicago Press, 1978.

———. "The Ottoman Conquest of Egypt (1517) and the Beginning of the Sixteenth-Century World War." *IJMES* 4, no. 1 (January 1973): 55–76.

Heyd, Uriel. *Studies in Old Ottoman Criminal Law.* Edited by Victor L. Ménage. Oxford: Clarendon Press, 1973.

Heywood, Colin. "Kastamonu." *EI 2.*

———. *Writing Ottoman History: Documents and Interpretations.* Aldershot: Ashgate-Variorum, 2002.

Hindle, Steve. *The State and Social Change in Early Modern England, c. 1550–1640.* Basingstoke and London: Macmillan; New York: St. Martin's Press, 2000.

Hodgson, Marshall G. S. *The Venture of Islam: Conscience and History in a World Civilization.* Vol. 3, *The Gunpowder Empires and Modern Times.* Chicago: University of Chicago Press, 1977.

Holt, P. M. "Khāʾir Beg." *EI 2.*

Howard, Douglas. "Genre and Myth in the Ottoman Advice for Kings Literature." In Aksan and Goffman, *The Early Modern Ottomans,* 137–66.

———. "The Historical Development of the Ottoman Imperial Registry (Defter-i Hakanî): mid-Fifteenth to mid-Seventeenth Centuries." *Archivum Ottomanicum* 11 (1986): 213–30.

———. "Ottoman Historiography and the Literature of 'Decline' of the Sixteenth and Seventeenth Centuries." *Journal of Asian History* 22 (1988): 52–77.

Hsia, R. Po-Chia. *Social Discipline in the Reformation: Central Europe 1550–1750.* London: Routledge, 1989.

Imber, Colin. "Canon and Apocrypha in Early Ottoman History." In Heywood and Imber, *Studies in Ottoman History in Honour of Professor V.L. Ménage*, 118–37.

———. *Ebu's-su'ud: The Islamic Legal Tradition*. Stanford: Stanford University Press, 1997.

———. "Ideals and Legitimation in Early Ottoman History." In Kunt and Woodhead, *Süleyman the Magnificent and His Age*, 138–53.

———. "The Legend of Osman Ghazi." In *The Ottoman Emirate (1300–1389)*, edited by Elizabeth Zachariadou, 67–75. Rethymnon: Crete University Press, 2002.

———. "The Ottoman Dynastic Myth." *Turcica* 19 (1989): 7–27.

———. *The Ottoman Empire, 1300–1650: The Structure of Power*. Basingstoke, Hampshire: Palgrave Macmillan, 2002.

———. "Suleyman as Caliph of the Muslims: Ebu's-Su'ud's Formulation of Ottoman Dynastic Ideology." In Veinstein, *Soliman le magnifique et son temps*, 179–84.

Isom-Verhaaren, Christine. *Allies with the Infidel: The Ottoman and French Alliance in the Sixteenth Century*. London: I.B. Tauris, 2011.

———. "Ottoman-French Interaction, 1480–1580: A Sixteenth-Century Encounter." Ph. D. *diss.*, University of Chicago, 1997.

Itzkowitz, Norman. *Ottoman Empire and Islamic Tradition*. New York: Alfred A. Knopf, 1972.

İnalcık, Halil. "Aḥmad Pasha Khā'in." *EI* 2.

———. "Comments on 'Sultanism': Max Weber's Typification of the Ottoman Polity." *Princeton Papers in Near Eastern Studies* 1 (1992): 49–72.

———. "Decision Making in the Ottoman State." In *Essays in Ottoman History*, 113–21. İstanbul: Eren, 1998.

———. "Dervish and Sultan: An Analysis of the Otman Baba Vilayetnamesi." In *The Middle East and the Balkans under the Ottoman Empire: Essays on Economy and Society*, 19–36. Bloomington: Indiana University Turkish Studies, 1993.

———. "Istanbul." *EI* 2.

———. "Kanun." *EI* 2.

———. "Mehemmed II." *EI* 2.

———. *The Ottoman Empire: The Classical Age 1300–1600*. New York: Praeger, 1973.

———. "Ottoman Methods of Conquest." *StIsl* 2 (1954): 103–29.

———. "The Ottoman Succession and its Relation to the Turkish Concept of Sovereignty," 37–69. In *The Middle East and the Balkans under the Ottoman Empire: Essays on Economy and Society*. Bloomington: Indiana University Press, 1993.

———. "Reis-ül-Küttâb." *İA*.

———. "State, Sovereignty and Law during the Reign of Süleymân." In İnalcık and Kafadar, *Süleymân the Second and His Time*, 229–48.

———. "Turkish Settlement and Christian Reaction, 1329–1361," "Ottoman Conquests and the Crusade, 1361–1421," "The Struggle for the Balkans, 1421–1451." In *A History of the Crusades*, edited by Kenneth M. Setton, vol. 6, *The*

Impact of the Crusades on Europe, eds. Harry W. Hazard and Norman P. Zacour, 222–75. Madison: University of Wisconsin Press, 1989.

İslamoğlu-İnan, Huri. *State and Peasant in the Ottoman Empire: Agrarian Power Relations and Regional Economic Development in Ottoman Anatolia during the Sixteenth Century*. Leiden and New York: Brill, 1994.

İzgi, Cevat. *Osmanlı Medreselerinde İlim. Vol. 1, Riyazî İlimler. Vol. 2, Tabiî İlimler*. Istanbul: İz, 1997.

Kafadar, Cemal. *Between Two Worlds: The Construction of the Ottoman State*. Berkeley: University of California Press, 1995.

_____. "The Myth of the Golden Age: Ottoman Historical Consciousness in the Post-Süleymânic Era." In İnalcık and Kafadar, *Süleyman the Second and His Time*, 45–57.

_____. "'Osmān Beg and His Uncle: Murder in the Family?" In Heywood and Imber, *Studies in Ottoman History in Honour of Professor V.L. Ménage*, 157–64.

_____. "The Ottomans and Europe." In *Handbook of European History, 1400–1600. Late Middle Ages, Renaissance, and Reformation. Volume 1, Structures and Assertions*, edited by Thomas A. Brady Jr. et alii, 589–636. Brill: Leiden, 1994.

_____. "A Rome of One's Own: Reflections on Cultural Geography and Identity in the Lands of Rum." *Muqarnas* 24 (2007): 7–25.

Kafescioğlu, Çiğdem. *Constantinopolis/Istanbul: Cultural Encounter, Imperial Vision, and the Construction of the Ottoman Capital*. College Park: Pennsylvania State University Press, 2009.

Kafesoğlu, İbrahim. *Türk-İslâm Sentezi*. Istanbul: Aydınlar Ocağı, 1985.

Karadeniz, Hasan Basri. *Osmanlılar ile Beylikler Arasında Anadolu'da Meşruiyet Mücadelesi (XIV.-XVI. Yüzyıllar)*. Istanbul: Yeditepe, 2008.

Karahan, Abdülkadir. *Fuzûlî'nin Mektupları*. Istanbul: İbrahim Horoz, 1948.

Kaufmann, Thomas. "La culture confessionnelle luthérienne de la première modernité. Remarques de méthode," *Études Germaniques* 57, no. 3 (2002): 421–39.

Kazıcı, Ziya. *Osmanlı'da Eğitim-Öğretim*. Istanbul: Bilge, 2004.

Keniston, Hayward. *Francisco de los Cobos. Secretary of the Emperor Charles V.* Pittsburgh: University of Pittsburgh Press, 1958.

Kerslake, Celia J. "The *Selim-nâme* of Celâlzâde Muṣṭafâ Çelebi as a Historical Source." *Turcica* 9–10, no. 2 (1978): 39–51.

_____. "Celalzade Mustafa Çelebi." *TDVİA*.

Kılıç, Mustafa. "Kemal Paşa-Zâdenin (İbn Kemal) Talebeleri." *Belleten* 58, no. 221 (1994): 55–70.

Kılıç, Remzi. *XVI. ve XVII. Yüzyıllarda Osmanlı-İran Siyasi Antlaşmaları*. Istanbul: Tez, 2001.

_____. *Kânunî Devri Osmanlı-İran Münâsebetleri (1520–1566)*. İstanbul: IQ, 2006.

Kılıçbay, Mehmet Ali. *Feodalite ve Klasik Dönem Osmanlı Üretim Tarzı*. Ankara: Gazi Üniversitesi İktisadi ve İdari Bilimler Fakültesi, 1982.

Kırzıoğlu, Fahrettin. *Osmanlı'nın Kafkas Ellerini Fethi (1451–1590)*. Ankara: Sevinç Matbaası, 1976.

Kim, Sooyong. "Minding the Shop: Zati and the Making of Ottoman Poetry in the First Half of the Sixteenth Century." PhD diss., University of Chicago, 2005.

Kinra, Rajeev Kumar. "Secretary-Poets in Mughal India and the Ethos of Persian: the Case of Chandar Bhān Brahman." PhD diss., University of Chicago, 2008.

Kittell, Ellen E. *From Ad Hoc to Routine: A Case Study in Medieval Bureaucracy.* Philadelphia: University of Pennsylvania Press, 1991.

Knecht, R. J. *The Rise and Fall of Renaissance France, 1483–1610.* London: Fontana Press, 1996.

Koch, Ebba. *Mughal Art and Imperial Ideology: Collected Essays.* New Delhi and New York: Oxford University Press, 2001.

Köprülü, Mehmet Fuat. "Bizans Müesseselerinin Osmanlı Müesseselerine Tesiri Hakkında Bâzı Mülâhazalar." *Türk Hukuk ve İktisat Tarihi Mecmuası* 1 (1931): 165–313.

———. *Some Observations on the Influence of Byzantine Institutions on Ottoman Institutions.* Translated and edited by Gary Leiser. Ankara: Türk Tarih Kurumu, 1999.

Krstić, Tijana. *Contested Conversions to Islam: Narratives of Religious Change in the Early Modern Ottoman Empire.* Stanford: Stanford University Press, 2011.

Kubinyi, András. "The Battle of Szávaszentdemeter-Nagyolazsi (1523): Ottoman Advance and Hungarian Defence on the Eve of Mohács." In *Ottomans, Hungarians, and Habsburgs in Central Europe: The Military Confines in the Era of Ottoman Conquest,* edited by Géza Dávid and Pál Fodor, 71–115. Leiden: Brill, 2000.

Kumrular, Özlem. "Campaña de Alemania: Rito, arte y demostración." In *L'Empire ottoman dans l'Europe de la Renaissance…,* edited by Alain Servantie and Ramón Puig de la Bellacasa, 191–214. Leuven: Leuven University Press, 2005.

———. "Osmanlı Sarayında ve Avrupa Siyasi Sahnesinde Venedikli Bir Sınır Diplomatı: 'Mir-i Venedik Oğlu' Alvise Gritti." *TTYY* 6 (Fall 2007–Winter 2008): 39–59.

Kunt, Metin. "The Later Muslim Empires: Ottomans, Safavids, Mughals." In *Islam: The Religious and Political Life of a World Community,* edited by Marjorie Kell, 113–36. New York: Praeger, 1984.

———. "Sultan Süleyman ve Nikris." In Kumrular, *Muhteşem Süleyman,* 93–99.

Küçükdağ, Yusuf. *Vezîr-i Âzam Pîrî Mehmed Paşa (1463?–1532).* Konya: n.p., 1994.

Kütükoğlu, Bekir. *Osmanlı-İran Siyasî Münasebetleri.* Istanbul: Edebiyat Fakültesi Matbaası, 1962.

Lambton, Ann K. S. "Quis custodiet custodes: Some Reflections on the Persian Theory of Government I." *StIsl* 5 (1956): 125–48.

———. "Quis custodiet custodes: Some Reflections on the Persian Theory of Government (Conclusion)." *StIsl* 6 (1956): 125–46.

———. "Justice in the Medieval Persian Theory of Kingship." *StIsl* 17 (1962): 91–119.

_____. "Islamic Mirrors for Princes." in *Atti del Convegno internazionale sul tema: La Persia nel Medieovo*, 419–42. Rome: Accademia nazionale dei Lincei, 1971.

Larkins, Jeremy. *From Hierarchy to Anarchy: Territory and Politics before Westphalia*. New York: Palgrave Macmillan, 2010.

Leaman, Oliver. *A Brief Introduction to Islamic Philosophy*. Malden, MA: Blackwell, 1999.

Lecoq, Anne-Marie. *François Ier imaginaire: Symbolique et politique a` l'aube de la Renaissance française*. Paris: Macula, 1987.

Lellouch, Benjamin. *Les Ottomans en Égypte: Historiens et conquérants au XVIe siècle*. Paris and Louvain: Peeters, 2006.

Lewis, Bernard. "Ottoman Observers of Ottoman Decline." *Islamic Studies* 1 (1962): 71–87.

Lewis, Geoffrey. "The Utility of Ottoman Fethnāmes." In *Historians of the Middle East*, edited by Bernard Lewis and P.M. Holt, 192–96. London: Oxford University Press, 1962.

Lieberman, Victor, ed. *Beyond Binary Histories: Re-Imagining Eurasia to c. 1830*. Ann Arbor: University of Michigan Press, 1999.

Lindner, Rudi Paul. *Nomads and Ottomans in Medieval Anatolia*. Bloomington: Research Institute for Inner Asian Studies, Indiana University, Bloomington, 1983.

_____. *Explorations in Ottoman Prehistory*. Ann Arbor: University of Michigan Press, 2007.

Lloyd, Howell A. *The State, France and the Sixteenth Century*. London: Allen & Unwin, 1983.

Loades, David. *Tudor Government: Structures of Authority in the Sixteenth Century*. Oxford: Blackwell, 1997.

Luttrell, Anthony. "The Hospitallers at Rhodes, 1306–1421." In Setton, *A History of the Crusades*, vol. 3, *The Fourteenth and Fifteenth Centuries*, ed. Harry W. Hazard (Madison: The University of Wisconsin Press, 1975), 278–313.

Mantran, Robert. "L'historiographie ottomane à l'époque de Soliman le Magnifique". In Veinstein, *Soliman le Magnifique et son temps*, 25–32.

_____. *Istanbul au siècle de Soliman le Magnifique*. Revised second edition. Paris: Hachette, 1994.

Mann, Michael. *The Sources of Social Power*. Vol. 1, *A History of Power from the Beginning to A.D. 1760*. Cambridge: Cambridge University Press, 1986.

Marcus, Kenneth H. *The Politics of Power: Elites of an Early Modern State in Germany*. Mainz: Philipp von Zabern, 2000.

Marlow, Louise. "Advice and advice literature." *EI 3*.

_____. *Hierarchy and Egalitarianism in Islamic Thought*. Cambridge: Cambridge University Press, 1997.

Masad, Mohammad Ahmad. "The Medieval Islamic Apocalyptic Tradition: Divination, Prophecy and the End of Time in the 13th Century Mediterranean." PhD diss., Washington University at St. Louis, 2008.

Masters, Bruce. *Christians and Jews in the Ottoman Arab World: The Roots of Sectarianism*. New York: Cambridge University Press, 2001.

Mathee, Rudi. "The Safavid-Ottoman Frontier: Iraq-i Arab as Seen by the Safavids." *Ottoman Borderlands: Issues, Personalities and Political Changes*, eds. Kemal H. Karpat and Robert W. Zens, 157–73. Madison: The University of Wisconsin Press/Center of Turkish Studies, 2003.

Mattingly, Garrett. *Renaissance Diplomacy*. Baltimore: Penguin, 1964.

Matuz, Josef. *Das Kanzleiwesen Sultan Süleymāns des Prächtigen*. Wiesbaden: F. Steiner, 1974.

McLeod, Bruce. *The Geography of Empire in English Literature, 1580–1745*. Cambridge: Cambridge University Press, 1999.

Ménage, V. L. "On the Constituent Elements of Certain Sixteenth-Century Ottoman Documents." *BSOAS* 48, no. 2 (1985): 283–304.

⸻. Review of *Tabakat*. *BSOAS* 47, no. 1 (1984): 154–57.

Meshal, Reem. "Antagonistic Sharī'as and the Construction of Orthodoxy in Sixteenth-Century Ottoman Cairo." *Journal of Islamic Studies*, 21, no. 2 (2010): 183–212.

Michaud, Hélène. *La Grande Chancellerie et les écritures royales au 16e siècle, 1515–1589*. Paris: Presses Universitaires de France, 1967.

Minorsky, Vladimir. "Shaykh Bālī-efendi on the Safavids." *BSOAS* 20, nos. 1–3 (1957): 437–50.

Mitchell, Colin Paul. "Am I My Brother's Keeper? Negotiating Corporate Sovereignty and Divine Absolutism in Sixteenth-Century Turco-Iranian Politics." In *New Perspectives on Safavid Iran: Empire and Society*, edited by idem, 33–58. New York: Routledge, 2011.

⸻. "Out of Sight, Out of Mind: Shah Mohammad Khodābanda and the Safavid *Dār al-enshā*." *Studies on Persianate Societies* 3 (2005): 65–98.

⸻. *The Practice of Politics in Safavid Iran: Power, Religion and Rhetoric*. London: I.B. Tauris, 2009.

⸻. "To Preserve and Protect: Husayn Va'iz-i Kashifi and Perso-Islamic Chancellery Culture." *IrSt* 36, no. 4 (December 2003): 485–507.

⸻. "Safavid Imperial *Tarassul* and the Persian *Inshā'* Tradition." *Studia Iranica* 26 (1997): 173–209.

⸻. "The Sword and the Pen. Diplomacy in Early Safavid Iran, 1501–1555." PhD diss., University of Toronto, 2002.

Mitchell, Timothy. "Society, Economy, and the State Effect." In Steinmetz, *State/Culture*, 76–97.

Miyamoto, Yoko. "The Influence of Medieval Prophecies on Views of the Turk: Islam and Apocalypticism in the Sixteenth Century." *JTS* 17 (1993): 125–45.

Mohiuddin, Momin. *The Chancellery and Imperial Epistolography under the Mughals*. Calcutta: Iran Society, 1971.

Moin, Ahmed Azfar. "Islam and the Millennium: Sacred Kingship and Popular Imagination in Early Modern India and Iran." PhD diss., University of Michigan, 2010.

Mordtmann, J.H. "İsfendiyar Oğlu." *EI* 2.

Muir, Edward. *Ritual in Early Modern Europe*. Second edition. Cambridge: Cambridge University Press, 2005).

Murphey, Rhoads. *Exploring Ottoman Sovereignty: Tradition, Image and Practice in the Ottoman Imperial Household, 1400–1800*. London: Continuum, 2008.

―――. "Ottoman Expansion, 1451–1556 II. Dynastic Interest and International Power Status." In *Early Modern Military History, 1450–1815*, edited by Geoff Mortimer, 60–80. Basingstoke, Hampshire: Palgrave Macmillan, 2004.

―――. "Ottoman Military Organisation in South-Eastern Europe, c. 1420–1720." In Tallett and Trim, *European Warfare, 1350–1750*, 135–58.

―――. *Ottoman Warfare, 1500–1700*. New Brunswick: Rutgers University Press, 1999.

―――. "Süleyman I and the Conquest of Hungary: Ottoman Manifest Destiny or a Delayed Reaction to Charles V's Universalist Vision." *JEMH* 5, no. 3 (2001): 197–221.

―――. "Süleymân's Eastern Policy." In İnalcık and Kafadar, *Süleymân the Second and His Time*, 229–48.

Murvar, Vatro. "Patrimonialism, Modern and Traditionalist: A Paradigm for Interdisciplinary Research on Rulership and Legitimacy," in Murvar, *Theory of Liberty, Legitimacy and Power*, 40–85.

Muslu, Emire Cihan. "Ottoman-Mamluk Relations: Diplomacy and Perceptions." PhD diss., Harvard University, 2007.

Müller, Ralf C. "Der umworbene 'Erbfeind': Habsburgische Diplomatie an der Hohen Pforte vom Regierungsantritt Maximilians I. bis zum 'Langen Türkenkrieg' – ein Entwurf." In Kurz et. al., *Das Osmanische Reich und die Habsburgermonarchie*, 251–80.

Necipoğlu, Gülru. *The Age of Sinan: Architectural Culture in the Ottoman Empire*. Princeton: Princeton University Press, 2005.

―――. *Architecture, Ceremonial, and Power: The Topkapi Palace in the Fifteenth and Sixteenth Centuries*. New York: Architectural History Foundation; Cambridge, MA: MIT Press, 1991.

―――. "Challenging the Past: Sinan and the Competitive Discourse of Early Modern Islamic Architecture," *Muqarnas* 10 (1993): 169–80.

―――. "From International Timurid to Ottoman: A Change of Taste in Sixteenth-Century Ceramic Tiles." *Muqarnas* 7 (1990): 136–70.

―――. "A Kânûn for the State, a Canon for the Arts: Conceptualizing the Classical Synthesis of Ottoman Arts and Architecture." In Veinstein, *Soliman le magnifique et son temps*, 195–216.

―――. "Süleymân the Magnificent and the Representation of Power in the Context of Ottoman-Habsburg-Papal Rivalry." *Art Bulletin* 71, no. 3 (1989): 401–427.

Neumann, Christoph. *Das indirekte Argument: ein Plädoyer für die Tanẓīmāt vermittels der Historie: die geschichtliche Bedeutung von Aḥmed Cevdet Paşas Ta'rīḫ*. Munster: Lit, 1994.

Nexon, Daniel H. *Struggle for Power in Early Modern Europe: Religious Conflict, Dynastic Empires, and International Change*. Princeton: Princeton University Press, 2009.

Newman, Andrew J. *Safavid Iran: Rebirth of a Persian Empire*. London: I.B. Tauris, 2006.

Niyazioğlu, Aslı. "On Altıncı Yüzyıl Sonunda Osmanlı'da Kadılık Kabusu ve Nîhânî'nin Rüyası." *JTS* 31, no. 2 (2007): 133–43.

Oborni, Teréz. "Die Herrschaft Ferdinands I. in Ungarn." In *Kaiser Ferdinand I. Aspekte eines Herrscherlebens*, edited by Martina Fuchs and Alfred Kohler, 147–65. Münster: Aschendorff, 2003.

Ocak, Ahmet Yaşar. *Osmanlı Toplumunda Zındıklar ve Mülhidler (15.–17. Yüzyıllar)*. Istanbul: Tarih Vakfı, 1998.

Okçuoğlu, Tarkan. "Nişancı Mustafa Paşa Camii." *Dünden Bugüne İstanbul Ansiklopedisi*, vol. 6, 87–88. Ankara: Kültür Bakanlığı; İstanbul: Tarih Vakfı, 1993–1995.

O'Leary, Brendan. *The Asiatic Mode of Production: Oriental Despotism, Historical Materialism, and Indian History*. Oxford: Blackwell, 1989.

Öz, Mehmet. "Ottoman Provincial Administration in Eastern and Southeastern Anatolia: The Case of Bidlis in the Sixteenth Century." In Karpat and Zens, *Ottoman Borderlands*, 145–56.

Özbaran, Salih. *Bir Osmanlı Kimliği: 14.–17. Yüzyıllarda Rûm/Rûmî Aidiyet ve İmgeleri*. Istanbul: Kitap, 2004.

Özcan, Abdülkadir. "Historiography in the Reign of Süleyman the Magnificent. In *The Ottoman Empire in the Reign of Süleyman the Magnificent*, edited by T. Duran, 165–222. Istanbul: Historical Research Foundation, Istanbul Research Center, 1988.

Özel, Oktay. "Modern Osmanlı Tarihyazımında 'Klâsik Dönem:' Bir Eleştirel Değerlendirme." *TTYY* 4 (Fall 2006): 273–294.

Özel, Oktay and Gökhan Çetinsaya. "Türkiye'de Osmanlı Tarihçiliğinin Son Çeyrek Yüzyılı: Bir Bilanço Denemesi." *Toplum ve Bilim* 91 (Winter 2001/2002): 8–38.

Özkoçak, Selma. "The Urban Development of Ottoman Istanbul in the Sixteenth Century." PhD diss., School of Oriental and African Studies, University of London, 1997.

Özvar, Erol. "Osmanlı Devletinin Bütçe Harcamaları." In *Osmanlı Maliyesi: Kurumlar ve Bütçeler*, vol. 1, edited by Mehmet Genç and Erol Özvar, 197–238. Istanbul: Osmanlı Bankası Arşiv ve Araştırma Merkezi, 2006.

Pagden, Anthony. *Lords of All the World: Ideologies of Empire in Spain, Britain and France c. 1500–c. 1800*. New Haven: Yale University Press, 1995.

Parker, Charles H. *Global Interactions in the Early Modern Age, 1400–1800*. Cambridge: Cambridge University Press, 2010.

Parker, Geoffrey. *The Military Revolution: Military Innovation and the Rise of the West, 1500–1800*. Second edition. Cambridge: Cambridge University Press, 1996.

Peirce, Leslie P. *The Imperial Harem: Women and Sovereignty in the Ottoman Empire*. New York: Oxford University Press, 1993.

———. *Morality Tales: Law and Gender in the Ottoman Court of Aintab*. Berkeley: University of California Press, 2003.

Perjés, Géza. *The Fall of the Medieval Kingdom of Hungary: Mohács 1526–Buda 1541*. Translated by Márió D. Fenyö. Boulder, CO.: Social Science Monographs; Highland Lakes, NJ: Atlantic Research and Publications, 1989.

Perry, John. "Cultural Currents in the Turco-Persian World of Safavid and Post-Safavid Times." In Mitchell, *New Perspectives on Safavid Iran*, 84–96.

Piterberg, Gabriel. *An Ottoman Tragedy: History and Historiography at Play.* Berkeley and Los Angeles: University of California Press, 2003.

Posch, Walter. "Der Fall Alḳās Mīrzā und der Persienfeldzug von 1548–1549. Ein gescheitertes osmanisches Projekt zur Niederwerfung des safavidischen Persiens." PhD diss., Bamberg University, 1999.

Poulantzas, Nicos. *Political Power and Social Classes.* Translated by Timothy O'Hagan. London: NLB, 1973.

Perdue, Peter A. "The Qing Empire in Eurasian Time and Space: Lessons from the Galdan Campaigns." In Struve, *The Qing Formation in World-Historical Time*, 57–91.

Pocock, J.G.A. "Texts as Events: Reflections on the History of Political Thought." In *Politics of Discourse: The Literature and History of Seventeenth-Century England*, edited by Kevin Sharpe and Stephen N. Zwicker, 21–34. Berkeley: University of California Press, 1987.

Raby, Julian. "Mehmed II's Greek Scriptorium." *Dumbarton Oaks Papers* 37 (1983): 15–34.

Rahimi, Babak. "The Rebound Theater State: The Politics of the Safavid Camel Sacrifice Rituals, 1598–1695 C.E." *IrSt* 37, no. 3 (September 2004): 451–78.

Reeves, Marjorie. *The Influence of Prophecy in the Later Middle Ages: A Study in Joachimism.* Oxford: Clarendon Press, 1969.

Reinhard, Wolfgang. *Geschichte der Staatsgewalt: eine vergleichende Verfassungsgeschichte Europas von den Anfängen bis zur Gegenwart.* Munich: C.H. Beck, 1999.

———. "Zwang zur Konfessionalisierung? Prolegomena zu einer Theorie des konfessionellen Zeitalters." *Zeitschrift für historische Forschung* 10 (1983): 257–77.

de Ridder-Symoens, Hilde. "Training and Professionalization." In *Power Elites and State Building*, edited by Wolfgang Reinhard, Theme D in Blockmans and Genet, *The Origins of the Modern State in Europe*, 149–72.

Robinson, Francis. "Education." In *Islamic Cultures and Societies to the End of the Eighteenth Century*, edited by Robert Irwin, vol. 4 in *The New Cambridge History of Islam*, edited by Michael Cook, 497–531. Cambridge: Cambridge University Press, 2010.

Rodríguez-Salgado, M. J. *The Changing Face of Empire: Charles V, Philip II and Habsburg Authority, 1551–1559.* Cambridge: Cambridge University Press, 1988.

Rossi, Ettore. "The Hospitallers at Rhodes, 1421–1523." In Hazard, *The Fourteenth and Fifteenth Centuries*, 314–39.

Röhrborn, Klaus. *Provinzen und Zentralgewalt Persiens im 16. und 17. Jahrhundert.* Berlin: Walter de Gruyter, 1966.

Runciman, W. G. "Empire as a Topic in Comparative Sociology." In *Tributary Empires in Global History*, edited by Peter Fibiger Bang and C.A. Bayly, 99–107. Basingstoke, Hampshire: Palgrave Macmillan, 2011.

Saatçi, Suphi. "Observations on Sinan's Mosques and Masjids in Eyüp." In *Eyüp Sultan Symposia I–VIII: Selected Articles*, 132–37. Istanbul: The Municipality of Eyüp, 2005.

Sağırlı, Abdurrahman. "Şâhnâme-i Âl-i Osman'a Göre Kanuni Döneminde Divân-ı Hümâyûn." In *Eski Çağ'dan Günümüze Yönetim Anlayışı ve Kurumlar*, edited by Feridun Emecen, 59–65. Istanbul: Kitabevi, 2009.

Sahin-Tóth, Péter. "A Difficult Apprenticeship. The Integration of Hungary into the Habsburg Monarchy in the 16th Century." In *The World of Emperor Charles V*, edited by Wim Blockmans and Nicolette Mout, 247–36. Amsterdam: Royal Netherlands Academy of Sciences, 2004.

Saray, Mehmet. *Türk-İran İlişkileri*. Ankara: Atatürk Araştırma Merkezi, 1999.

_____. *Türk-İran Münâsebetlerinde Şiiliğin Rolü*. Ankara: Türk Kültürünü Araştırma Enstitüsü, 1990.

Savory, Roger M. *Iran under the Safavids*. Cambridge: Cambridge University Press, 1980.

Schilling, Heinz. "Confessionalization: Historical and Scholarly Perspectives of a Comparative and Interdisciplinary Paradigm." In Headley, Hillerbrand and Papalas, *Confessionalization in Europe*, 21–35.

_____. *Konfessionskonflikt und Staatsbildung: eine Fallstudie über das Verhältnis von religiösem und sozialem Wandel in der Frühneuzeit am Beispiel der Grafschaft Lippe*. Gütersloh: Gütersloher Verlagshaus Gerd Mohn, 1981.

Schilling, Heinz and Heribert Smolinsky, eds. *Der Augsburger Religionsfrieden 1555. Wissenschaftliches Symposium aus Anlass des 450. Jahrestages des Friedensschlusses, Augsburg, 21. bis 25. September 2005*. Münster: Aschendorff; Gütersloh: Gütersloher Verlagshaus, 2007).

Schimmel, Annemarie. *The Empire of the Great Mughals: History, Art and Culture*. Translated by Corinne Attwood. Edited by Burzine K. Waghmar. London: Reaktion: 2004.

Setton, Kenneth M. *The Papacy and the Levant, 1204–1571. Vol. 3, The Sixteenth Century to the Reign of Julius III, vol. 4, The Sixteenth Century from Julius III to Pius IV*. Philadelphia: American Philosophical Society, 1976–1984.

_____. *Western Hostility to Islam and Prophecies of Turkish Doom*. Philadelphia: American Philosophical Society, 1992.

Sinclair, Tom. "Administration and Fortification in the Van Region under Ottoman Rule in the Sixteenth Century." In *The Frontiers of the Ottoman World*, edited by A.G.S. Peacock, 211–24. Oxford: Oxford University Press, 2009.

_____. "The Ottoman Arrangements for the Tribal Principalities of the Lake Van Region of the Sixteenth Century. In Karpat and Zens, *Ottoman Borderlands*, 119–43.

Smith, Adam T. *The Political Landscape: Constellations of Authority in Early Complex Polities*. Berkeley: University of California Press, 2003.

Sohrweide, Hanna. "Dichter und Gelehrte aus dem Osten im osmanischen Reich (1453–1600). Ein Betrag zur türkisch-persischen Kultur geschichte." *Der Islam* 46 (1970): 263–302.

_____. "Der Sieg der Safawiden in Persien und seine Rickwürkungen auf die Schiiten Anatoliens im 16. Jahrhundert." *Der Islam* 41 (1965): 95–223.

Somel, Selçuk Akşin. *The Modernization of Public Education in the Ottoman Empire, 1839–1908: Islamization, Autocracy, and Discipline.* Leiden: Brill, 2001.

Spiegel, Gabrielle M. *The Past as Text: The Theory and Practice of Medieval Historiography.* Baltimore: Johns Hopkins University Press, 1997.

_____, ed. *Practicing History: New Directions in Historical Writing after the Linguistic Turn.* London: Routledge, 2005.

_____. *Romancing the Past: The Rise of Vernacular Prose Historiography in Thirteenth-Century France.* Berkeley: University of California Press, 1993.

Strong, Roy C. *Art and Power: Renaissance Festivals, 1450–1650.* Berkeley: University of California Press, 1984.

Subrahmanyam, Sanjay. "Connected Histories: Notes towards a Reconfiguration of Early Modern Eurasia." In Lieberman, *Beyond Binary Histories,* 289–316.

_____. "The Fate of Empires: Rethinking Mughals, Ottomans and Habsburgs." In *Shared Histories of Modernity: China, India and the Ottoman Empire,* edited by Huri İslamoğlu and Peter C. Perdue, 74–108. Delhi and London: Routledge, 2009.

_____. "Turning the Stones Over: Sixteenth-Century Millenarianism from the Tagus to the Ganges." *The Indian Economic and Social History Review* 45, no. 2 (2003): 129–61.

_____. "Written on Water: Designs and Dynamics in the Portuguese *Estado da Índia.*" In *Empires: Perspectives from Archaeology and History,* edited by Susan E. Alcock et. al., 42–69. Cambridge: Cambridge University Press, 2001.

Subtelny, Maria E. "Husayn Va'iz-i Kashifi: Polymath, Popularizer, and Preserver." *IrSt* 36, no. 4 (December 2003): 463–67.

_____. "A Late Medieval Persian Summa on Ethics: Kashifi's Akhlaq-i Muhsini." *Ibid.,* 601–14.

Sutter Fichtner, Paula. *The Habsburg Monarchy, 1490–1848: Attributes of Empire.* New York: Palgrave Macmillan, 2003.

Sümer, Faruk. *Safevi Devletinin Kuruluşu ve Gelişmesinde Anadolu Türklerinin Rolü. Şah İsmail ve Halefleri ile Anadolu Türkleri.* Ankara: Selçuklu Tarih ve Medeniyeti Enstitüsü Yayınları, Güven Matbaası, 1976.

Szakály, Ferenc. *Lodovico Gritti in Hungary 1529–1534: A Historical Insight into the Beginnings of Turco-Habsburgian Rivalry.* Translated by Dániel Székely. Budapest: Akadémiai Kiadó, 1995.

_____. "Nándorfehérvár, 1521: The Beginning of the End of the Medieval Hungarian Kingdom." in *Hungarian-Ottoman Military and Diplomatic Relations in the Age of Süleyman the Magnificent,* edited by Géza Dávid and Pál Fodor, 47–76. Budapest: Loránd Eötvös University, 1994.

Şahin, Kaya. "Âşıkpaşa-zâde as Historian: An Analysis of the Tevârih-i Âl-i Osman [The History of the Ottoman House] of Âşıkpaşa-zâde." MA thesis, Sabancı University, 2000.

_____. "Constantinople and the End Time: The Ottoman Conquest as a Portent of the Last Hour." *JEMH* 14, no. 4 (2010): 317–54.

_____. "Imperialism, Bureaucratic Consciousness and the Historian's Craft: A Reading of Celālzāde Muṣṭafā's *Ṭabaḳātü'l-Memālik ve Derecātü'l-Mesālik.*"

Forthcoming in *Writing History at the Ottoman Court: Editing the Past, Fashioning the Future*, edited by Emine Fetvacı and Erdem Çıpa. Bloomington: Indiana University Press, 2013.

_____. "In the Service of the Ottoman Empire. Celalzade Mustafa (ca. 1490–1567), Bureaucrat and Historian." PhD diss., University of Chicago, 2007.

_____. Review of Dale, *The Ottomans, Safavids, and Mughals*, *IJTS* 17, nos. 1–2 (2011): 196–99.

_____. (with Cornell H. Fleischer). "Süleymân the Magnificent." *The Princeton Encyclopedia of Islamic Political Thought*, edited by Gerhard Bowering et. al. Princeton, NJ: Princeton University Press, 2012.

Şevik, İsa. "Şah Tahmasb (1524–1576) ile Osmanlı Sarayı Arasında Teati Edilen Mektupları İçeren "Münşe'ât-ı 'Atîk"in Edisyon Kritiği ve Değerlendirilmesi." MA thesis, Dokuz Eylül Üniversitesi, 2008.

Tanner, Marie. *The Last Descendant of Aeneas: The Hapsburgs and the Mythic Image of the Emperor*. New Haven: Yale University Press, 1993.

Terzioğlu, Derin. "How to Conceptualize Ottoman Sunnitization: A Historiographical Discussion." Paper presented at The Alevi-Bektashi Communities in the Ottoman Realm: Historiography, Sources and Paradigms, Boğaziçi University, 13–15 December 2011.

Tezcan, Baki. "Ethics as a Domain to Discuss the Political: Kınalızâde Ali Efendi's Ahlâk-ı Alâî." In *Proceedings of the International Congress on Learning and Education in the Ottoman World: Istanbul, 12–15 April 1999*, edited by Ali Çaksu, 109–20. Istanbul: IRCICA, 2001.

_____. "Ethnicity, Race, Religion and Social Class: Ottoman Markers of Difference." In *The Ottoman World*, edited by Christine Woodhead, 159–70. London: Routledge, 2012.

_____. "Lost in Historiography: An Essay on the Reasons for the Absence of a History of Limited Government in the Early Modern Ottoman Empire." *Middle Eastern Studies* 45, 3 (May 2009): 477–505.

_____. "The Politics of Early Modern Ottoman Historiography." In Aksan and Goffman, *The Early Modern Ottomans*, 167–98.

_____. *The Second Ottoman Empire: Political and Social Transformation in the Early Modern World*. Cambridge: Cambridge University Press, 2010.

Theunissen, Hans. "Ottoman-Venetian Diplomatics: the 'Ahd-names. The Historical Background and the Development of a Category of Political-Commercial Instruments together with an Annotated Edition of a Corpus of Relevant Documents." *Electronic Journal of Oriental Studies* 1, no. 2 (1998): 1–698.

Tietze, Andreas. "Muṣṭafā 'Ālī of Gallipoli's Prose Style." *Archivum Ottomanicum* 5 (1973): 297–319.

Tilly, Charles. *Coercion, Capital, and European States, AD 990–1992*. 2nd printing. Cambridge, MA: Blackwell, 1992.

Turan, Ebru. "The Marriage of İbrahim Pasha (ca. 1495–1536). The Rise of Sultan Süleyman's Favorite to the Grand Vizierate and the Politics of the Elites in the Early Sixteenth-Century Ottoman Empire." *Turcica* 41 (2009): 3–36.

_____. "The Sultan's Favorite: İbrahim Pasha and the Making of the Ottoman Universal Sovereignty in the Reign of Sultan Süleyman (1516–1526)." PhD diss., University of Chicago, 2007.

_____. "Voices of Opposition in the Reign of Sultan Süleyman. The Case of İbrahim Pasha (1523–36)." In Ousterhout, *Studies on Istanbul and Beyond*, 23–35.

Turan, Şerafettin. "Celal-Zade." *İA*.

_____. "Kemalpaşazade İbn-i Kemal." *TDVİA*, volume 25.

_____. *Kanuni Süleyman Dönemi Taht Kavgaları*. Revised 2nd edition. Ankara: Bilgi, 1997.

_____. "Rodos'un Zaptından Malta Muhasarasına." In İğdemir, *Kanunî Armağanı*, 49–79.

Turner, Bryan S. *Weber and Islam: A Critical Study*. Boston and London: Routledge and Kegan Paul, 1974.

Turner, Ralph V. *Men Raised from the Dust: Administrative Service and Upward Mobility in Angevin England*. Philadelphia: University of Pennsylvania Press, 1988.

Uluçay, Çağatay. "Yavuz Sultan Selim Nasıl Padişah Oldu?" *Tarih Dergisi* 6, no. 9 (March 1954): 53–90; *Tarih Dergisi* 7, no. 10 (September 1954): 117–42; *Tarih Dergisi* 8, nos. 11–12 (September 1955): 185–200.

Uzunçarşılı, İsmail Hakkı. "Onaltıncı Asır Ortalarında Yaşamış Olan İki Büyük Şahsiyet: Tosyalı Celâl zâde Mustafa ve Salih Çelebiler." *Belleten* 22, no. 87 (1958): 391–441.

_____. *Osmanlı Devletinin İlmiye Teşkilâtı*. Ankara: Türk Tarih Kurumu, 1965.

_____. *Osmanlı Devletinin Merkez ve Bahriye Teşkilâtı*. Ankara: Türk Tarih Kurumu, 1948.

_____. *Osmanlı Devletinin Saray Teşkilâtı*. Ankara: T.C. Atatürk Kültür, Dil ve Tarih Yüksek Kurumu, 1984.

_____. *Osmanlı Tarihi. Vol. 2, İstanbul'un Fethinden Kanunî Sultan Süleyman'ın Ölümüne Kadar*. 3rd imprint. Ankara: Türk Tarih Kurumu, 1975.

Üstün, İsmail Safa. "Heresy and Legitimacy in the Ottoman Empire in the Sixteenth Century." PhD diss., University of Manchester, 1991.

Vali, Abbas. *Pre-Capitalist Iran: A Theoretical History*. New York: NYU Press, 1993.

Varlık, Nükhet. "Disease and Empire: A History of Plague Epidemics in the Early Modern Ottoman Empire (1453–1600)." PhD diss., University of Chicago, 2008.

Vatin, Nicolas. "The Hospitallers at Rhodes and the Ottoman Turks." In *Crusading in the Fifteenth Century: Message and Impact*, edited by Norman Housley. 148–62. London: Palgrave-Macmillan, 2004.

_____. *L'Ordre de Saint-Jean-de-Jérusalem, l'empire ottoman et la Méditerranée orientale entre les deux sièges de Rhodes (1480–1522)*. Paris: Peeters, 1994.

_____. *Rhodes et l'ordre de Saint-Jean-de-Jérusalem*. Paris: Éditions CNRS, 2000.

Veinstein, Gilles. "L'hivernage en campagne: talon d'Achille du système militaire ottomane classique. A propos des sipāhī de Roumélie en 1559–1560." *StIsl* 58 (1993): 109–48.

Viallon, Marie F. *Venise et la porte Ottomane (1453–1566): un siècle de relations véneto-ottomanes, de la prise de Constantinople à la mort de Soliman.* Paris: Economica, 1995.

Walker, Greg. *Persuasive Fictions: Faction, Faith, and Political Culture in the Reign of Henry VIII.* Aldershot: Ashgate, 1996.

Wallerstein, Immanuel. *The Modern World-System.* Vol. 1, *Capitalist Agriculture and the Origins of the European World-Economy in the Sixteenth Century.* New York: Academic Press, 1974.

Walsh, John R. "The Historiography of Ottoman-Safavid Relations in the Sixteenth and Seventeenth Centuries." In Lewis and Holt, *Historians of the Middle East,* 197–211.

———. "The Revolt of Alqās Mīrzā." *WZKM,* 68 (1976): 61–78.

Whimster, Sam and Scott Lash, eds. *Max Weber, Rationality, and Modernity.* London: Allen and Unwin, 1987.

White, Hayden V. *The Content of the Form: Narrative Discourse and Historical Representation.* Baltimore: Johns Hopkins University Press, 1987.

White, Sam. *The Climate of Rebellion in the Early Modern Ottoman Empire.* Cambridge: Cambridge University Press, 2011.

Williamson, Arthur H. "An Empire to End Empire: The Dynamic of Early Modern British Expansion." *Huntington Library Quarterly,* 68, nos. 1–2 (March 2005): 227–56.

Winter, Michael. *Egyptian Society under Ottoman Rule, 1517–1798.* London: Routledge, 1992.

Winter, Stefan. *The Shiites of Lebanon under Ottoman Rule, 1516–1788.* Cambridge: Cambridge University Press, 2010.

Wohlfeil, Rainer. "Grafische Bildnisse Karls V. im Dienste von Darstellung und Propaganda." In *Karl V. 1500–1558: neue Perspektiven seiner Herrschaft in Europa und Übersee,* edited by Alfred Kohler, Barbara Haider and Christine Ottner, 21–56. Vienna: Verlag der Österreichischen Akademie der Wissenschaften, 2002.

Woodhead, Christine. "After Celalzade: the Ottoman Nişancı c.1560–1700." In *Studies in Islamic Law: A Festschrift for Colin Imber,* edited by Andreas Christmann and Robert Gleave, *Journal of Semitic Studies,* supplement 23, 295–312. Oxford: Oxford University Press and Manchester University Press, 2007.

———. "An Experiment in Official Historiography: The Post of Şehnameci in the Ottoman Empire, c.1555–1605." *WZKM,* 75 (1983): 157–82.

———. "From Scribe to Litterateur: The Career of a Sixteenth Century Ottoman Kātib." *Bulletin of the British Society for Middle Eastern Studies* 9, no. 1 (1982): 55–74.

———. "Murad III and the Historians: Representations of Ottoman Imperial Authority in Late-16th Century Historiography." In Karateke and Reinkowski, *Legitimizing the Order,* 85–98.

———. "The Ottoman Gazaname: Stylistic Influences on the Writing of Campaign Narratives." In Çiçek, *The Great Ottoman-Turkish Civilisation,* 55–60.

————. "Ottoman İnşa and the Art of Letter-Writing. Influences upon the Career of the Nişancı and Prose Stylist Okçuzade (d. 1630)." *Osmanlı Araştırmaları* 7–8 (1988): 143–59.

————. "Perspectives on Süleyman". In Kunt and Woodhead, *Süleyman the Magnificent and His Age*, 164–90.

————. "Reading Ottoman *Şehnames*: Official Historiography in the Late Sixteenth Century." *StIsl* 104–105 (2007): 67–80.

Woolf, Daniel. *The Social Circulation of the Past: English Historical Culture, 1500–1730*. Oxford: Oxford University Press, 2003.

Woods, John E. *The Aqquyunlu: Clan, Confederation, Empire*. Revised and expanded edition. Salt Lake City: University of Utah Press, 1999.

————. "The Rise of Tīmūrid Historiography." *Journal of Near Eastern Studies* 46, no. 2 (April 1987): 81–108.

Yates, Francis A. *Astraea: The Imperial Theme in the Sixteenth Century*. London and Boston: Routledge and Kegan Paul, 1975.

Yıldırım, Rıza. "Turkomans between Two Empires: The Origins of the Qizilbash Identity in Anatolia (1447–1514)." PhD diss., Bilkent University, 2008.

Yıldız, Sara Nur. "Persian in the Service of the Sultan: Historical Writing in Persian under the Ottomans during the Fifteenth and Sixteenth Centuries." *Studies on Persianate Societies* 2 (2004): 145–63.

Yılmaz, Hüseyin. "The Sultan and the Sultanate: Envisioning Rulership in the Age of Süleyman the Lawgiver (1520–1566)." PhD diss., Harvard University, 2004.

Yılmaz, Mehmet Şakir. "'Koca Nişancı' of Kanuni. Celalzade Mustafa Çelebi, Bureaucracy and 'Kanun' in the Reign of Süleyman the Magnificent (1520–1566)." PhD diss., Bilkent University, 2006.

Yurdaydın, Hüseyin Gazi. "Bostan'ın Süleymannâmesi." *Belleten* 19, no. 74 (1955): 137–202.

————. *Kanunî'nin Cülûsu ve İlk Seferleri*. Ankara: Türk Tarih Kurumuı, 1961.

Yücel, Yaşar. *Anadolu Beylikleri Hakkında Araştırmalar 1*. Second edition. Ankara: Türk Tarih Kurumu, 1991.

Yücesoy, Hayrettin. "Justification of Political Authority in Medieval Sunni Thought." in *Islam, the State, and Political Authority: Medieval Issues and Modern Concerns*, edited by Asma Afsaruddin, 9–33. New York: Palgrave Macmillan, 2011.

Zagorin, Perez. *Rebels and Rulers, 1500–1660. Vol. 1, Society, States, and Early Modern Revolution: Agrarian and Urban Rebellions*. Cambridge: Cambridge University Press, 1982.

Zaller, Robert. *The Discourse of Legitimacy in Early Modern England*. Stanford: Stanford University Press, 2007.

Zilli, Ishtiyaq Ahmad. "Development of *Inshā* Literature to the End of Akbar's Reign." In Alam, Delvoye, Gaborieau, *The Making of Indo-Persian Culture*, 309–49.

Index

Titles in the series:

Made in the USA
Las Vegas, NV
05 September 2021